FIVE LINES, FOUR SPACES

Five Lines
Four Spaces

The World of My Music

GEORGE ROCHBERG

Edited by Gene Rochberg and Richard Griscom
Introduction by Gene Rochberg

UNIVERSITY OF ILLINOIS PRESS
URBANA AND CHICAGO

Publication for this book was supported in part
by a grant from the National Endowment for the Arts.

Library of Congress Cataloging-in-Publication Data
Five lines, four spaces : the world of my music /
edited by Gene Rochberg and Richard Griscom ;
introduction by Gene Rochberg.
p. cm.
Includes bibliographical references and index.
ISBN 978-0-252-03425-1 (cloth : alk. paper)
1. Rochberg, George. 2. Composers—United States—Biography.
3. Rochberg, George—Criticism and interpretation.
I. Rochberg, Gene. II. Griscom, Richard.
ML410.R6255A3   2009
780.92—dc22 [B]   2008034989

To Hans Weisse and George Szell
my first composition teachers
at the Mannes School of Music in
New York City, New York
and
To Rosario Scalero and Gian Carlo Menotti
my teachers at the Curtis Institute of Music in
Philadelphia, Pennsylvania
With loving regard and great admiration

GEORGE ROCHBERG

CONTENTS

Illustrations follow page 142.

ACKNOWLEDGMENTS

Grateful thanks is extended to dear friends, family, eminent musicians, and critics—ardent supporters and detractors alike—who constituted the world of the composer George Rochberg's life and times and gave it rich meaning. Special thanks go to the following for their contributions to *Five Lines, Four Spaces:*

The National Endowment for the Arts, Washington, D.C., for their publication subvention.

Pendragon Press for the use of the chronology from *George Rochberg: A Bio-bibliographic Guide to His Life and Works,* by Joan DeVee Dixon.

Theodore Presser Company for the use of information from their catalog of the published works of George Rochberg and for their generosity in the use of the Rochberg files.

Jeremy Gill for preparing the figures and the music notation.

Michael Garber for the use of his photographs.

Beverly Holmes for her assistance in preparing early drafts of *Five Lines, Four Spaces.*

Alan Gillmor, professor emeritus of Carleton University, Ottawa, Canada, and editor of *Eagle Minds* (the selected correspondence between George Rochberg and Istvan Anhalt), for reading a draft of *Five Lines, Four Spaces* and preparing the index.

Robert Reilly, musician and critic, for his loyal support and encouragement.

Richard Griscom, head of the Otto E. Albrecht Music Library at the University of Pennsylvania, for preparing the book for publication and making the initial contact with Laurie Matheson at the University of Illinois Press. He gave unstintingly of his time and offered advice in every aspect on the way to publication. His efforts and profound insights have made possible what we hope will be a valuable and highly significant addition to the catalog of books on music.

Note: An unabridged, unpublished version of *Five Lines, Four Spaces* can be seen on request at the Sacher Archives in Basel, Switzerland, along with the manuscripts and sketches of Rochberg's major oeuvre. Another copy is held in the American Music Collection at the New York Public Library for the Performing Arts.

George Rochberg's memoirs, *Five Lines, Four Spaces,* do not focus on recountings of his personal life but rather on the panorama of the life he lived in music. Music was the world he loved, and there he experienced life to the fullest extent, giving and taking of its great riches. When he died, May 29, 2005, he left, besides his books, a huge body of extraordinary music in many categories—chamber ensembles, seven string quartets, six symphonies, solo pieces, songs, and one opera.

He also left an indelible mark on the thinking of young composers who were his students, inspiring them with his example and his potent ideas regarding the direction the art of music should take. His essays show how intensely mindful he was of the legacy left by the greatest composers of the past, and he used this legacy wisely, adding to it works of his own making. Truly he was unique among artists—functioning significantly and with passion in the public sphere, yet giving generously to students and finding time for family and friendships.

These memoirs have much to reveal of the contentious and combative atmosphere prevalent in artistic circles, where craft and language were of central concern. In these frequently fierce battles Rochberg played a major role—making possible the continuation of a vital, healthy approach to creating art and loosening the grip of a sterile avant-garde. What he taught and accomplished exerted a powerful effect on his own generation, as well as on the young who followed his example into a less restrictive, freer world in which to realize their ambitions.

In his late seventies, sensing his diminishing energies and the inability to sustain a composing schedule, he turned exclusively to writing about music and musicians (many of them beloved friends) who made his music come alive with brilliant performances and sensitive recordings. He tells of the lively discussions concerning the craft of music, which he felt was being imperiled with foolish tampering by those whose intentions and philosophy it was to "make it new."

Throughout his career he was commissioned to write works for outstanding soloists and orchestras, and the descriptions of those events give an unvarnished truth of fabulous occasions. It was clear his character, his quality, along with his remarkable gifts, were recognized and rewarded by many honors and the sincere appreciation of audiences. He was also singularly fortunate for the performers who championed his work and made it possible for him to enjoy success in his lifetime. His music brought his family the greatest joys and gave them the strength to survive and overcome searing grief and deepest sorrows.

Weeks before he died, Rochberg completed his memoirs. He selected those events, incidents, and ideas he deemed of major importance, and these words constitute a partial autobiography—the rest is embedded in the notes between the lines and spaces of the scores where his music lives for him.

Gene (Mrs. George) Rochberg
Dunwoody Village
Newtown Square, Pennsylvania
August 2008

PART I

CHAPTER 1

"Save Something for the End"

Second Symphony and George Szell

I've long forgotten why I was walking on Chestnut Street in Center City Philadelphia, but I do remember suddenly hearing my name repeated several times
over, "Roschbergh, Roschbergh!" in a distinctly Mitteleuropa accent. There, not
many steps away and easily distinguishable in the crowd, stood George Szell,
the conductor of the Cleveland Orchestra, wearing a homburg hat and a natty
coat with a fur collar. Altogether the figure of a man totally self-possessed, carrying himself with a bearing that could only have been acquired in the highly
sophisticated and cultivated urban society of pre–World War II Europe. He had
picked me out of the crowd and obviously remembered me clearly. Apparently
he was as surprised and delighted to see me after so many years—sixteen—as I
was to see him.

Before being drafted into the army in 1942, I had been one of three students
studying with Szell at the old Mannes Music School on East Seventy-fourth Street
in New York City. During my three years at Mannes, the school occupied a gracious
town house on a genteel, quiet street probably dating back to the beginning of
the first two decades of the twentieth century. My first composition teacher, Hans
Weisse,[1] like so many musicians, artists, and intellectuals, had been driven out of
Europe—in his case, Vienna—by Hitler and his viciously insane Nazi regime. At
the time, I was young and naive and gave no thought to things like Weisse's professional background. I cared only that I would be studying composition with a
man who was himself a composer, a thorough musician, and an excellent pianist.
I studied Bach in a way I'd never dreamed possible. Most of all, Weisse could teach
me what I hungered to know about the mysteries of writing music.

Later I learned he was a friend, student, or disciple—perhaps all three—of Heinrich Schenker and, through the grapevine, that it was Weisse and Felix Salzer, also then teaching at Mannes, who were strong advocates of the principles and theories of Schenkerian tonal analysis, which eventually spread like wildfire throughout American musical academia. At the time Schenkerian analysis had no interest for me. The truth was, no system of analysis ever seriously engaged me, then or later. But when I did come to grips with Schenkerian thinking, I found it particularly abhorrent, especially as practiced by hidebound academic theorists. There was a doctrinal zealotry about them that substituted an almost theological rigidity of method for realizing, musically and imaginatively, the miracle of the totality of design of a composition. Schenker's three-step, layer-by-layer reductive revelation of the tonal truth was applied starting from "the foreground," passing through "the middleground," and finally—and tortuously—arriving at "the background," yielding the fundamental line, the *Urlinie,* the primal tonal cadence that summed up all the pitch motions traced out from the surface of the music (as experienced) to its ultimate, logical, symbolic, Schenkerian tonal reality—truth, understood analytically.

Nonetheless, Schenker conveyed something of greater importance to me than analytic particularities: namely, that a composition was an organic, structural whole, a totality of design that had the power to live in the ear, persuade the mind, warm the heart and soul. Schenker's work corroborated something I knew intuitively.

In our lessons Weisse never once spoke about Schenker. Why he didn't remains an open question even at this late date. Perhaps it was because he understood that teaching by indirection and suggestion is more productive of desired results than the more obvious, dogmatic, proselytizing approach. It also had the unintended benefit of immunizing me against the Schenkerian cult that arose and literally took over theory teaching in countless faculties throughout America. When I entered university teaching in 1960, Schenkerism was already deeply entrenched, a doctrine and a faith not to be challenged. Looking back, I am grateful to Weisse for not attempting to indoctrinate me. Perhaps he sensed that I was, besides being shy, independent in spirit; and that while this independence would make me resistant to overt, dogmatic instruction it would keep me open to subtler forms of being nudged and guided in desirable directions.

Weisse loved the music of Brahms. In 1939–40, with the ascendancy of the New Viennese School, this was not so remarkable—especially if you were from Vienna. I remember the bitter tale he told of how he had offered a group of his works to Universal Edition, the great publishing house in Vienna. The editors said they would be only too glad to publish provided he would allow them to come out as recently discovered works by Brahms himself. If not, they would have to return them. Which is what happened.

During the second year of my work with Weisse he began suffering violent headaches. Several times I would come for a lesson only to take the bus back to New Jersey because he was too ill to see me. Not long afterward, this man whom I'd come to love and admire and whose music I was just beginning to know was diagnosed with a brain tumor. He died despite an operation it was hoped would save him. I was devastated. His death was the first great personal loss in my life. I was too anguished to attend a memorial service for him at the Mannes school.

To fill in temporarily for Hans Weisse's loss, Leopold Mannes,[2] now running the school because of his father's failing health, took over the task of teaching composition. Where Weisse was European to the core, Leopold Mannes was American in look, manner, and physical appearance, though his family had deep roots in Europe. His mother, Clara Damrosch, was the sister of Walter Damrosch, who had been the conductor of the New York Philharmonic. Leopold was a fine pianist, though not a composer. Just as Weisse had been generous-hearted in my direction, so also was Leopold Mannes. Unhappily, my studies ended when I was drafted into the army in 1942.

In July 1945, after three long years in the army, I returned home. I was with my wife Gene again and saw my little boy Paul for the first time. On fire to get back to music and desperate to make up for lost time, I went to see Leopold Mannes to talk about resuming my studies. Knowing how intent I was on mastering my craft, Leopold advised me to study with Rosario Scalero at the Curtis Institute of Music in Philadelphia. Scalero was not only the greatest teacher of counterpoint then living (*pace* Nadia Boulanger), he could also trace his spiritual/musical genealogy back to Brahms and was the last living link to an age-old tradition from Brahms to Joseph Haydn, the theorist Johann Fux, and earlier times.

In his early years he had lived in Vienna as a professional violinist and composer, and while there he became a member of Brahms's circle. Among the cantus firmi he gave his students to work with was one in D minor by Brahms himself (D–F–E–D–G–F–A–G–F–E–D). From October 1945 to May 1946, knowing this would be Scalero's last year at Curtis, I worked like a demon on all the old forms of counterpoint—canon at all intervals, double and triple invertible counterpoint, single and double fugue, chorale prelude (often in canonic imitation), *cori spezzati* ("broken chorus," that is, antiphonal responses) for eight-part double chorus— twelve and fourteen hours a day mostly away from the piano. Scalero retired to a picture-book medieval castle on a hill overlooking a village in the Piedmont region of northern Italy, which he had modernized with plumbing.

Five years later while I was a fellow at the American Academy in Rome in 1951, Gene, Paul, and I visited Scalero. He was then eighty, straight as a tree, the image of the *signore,* beret on his white head, cane in his gnarled hand as he walked slowly with us through the village. I remember showing him my First Symphony. After perusing the opening pages, he asked, "Why you are making these seconds?!" I knew why, of course, but found it impossible to convey to this grand old musician who still thought Debussy's music was "a pink fog." Those few days with him were the last time I saw him.

When I sent Leopold Mannes the two-piano version of the Capriccio movement of my First Symphony, he seemed completely baffled by it, for in the note he sent me he said, "This is the craziest music I've ever seen." Not a remark to be taken lightly from a man like Leopold Mannes, nor encouraging to a young, still-insecure composer. If anything, it was the kind of reaction that demanded some soul-searching, to explain to myself more than to Leopold what I was after, what I was trying to say. Today I look back on his remark as virtually twin to Roger Sessions's almost identical statement as we walked away together, just after hearing a performance of my *Music for the Magic Theater* given by the contemporary music group of the Aspen Festival. "George," he said in his always thoughtful, deliberate way, "that's the strangest music I've ever heard." Perhaps Roger was identifying something Leopold had caught in the Capriccio, some quality or characteristic that seemed right and natural to my ear but not to theirs.

It was in the 1940–41 season that George Szell came to the Mannes Music School, invited by Leopold to teach composition. Szell had found himself stranded by the outbreak of war in Europe while guest conducting in South America, and Leopold's invitation saved the day for him, as it provided the opportunity to establish himself in New York and, eventually, the United States. Almost immediately he was invited to conduct Toscanini's NBC Symphony, and in 1946 he became the full-time conductor of the Cleveland Orchestra, which, in his capable hands, soon developed into one of the great American orchestras.

And now years later, in 1958, here was George Szell on Chestnut Street in Philadelphia. We greeted each other most cordially, with genuine pleasure. Truthfully, I was completely amazed at his wonderfully open, friendly manner, quite the opposite of how I remembered him in my student days—distant, cold, detached. A kind of diffidence seemed to envelop him then. No doubt he was preoccupied with his own unsettled situation after arriving in New York, and I misinterpreted this as coldness and indifference. That he was a superb, brilliant musician was immediately evident. Perhaps of the three musicians I worked with at Mannes he was the most brilliant. Szell once told me that he had wanted to be a composer, had even written works that Universal had published, but admitted sadly that he realized while still a young man that he "had nothing to say." This confession to me—his student—showed a side of him that I was unable to interpret at the time. For one thing, by taking me into his confidence, he was not only showing genuine trust in me but also showing the side of himself that ran completely counter to my mistaken notion that he was cold and indifferent. For another, his admission to his student some twenty years his junior that he had nothing to say as a composer suggests not only the strength of his personal integrity, but also that he believed I did and, just possibly, it was his responsibility to help me find the way to say it. Had I realized all this in 1941–42, I would have felt less tortured by the more forbidding, off-putting aspects of Szell's personality, for he was not easy to approach, and in my early twenties I was reticent and no psychologist of human behavior.

In the two seasons I worked with Szell I produced a large torso of a never-to-be-completed one-act opera based on William Butler Yeats's *The King's Threshold*. Besides the piano-vocal score, which kept growing week after week, there were many pages of orchestration sketched. My enthusiasm for the character of the poet, Seanchan (pronounced "Shanahan"), who carries on a symbolic sit-down strike on the palace steps because he demands to be restored to his rightful place at the high table of the king, thereby restoring poetry to *its* rightful place in the king's realm, was great indeed. Unfortunately, I had not yet learned that for purely poetic reasons a dramatic-verse play intended for the spoken stage had more words than needed for a musical setting to be sung onstage. I dropped the project because I knew I would never meet the deadline for submitting the work on time to the competition I had intended to enter.

Another work I wrote under Szell's guidance was a large set of piano variations "on an original theme." Or as Brahms designated his op. 21, no. 1, "über ein eigenes Thema." Translated roughly, "on a theme of my own," that is, original. My designation, like Brahms's, was to make a clear distinction between, for example, variations on "America" such as Charles Ives produced or "on a nursery theme" such as Ernst von Dohnányi wrote for piano and orchestra or the many sets Beethoven composed throughout his lifetime on themes by other composers, his best set of this type being unquestionably his *Diabelli Variations.* My set of theme, twelve variations, and finale grew out of a fascination with two separate strands of study and experience. I spent endless hours in those early years at the piano poring over the works of the masters and always found myself drawn deeper and deeper into the realm of variation technique. What excited and moved me profoundly was the discovery of the great principle that lies as much at the core of science and philosophy as it does of music: that there is an unchanging essence in life that paradoxically takes on or is the source of a constant series of ever-changing surfaces and exteriors. Blake captured the identical idea in his epigrammatic observation: "Eternity is in love with the productions of time."[3]

Within that essential intuitive understanding I saw that sameness could be disguised, altered, reshaped in as many different ways as one (or nature) could invent, endless, in fact; and yet organic wholeness, that which held all such differences in an integral musical structural relationship, was anchored in the particularities of melodic and harmonic characteristics of the theme, its musical genome, its DNA, its neurology. No matter how far afield one went inventing variations, one could theoretically go on forever so long as the essential nature of the theme remained present somewhere, somehow—whether deep in the folds of the musical tissue or closer to its surface, and thereby more immediately perceivable.

Another side of my fascination with variation came from my experience playing jazz from the time I was fifteen into the years I studied at Mannes. Obviously, it was a totally different kind of music making within a wildly different milieu. The seedy bars, taverns, clubs, and roadside rests that coincided with the dark, traumatic times of the Great Depression reached into and affected every corner of American life. From playing jazz I learned to improvise, since improvisation is its lifeblood. There is no fixed, final form to a piece of jazz. Its very malleability and endless variability do not permit it to be frozen into a single shape. Jazz is a way of playing, for example, a tune not fixed in a final form—actually, there is no ultimate form to a piece of jazz as there is to a piece of classical music. Jazz is the expressive art of performers of an existent standard repertoire where fixed identity is less important than inspired variation, while classical music is the expressive art of an individual composer and exists as an unvarying notated identity.

However dark the times of the 1930s, the air rang with hit songs pouring out of Tin Pan Alley, Broadway musicals, and especially Hollywood extravaganzas, costly excuses for songs and singers, dancing and dancers, troupes of beautiful young women and paper thin plots stringing them all together. Looking back, without those songs and movies, I am convinced America could not have survived the depression. They combined to produce a kind of romantic aura around a dark center, which made life bearable.

It was in that world I learned to play jazz and how to improvise. At the same time I ingested and breathed in hundreds, if not thousands, of songs that still sing in my head. In the midst of all this I discovered that the great "theme" for jazz improvisation going back generations is the twelve-bar blues, locked into a specific, elemental harmonic progression, adaptable in other directions and to other tunes, but at its best and purest only in and of itself.

When the call from the draft board to leave for basic training came in November 1942, it brought to an abrupt close what had been for my wife and me an idyllic period in New York. Because this part of my story concerns Szell and my Second Symphony, before continuing with Philadelphia in 1958, there are some special moments at the Mannes Music School I still need to describe in order to give a more complete picture of my relation to Szell in that earlier time.

One remarkable afternoon Szell and Leopold Mannes got together to make music. Playing at two grand pianos side by side in one of the larger studios, they went through an incredibly exciting reading of Richard Strauss's *Elektra,* or perhaps it was *Salome.* I had been dragooned into turning pages, and at the rate they ate through the pages I was as busy as they were. It was a fantastic display of a kind of musicianship I had never before witnessed or experienced. Totally spontaneous, the music poured forth in waves of an oceanic Straussian surge. In great, good high spirits a joyous generosity filled the studio regardless of the vengeful agonies *Elektra* or *Salome* projects. Those two incomparable musicians, one born and bred in Europe, the other in America, wrung extraordinary drama from two concert grand pianos. I felt as though I were in the presence of gods.

Another time even more critical to my later development was the lesson with Szell that turned on an impromptu discussion of the great importance to the performer—more precisely the conductor—to, as Szell put it, "save something for the end." It is a given that the performance of a concert, an opera, any single, large work requires enormous expenditure of mental, physical, and psychic energy. How this energy is disposed, how it is expressed, whether in one controlled burst or a series of shorter bursts with potentially serious depletion following each, or in carefully planned and balanced release of what the performer intuitively understands he or she is being called on to give—these are vital, indeed, crucial matters, that affect the outcome of musical performance. Szell's point was that one must keep something in reserve; one should not, out of uncontrolled enthusiasm, give all one's substance away too quickly or too early. There was always yet more to shape and project into convincing performance. Therefore, his dictum: "Always save something for the end."

This way of understanding the design of a performance took deep root in me and ultimately presented itself in the form of a principle so basic to my way of thinking that it literally affected how I approached the design of any composition I undertook. By converting Szell's idea of how to design a performance, I arrived at the idea that the design of a composition must make convincing to its performers the structural dispositions and proportions of its ideas, phrases, sections, and movements, as well as its particular processes of emergence of musical substance that combine to make a created form and identity of real and deeply felt mental, physical, and psychic energies. It is not necessary to be a composer to recognize that a large design can be accomplished only over long stretches of time, especially if the work in question emerges slowly through endless sketches and many drafts, and one has to deal more than once with the "Y" dilemma. Taking the left or right fork of the Y has, as I discovered, major consequences for the design of a work. Add the questions "Where do I begin? How do I end this work?" Then one realizes how important Szell's idea of "saving something for the end" becomes in actual practice.

Beginnings and endings are absolutely crucial to a convincing design. Once discovered, work can begin to fill out meaningfully the seemingly endless span between the two. While still quite young, I realized that repertoire instrumental works often suffered severely from "last movement-itis." This seemed especially true of Brahms, who generally placed the greatest emotional and structural weight on his monumental first movements and the least on his last. To my taste, especially faulty in this regard are his First and Second piano concertos, as well as his Violin Concerto. It is by no means true of his First Symphony, nor of his Second and Third, but I have never been able to reconcile myself to the perfunctory manner in which he brings to a close the final measures of his still-amazing Fourth Symphony. It seems also at times that Haydn and Mozart have a tendency to rely too heavily on formulaic conventions when they bring allegro or vivace movements to a close. By contrast, Beethoven was the first great conscious designer of endings and especially of last movements. To cite only the end of the remarkable variation last movement of the "Eroica" Symphony, plus the glorious coda of the giant sonata-form first movement, is to show the idea in its most ideally realized incarnation.

When Szell's idea joined forces with my early diagnosis of "last movement-itis," the two combined into powerful principles of design that guided me through my early maturity and beyond. And serendipitously, I gave back to Szell my understanding and interpretation of his idea of "always save something for the end" in the summation ending of my Second Symphony, which he chose to perform.

What made New York possible, what gave the last year—from September/October 1941 to October/November 1942—its virtually magical, idyllic quality, at times even a sense of heightened superreality, was being married to Gene Rosen-feld. We met as students at Montclair State Teachers College in February 1939, the same year I began my studies with Hans Weisse. We fell madly in love and could no more imagine a life without each other than we could a world without the sun, moon, and stars, an earth without rain, grass, trees, and flowers.

That spring I graduated from Montclair, and we would have married had it not been for the rigid Victorian college code that threatened dismissal of any coed who married while still a student. Gene had two more years before she could get her degree, and though we were starry-eyed, we were also realistic enough to understand we had to deal with external problems and obstacles in our path. The summer Gene graduated we took a Greyhound bus to Minneapolis, where we stayed with our dear friends Herb and Mitzi McClosky. There were only five people at our civil wedding: ourselves, the McCloskys, and Judge Bennyhof officiating.

On returning to New York City, we moved into a fifth-floor walk-up on West Ninety-third and Amsterdam Avenue and began a life together that after sixty-five years still has its magic. Now we laugh about the slanting floor of our one-room apartment on what we called "Ninety-free Street" and the mice that came out of the hole behind the old-style, noble, ebony-black Mason and Hamlin upright piano I'd bought with my hard-earned money years earlier. Unfortunate mice, when they thought all was quiet and the night belonged to them, they couldn't know I was waiting for them—with a broom.

New York in 1941–42 was hardly today's New York. Then, living was possible on very little money. Food was cheap and preservative-free, and it was possible to walk across Central Park in the dark in any direction without fearing for your life. Concerts were either free or inexpensive. Society was civil; people showed a decent respect for each other and themselves. While there may have been guns and drugs, they hadn't yet penetrated into the veins and arteries of a dysfunctional society. There were plenty of cars, taxis, and buses, but not in such profusion that gridlock and bumper-to-bumper traffic were the rule. In fact, New York was still beautiful in the central areas of Manhattan, and one could walk for miles, north and south, east and west, and enjoy looking at everything.

Luigi Dallapiccola once described how he loved walking around New York when he visited in the early 1950s. There you could dream big dreams and work hard to become a composer, a painter, a poet, a writer—even if no one knew who you were or why you were there. Life was serious, full of purpose to create art—good and lasting, if possible. Culture was a long way from becoming eviscerated, trivialized, or extruded and trashed as the twentieth century reveals. There were at least five major newspapers that reported events of interest and significance, and the music reviews—whether you agreed with the critics or not—were written by people with tough standards and tastes who had the courage to speak their minds. Virgil Thomson wrote intelligently no matter whether he liked what he heard. His English, or I should say his American, went straight to the point, no self-consciousness, no fancy footwork. Olin Downes, stodgy though he was, opened his Sunday column to living issues. I distinctly remember an exchange with Arnold Schoenberg that had a kind of dignified rage. Wonderful movies were shown at the Thalia. Museums, where you could see the great art of the past and the recent present anytime you wanted, were free.

At the end of our resources, miraculously we became house sitters for a Mrs. Terry's elegant twenty-five-room town house on East Ninety-sixth Street between Madison and Fifth—this was a fairy tale in itself. Our lives continued as before, and our activities did not change. Gene still went to Macy's every day to work in "book information," and I continued to give piano lessons in Brooklyn and in New Jersey, occasionally playing a jazz date. However, where and how we lived had changed radically. It was as though we had been catapulted into another world where we were rich beyond our wildest imaginings, yet we had not a penny more than we'd had before. From April to October 1942, we lived in a euphoric state, giving occasional parties to which it seemed every young musician in New York showed up bringing food and drink. There were frequent hearty Sunday breakfasts in the kitchen with friends sitting around a large table eating and drinking pot after pot of coffee. In those dreamlike months we even had a wedding in the ballroom for two dear friends.

Returning to Philadelphia and the surprise meeting with Szell in 1958, the first thing he asked was, "Where can we talk?" We were only a stone's throw from the downtown music store of the Theodore Presser Company, the music publisher where I was then chief editor and director of publications.

Presser's main offices were in Bryn Mawr, one of the suburban towns on the Main Line railroad that linked them to Philadelphia. John Haney, president of the company's board of directors, told me when I began working there in 1951, with great booster pride in his high-pitched voice, "Presser is the Woolworth of the music business." I received this news with the shock of the totally unprepared, having just returned from Italy and the American Academy in Rome, where all I did for a year was think, suffer grave doubts and anxieties, combat stomach distress, and try to write music.

I wasn't at all prepared for Haney's proud coupling of Presser—the place where I had accepted a job only because I needed to support my family—with Woolworth, the great five-and-dime emporium of Depression USA. What jarred me was his casual joining of what I loved passionately, "music," with what I loved least of all things possible in this world, "business." His phrase "the music business" fell with painful dissonance on my ears, and his likening Presser to Woolworth sounded a bit ominous, though I confess there was an oddly humorous ring to the metaphoric comparison. By the time of my wholly chance meeting with Szell, Presser had established itself as one of the leading American publishers of contemporary music with connections internationally. Its "Woolworth" days had passed into history along with its two-page piano pieces for beginners and *Etude* magazine.

I found a room in the Presser store where Szell and I could make ourselves comfortable and talk undisturbed. He wanted to know everything that had happened to me since we'd last seen each other and kept pressing me about my music. What had I written? What could I show him? When could he see it? The warmth of his personal interest broke through my normal reserve. I told him about my two symphonies, the first written in 1948–49, the second completed in 1955–56. For purely practical reasons, it was important that Szell know that the First Symphony had already been given its premiere earlier that year (March 1958), by Eugene Ormandy and the Philadelphia Orchestra, and that immediately following the first performances Ormandy had taken it to New York. I don't remember if I explained to Szell that I had cut the original five movements of my First Symphony down to three and that it was the shorter version Ormandy had played. Actually, I never got over the radical surgery I had performed on my own work, and it was many years before I was able to restore the symphony to its original form. At the age of thirty, when I wrote it, I had allowed myself to be persuaded by very bad advice: "No one's going to play an hour-long symphony by a young, unknown composer. Cut it down to practical size"—and so forth. I don't think I told Szell any of this then, or even that I regretted exceedingly having followed my colleagues' expedient advice.

Wanting Szell to have some idea of what to expect before seeing the scores of both symphonies, I described as best I could their general characteristics. I laid stress on the essential tonal nature, understood in the broad sense of Stravinsky and Bartók, of the First Symphony, but at the same time its clear tendency to play around the edges of the borderland between the tonal and the atonal worlds, even verging on the twelve-tone realm at times. I told Szell that the Second Symphony had neither been performed nor spoken for and described how much closer to my present way of thinking it was than my First, which had been an important stepping stone. My Second was a full-scale twelve-tone (or serial) work with essentially four movements linked by brief interludes into a thirty-minute uninterrupted musical whole. I began sketching it between 1952 and 1954 while working on other things. In fact, I had begun thinking of it as soon as I had written my first twelve-tone music in 1952, a work for solo piano called *Twelve Bagatelles*. I finally returned to my symphony in the winter of 1955 and worked on it until it was completed in the spring of 1956.

Szell's interest in my description of the Second Symphony being a twelve-tone work must have been very keen. He knew, as I did, that in 1958 writing twelve-tone music was not at all respectable; not only that, it was considered a form of trafficking with the devil. Somehow it smacked of something disreputable, an ugly aesthetic anomaly whose composers were highly suspect, practitioners of a black art dangerous to society and civilization. Arnold Schoenberg, its "inventor" as he ironically called himself, was persona non grata in virtually all music circles except the most avant-garde.

While Stravinsky had adopted the twelve-tone or serial method as his own in his late years (and only after Schoenberg had died in 1951), even he, the longtime hero of modern music, could not remove its onus. By 1958, however, it had captured the hearts and minds of the young postwar European generation of composers who adopted serialism as a way of filling the cultural vacuum created by the disruptions of World War II. In America, its practitioners and adherents were few and far between. When I began wrestling with the purely technical problems of the twelve-tone method, I knew none of the other composers who were involved with it. And when I attempted to make contact with a number of them, they were standoffish. In time I learned that my reasons for adopting the twelve-tone method couldn't have been more different from any other composer's—European or American.

Whatever reasons may have motivated others, mine had absolutely nothing to do with being avant-garde or playing the radical. I needed a language expressive and expansive enough to say what I had to. My war experience had etched itself deep into my soul, and afterward I lived with an ever-sharpening awareness of the approach to the abyss I saw in a world coming apart at the seams. I was distressed at the growing slovenliness of people's bad thinking and grew increasingly nauseated by a rising tide of narcissism that surfaced in public comments and statements by leading artists and writers of the day. Even worse were the works being produced in a never-ending stream of bad taste, bum ideas, and sloppy craftsmanship. There was no recourse but to pursue my own purposes stubbornly and ignore the unraveling going on around me.

What was Szell thinking as I told him how I saw the musical situation and my part in it? Impossible to say, but I can at least conjecture that he understood, that he seemed sympathetic to my position. Above and beyond that and depending on his eventual reaction to both my symphonies, he may have considered or even seen some special merit in presenting to a conventional audience a new score whose totally unconventional nature might arouse more than the usual short-lived flurry of interest shown a new work by an American composer and might even produce some afterlife beyond the brief glow of the aura of a first performance.

On returning to my office in Bryn Mawr, I immediately arranged to have both symphonies sent to Szell. Shortly afterward, Szell called me at Presser, and as though it were a perfectly ordinary, everyday thing to say, he announced, "Roschbergh, I am going to do your Second Symphony." There was pleasure in his voice, and I could hardly contain myself at the wonderful news. I thanked him most warmly, and then we talked practicalities. I had learned that Szell was very precise and knew even the grandest things depended on organizing all the details involved. He already knew when he would perform my symphony and when he would need additional copies of the score and when the parts for his orchestra players should be ready and, finally, when he planned to begin rehearsing the work. He had already scheduled performances for February 26 and 28, 1959, in Cleveland. Rehearsals were to begin just as soon as I could get the parts to the orchestra librarian. Immediately I arranged for the parts to be extracted, proofread, and reproduced. Accuracy was absolutely of the essence. Mistakes in orchestra parts wasted precious time in rehearsal and aggravated nerves. They had to be avoided at all costs. My anticipations were heightened by the fact that February 1959 was right around the corner. It had been a long wait, almost ten years, between the time I'd written my First Symphony and Ormandy had performed it. But here was the Second, still very fresh in my mind, about to see the light of day. The routine of everyday work publishing other composers' music kept my nerves and growing impatience in check.

Once rehearsals in Cleveland began, Szell told me that he had already spent hours taking his orchestra through my symphony by literally stealing time from rehearsals for other concerts. Hardly usual practice, but if the stakes are high enough—and obviously Szell thought they were—a conductor will sometimes do just that. From the first rehearsal, it became eminently clear that he knew my symphony inside and out and had planned exactly how he would conduct it. I like to think he recognized his dictum "Save something for the end" in the way I brought together and summed up all the principal gestures and motifs and lifted them to the highest possible peak of emotion in the last five or six minutes of the work. I had a profound sense of security, a feeling of absolute confidence in Szell and his musicians. Some of them had studied counterpoint with me in the late 1940s at the Curtis Institute or, if not counterpoint, then that monster anomaly known as "form and analysis."

The question of form, its morphology, how the logic of phrases, sections, movements becomes a function of an unfolding, successive whole—and its psychology—
and how interest in the unfolding of successive events is achieved and maintained
throughout a work: these are crucial matters in the design of a composition. And
since the morphological and psychological aspects of the process of forming vital
structure are intimately involved with the character and nature of ideas, it has always
seemed to me that only musical ideas with strong profiles of identity ultimately
satisfy the demands of both the logic of internal relationship of structural functions
and the interest demanded of the unfolding of these successive functions. Musical
ideas—"happiest motifs," Delacroix calls them in his journal⁴—are what sound in
our heads and in our ears when we are composing. For the performing musicians,
they are what sing in their heads and ears as they wrestle with the problem of how
best to project the work of which these ideas are the living substance, the organic
essence. When a composer is lucky enough to have such memorable, identifiable
musical thoughts, the chances are quite good that the same will eventually happen
in the heads and ears of his listeners.

Using the ancient brute method of trial and error in my pursuit of the morphology of formal design and the psychology of musical ideas and their relation to each
other in composition, I grew more and more keenly aware of the physiognomy
of ideas, their profile, their cut, their identifying characteristics.

So it was that in designing the Second Symphony I decided against the multimovement sequence of my First Symphony in favor of a large, multisectioned
design with only one beginning and one ending. The beginning gestures and
ideas of such a totally integrated design as I planned would have to stand for the
entire work; and the ending of such a formal design would of necessity have to
stand as the apotheosis, the gathering up and summation of the intellectual and
emotional forces that characterized the entire work.

Given these conditions, therefore, new meaning attaches to beginning and
ending a work. What lies between must be organically tied, related to the whole,
and must be powerfully absorbing. In addition, because the work was twelve-tone,
I found ways of organizing the row based on hexachords in such fashion that its
transpositions through inversion could take on an analogical relation to tonal
centers through *locus,* so that different ideas and gestures embodying events had
a relationship to a scheme of tonal *loci*—that is, they had the status of "keys" in
the old tonal sense.

Still further, because I have always been fascinated by what happens when slow-
moving music is pitted rhythmically against faster-moving music, I found a way

to combine slow and fast speeds in the "save something for the end" summation by increasing the number of repetitions of the assertive opening figures of the work layered over and against slow-moving masses of strings and brasses. The tension between the two mounts, the climactic plateau is reached, breaks, and spills out its energy—then dissolves to the last phrases, which are emotionally dark, exhausted.

Not once did Szell ask anything about the twelve-tone organization of the music. He approached the symphony exactly as I would have wanted: as music that expresses itself in large, dramatic gestures that reach for unattainable heights, plunge into dark regions, catch fire, and burn with ferocity. By the time of its premiere, the Second had miraculously taken on, in Szell's hands, the quality of a work in the grand Romantic tradition that Szell and his orchestra had played many times before, knew intimately, and believed in thoroughly. There was none of that soulless, self-consciousness of playing "new music" that has plagued music in the twentieth century and that I have come to abhor.

As far back as I can remember, I have felt this attitude to be among the deep-seated but almost never acknowledged causes of why, from its very inception, modernism in music was prevented from ultimately flowering into a repertoire of works that combined intellectual power with concrete emotional power and lent itself to exciting performance levels of real gratification, not only for performing musicians but also for listeners, even as the music retained its identity as a music obviously different in syntax and semantic from nineteenth-century music.

Years later, in the 1990s, a performance of the Second Symphony completely opposite to Szell's took place with Paul Dunkel conducting the American Composers Orchestra. Against all caution and advice I had offered, Dunkel played the identical work, notes, and orchestration so that it came out sounding avant-garde, serial—in short, like a performance of "new music," born in America in the twentieth century. Hard-edged modernism triumphed over emotionally expressive romanticism. What had been expansive was flattened out, what sang lost its lyricism. A kind of strict musical accounting won out over what was uncertain, in pain, struggling with being human. Where Szell had been open and large-gestured, Dunkel was tight and compressed; where Szell had allowed wind solos to take on the hues of individual coloration, creating a rich, kaleidoscopic instrumental palette, Dunkel tended to depersonalize and homogenize this palette into a single wind color. Where Szell had made his strings passionate, tender, ferocious, soaring by turns, Dunkel made them hard, without expressive gradation, metallic. Nor can it be said that these differences had to do essentially with the disparity of age and experience between the two or the nameable and unnameable distinctions between the orchestras. Something deeper is at stake, primarily the opposite characteristics, as I see them, between two musical cultures, the European and the American.

Here in America we seem to have been largely insensitive to, and unaware of, two inescapable realities: first, our total adoption of the repertoire, its history, and its great changes in language and style as though we ourselves had had a hand in its creation rather than simply accepting what had been produced in Europe over the centuries as an incredible legacy; second, our almost blithe indifference to the widely differing basic chemistries, tensions, and strengths and weaknesses of the European soul and our own, the American. Even granting those inevitable instances where American composers and performers are the descendants of mainly European immigrants at least through the time of my own generation, these different chemistries and psychic attributes reveal themselves readily in the vast compositional disparities of musical expression between the two Western cultures and, just as strongly, in how both new twentieth-century music and repertoire music are played.

Szell approached his performance as a European born in the nineteenth century into the romantic repertoire and its performance traditions. Dunkel played my work as an American born into twentieth-century modernism that had stripped away all the outer layers of an earlier romantic approach in favor of a head-on collision with the hard realities of pitch structures and their organization rather than expression as the principal reason and goal of writing and performing music.

The premiere of my Second Symphony was unique in its own way. There was a sense that the work had made a strong impression. At the reception that followed, Szell himself was more relaxed than I'd ever seen him. He was quite animated and extraordinarily voluble—basking in the admiration of people with whom he felt completely at ease. He knew he had brought off my symphony brilliantly. Such times produced a kind of haze in me. I heard and saw everything as though through a film of soft gauze. All conversation seemed remote, distant. Toward the end of the evening Szell, still holding forth, amazed me by launching into the most outspoken, strongest tirade imaginable against his fellow conductors. I was especially startled by the saltiness of his language: clearly master of good old Anglo-Saxon four-letter words, he knew exactly how to use them! He rose to a particular *crescendo agitato* when he zeroed in specifically on Eugene Ormandy. Obviously no love was lost between them. Certainly there was none from Szell to Ormandy; and, as I learned later, none from Ormandy, who referred to Szell snidely as "the other George."

Szell's second momentous decision was to take my Second Symphony to New York with his orchestra. Not only was it uncommon for a conductor of Szell's stature to present a new work by a young composer to New York critics and audiences, it most certainly was not a common occurrence if the work in question was what in the late 1950s and early 1960s was still thought of as radical and avant-garde. New York was then and remains to this day the nerve center of American culture, musical and otherwise, and, by a kind of natural extension, of Western and world culture as well. For in the decades following the end of World War II, America became a world power and leader, not only in cultural matters, but in all things that drive the engine of modern human existence and enterprise.

But inside the outer skin of things, something deeply personal was happening in me: the sense that my work—which is also myself—had passed a great and critical test. The feeling was inevitably compounded of euphoric sensations often simultaneous with their opposites, fearful scenarios of disaster and failures, rejections and ridicules yet to come. Such combinations of polarities of opposites have haunted me all my life. And with them, the periodic inner awareness that I am being tested, or about to be tested. The concomitant sensations of having passed the test or not, with the accompanying euphoria of coming through or falling on my face, is almost exactly the same—whether I am about to embark on a new work, or already engaged on one, or my work has been completed and is about to be performed in public. That is one major side of my sense of being tested. The other—which always parallels the first—is bound up, warp and woof, with what happens to any human being who faces life without defenses against the inner and outer forces with which he must contend. Beyond that, to whatever levels we may ratchet up the individual intensities of our lives—composing included— all is a test because there are no certainties where it counts most. Science and technology cannot help.

Szell played my Second Symphony in Carnegie Hall in the spring of 1961 with the Cleveland Orchestra. During that time he said to me, "We own it now. It's ours. It belongs to us." I was profoundly touched, happy to share with Szell and his orchestra the spiritual possession of my work. Later backstage, Szell told me again how he felt about my symphony: "It took me eleven years to prepare this orchestra to be able to play a work like yours."

One of the strongest images I retain from that intense time is going into Szell's room during a rehearsal break just as he was madly tearing the skin off an orange and shoving the fleshy fruit into his mouth in big chunks. He laughed delightedly when he saw me and explained that eating oranges in rehearsal breaks and performance gave him just the extra energy charge he needed to keep going. His enjoyment was refreshing to see.

But the best moment of all, the keenest memory of that fantastic time, was when Gene and I walked into the La Scala Restaurant on West Fifty-sixth Street to have dinner. As we were being shown to a table, we were greeted by a chorus of men's voices giving forth in lusty unison—and all the right pitches, too—the opening three clipped phrases of my Second Symphony! I couldn't believe my ears. A crowded restaurant, and sounding *fortissimo* above the din and noise of people talking, my music being sung out joyously, forcefully! We turned to see where it was coming from, and there, having dinner, were members of the Cleveland Orchestra, grinning from ear to ear. They had seen us and spontaneously decided to greet us this way. Gene and I, delighted beyond words, went over to meet them. I introduced Gene, and each in turn told us who he was and what instrument he played. In a lifetime of working with performers, this remains one of those shining moments, an unforgettable form of personal and professional tribute from the toughest-minded musicians in the business—orchestra performers. Their goodwill and enthusiastic valuation of my music is worth more to me than the finest review of a critic or a standing ovation from an audience.

The excitement of the response to my Second Symphony that spring night in 1961 is directly connected to the events that followed. Backstage at Carnegie Hall literally overflowed with well-wishers, friends, and colleagues, among them William Schuman and Aaron Copland, who were particularly cordial. My work had evidently made a strong impression. I can only surmise from subsequent events that it was Bill Schuman who had a major hand in the decision of the Naumburg Foundation to grant my work the recording award that led to its performance and recording by the New York Philharmonic in 1962.

Parallel with the recording award to my Second Symphony, the Naumburg Foundation announced a conductor's award to Werner Torkanowsky, a young ballet conductor, which provided him with the opportunity to conduct the New York Philharmonic in a single live performance of my symphony before recording it with the Philharmonic for Columbia Records. Whatever the reasons—whether inadequate preparation on his part, lack of understanding of my symphony, an essential nonseriousness of his nature—the initial rehearsal revealed serious problems. Things kept breaking down. My first intuitive sense of the man, that he lacked the kind of substance that inspires confidence, was unfortunately proving to be true. In the remaining rehearsals and live performance it became clear that it was the orchestra that pulled Torkanowsky through, rescued him, not for his sake, but out of a need to "save the honor" of the New York Philharmonic. I caught wind of their collective resolve to save the situation just before the recording session got under way a few days after the Carnegie Hall performance.

When I walked into the recording session, a group of five or six of the Philharmonic players, looking serious and determined, came to me. I didn't know quite what to expect or make of it. Saul Goodman, the orchestra's timpanist, acted as their spokesman. Clearly there had been prior discussion of whatever was on their minds and they had agreed on this way of carrying out what had been decided. From Saul's remarks I had a clear sense that he was speaking for the entire orchestra and not just a small group. "Don't worry, George," he said. "We want you to know that we understand the situation and the whole orchestra is behind you. No matter what happens, we're going to play your work so it comes out right." Not only what Saul Goodman said, but the determination with which he said it, assured me of the absolute resolve the orchestra had taken. I was immensely moved by this incredible gesture, and I was not insensible to the feelings toward me and my music that it conveyed. I shook hands with Saul and his colleagues, thanked them for their fantastic show of solidarity and expression of support, and wished all *buona fortuna.*

The recording session did, in fact, realize its purpose by producing (with the important help of John McClure and Tom Shepard of Columbia Records) a true representation of my Second Symphony.[5] And this I owe entirely to the players of the New York Philharmonic, a tough-minded, sturdy, committed ensemble of first-rate musicians endowed with a remarkable sense of probity.

I turn aside to try to describe the desperately threatening undercurrent that underlay and enveloped our family life from 1959 to 1964, virtually concurrent with Szell's first Cleveland performance of my Second Symphony. The winter that had New York in its grip in January 1962 was nothing compared to the winter in our souls. In the spring and summer of 1959, Gene and I began to realize that our son, Paul, was not well. He was fifteen years old and already writing poetry of striking imagery and astonishing insights, and yet there were signs that something was seriously wrong. Paul, too, was aware of some unnamable dread eating away at his vitals. His stoicism and bravery in the face of what he endured from the time of his first operation in October 1961 to the time of his death from a brain tumor in November 1964 was cataclysmic for all of us.

The undertow still drags at us and colors our existence, our perceptions, and our understandings. When Paul's illness took over our lives, we knew we had to maintain as much stability in our family as we were capable of. So when he could, Paul continued his studies, wrote poetry, and even graduated from the Haverford

School. Our daughter, Francesca ("Chessie"), was going to school and became very serious about ballet dancing; Gene kept the life of our family together, and I worked hard at building and shaping a new Department of Music at the University of Pennsylvania. Composing was at a virtual standstill. We had to match Paul's heroism, his unbelievable fortitude in the face of death, but his death remains forever irredeemable and we continue, inconsolable.

Life went on, and while in New York on a free night before the recording session, I decided to visit Edgard Varèse. When I phoned, Louise Varèse answered and said they were home that evening and would be very happy to see me. I had not yet met Louise but knew her translations of Rimbaud's poetry.[6] It was almost two years since Varèse and I had first met in Canada in August 1960 at an international symposium sponsored by Canadian composers. The sponsors had the wonderfully good sense to hold the symposium at Stratford the same time as the Stratford Shakespeare Festival. There we saw at least two powerfully effective productions of Shakespeare: *Romeo and Juliet* and the rarely played *King John*. Varèse, then in his late seventies, had come with Fred Prausnitz, the conductor, and some other people. I had been invited as a participant in the proceedings along with other American composers including Ernst Krenek, Gunther Schuller, and Aurelio de la Vega. Among the Canadian composers attending were John Weinzweig, Harry Freedman, Harry Somers, and Istvan Anhalt. Also present were Luciano Berio from Italy, Henri Dutilleux from France, Iain Hamilton from England, and Karl-Birger Blomdahl from Sweden. I formed immediate friendships with Istvan Anhalt and Aurelio de la Vega that we happily continue.

The circumstances under which I first met Varèse were the best possible—at a performance of my *Duo Concertante* for violin and cello. The performers were first-rate Canadian musicians who played with passion. After taking my bows and thanking them, someone brought me to Varèse, who was standing in the wings with his friends. He looked at me with great warmth, smiling; he shook my hand and then said two words that still echo in me: "Golden music." He spoke ardently, said other things I was happy to hear, but those first two words rang with magic for me. Words spoken directly to me by an older composer whom I admire greatly are rare and precious. In a lifetime I can recall only one other phrase that still rings with the same magic as Varèse's. That was Luigi Dallapiccola's "*ottimo lavoro*" ("supreme achievement") after I'd played for him my 1949 Second Piano Sonata in his home in Florence in May 1951.

The bond between Varèse and me had been established by that happy encounter in Canada, and I wanted to renew it. The January of 1962 was winter as I remember it growing up across the river in northern New Jersey—harsh, unrelenting, with constant low temperatures and piles of snow. Varèse lived in the Village on Eighth Street near Sullivan, and as I walked toward his place the wind cut like a knife. I had almost passed an Italian bakery but stopped to look in the window. What drew me was the sight of more panetones than I'd ever seen before.

The sight of them evoked my still-warm memories of Italy in 1950, the year Gene, Paul, and I had lived there. I entered the shop—the sudden warmth of it combined with the good odors of wonderfully fresh baking was immensely satisfying—and bought one of the extra-large panetones, carrying it triumphantly down the street. When I rang the bell of Varèse's apartment, Louise opened the door and greeted me saying something like, "What have you got there?" I responded, "A panetone. I thought you and Varèse would enjoy it." She laughed and said, "Oh no, we don't eat it. You'll have to eat the whole thing yourself!" By then we were in their apartment and Varèse and I were greeting each other like old friends. He seemed much older than when I'd last seen him. Louise was clearly concerned, keeping a solicitous eye on him. She was a charming woman, delicately made with a refined, patrician face. In her quiet manner there was firmness, clarity, and an appealing openness.

A wood fire was burning in the fireplace in their living room. High up, displayed on the walls, were all kinds of percussion instruments, most of them quite exotic, probably African or Asian. The warmth the fire gave off and the brandy Louise offered made me feel comfortable and at ease. I had a small piece of panetone, but neither Varèse nor Louise touched it. In the course of the evening I made a trip to the bathroom, which was also a library. The room was stuffed with books. A rather unexpected sight for a room normally devoted to other, more basic needs.

That evening Varèse told one fascinating story after another about his early years in New York, which created the close-up sense and feel of the 1920s and early 1930s that I knew only from reading and hearsay. Each story had a clear yet unconscious pattern. Each started by Varèse—and Louise gently breaking in from time to time supplying a necessary detail of fact or memory—telling how he'd met someone with wealth or position (or both) in New York society who was initially interested in him and his career and, at the same time, in helping him realize his project to advance the cause of new music in America, only to end in grave disappointments, broken promises, and abrupt estrangements and parting of the ways. It was all too painfully human.

After Varèse's death in 1965 at the age of eighty-two, Louise gave me a Karsh photo of Varèse that still hangs in my study not far from Bartók's. I can never forget how distressed I felt when she described how in his late years Varèse used to have violent nightmares from which he would wake up screaming, "I'll kill him, I'll kill him!" It was his father he dreamed of killing, because he could not forgive him for frustrating his early ambitions to be a composer. The ferocity of such feelings surely must have worked its way into Varèse's music and gave it its particular tactility, claw, and edge, which were intensely real, quite the opposite of the fabricated ferocity of Stravinsky, who, like Richard Strauss in another aesthetic realm, was a master of the posed, of the simulacrum of the real thing.

There is no posing in Varèse. He was the "last of the romantics." I believe he saw himself as the "artist as hero" who contends against the world and goes down to defeat. Key to this sense is the very kind of self-image early nineteenth-century romanticism had encouraged and fostered—not only in composers, but also in writers and artists. This sense flowered into full bloom in the late decades of that century and continued into the early decades of the twentieth, not as "romanticism" but as "modernism." Which is to say, the sense of being the artist-hero supported by a powerful sense of unique individuality shifted its attachment from a complete immersion in the beliefs associated with the romantic movement to as complete an immersion in beliefs now tied to the convictions of the modernist movement. Orthodoxies beget orthodoxies, and it is not uncommon to switch passionate allegiances from one set of beliefs to their exact opposites. Modernism, when it began in the first decades of the twentieth century, was the last and perhaps most blatantly blaring form of romanticism of a century earlier—and, while stylistically its complete opposite, it was psychologically identical in its insistence on the primacy of the individual ego. It is precisely in that sense that Varèse is the "last of the romantics," for even as a modernist, he *lived* as a romantic, seeing himself as the defeated victim of a personal fate against which ultimately he could only rage. A strange interlude.

CHAPTER 2

A Concert of Music

Caprice Variations for Solo Violin

The story of how my *Caprice Variations* for solo violin came into being and how it continues to take on new life in new forms involves many people, places, and circumstances spread over a wide arc of time.

Two people, totally unbeknownst to each other, Daniel Kobialka, a young, gifted violinist, and our daughter, Chessie, then a young ballet dancer with the Buffalo Ballet Company, were—directly in the one case, indirectly in the other—responsible for initiating the impulses that led to the "CVs," as they've come to be called. Dan Kobialka was the catalyst for my even thinking of writing a solo violin work, and Chessie, unwittingly, had a central role in the form the CVs took as a huge set of variations on the theme of Paganini's 24th Caprice for solo violin.[1]

In the late 1960s I met Dan Kobialka and his younger brother Jan, both in their early twenties. Jan, an excellent cellist, matched his brother in musicality, temperament, and technique, and together they made a first-rate duo. I coached them for a recording of my *Duo Concertante,* which they did in 1969 for Advance Recordings.[2] It was Dan who planted the idea of my writing for solo violin, and when the CVs were published I dedicated them to him.

Chessie became the guiding angel/spirit who directed the nature of the work I was eventually to write. In 1968 at sixteen, Chessie joined the Buffalo Ballet, a newly formed company of exceedingly talented young dancers. Kathleen Crofton, who had been affiliated with the London Sadler's Wells Ballet, was founder and director. She had the requisite toughness and, though kind, never failed to tell a dancer who wasn't giving her all, "There's always the wayside, dearie. There's always the wayside." The girls knew what that meant! They didn't need a translation.

It was the summer of 1969 that the Buffalo Ballet Company was invited to perform at Jacob's Pillow in the Berkshires. Gene and I were glowing for Chessie, because she was to be featured as one of the two "grey girls" in *Les biches*, the famous dance choreographed to Poulenc's music in the 1920s by Nijinska, sister of the ill-fated Nijinsky. Also planned for the Jacob's Pillow program was a new ballet to piano music of Brahms. As fate would have it, Nijinska chose to choreograph parts of Brahms's two books of variations for piano solo on Paganini's 24th Caprice.[3]

No longer young, Nijinska was short, round, and intimidating to the young dancers. She rehearsed the company wearing several sweaters and what looked like an old robe. Through layers of Russo-French idioms, syntax, accent, and the famous hand gestures, Nijinska managed to convey her choreography to the dancers, who responded with rapt attention and devotion.

Gene and I attended all five performances scheduled for Jacob's Pillow. We wanted to spend as much time as possible with our daughter and to enjoy her beautiful dancing. Had we planned only to attend the premiere plus one performance there might never have been any CVs, but by the time the last performance ended I was totally in thrall to Brahms's *Paganini Variations*. The work had taken complete hold of me—especially the harmonic structure of the Caprice theme itself. While familiar with virtually all the works based on Paganini's Caprice, I found myself making mental comparisons, for example, between Brahms's variations and Rachmaninoff's *Rhapsody* for piano and orchestra[4]—to my taste one of Rachmaninoff's better works, and Brahms's variations and Lutosławski's two-piano set.[5] Rachmaninoff's treatment I thought far richer harmonically and emotionally than Lutosławski's. But Brahms's was superior to all the others, including Paganini's own variations on his Caprice theme.

After returning home I began sight-reading at the piano—for I had never studied Brahms's sets—both books of his variations, noting particularly the ones that caught my fancy. I was especially interested in Brahms' harmony and all the ways he found to flesh out and vary the large, open-framed harmonic structure of the Caprice theme. Never having been a Schenkerian, my "analysis," how I approach an understanding of musical structure whether "in the large" or "in the small," exists on quite a different plane from the abstract reductionism underlying Schenker's premises. I need concrete tangibilities and palpabilities I can hear and feel. (A famous story is told about Schoenberg's reaction to Schenker's analysis of Beethoven's "Eroica" Symphony that a friend once showed him. After looking it over he asked, "But where are my favorite melodies?")

It is a lifelong predilection when thinking about composition to insist on being able to hear inwardly and to join that inward hearing directly with what I am able to comprehend analytically. In this instance I wanted to grasp the absolute fundamental harmonic frame that supports the bare-bones structure of the harmonic progression making the Caprice theme a self-contained, starkly simple, yet densely packed, single musical thought. Harmonically understood, its phrases are primary to what we mean when we say "tonal." The very fundamental simplicity and primordial nature of its progressions provide the perfect frame and scaffolding for every possible kind of harmonic adventure without losing touch with its unchanging core. This meant I was able to push close to the tonal periphery as well as to break through that tonal envelope into the atonal world on the other side yet still feel connected to the tonal frame of the Caprice theme. Thus I could join together in a single large context the antipodes that most musicians and composers still automatically assume are logically antithetic to each other. I was searching for ways to anchor atonal adventures in tonal thinking.

During this entire process, I returned again and again to the realization that the model for understanding Paganini's theme as an *Ur*-structure came from my early fascination with Beethoven's two "Eroica" variation sets: the last movement of the "Eroica" Symphony and the earlier piano set, op. 35.[6] Where did Beethoven find such an idea as his "theme"? Was this theme for both sets actually a theme as understood in the melodic sense, or was it a stripped-down, denuded skeletal frame outlining the primordial nodal points of harmonic motions to be more fully realized in the variations built on this scaffolding?

Beethoven, we have to surmise, was quite familiar with the chaconne and passacaglia ground basses of the baroque composers over which they hung endless chains of decorative variants in as many voices as suited their purpose. But in a more particular sense the idea is inherent in the harmonic motion and underlying bass line of the "Prometheus" theme from an earlier work, a ballet score of the same name.[7] This "Prometheus" theme is a lyrical effusion of the young Beethoven that, by itself, might neither suggest nor provide the adventures we find in both "Eroica" sets in which Beethoven engages. But the stripped, bare bass line achieves precisely that. By no means is it a reversion to older baroque practice, but it does suggest rather strongly that Beethoven was thinking of the old chaconne/passacaglia ground basses and what could be done with them.

But if that were all, we would miss deeper strata of Beethoven's intense awareness of baroque practice, among them, for example, his passion for counterpoint, particularly double invertible counterpoint. In this he continues a direct carryover and inheritance from Haydn and Mozart, both of whom had an equal passion for the devices of baroque contrapuntal technique. But it is in Beethoven's dramatic transformation of the fugue that he carries his rethinking of baroque practice to levels not even dreamed of by Bach or Handel, let alone Haydn or Mozart. The flowering of Beethoven's new vision of what fugue might become as a vehicle of musical intensification into high emotional drama, paradoxically realized through unique intellectual mastery, surely includes op. 35's fugue and reaches its peak in the fugues of the late chamber works, the Ninth Symphony, and the *Missa Solemnis*. But still greater levels are erected in the fugues of the "Hammerklavier" Sonata, op. 106, and the Sonata in A-flat Major, op. 110. It is from this point of view I see the construction of the "Eroica" variation sets' bass line resting solidly on the model of the old baroque chaconne/passacaglia ground basses.

A good set of variations needs an actual or implied fundamental harmonic frame large enough and sufficiently open to permit filling out, expanding, compressing, substituting, even bending out of shape so long as the frame remains fundamentally stable even as it seems to undergo change. Its transformation is akin to a kind of musical topology. Beethoven's "Eroica" variations theme is a perfect model of such a scaffolding, Paganini's Caprice theme another.

Once the Caprice theme became second nature to me, I began another process: tracking down and mentally identifying melodic incipits in past works whose implied harmony matched hand in glove the initial tonic/dominant motion of Paganini's harmonic frame. Interesting things began turning up; possibilities that appeared to have no immediate relationship began to connect. In this way I built up a small "library" of incipits to work with. I wanted to show that regardless of when melodic ideas have been composed, there exists below the shifting historical surface of style a capacity for drawing melodic images from an unchanging "collective unconscious" that connects all individual melodic-harmonic image making to a larger, nonindividual whole.

By the time I was free to write the CVs it was January 1970. I had spent hours in another kind of preparation: studying carefully the solo violin music of J. S. Bach and Eugène Ysaÿe for their treatment of soloistic technique. Though some reviewers and commentators have referred to the CVs as a "history of writing for the solo violin," my intention was to explore not history per se, but every possible violinistic technical device that appealed to me in order to write variations in every direction, tonal in all its manifestations including the chromatic, and atonal in its wide range of possibilities without necessarily relying on twelve-tone or serial methods. Chromaticism clearly anchored in tonality strongly suggests, of course, nineteenth-century romanticism; whereas atonal chromaticism, set free from key centers, is one of the principal modes of modernism whether or not there is a row or a series present. Dissonant tonality, "invented" principally by Stravinsky, is made so by displacing and metrically misaligning conventional melodic/harmonic agreements that result in distorted tonal perspective, throwing the perspective off-center so it is heard as though aurally askew. Dissonant tonality shares with the cubism of Picasso and Braque the reordering of disassembled features and elements—in painting, of faces, bodies, and objects; in composition, of chords and scales—new and unexpected juxtapositions and reconfigurations that baffle or disorient conventional norms of perception.

Wherever we have lived I've always had a favorite couch where I often rest, think, and compose. With my eyes shut tight, I hear far better than when they are open. The CVs were composed entirely this way—on my favorite couch. It's like listening to a radio broadcasting in my head. Almost everything I've written happens this way—my "radio" turns on automatically and shuts off only when the work I'm obsessed with is completed. It is then and only then that the "radio" ceases broadcasting. My "radio" broadcasts only from a single station—my inner ear. In this way I sketched three, four, and sometimes five variations a day. It was as though they came virtually ready-made. And when they flashed across my mind and took shape in my inner ear I would dash up to my studio to put them on paper, to capture them in flight before they might fade—which sometimes did happen, leaving only ragged, disjointed fragments behind. The real difference between working this way—a kind of daydreaming—and nightdreaming is that the nightdream is lost at the moment of daytime consciousness. I have dreamed music all my life—I suspect many composers do—quite fantastic dreams of exquisite music, but not once have I remembered in awakened consciousness what I heard in sleep.

Dreams of music are not the strangest of my recurrent dreams, but they surely exist in a category all by themselves. Music transforms into unearthly landscapes, or nature transforms into unearthly music, and usually in one of two forms. In the one, I am in an incredibly beautiful place of trees, fields, and hills. Water is often part of such surreal, "natural" landscapes. (In the dreaming everything seems perfectly natural.) Wondrously, the trees and fields, hills, and water begin to make their own music—a sounding of the purest instrumental music that possesses a quality of delicacy of texture and design of shapes and phrases impossible to describe. Most remarkably, in a dream I know in the conscious sense of clear awareness that I have never heard such music before; it seems unlike any human music ever composed. It is an Edenic music. In the other I see large sheets of music, not music as we know it in the nondream world, but notated as landscapes, or as cityscapes combined with landscapes, and rendered as special kinds of unearthly scene painting delicately etched in color, never black and white. Certainly always mysterious, unlike anything I've ever seen in waking consciousness. At times they sound—at times not. But whether they sound or not, they are always "music." I long desperately to be able to convert what I see on the page into living sound, and there is the uncanny sense that I know I am dreaming and when I awake I will have the power to "translate" what I have seen in the dream into the actual music it represents pictorially. But no, it has never happened. Only once in waking life have I had the remarkable experience of discovering in the phenomenal world of nature the living counterpart of a piece of music I have loved since my early twenties.

This occurred when my wife and I were driving through Jackson Hole in Wyoming. In the near distance, looming against the vast, blue sky, were the gray-brown, jagged peaks of the Tetons, the tallest thirteen thousand feet high, each peak shaped like a huge projectile pointing into the sky, one after another. Suddenly—as I took in this astonishing scene—I heard the jagged, sky-reaching theme of Beethoven's *Grosse Fuge,* op. 133, the one that comes in as upbeat to measure 31. Each was the magical image of the other, each as real as the other, the one a natural, earthly phenomenon, the other an incredible musical gesture, nature refracted through the human soul and psyche and formed by the spirit. That image of the Tetons as the reflection in nature of Beethoven's rugged fugal theme or the mirror image of the two remains with me as an epiphany, a blazing moment of revelation, linking itself to my recurrent dream.

Years later in Australia I met and talked with an ethnomusicologist who was working with Aborigine earth music. As she described the Aborigine concept of earth music, itself a form of dreaming, I experienced once again the extraordinary quality of my own dreams, the uncanny connection between the Tetons and Beethoven, and the forms the earth takes in nature and how dreamlike they translate into music in phenomenal existence.

Now, when I think of my couch, especially in connection with the CVs, I remember William Wordsworth, the much-scoffed-at poet, parodied in verse by his contemporaries. The association is far from idle, for Wordsworth also had a couch on which he presumably rested, based on the evidence of the lines "And oft when on my couch I lie in vacant or in pensive mood," from the famous "I Wandered Lonely as a Cloud." Years ago Gene and I actually saw Wordsworth's couch at his house in Rydal Mount in the Lake District of England. It was well over six feet long, square-cut, and covered with some kind of cracked black material I took to be worn-out leather. The reference to it in the last stanza of his 1804 "Daffodils" poem "I wandered lonely as a cloud," is all the evidence I need that Wordsworth preceded me as a "couch composer."

Before continuing to describe the performers of the CVs and their performances, it becomes necessary to introduce the thorny aspect of my break with
modernism. It is a matter of sufficient magnitude to warrant returning to any
number of times. Here I wish to discuss it only in general terms as it relates to
the CVs. Considerably more will emerge when I discuss my Third String Quartet,
which was, in some regards, a direct outgrowth of the CVs and inevitably gives
the reasons why I abandoned the exclusive use of modernism.

The story begins in the early sixties and overlaps the time in 1963 when I turned
away from twelve-tone composition. It was the outgrowth of a *powerful positive,* balanced inversely by an equally *powerful negative.* It is quite impossible to
describe in any detail my subjective states and the perpetual internal debate that
took place in me during the period in which I had grown painfully aware of the
extreme limitations of modernism. Certainly I felt I could go no further in a form
of musical expression that lent itself too readily to the indeterminate and abstract
in both projection and perception. I came to a dead-end. Nor was I interested in
the overt attitude so visibly evident among my contemporaries of being at the
"edge" just for the sake of being there. It all struck me as empty posturings that
ended in bad music and worse art. This was also the time of the "night of the soul"
with all its fears and anxieties. Our family was in a fierce struggle with the mortal
illness that was threatening our son Paul's life. For five years Paul's heroic fight to
live and write poetry never wavered, and his example became the model for all
we did and thought. Although his brave memory sustains us still, after his death
we would never be the same, and my music had to change.

In what follows I want to state the *positive* without being exhaustive in its myriad
ramifications. Music in the West developed over long centuries as an essentially
inclusive art, without necessarily discarding past practices along the way. This cumulative, evolving inclusivity allowed for processes of increasing subtlety and sophistication in the means of craft, specifically in polyphony and harmony, carried
forward and handed down from generation to generation as a rich and growing
tradition based on disciplined knowledge and practice. These processes made it
possible for tonality as a language of musical speech and expression to grow through
evolving stylistic changes instead of beginning anew with every change.

By the mid-twentieth century, concert programming, reflecting in an unself-
conscious way this principle of historical inclusivity, offered audiences the widest
possible range of works from different periods, including works by living composers. The development of atonality was *not* antithetic to tonality but was, on
the contrary, a necessary extension of musical thought into previously avoided
borderland states of consciousness—essentially dark, unstable, psychologically

covering a spectrum from neurosis to psychosis in human life and now open to musical expression as, for example, in Bartók's *Miraculous Mandarin,* Alban Berg's *Wozzeck* and *Lulu,* Schoenberg's *Pierrot lunaire* and *Erwartung,* and Stravinsky's *Le sacre du printemps.*

Everything I have pointed to can be understood as movement consciously directed away from the abstract and toward the concrete, toward the palpable and memorable as opposed to that which is thought rather than felt, merely heard rather than perceived and registered, therefore resistant to memorability. By now, whatever modernism has produced of value as possible forms of expression has been absorbed into the cumulative, ongoing stream of historical inclusivity.

The *negative* can be stated in what follows, also without being exhaustive in its branching ramifications. Modernism from its inception sought to obliterate all vestiges of the past in all art, not just music. This campaign of "aesthetic cleansing" was periodically proclaimed throughout the century, first by Italian Futurists, later by propagandists like Ezra Pound who not only wanted to "Make It New!" but who also became a fanatic fascist, fighting with words against the survival of political democracy. Modernist zealots such as Apollinaire in France, who published lists of "*merde à*" all the monuments of art of the past and "*rose à*" his contemporaries in the adventures of the new art. Chief among them were D'Annunzio in Italy, whom Mussolini aped in gesture and public display, and Clement Greenberg, who celebrated (in the 1950s) the arrival of the two-dimensional flatness of abstract expressionism in the post–World War II United States. Consistent with such a generalized program Anton Webern could, for example, in the 1930s in his private lectures called "The Path to the New Music"[8] declare "the death of tonality" as necessary in order to make way for the twelve-tone method of composition devised by Schoenberg. With "the death of tonality" came also "the death" of the use of common triads and chords, scales and arpeggios—virtually all stepwise pitch motion except for the chromatic half step and its octave displacements. An ideology of exclusion developed in the first half of this century and fostered the continuing evolution of exclusionary tactics pronounced by false prophets such as Boulez, who praised amnesia in regard to the past of music, and Cage, who proposed the virtual anonymity of composition via chance procedures, thus, in theory, disallowing any visible individual fingerprints discoverable in "work" thus "composed."

The narrowing of thought and gesture led to the destruction of the possibility of multiplicity of ideas, images, and means in favor of single ideas, images, and means. Such conscious reductionism and renunciation led to aesthetic "downsizing" resulting in bare surfaces where only cold abstraction could subsist. Intellectual coldness replaced emotional heat, paucity and parsimoniousness took the place of richness and largesse, the resulting stinginess inhibited outpour, emotional generosity. Ideological posturings fostered by the politics of both left and right by fascist/communist dictatorships and tyrannies had their counterparts in aesthetic ideological posturings that attempted to define and control what art and artists could and could not do. Aesthetic ideological repression cropped up in disguised ways also in democratic societies and attempted to tyrannize those who refused to join in the politicization of aesthetics and art. Inevitably, modernism had to die of its own lack of inner spirit and nourishment. The bitter, acrimonious modernist proselytes and zealots who still linger on in academic nooks and crannies in Europe and America will ultimately dry up and blow away because modernism as an avant-garde no longer has a necessary or vital function to perform in world culture.

Out of this internal debate I carried on between the two sides of the modernist dilemma came, in writing the CVs, a resolution of the problem as I saw and felt it, an "answer" in musical terms that attempted to show how it was possible to represent different and seemingly opposite worlds in the same work, and simultaneously show that the technical and linguistic means that derived from seemingly exclusionary traditions—the tonal excluding the atonal, the atonal the tonal—were false not only in theory, but in practice, as well. They were, in fact, compatible in much the same way the human face that smiles and sheds light and warmth can be the same face that frowns and threatens. Regardless of the obvious differences between the emotional sources of the "contemporary" variations and the more "traditional" ones, the former, though couched in more atonal terms, are nevertheless cast in structural forms that are clear analogues to Paganini's *Ur*-frame. That, after all, was the point of trying to show that aesthetic reconciliation between opposites was possible.

The first complete performance of all fifty CVs was given by Lewis Kaplan soon after they were finished, not in a concert hall, but as a live broadcast over radio station WBAI in New York, April 1970. The broadcast began with Eric Salzman introducing Lewis and saying a few words about the CVs, and then Lewis proceeded to play. It may not have been the most polished of performances, but it conveyed great conviction because the violinist believed wholeheartedly in the work, in the rightness of its combination of the old and the new, the tonal and the nontonal. He played with the spontaneity and freshness of "the first time." Clearly he communicated this to the studio audience, who returned exactly what a committed performer wants and needs: rapt, serious, focused attention. Many in the audience were musicians; some were composers. I couldn't have asked for better.

Stamina, pacing, managing the emotional highs and lows of tension and release as well as psychic energies and their dispositions—these are bound to play crucial roles in producing a musically engrossing performance of an approximately seventy-five-minute solo violin work such as the CVs. If it were to be done at all, the performer would have to possess the kind of musical prowess that takes an audience with him, the courage to override conventional habits of programming such a long, demanding work, and an unswerving dedication to the music itself. Miraculously, there was such a musician who entered my world in the late 1990s—Peter Sheppard Skaerved. At the time we met, Peter was already working up the CVs and asked for my guidance. I was immediately taken with his musicality, personal warmth, exuberance, and great intelligence. Everything about the violinist was charged with energy. He took to the mixture of the tonal and the atonal without a blink. I couldn't quite believe it when he began telling me in letters from Sarajevo, Zagreb, and other cities in the former states of Yugoslavia that he was playing the entire CVs to astonishingly enthusiastic audiences. As time went on, the geographic circle of his performances spread to include western China, Turkey, and Mexico.

During this period Peter must have determined to record the whole work for Metier, a British label. On August 28 and 30, 2000, he recorded a ninety-minute version, necessitating two CDs.[9] (After many live performances, Peter felt it was essential to honor all the repeat signs I had written into the score.) When he was asked to give a concert of my violin and piano music at the Venice Biennale in September 2003, he programmed the ninety-minute CVs version along with my Sonata for Violin and Piano (1988) and the *Rhapsody and Prayer* (1989) for violin and piano, both of which he performed with pianist Aaron Schorr. It went so well that Peter decided to arrange an American tour with the same program. The first stop was Swarthmore College in February 2004, which gave me the opportunity to hear him do the entire CVs live. It was an amazing display of sheer technical prowess and bravura, emotionally rich in projection, musicianly to the nth degree. Peter has a thoroughly personal way of performing—especially solo music. Extraordinarily free and unstudied in his physical motions, his body is loose yet graceful. The marvel is that his playing is always controlled; he knows exactly what he wants with each figure, phrase, musical gesture. For ninety minutes he held the rapt attention of an unusually knowledgeable, sophisticated audience. It was a great triumph for him as well as the work he delivered with such love and understanding.

The professional concert life of the CVs had begun when Zvi Zeitlin played a set of twenty-three or twenty-four variations at Hunter College in New York, February 28, 1976. Wisely, Zvi's decision to limit himself to a substantial group rather than play the entire work proved to be right. This was the best way to test them before a New York audience. Because they responded to his performance with great enthusiasm, he was encouraged to think seriously about recording the entire work. A bold step, indeed. When Zvi informed me that Musical Heritage had agreed to record the work, I was immensely pleased.[10] In preparation for the recording sessions scheduled for June 1976 at Zvi's home base, the Eastman School of Music in Rochester, New York, I invited him to stay with us in at our home in Newtown Square so we could work together in comfortable, relaxed circumstances. Our purpose was to polish those CVs he had not played in New York and to refine the ones he had; also to decide the order of succession of the fifty variations. Though potentially, various satisfactory orders are possible, one of the important factors in arriving at a musically viable succession of the CVs, especially in their entirety, is the idiosyncratic temperament of the performer making choices and how that order fits his particular temperament. Also, on reflection, a concert order is bound to be different from the one suitable to recording. This proved to be the case when Eliot Fisk made a CD of his own transcription/recomposition of the CVs for guitar.[11]

June came, and I went to Rochester to stay with Zvi while we recorded. Three successive sessions were scheduled for late evening to take advantage of the quiet that descends on most cities—and, in this case, the Eastman School itself, where recording would take place. During the day Zvi and I worked on the variations he would record that night. Much time was needed—three full-length sessions, each hours long, allowing Zvi to do as many "takes" as necessary to make sure everything was "covered," as the lingo has it.

The next stage in this indeterminate, undetermined unfolding of the CVs story took place in 1983 at Carnegie Hall, where the International American Music Competition for violinists cosponsored by the Rockefeller Foundation and Carnegie Hall was in progress. A list of twentieth-century works for violin by American composers, which included the CVs, provided the repertoire from which the competing violinists could choose their programs. One of the judges was Gidon Kremer. He heard one of the contestants play a group of the CVs and immediately decided to look into them with the idea of performing them himself. Considering Kremer's volatile temperament—not surprising.

On January 13, 1985, Gidon Kremer included a substantial number of the CVs on a recital at Carnegie Hall. It was then that I first met him. I was astounded at how he played—with a kind of electric, nervous energy lending an aura of shifting colors, certainly not given to many violinists or string players generally. His phrases inscribed plastic shapes in the air that seemed to take on visible, material form. He could release torrents of wild, abandoned gestures that, while bordering on losing control, never did. Not many months later I received a letter from a Japanese friend who described Kremer's performance in Tokyo of the same set of CVs. She wrote that the music made her "shiver."

In 1986, Gidon recorded for Deutsche Grammophon twenty-four CVs—possibly the same group he played at Carnegie Hall—as part of a solo violin CD, each work of which had some connection to Paganini. Hence the title of the CD: *A Paganini: Virtuoso Violin Music*.[12] The front cover has a photo of Gidon, his scraggly hair almost down to his shoulders, the violin tucked under his chin, fingers on the strings, the bow poised as though in action. On either side of him stood tall candelabra with large, burning candles and two attendants in court dress. Clearly all intended to depict a nineteenth-century scene.[13]

Gidon Kremer's extensive, even intensive, relation to the CVs reached its summit early in May 1992. A farewell concert for Riccardo Muti, the Philadelphia Orchestra's music director, who was leaving to return to Milan, Italy, included on its roster of guests Gidon Kremer. The event was telecast on one of the major TV networks, so Gene and I decided to watch it in the comfort of our own home. The program was essentially a potpourri of things, mainly arias from Italian opera. Muti sat stage right, a foot or so down from the last stands of the first violins. It was a dull, lackluster affair until Gidon burst from the wings offstage left, virtually dancing his way across to where Muti was sitting, playing the CVs for all he was worth. It was a great performance, but more than that, it was a "show," almost vaudevillian as he bobbed and weaved like a prizefighter pouring out the CVs, one after another, demonically, his face lit up with smiling laughter as he went. The effect, so readily visible on the TV screen as the cameras panned back and forth, was positively electric. Muti had the look of a man who didn't know what hit him. His jaw dropped with the shock of the explosion that was Kremer's performance. Indeed, there was something wonderfully free and released in it. Finally Gidon finished with a grand flourish. There was an uproar from the audience and wild appreciation from the orchestra. No one, least of all Muti, could have anticipated the phenomenon of Gidon Kremer's mad intensity of projection.

Into this tale enters one of the liveliest spirits of all in American music-making, the great guitarist Eliot Fisk, the inheritor—literally and figuratively—of Andrés Segovia's mantle. Apparently Eliot learned about the CVs in the early 1990s from his good friend and colleague at the Mozarteum in Salzburg, violinist Ruggiero Ricci. I had not brought them to Eliot's attention for the simple reason I was preoccupied with new works I was doing for him and hadn't even thought of the CVs as potentially transcribable for solo guitar, even though I knew that a good deal of the repertoire for present-day concert guitarists is made up of transcriptions of solo violin music—such as J. S. Bach's six Sonatas and Partitas (BWV 1001–1006). Clearly classical guitarists are more aware of this than composers who, like myself, are not guitarists. It was Eliot who taught me the obvious but rarely noted fact that the cross-string technique of violin playing, which arpeggiates tonal chords and even dissonant atonal, highly chromatic ones is one of the principal carryovers from violin playing (bowed) to guitar playing (plucked and strummed). Added to that was the ability to write for the violin in such a way as to accompany a melody with supporting chords or figures. This, too, lends itself readily to the guitar. In the Bach Partitas there are, for example, fugues and contrapuntal passages for two and three voices. This, too, can be replicated on the guitar. And of course, the violin technique of playing two-, three-, and four-part chords simultaneously (or in broken fashion) translates directly into guitar playing. Already a master transcriber of old music from violin to guitar, it was no mystery for Eliot to go about working up a guitar version of the CVs.[14]

Eliot frequently consulted me via airmail from Europe and phone calls from anywhere and everywhere, plus working visits where he would show me what he was doing and I could respond with suggestions or simply marvel at his grasp and understanding. Inevitably the sound of the CVs on the guitar automatically gave them new and different qualities, often quite unexpected. Many of the CVs lent themselves immediately to the guitar, whereas others had to be reworked, not as composition, but to arrive at what was idiomatic for the guitar while fully retaining the musical sense of the original.

I still find what Eliot achieved brilliant. His approach is as much "recomposition" as it is "transcription" and remains completely idiomatic for the guitar while retaining the characters and qualities of the original CVs. His grouping for recording purposes (June 6–8, 1993, in England) is striking and ingenious.[15] But two important aspects need pointing out and stressing. First, before he began work on the CVs, Eliot had already transcribed all twenty-four Caprices for solo violin of Paganini.[16] I did not hear the recording of his Paganini transcription until after he had recorded the CVs, but when I did, I understood instantly what had driven him to undertake so mammoth a task as transcribing my work. It *had* to be preceded by the Paganini transcription to be done at all; the later one depended on the experience of having accomplished the earlier one. In the case of both sets of transcriptions, Eliot wisely tried out groups of them in his concerts, undoubtedly to get the feel of their projection and to gauge their effect on audiences. What he did with the Paganini Caprices is an astonishing feat, musically and technically.

In the Paganini the guitar sounds much bigger acoustically both in concert and recording. This leads to the second and related point: I still do not comprehend rationally why his transcription/recomposition of the CVs enlarges the sound of the guitar to double or even triple its "normal" acoustical size as physical sound and as idiomatic possibilities. Perhaps it is only an illusion. But if it is, it is indeed strange that in those regards—sound and idiom—Eliot's Paganini confirms my CVs and vice-versa where unforced enlargement is concerned. It is as though he takes the guitar to a new acoustical/technical plateau, stretches it to the very edge of what it is physically capable of being and doing. In every way his CVs are a tour de force that has proven itself over and over in concert form.

Perhaps the reason was sheer proximity in time that made me turn to the CVs when I started to think about writing my Third String Quartet. Other factors went into the early stages, but that was one of the principal ones. And it would have been perfectly natural in any case, the CVs having been completed February 1970, and the actual beginning of work on the quartet dating from December 1971. Nothing else came between—the CVs remained fresh and alive for me. Psychologically, I had become familiar with the signs of certain processes that operated independently in me—visible and traceable in the aftereffects and affects on my consciousness of the music I had most recently completed. These were often long-lasting and extraordinarily palpable. I continued feeling the music in me as alive in itself, a substance that would go on living beyond itself, something yet to be born. But another tendency operated. As often as not, I consciously and determinedly frustrated this afterlife by going in a direction completely opposite to the qualities and characteristics of the last work done; I had a positive abhorrence of merely replicating what I'd already written, of falling into the habit of repeating gestures, figures, designs. In this I was fully aware I was rejecting outright a process of self-replication I heard and saw all around me in the successive new works of composer colleagues—and even more obviously among the painters and sculptors of the abstract expressionist school, for whom self-replication had become a way of being and functioning. I marveled that composers and artists of the avant-garde persuasion had fixated on self-identity via a single, consistently recognizable style-idea as his or her trademark and signature. I preferred the freer, wilder image of the ruthless, protean, shape-shifting buccaneer of twentieth-century painting—Picasso—who made more than one revolution in his time with perfect equanimity.

Before the actual writing of the Third String Quartet, I allowed myself to be drawn back into the CVs for both stimulation and provocation—and as a source of ready-made ideas that could serve as jumping-off places for inventing new ways of making use of them through enlargement, expansion, and textural and gestural enhancement. For the new quartet I had decided on a large-scale, five-movement design for which I wanted sharply differing ideas, atmospheres, and environments, not only for each movement, but also for sections within separate movements. To a large extent, this decision was predicated on the urge to write a work whose proportions juxtaposed, on a very broad scale, strongly marked tonal and atonal polarities. Here I was continuing what I had already begun in the CVs, projecting yet further my sense that the tonal and atonal faces of music were nonetheless intimately related by the opposite tendencies inherent in essential polarities, an idea that grew in significance as I observed it in both nature and art. In this way the CVs became a sourcebook not only for the quartet but for later works.

Tracing out the specific CVs that engendered major aspects of the quartet will underscore the essential polarities of the tonal and atonal physiognomies that marked the new work as a departure from old modernist thinking and undoubtedly helped produce the initial shock that greeted its first public appearance. What was innocent enough in its birdcall repetitiveness as no. 18 of the CVs changed radically when it took the amplified form of harsh, unrelenting, four-part chordal parallelisms of tritone-separated fifth intervals, E♭–B♭/A♮–E♮, in the opening gesture of the first movement, "Introduction: Fantasia." (Tritone-related fifths, this time A♭–E♭/D♮–A♮, provide the essential harmonic ostinato environment in the second movement "March" rhythmic fancy whose pattern came to me directly after seeing Charlie Chaplin's *Modern Times*.)

The fifth movement, "Finale," which lives entirely through successive juxtapositions of the atonal and tonal "Scherzos and Serenades" of its subtitle, draws its primary scherzo, nontonal, rhythmically asymmetric idea directly from no. 19 of the CVs and is expanded for 150 measures at the outset of the movement and comes back as the elongated coda of the movement (and the entire work) starting at measure 515 and ending with measure 779. All the other materials of the "Finale," the tonal "Serenades" and tonal "Scherzo," have no relation at all to the CVs. The large middle of the quartet, which comprises the variation movement, owes almost everything to the CVs. First of all, its "theme" is an expanded, freshly invented version of CV no. 36, which determines the key of the movement, A major.

The key of A major has an indefinable quality—quality more than color; although I can imagine someone else hearing what I am calling "quality" as "color"—an indescribable-in-ordinary-language state of purity bordering on another indescribable state, that of the soul detached from the gross materiality of the phenomenal world, an inner condition of luminosity, a sense of the numinous. (My *Ricordanza* for cello and piano, also in A major, has something of the same luminosity.) Of the six variations that complete the third movement, four CVs were sources for three: nos. 37, 23, 29, and 30. The fourth movement, "March," which is both a variant and continuation of the second-movement "March," takes a brief episode from CV no. 33 and expands it far beyond its simpler initial appearance.

I've described how I used my CVs as a sourcebook for the Third String Quartet—more to show how an already existent work of one's own may serve as a launching pad for a new and different work, not through self-imitation and replication but rather by taking off from the existent work in wholly "other" directions with entirely "new" intentions and results. In much the same way I am convinced that by allowing oneself to be influenced by those who have preceded us or by our contemporaries, the fear of losing one's "originality"—which haunted the modernists—would have evaporated in the warmth of admiration for work done by others. It was a groundless fear, an extreme position of the superromanticism of excessive individualism fostered by the new twentieth century.

Not every telling requires a coda. But in this particular instance one presents itself in a perfectly natural way with the recent recordings of small groups of CVs by the violinist Michelle Makarski, recordings of special sensitivity, polish, and expressivity. In June 1997 I received a letter and CD from her. The CD bore the title *Caoine* and included in its program ten of only the contemporary-sounding CVs.[17] Stephen Hartke, her friend and the composer of the music from which the title was taken, had "steered" her "toward recording some of [the] *Caprice Variations* on the enclosed CD." In her letter she describes parenthetically the curious coincidence of birdsong mingling with the opening variation (no. 18) of the set she chose: "(. . . if you think you hear chirping mid-way through the opening variation, you are not mistaken. The birds in the eaves of the monastery chapel seemed to be responding to what I was doing—and at virtually the identical pitch levels—so we obligingly left them in!)." And no wonder. For what the birds were responding to is itself based on birdcalls I had heard from the stand of trees beyond our back lawn.

Two years were to pass until March 1999, when I received another letter from Makarski, telling me she was planning another solo CD and meant to include, this time, four of the tonal, expressive, and slow CVs that, as she wrote, "were not recorded by Kremer and so only appear in Zeitlin's and Fisk's complete versions." Since I had to be in New York on April 22, I arranged for us to meet for a morning working session. I liked her immediately for her seriousness and nervous intensity mixed with warmth. As we worked, her playing grew stronger and more controlled, her phrases more expressive and plastic. It was a good session, and after an hour and a half we both felt she was ready to record.

On listening to the second CD[18] I was pleased to hear Michelle's delicately refined performance of the tonal CVs sounding in the context of atonal pieces by Luigi Dallapiccola, Luciano Berio, and Goffredo Petrassi. It was a telling touch of aesthetic judgment and balance resulting from a keen sense of sharp contrast of opposites to offer contemporary-sounding CVs in the chiefly tonal program of her first CD and unquestionably tonal CVs in the more abstract twelve-tone/serial program of the second CD.

A Distant Music
Serenata d'Estate

Memory plays tricks. So whether Gene and I were actually out walking that soft, beautiful evening in Venice when I heard or dreamed I heard—wafting across the waters of the canals—the exquisite half sound of a distant flute and a plucked guitar or mandolin hardly matters now. The music I thought I heard remains dreamlike, perhaps of my own making—a half-conscious reaction to the spell of that Venetian night. Out of its memory came the impulse for the *Serenata d'Estate* (Summer Serenade), which I wrote in 1955.

With the flute as principal voice, a duo of plucked harp and guitar mixes with a trio of violin, viola, and cello to provide the warm colors, textures, and atmosphere for a single-movement, multisectional work that rarely rises above whispered lines and interlocking, mottolike melodic and metric/nonmetric figurations. As musical expression it owes far less to the distraught passions of expressionism—it is row music in every sense—than it does to the supremely subjective, subtle hues, and symbolist sensibilities of the *fin de siècle:* in poetry—Mallarmé, Verlaine, Rilke; in music—Scriabin, Debussy, early Bartók. The *Serenata* is in the same removed realm as its darker spiritual cousin *Night Music.* Both belong to a pantheist, animist world ruled by gods and spirits not necessarily well disposed toward or even concerned with human wishes and desires. In that imagistic world I also place my *Slow Fires of Autumn, To the Dark Wood, Imago Mundi, Black Sounds, Contra Mortem et Tempus,* and *Tableaux.*

All these works adhere to the imagistic interplay of ideas where rapid shifts and changes establish an unpredictable, ongoing form—different in each instance—that takes its shape from the play of images. No particular way for proceeding exists—

except for what can be imaginatively extrapolated from the American poet Charles Olson's urgent exhortation that "one perception must immediately and directly lead to a further perception . . . ,"[1] which in turn must lead to another . . .

The only rehearsal of *Serenata d'Estate* took place just before the players went onstage to give its first performance May 4, 1958 at New York's Ninety-second Street "Y" in a concert sponsored by "Music in Our Time," one of those short-lived splinter groups that sprang up all over the country with the sole purpose of presenting new music, new directions, and new modes of performance to small, passionately devoted audiences. Often a spontaneous, harum-scarum informality characterized their presentation—and this was one of those times. There is a scene in the Marx Brothers movie *A Night at the Opera* that takes place on a trans-Atlantic liner where Groucho is assigned a broom closet for a "cabin." Within seconds, people are piling into a space hardly big enough for one person, climbing and tumbling over each other—chambermaids, plumbers, waiters carrying trays of food and drink, a veritable shipboard bedlam. The *Serenata* rehearsal was hardly tumultuously comedic, but in retrospect, it reminds me of that broom-closet-for-a-cabin scene. Eight of us crammed into an oddly shaped space, a leftover "closet" of sorts, a weirdly distorted modernistic out-of-perspective parallelogram, which presumably served also as a dressing room. It was just offstage, and there the conductor Arthur Winograd, six players—one with a harp, another a guitar, the rest with flute and stringed instruments—and myself were supposed to rehearse. With barely enough room to breathe, amazingly, good spirits prevailed and physical discomfort gave way to musical focus. Arthur Winograd was a natural conductor and fine musician (from 1945 to 1954 he'd been cellist of the Juilliard String Quartet). The players were young freelance musicians who thrived in the free-for-all that was New York then. The twenty-or-so-minute rehearsal over, Winograd and the players went directly onstage. I slipped into the hall. The performance, professional in spirit though not the most polished, established a tranquil, hushed, magical presence.

By its very contained nature and calm, quiet voice, the *Serenata* is not the kind of music to stir an audience to noisy enthusiasm. (At least, not back in the late 1950s.) Whatever else may have been on the program, I remember only a longish, all-out—as far as volume of sound was concerned—experimental tape piece by Vladimir Ussachevsky. It was a kind of musique concrète, an early form of electronically generated and manipulated sound-design composition. The loudspeakers on either side of the stage were the "performers" projecting electronic sounds. Completely without any "personality"—they were cold, passive vehicles through which sound complexes would be transmitted as identically the same vibratory substance on their fiftieth as on their ten-thousandth repetition. Beyond the variety of different timbres, register combinations, and dynamic levels (mostly loud, and presumably intended as heightened dramatic moments), it would be impossible to speak of musical ideas in any traditional sense.

When the musical part of the program was over, Max Polikoff, director of "Music in Our Time," invited the audience to stay for a panel discussion. The eagerness of the audience was unmistakable. (As time went on, pre- and post-concert discussions and interviews with composers and performers became established features of concerts, particularly when contemporary music was performed.) I had a hunch that few, if any, questions would be asked about the *Serenata d'Estate*. Despite its twelve-tone palette, as music it was the absolute reverse of an attention-getter; its outward demeanor was too intimate, too modest. By its very unexpected quality of fantasy missing from the usually stringent, severe serial music, it contradicted the unspoken, curiously held notion that grace of manner and beauty of sound were somehow antithetic to twelve-tone expression.

All the questions from the audience were addressed to Ussachevsky. People wanted to hear about how an electronic piece was made, what equipment—from a purely engineering point of view—he had used, how he had arrived at the sound design of the piece, and what all this meant for the future of music.

Ussachevsky, a large, pleasant-faced, sober man, genuinely believed that electronic music was the inevitable, inescapable path composers had to take. He liked being part of the significant new developments that were under way, and clearly, I stood outside this new utopia, looking on askance. For one, I actively disliked its dependence and reliance on technology and its potential for mechanical manipulation of sound-for-its-own-sake. Even more, I abhorred the dead-sounding "voice" of electronics. Musique concrète, if any interest in it still remains in this new century, is merely a historical curiosity. Varèse's *Poème électronique* is the only work I know of arising from that experimental genre that still has interest *as music* and therefore maintains a continuing presence.

Serenata d'Estate continues to go its quiet way through this increasingly strange and mysterious world, surfacing in chamber ensemble performances in unpredictable places, most recently on a program of Sequitur, a new music group founded by Harold Meltzer, in the Miller Theater, New York City, on April 28, 2000.[2] It was a particularly magical performance that transformed the atmosphere in the hall and wrapped the audience in its spell.

The years between the *Serenata*'s initial performance in the spring of 1958 and the recent one in the spring of 2000, for some inexplicable reason, appear to have enhanced its charm and magic and intensified an audience's sense of its special voice. If it is possible to say so, this performance was even closer to the summer-night spirit of the work than its first Nonesuch recording of 1968 by the

Contemporary Chamber Ensemble led by Arthur Weisberg—a rare document of one of my personal favorites.[3] Happily, its life has been prolonged by having been included in a CD anthology of twentieth-century chamber works issued by Nonesuch in 1990, thus achieving what used to be called "posterity"—itself only an infinitesimal portion of another immeasurable quantity called "eternity." Posterity being what in music, according to a statement attributed to Brahms—apocryphal, no doubt—comes to a work if it lasts more than twenty years.

The Last Gershwin Prize

Night Music and Dimitri Mitropoulos

Phone calls can sometimes be invested with the magic of messages sent by the gods who, invisibly and mysteriously, weave our fates on their golden looms. Almost as though it were a latter-day annunciation, such was the whispered phone call Gene received one morning in 1952 saying that I had won the George Gershwin Memorial Award for my orchestral work *Night Music* and that it had to be kept secret until the official announcement appeared in the newspapers. But the committee wanted me to know . . . and how could I be reached . . . the messenger wanted the pleasure of telling me the news himself. Gene gave him my number at Presser, but by then I was at lunch, blithely unaware that soon I would receive the phone call that changed our lives. This "divine" messenger of the gods told me with suppressed excitement what earlier he had told Gene. Besides the money prize, there would be a performance of my *Night Music* by Dimitri Mitropoulos and the New York Philharmonic. By the time our conversation ended I was in a state of euphoric shock. The public announcement of the Gershwin Award came in December 1952, some seven months after the birth of our daughter, Francesca, who quickly became our "Chessie." Our "darling bud of May"—as in Shakespeare's incomparable sonnet. Those phone calls brought about changes that propelled us into a new and better life.

Two years earlier we had gone to Rome when a fellowship from the American Academy in Rome made possible a studio for me to work in and a Fulbright fellowship provided a stipend for us to live on. Among the things I brought with me was the score of my First Symphony, written in 1948–49. I wanted to concentrate only on the first of the symphony's two slow movements, second in the order of the original five, which I decided to remove and treat as a separate and independent work. It was then I gave it the title *Night Music,* more in the spirit and sense of the "night pieces," for example, in Bartók's String Quartet no. 5 and *Music for Strings, Percussion, and Celesta* than in Mozart's *Kleine Nachtmusik* or Chopin's Nocturnes. It became the first of a number of works I wrote in which the atmosphere and evocation of nature and its elusive, brooding, darkly pervasive moods were central.

The night we drove into Rome after coming down from Perugia in the Umbrian hills was unforgettable. All the apartment windows were ablaze with candlelight: Pope Pius XII had declared that day in October 1950 "Anno Santo," the Holy Year of the Ascension to Heaven of the Virgin Mary. The sight was unbelievably dazzling, a never-to-be-forgotten introduction to the Eternal City. Weeks earlier I had been in Rome looking for an apartment. But now it was a different city, magically alive, festive, and unreal in the shimmering glow of millions of burning candles.

That Christmas a party of fellows from the American Academy went to the Vatican to join the crowd of Italians waiting impatiently for the pope to appear. Suddenly a cry went up on all sides: "Papa, Papa, Papa." And there, carried on a litter like an ancient Eastern satrap, was Pope Pius XII, a thin, wiry, smiling, small man scattering blessings as he went. The crowd went wild. Men, women, and children shouting, crying for joy. It was fantastic to be there. We, the unbelievers among a throng of believers, witnessing the pageantry and drama of religion at its most glamorous, drenched in indelible images.

When I had arrived in Rome a few weeks earlier to find a place for us to live, I went straight to an address I had for Gian Carlo Menotti, who was there filming a version of his opera *The Medium,* which had caused a sensation in its run on Broadway.[1] Tom Schippers, who was conducting the music for the soundtrack, was staying at Menotti's apartment, and after our mutually surprised greeting he told me where I would find Gian Carlo. Somehow I found my way through the great sprawl of Rome to Cinecittà. Gian Carlo couldn't have been kinder and more cordial. The minute I told him I needed help finding an apartment he offered his secretary, a young Italian in his twenties who knew Rome inside out and could show me where to look.

Gian Carlo's secretary certainly knew his Rome! By the end of an exhausting day I had lost track of how many apartments I had seen or where they were. I stayed the night with his family, who were kind enough to put me up, and the next morning, after a quick breakfast, we set out once again. I was determined not to return empty-handed to Perugia, where Gene and Paul were waiting for me. This time luck found me, or I found it. Off the Piazza Annibaliano, on the Corso Trieste, a main artery of northeast Rome, I saw an *apartamento di lusso* with six rooms plus a veranda overlooking a large courtyard. My instincts told me this would serve our needs and be acceptable to Gene. The fact that it was at the opposite end of Rome from my studio seemed less important than that my family be comfortable.

Our apartment belonged to a matronly Italian lady, not exactly at ease with the idea of renting her deluxe, marble-floored, fully furnished place to a young American family. When I learned her name was Signora Archi—translated "Mrs. Strings," as in musical instruments—the coincidence was cause for secret delight. Quickly we learned she wanted a great sum of cash, one month in advance, and one month in escrow to cover any damages. So back we went to Cinecittà, where I told Gian Carlo what I needed to seal the bargain. He quipped that he didn't carry that kind of money on him . . . but . . . wait a minute . . . he would talk to his producer . . . perhaps he had it. Minutes later Gian Carlo appeared with his producer, a pleasant-looking American businessman, and, after introductions, the producer handed me a huge wad of Italian lire. My expressions of thanks were lightly countered by remarks from Gian Carlo and his producer about whether or not, when or if, they would ever see the money again. The gentle raillery helped relieve my tension. I thanked the secretary for his indispensable help and, stuffing the money into my jacket pockets, went off to complete my arrangements with Signora Archi. That accomplished and papers signed, I took the train back to Perugia to give Gene and Paul the good news.

Why I didn't write Gian Carlo a check for the amount he had loaned me, I can't imagine, but when my next Fulbright check arrived I went to the Banca d'Italia e America—where we had an account—and had them count out precisely the same amount of lire I'd borrowed. Somehow it seemed more appropriate that way. When Gene and I arrived at Cinecittà, Gian Carlo was shooting a scene. In the first break I went up to him, *molto serioso,* and handed him the same-sized wad of lire his producer had given me. Gian Carlo looked at us, broke out laughing, and said, "I won't even bother to count it. I know I can trust you." "Mrs. Strings" had asked for hundreds of dollars in advance. At 620 lire to the dollar, the exchange rate in 1950, ten dollars translated into 6,200 lire, 100 dollars into 62,000 lire, and so on. The bundle of money I had initially walked off with from the Cinecittà set was now returned and indeed looked big enough to choke a horse!

Once settled into our new quarters I began a daily routine of commuting to my studio at the academy. Happily I found a professional music copyist—a trustworthy craftsman, well schooled, and with a good hand. We managed to communicate, even though my Italian was no better than his English. Still, with music as our common bond we managed. He took my rough pencil score of *Night Music* and produced a beautiful ink score. It was from his master tissues that the score Mitropoulos used was reproduced and later became the basis for the printed study score. When the score was completed, and I had established a good working relation with my Italian copyist, I had him extract orchestral parts for the *Night Music*. Since we were leaving Rome to return to the States in July 1951 and the parts were not yet finished, I asked my friend Ulysses Kay, who had a studio apartment at the academy, if he would keep an eye on the work as it progressed. Ully did more than that: he even proofread parts to make sure that errors, inevitable in the course of copying, were corrected. For one composer to do for another what Ully Kay did for me went far beyond the call of ordinary friendship; it was an act of pure altruism, worthy of celebrating in memory here.

That year in Italy, 1950–51, was the great watershed in the development of my music, my mind, my soul. Everything in me stretched: the circumference of my perception of the world around me, of myself in relation to that enlarged world, of the continuing power of the old music as I realized it afresh, as well as of the absolute necessity of coming to grips with the problem of new music and its still-unknown possibilities—a sense that flashed through me often—and, above all, of the gnawing uncertainty of my place in it. None of this would have been possible back home. It took the geographic and psychic-spiritual distance of Italy from America, the inner mental and emotional space they opened up, to allow the new perspectives to form, develop, and produce a harvesting of new and enlarged perceptions I had been incapable of before coming to this land I came to love. It was there in Italy I came face-to-face with the problem that still obsesses me, the same problem that haunted not only the whole of the twentieth century but that remains unresolved in the new millennium: *modernism.*

The supreme importance of my first Italian experience came back to me with redoubled intensity in May 1996 when Gene and I returned to Italy—and Rome—for the first time together since we'd lived there in 1950–51. We stayed at the American Academy only a few days, but what memorable days they were. I tried to encapsulate their vividness in my May 19 journal entry written after arriving home:

> What is uppermost in my not-yet-lively mind is to recount the totally sleepless night—the first of two—between May 8 and May 10 when we left with [pianist] Sally Pinkas for Como by train. It may have been the fact of the foam rubber pillow . . . which made it impossible for me to sleep. I think . . . it was the *re-membering,* so vivid, so detailed, so "live" of 1950, coming down to Rome from Perugia in early October with Mims [wife Gene] and [son] Paolo, he at six, so

full of interest and curiosity, loving it all, and I, naive, totally so, each of us in our own way bowled over by Italy, by the Academy, by the whole experience . . . Had we been tougher, more worldly, we wouldn't have been so impressed by everything; mostly our feelings were *wonderment* that we were even *there* . . . now Italian millionaires . . . Back home we were struggling . . . living principally on $60.00 a week from the Curtis Institute of Music (no pay for holidays, vacations, etc.). What I felt as I lay there was the powerful sense that it was coming to Italy, to Rome, the separation from America and our life before the separation that was crucial, absolutely so, because our lives changed fundamentally and profoundly afterwards. The deepest change was in me, in my work . . . I opted emotionally, spiritually for the deep-sea diving . . . people called "twelve-tone." All this happened *before* we left on our trip to Firenze, before I met Dallapiccola, was, in fact, the reason I wanted to meet him. I had not yet met another living musician who had adopted organized atonality as his language. Meeting D. made my own decision more real, more human, removed it from being a calculated, rational act—which it obviously never was nor could have been, given my crazy, over-intense emotionalism which drives my "intellectual" and musical life, and not the other way around . . . In short, here I was, closing the circle, back for a concert of Sally's (with the *Partita-Variations* and *Four Short Sonatas*) and a luncheon in my honor . . . and I kept asking myself why is Italy so important at the major nodal points of our lives, why Italy? Some unfathomable connection between Italy and us (including our Paolo and our Francesca)? Some deeper sense in me rejects the notion of coincidence. . . .

Such were my ruminations that night and the next. Retracing, reliving years long past. Suddenly on the verge of another great life change—and once again in Italy. Fate, destiny, coincidence? Or living a predetermined pattern over which neither Gene nor I have any control? I still am pursued by feelings and deep undercurrents of unidentifiable sensations that *something* is at work shaping our personalities and lives in ways that no explanation of science can offer or match. I've searched in the writings of Emanuel Swedenborg—and marveled. I take William Blake's "visions" totally seriously—yet I find nothing to support them either in logic or reason. I am still drawn back to read again and again William Butler Yeats's *A Vision*—his astonishing and astonishingly beautiful account(s) of his inner travels in the world of the occult and the strange findings he related—a wholly different kind of Gulliver. Somehow when the veil parts, we see through a crack for the briefest part of a second—it happens through art, through music. And all my torments and struggles in Italy and afterward somehow had to do with *not* allowing modernism to rob me of those fleeting, magical glimpses and awarenesses—or their possibilities of even occurring.

If modernism remains a major question for the culture of the West, should it not, like all questions worth pursuing, find its answer? Some questions—and I have come to believe modernism is one of them—are too intrinsically complex to give way to single-minded answers or simple-minded solutions. Where music and art are concerned, human beings who have the capacity to deal with *res severa* (serious things) must keep wrestling with the questions of what they are and what art is as long as both continue. Sadly, where modernism is concerned it appears that for many, no such problems exist.

With the news of the Gershwin Award I began working with my Italian copyist to prepare a beautiful autograph score and parts of *Night Music* that would be used for the New York Philharmonic performance with Mitropoulos. When rehearsals began for the April 23, 1953, premiere I had the parts ready and completely accurate. Mitropoulos told me when we met that since he had already decided to do the work for its own sake, he was particularly delighted when he was approached by the Gershwin committee. This fact remains a puzzle, because I cannot piece together by what means he would have gotten the score prior to the Gershwin prize. Whatever the case, what Mitropoulos told me cast the situation in a new and different light.

Mitropoulos was a quiet, undemonstrative, self-contained man with a simple and gentle demeanor. All kinds of stories were circulated about him—how he lived a monklike existence, how he led a contemplative life obsessed only by music. That he was a fine musician and more than merely an able conductor was borne out at the first rehearsal. I was stunned by the realization that he was directing the rehearsal completely from memory. There was no score laid out for him on a stand to refer to. Each note and every rehearsal letter were in his head. When he wanted to go back over a passage, he would say with unfailing politeness, "Please, ladies and gentlemen, take it from three measures after letter D," and offer a brief comment or two as to what he wanted.

No rehearsal of a work of mine has ever left such an indelible impression on me. It also bespoke the deepest kind of responsibility on Mitropoulos's part toward the preparation of a work by a relatively unknown composer. He treated it as an existent, musical reality, and his decisions in regard to tempi and orchestra balances were unerring. It was as though he knew what was in my own mind. I listened enthralled at how the colors of the orchestration took on life and shifting light and shadow under Mitropoulos's guidance. Of especial beauty and passionate delivery of line and expressive scenario was the principal cellist Laszlo Varga's playing of the solo cello part that forms the large middle panel of the triptych design of the work. I had found a special way to establish an emotionally neutral yet warm and throbbing, mysterious, dark textural backdrop of strings, harp, and percussion played at the softest possible dynamic level (*ppp–pppp*), against which the solo cello raised its passionate human cries followed by muted low brasses' dark, responsorial figures. This huge atonal harmonic pedal, which covered the virtual audible range of registers from low to high raised by the strings, harp, and percussion, played its thoroughly unchanging and indifferent role, ignoring whatever the cello was saying or the response of the brass.

Back in 1948–49 it had been a struggle to realize this particular part of the work. I wanted the musical metaphor of what I had come to see as a fundamental reality of human existence: the total indifference of nature to human beings, to our ever-flowing, strange river of consciousness, suffering all the overwhelming states as we live out our lives. Nature not only ignores us, its laws are—despite our science—beyond our capacity for comprehension and outside the limits and means of our intelligence and perception. It is against that indifferent reality, the individual—the solo cello—must live out his or her baffling life. I have forgotten how many versions I sketched. I was obsessed. The idea would not let go. I had to keep at it, until it came to me. Often I was on the verge of giving up, but I persisted, hoping against hope it would eventually reveal itself.

Literally at my wit's end, it seemed hopeless that I'd ever find the right solution. On my way to teach at Curtis one day I stopped for lunch at a drugstore. Sitting there, munching my sandwich at the counter, feeling low and depressed, suddenly, as though the heavens opened up, I heard, I saw what I'd been looking for for weeks, even longer. What I had so desperately wanted, and what had eluded me at every turn, presented itself—a gift from the gods. My problem had solved itself. Euphoria lifted me. I finished my lunch, walked to Curtis a few blocks away, taught my counterpoint classes, and then went home to write it down. It had all the earmarks of a true epiphany, one of those rare times in a composer's life that justifies the most stressful, strenuous effort to reach that state of shining openness where the right way seems almost to dream itself into existence. The language of the cello soliloquy foreshadowed the decisions I later made in Rome in the high, whitewashed walls of the studio where I worked. These decisions were to cast my lot with the extremes of expressionism, with heightened, intensely personalized modernist projections of angst and forebodings of terror (first heard in the ghastly, ghostly war music of trumpets and drums in the Agnus Dei of the *Missa Solemnis* [mm. 170–89], Beethoven's strange prophecy of the next century—ours), and try to speak in the stripped-down syntax of the twelve tones.

After the premiere of my work by the New York Philharmonic, brilliantly conducted by Mitropoulos, I rejoined my family in the audience to hear the final work on the program, the glorious, sunlike Beethoven Fifth. Ever since I first heard it as a boy of ten or eleven it has always seemed to me a magical given, not at all the work of a human being, but something that sprang into existence full-blown like Aphrodite from the head of Zeus—though history and sketchbooks tell us otherwise. When the concert was over and we were leaving the hall, my mother said to Gene, referring to my music, "It's nice, but why can't George write like Beethoven?" In its very simplicity and directness she had asked *the* central question of the century, central because in it were inherent all the thorny problems that came with the onset of modernism. Every imaginable kind of composer, artist, writer, intellectual—traditionalist and avant-gardist—had been wrestling since the early decades of the century with those very questions that had arisen with breaking away from the long past. Without knowing a thing about the acrimonious, contentious side of all this, my mother had intuitively found the core problem: how does one continue to try to make serious art when strong forces contend against each other in opposite directions, forces represented simultaneously in music by the ongoing vital presence of Beethoven and Brahms side by side with the more recently established presence of Stravinsky, Schoenberg, and Bartók, composers who have broken the language of music wide open?

First-time experiences retain a sense of magical freshness that seem never to diminish or fade with the passage of time. So it was for me with having an orchestral work performed for the first time by a world-class conductor and a great orchestra. To hear that monster machine of strings, winds, brasses, and percussion we call "the orchestra" come to life through the sounds of one's own music—that is indescribable. (Perhaps that explains why Bruckner, when asked about a particular passage during a rehearsal of one of his symphonies, is reported to have said: "Just play, just keep playing.") Ultimately the orchestra is chameleon-like. Depending on the idiosyncrasies and qualities of the composer's music, it takes on a different sound, character, color, and texture. There is no way to explain this rationally.

Hearing the *Night Music,* I recognized for the first time the qualities of my own "orchestra" sound, its textures and timbres, the dark radiance they give off, which I hear as one of the distinguishing characteristics of my orchestral music; and even when the language is the same as or similar to that of other composers, it remains indelibly my voice. This kind of recognition is not unlike the feeling in dreams when one is acutely aware that the dreamer is not another but oneself. In dreams we indisputably recognize and know our own essence as a constant presence.

The spring of 1953 brought about a complete change in where and how our family of four lived. We moved to the suburbs, away from Philadelphia with its cramped apartment life, summer heat and humidity, foul air, and dirty streets. We traded it all gladly for our first house in the midst of grass, flowers, trees, birds, fresh air—a saltbox just big enough to accommodate us four. The effect on Paul, then eight, was wonderful to see. It was as though he had been sprung loose into a world he could love. Chessie, one year old that spring, took her first steps in the still mostly bare living room, her little arms up in the air, her round shining face flushed with triumph and joy. Gene ruled gently and kindly over her new domain with great energy and happiness. As wife, mother, manager, and designer of her first home, she at last had free rein, the only constraint on her vivid imagination being the limits of our income.

We came to Newtown Square at the point of the first major development into genuine suburbia with roadways and streets—but no sidewalks. Today Newtown Square retains its countrified, suburban look but it has matured, grown in, and succumbed to commercialism. Two-lane roads have been replaced by six-lane, freeway-style roads connecting the cardinal points where people live, work, and battle unbelievable traffic.

The morning after the first performance of *Night Music*, the then five New York newspapers carried reviews. One in particular, in the *New York Herald Tribune*, infuriated me. It came from the acid pen of Arthur Berger, a young composer serving time as a music critic. It was a nasty, trivializing piece with a curiously personal edge to it. What offended me was not so much its display of arrogance or its parti-pris tone, but his refusal to take *Night Music* seriously.

This was a crucial and divisive time in American music. Animating and agitating the aesthetic positions of composers of my generation in the early 1950s were primarily two loyalties and two loosely defined camps. The larger and more visible one orbited around the music and compositional practices of Igor Stravinsky with a strong secondary gravitational pull toward Aaron Copland—in those years often referred to as the "dean of American Music." Berger belonged to this group, which also included Leonard Bernstein, Lukas Foss, Irving Fine, and Harold Shapero. Obviously each had his individual personality and talent, but all were in close agreement with the neoclassical tonal principles of Stravinsky's music. Copland, too, drew some of his strengths from the Stravinskian world; but with *Appalachian Spring*, he had begun the process of simplifying the surface of his music with a view to creating a vernacular, nationalistic "American" style. He succeeded, if one judges on the basis of his ballet scores, *Billy the Kid, Rodeo,* and others.

The nexus of Copland's position in the 1940s and 1950s was Tanglewood, and it was there that young composers came to study, to compose, to absorb the influences of the tonal world refracted through Stravinsky's neoclassicism and Copland's American populism. Serge Koussevitzky was the great nurturing musical spirit that hovered over, protected, and nourished Tanglewood. Out of choice I never entered this world. In the late 1940s, after a blazing performance by the Philadelphia Orchestra of Tchaikovsky's Fourth Symphony led by Koussevitzky, the pianist Seymour Lipkin introduced me to the grand old man. In his most kindly, courtly manner, Koussevitzky said, "You should come to Tanglewood this summer." I thanked him but explained I already had other plans. In fact, I had no other plans—except to work on my First Symphony. But the real reason Tanglewood did not appeal to me was my total lack of sympathy for the Stravinsky–Copland ethos that dominated Tanglewood.

The smaller camp was made up of individuals who functioned in their own orbits and hardly knew each other: Ernst Krenek in California, Wallingford Riegger in New York, and closer in age to me, Milton Babbitt and George Perle, both much more involved in the theory of twelve-tone and serialism than I was initially. My theoretical interests developed later but took a different path from either of theirs. Each in his own way, myself included, was struggling with mastering the twelve-tone praxis. Its propensities toward cold, abstract structures with little or no emotional content held no interest for me at all. At that point I was drawn to the highly charged chromatic intensities of the twelve-tone palette and its potential extremes of expressionism. By the late 1940s I was on the verge of entering that world, and after 1952, finally I did. *Night Music* was one of my first realizations toward this expressionistic way of working. That was what Berger had heard and rejected. It would have gone against the grain of his aesthetic loyalties to have found my work viable in any way.

Ironically, it is now history that after Schoenberg died in 1951, Stravinsky began to compose twelve-tone or serial music and the coterie of American loyalists, no doubt completely caught off-guard by Stravinsky's sudden switch to the opposite camp, did what they could to adjust to the new reality. Even Copland attempted to write music that he lightheartedly referred to as "twelve-tony." This was on the occasion of displaying his new piano quartet for Ulysses Kay, myself, and our wives after dinner with him at the Villa Aurelia, where in 1950–51 he was composer-in-residence at the American Academy in Rome. What impressed me was not so much the music per se but the pianistic skill with which he made a complex score intended for piano, violin, viola, and cello come to life.

It would not be an egregious error of either fact or judgment to say that America, on the threshold of the millennium, was one vast market with every conceivable advertising device and technique at its command; and that everything happening was ruled by the corporate values and principles of a market mentality, including its entertainment-driven cultural life and what is referred to generally as "classical music" (to distinguish it from the music of pop or mass culture). Additionally, this business-oriented, market-dominated culture spawned an odd and very American notion—rational on the face of it but wrong in every regard I can see—that throwing money at social ills and problems or cultural goals will bring about and effect the cures or ameliorations desired. The idea of throwing money at culture is exactly the premise that led to, in the 1950s, doling out large sums from the coffers of giant foundations, notably Rockefeller and Ford, to the composers of America in the form of commissions, particularly for orchestra. One of the principal venues for the disposition of such funds to commission and record new works was the Louisville Symphony Orchestra, led in those years by Robert Whitney.[2] This part of my story recounts the strangely oblique way in which my own music was drawn into the wide net cast by Whitney and the Rockefeller–Louisville program.

It was in 1956 that I received a Guggenheim Foundation fellowship, ostensibly to fulfill a commission from the Koussevitzky Foundation. This became the genesis of my *Dialogues* for clarinet and piano, a spare twelve-tone work, abstract in spirit, the first of my dodecaphonic pieces to reflect my fascination with the music of Anton Webern. The hitch was that I could use only half of the Guggenheim, since I was able to take only a six-month leave from my publishing job. Even so, the prospect of six months free for my own work was just the tonic I needed. The question was: where to go?

By pure coincidence it was the time of the crisis caused by the imminent takeover of the Suez Canal by Britain, France, and Israel that Eisenhower, then president, prevented from going forward. We were unwilling to subject our family to the possibility of being anywhere near another European armed conflict, so instead we turned our eyes southward toward Mexico. The prospect of Mexico seemed all the more inviting since we could drive the roughly seventeen hundred miles from the Philadelphia area to Mexico City and visit friends along the way.

Entirely on our own, with no timetable except for one appointment, we took our sweet time and meandered westward and south over a period of about seventeen days. We stopped in Washington, D.C., to sightsee with the children, then swung over to Cincinnati to visit our old friends the Daracks.[3] Continuing, we spent a couple of days in Paris, Tennessee, with Allison Nelson and Harry Neal, colleagues and friends from Curtis who had formed a duo-piano team and for whom I made a two-piano version of the Capriccio movement of my First Symphony.

It seemed to make sense to try to see Robert Whitney in Louisville, Kentucky, as we drove on our way to Mexico. I wanted to talk to him about the possibility of a Rockefeller commission. It's difficult to describe my basic reluctance to do anything that smacked of self-promotion. I had witnessed the parade of the gifted and ungifted alike being diminished or destroyed by the pressures to promote themselves and their work, too often resulting in producing self-delusional substitutes that passed for art. In order to preserve integrity and seriousness of purpose I found it essential to divorce myself as much as possible from the self-promotional cultural circus that had become America in the postwar years.

So it happened that with great effort before we set out on our journey, I forced myself to arrange an appointment with Robert Whitney. He seemed pleased to see me; in fact he was quite affable, talked a blue streak about the Rockefeller programs, citing facts and figures that, while interesting in themselves, palled on me. These preliminaries out of the way, Whitney came straight to the point, and what he said was refreshingly frank and open: "I've been badgered and pestered by every composer from one end of this country to the other—by phone, by telegram, by letter, over and over—they never give up—except for one, and that's you. . . . You're the only composer in the whole country I never heard from, the only one who never called or wrote or tried to get to me one way or another." He paused, then resumed: "I'll tell you what I'll do. The commissioning funds are all used up, but we have a rotating royalty fund on our recordings which allows us room to record works we didn't commission but that we think should be in our catalog." Another pause, then: "I'm going to record your music. Now, what would you like me to do? How about your *Night Music?* Let's start with that and think about doing something else later." In fact, in 1963 he recorded the three-movement version of my First Symphony.[4] The spontaneity of his decision, his decisiveness, his cordial manner were reassuring. What came across was the sense that he was literally making up his mind as he moved rapidly from stage to stage, thinking out loud as he went. I couldn't have been happier with the outcome of my visit.

Whitney programmed *Night Music* for his regular concerts in preparation for recording, and while he was a capable conductor, he was no Mitropoulos. His orchestra was efficient, and, like many regional American orchestras, thoroughly professional but rarely exciting or stirring in its delivery. Grace Whitney, Robert's sister, as principal cellist, was assigned the cello solo, the centerpiece of *Night Music.* Unfortunately, she was no Laszlo Varga,[5] nor was she Lorne Monroe, principal cellist of the Philadelphia Orchestra, who played it later with Ormandy. Grace managed the notes, but not the music. What was missing was the passionate utterance the solo demands, the capacity to shape the line inherent in the emotional scenario. Even with the best of intentions, neither the live performance nor the recording rose to the level of intensity the work requires to speak fully.

Years passed and other performances of *Night Music* took place, notably by

Eugene Ormandy and the Philadelphia Orchestra in 1961 and Erich Leinsdorf with the Boston Symphony in 1966. I remember best the critical survey a young composer made of the Louisville project. He named a half-dozen works he considered the cream of those compositions that, in his view, justified the whole Rockefeller–Louisville program. Among them he placed my *Night Music*—which gave me great satisfaction. Nor was the irony of its inclusion in his "short list" lost on me. He had assumed, erroneously of course, that *Night Music,* like all the other works, had been commissioned for the Louisville Orchestra. He couldn't possibly have known that the fact that it was recorded by Louisville was the serendipitous outcome of my decision to stop in Louisville to see Robert Whitney on our way to Mexico.

CHAPTER 4

After and Before

Twelve Bagatelles and String Quartet no. 1

On January 10, 1953—the dead of winter—there had been a terrific snow and ice storm in New York. That night I was to give the first performance of my Twelve Bagatelles for Piano on a Composer's Forum concert which also included the first performance of my String Quartet no. 1. We were driving from Passaic, New Jersey (where I'd grown up), on dangerously icy roads, and at times, traffic slowed to a crawl. My brother—"Rock," since his college days—was driving us (his wife, Gene, and me) to the concert.

Rock had been the first musician in the family. When he was about seven and I four, he began violin lessons. How he felt about them I never knew—but they fascinated me. I sat quietly, watching and listening. Each lesson had that special, magical moment when Rock's teacher—in those years music teachers, like family doctors, came to your house—would take out an oblong, maroon-covered, manuscript notebook, open it, and, making large, egg-shaped ovals—in other words, whole notes—write out in pencil a new scale, first up, then down. It was pure magic to me. I waited for that moment at each lesson. The sight of those five lines and four spaces—the musical staff—on which you could write symbols that marched up and then down, and make them sound on the violin, was exciting, and more marvelous than anything I could imagine.

Perhaps what musical notation shares with all scripts, handwritten or not, in every ancient and modern culture is the magic of trying to capture every possible shade and nuance of human expression and feeling that musical notation and words are capable of evoking. There I agree with Felix Mendelssohn. He was the first I know of to say unequivocally that music is much more precise as to meaning than words. What I sensed as a boy of four still holds; the five lines and four spaces of the staff contain worlds of magic that is, as far as we can project into the future, endless in its potentially infinite variety of ways and expressions to delight the ear and move the heart.

With Rock driving in that bitter winter weather, we finally made it to 116th Street and Broadway and the McMillin (now Miller) Theater just as my part of the concert was to start. I rushed backstage, where people were nervously waiting. There were hurried greetings, words of relieved concern. I tore off my coat, took a couple of deep breaths, and propelled myself onstage. Perhaps it was just as well I didn't have to wait before going on; it spared me the agony and buildup of nervous tension and anxiety that could have wrecked my playing. Truth was, though I could play the bagatelles in my sleep if I had to—every note inscribed on my memory circuits—I lacked the temperament of the true performer who needs and enjoys the adrenaline rush of putting on a show and winning an audience over. In memory, at least, it seems to me I brought the work off: its quixotic mix of warm and dark, cold and sardonic, lyrical and rhetorical moods and atmospheres—judging from the comments of colleagues and well-wishers, and even from the reviews that came out a few days later—had made its point. My personal part in the concert over, I could sit back and give all my attention to the performance of my First Quartet by the Galimir Quartet, made up of Felix Galimir and his three sisters. They gave a splendid, thoroughly polished, and convincing performance. I like to think the Galimir Quartet was the beginning of my good luck in first-class performers who played my music with heart and soul because they believed in it. So began the "official" introduction of my music to New York City—although it had already had its unofficial debut years earlier at the MacDowell Club—somewhere between 1941 and 1942.

All through the prewar years I had composed a number of art songs, all of which I sang myself. I had what Mildred Ippolito, an opera singer with the Hippodrome Opera Company in New York, called a "basso cantante" voice—a high baritone, though I could produce solid low D's, E's and F's in the "basso profundo" range, as well. Once I had auditioned for the college choir, and was accepted for the bass section, I decided to study voice, which is how I came to take lessons with Mildred Ippolito. I was seventeen then, determined to be a composer—even though Mildred kept urging me to think seriously about becoming an opera singer. Hardly a lesson went by without her mentioning it, and without my reaffirming my ambition to be a composer. I simply couldn't connect the image of an opera singer with myself;

my natural reticence wouldn't allow me to make a connection with becoming a performer of any kind—singer, pianist, or conductor.

Around the same period I had begun to entertain the idea of trying to find a publisher for my songs. That in mind, I talked to Leopold Mannes, who arranged for me to show my work to the composer Wallingford Riegger,[1] then an editor at Carl Fischer, one of the major New York music publishers. Riegger was probably in his forties, a kindly, calmly serious man. I went to his office and sang and played a group of my songs for him. His response was very positive—but under the circumstances, discouraging; for what he said was, while he liked the songs very much and thought they were good art songs, they were "too good" to be "commercial"—that is, to earn any money for Fischer or me, so reluctantly he had to turn them down. It was my first refusal by a publisher, but not my last.

A few years passed, and one day a letter arrived from Riegger inviting me to take part in a MacDowell Club concert for young American composers. He asked if I would be willing to sing and accompany myself in a group of my songs. I was enormously pleased at his invitation and accepted. Try as I might, I find it impossible to recall that concert, the reception of my songs, or my performance of them. One memory remains, that of Ursula Mamlok[2]—also then studying with Szell—being in the audience. During those years before I was drafted into military service, Gene and I saw a good deal of Ursula and her parents, who were refugees from Hitler's Germany. Ursula was a rarity among composers back then, a sensitive woman and highly talented.

The pairing of the first performance of my String Quartet no. 1 with my Twelve Bagatelles for Piano on the program at the McMillin Theater was neither random nor happenstance. It could be described as the *before* (the quartet) and the *after* (the piano work) of a tectonic shift in my compositional outlook, *seismic* in its impact on my music and myself. Like its metaphoric geological parallel, this musical tectonic shift was no simple mechanical replacement of one set of conditions with another equally as good—or even better, because newer—but was fraught with deep unseen changes, resulting from unknown, even arcane processes, with sharply differing visible-on-the-surface consequences both in the metaphoric physical model and in my new way of working. In a human life, though the time-scale is micro, not macro, the internal alterations of such a change are felt as cosmic, no less vast than the physical model. These grew out of the subterranean ebb and flow of tensions, feelings of anguished doubt, and deep anxiety as I pondered for years the profound changes that had occurred in music before and since I was born in

1918; what they implied, what it meant to try to continue composing in the face of diastrophic upheavals in musical languages and wildly antagonistic aesthetic positions and posturings. In the many-splendored world of art—especially in the postmodern days of the late twentieth century—there is always the latter, and an ever-avid public ready for yet another side show.

But the temporal aspects of the shift need to be narrowed still further to the *just before* and the *right after*: the First String Quartet gathered up in a single work everything I had attempted and had been concerned with—from at least 1939 on to 1950—that related to opening my initial tonal orientation more and more to chromatic and atonal extensions with stabs at what were tentative, even timid probes in the direction of twelve-tone possibilities, immediately followed by—in the space of a few weeks in May–June 1952—an open declaration of composing with twelve-tone rows in the form of the bagatelles. This carried with it enormous consequences for me, not least the conscious banning of all the old trappings and habits of mind of tonal thinking, and accepting new conditions of melodic/harmonic thinking and composing that entailed making new gestures and textures while conceiving new designs in compositional structure allowing maximum clarity and coherence of projection.

With the Twelve Bagatelles began a series of twelve-tone works that, like spokes of a whirling wheel, radiated out in different directions with each successive work, no two going over the same ground twice, musically, formally, or in terms of instrumentation (except for the bagatelles and the 1956 *Sonata Fantasia*—both solo piano works). My old passion for making variations took on renewed energy and enlarged scope with the manifold possibilities I saw inherent in the principles of the row. I loved the challenge of adhering as closely as imagination and technical control permitted to one or another configuration of the twelve notes while finding in the combinations of row transpositions, inversions, and retrogrades seemingly limitless ways to present such configurations in memorable continuities. Once again I responded with keen intellectual and emotional pleasure to the presence of the fundamental principle underlying all variation processes over an unchanging core, whether harmonic progression, bass line, theme, or twelve-tone row, to make memorable continuities, if possible, that flowed from the core in a veritable procession of shifting musical shapes.

The Twelve Bagatelles represent a more intuitive way of dealing with the row, still primitive rather than elegant. As yet, I was not aware of the possibilities of treatment, melodically and harmonically, of the hexachord principle. That came later, and when it did I was able to work the row technique with greater sophistication and conscious control, pitting groups of six tones against each other or combining them in complementary ways that yielded richer results.

The secrets of the hexachord came to me in a sudden rush in the summer of 1954 following much digging, score studying, and analysis. I formalized my findings in *The Hexachord and Its Relation to the 12-Tone Row,* published in 1955.[3]

Chronologically, then, the Twelve Bagatelles came directly on the heels of the quartet begun in Rome and finished two years later in Philadelphia, May 1952. The bagatelles came much faster, between June 7 and September 19, 1952. In fact, after long preparation and improvising daily on rows in progress, the first eight bagatelles burst forth, each in a single night. The last four were written more slowly and deliberately between August and the middle of September. Between these two groups of eight and four I made a trip to Tanglewood in July, ostensibly to meet new young composers, hear their music, and possibly find publishable works. But my real purpose was to see Luigi Dallapiccola, who was teaching that summer. More particularly, to show him the bagatelles I had already put on paper. My external "mission" as editor for Presser and my personal one to see Dallapiccola again came together and jibed harmoniously. Through Luigi I met Luciano Berio, then about twenty-seven, and a young Turkish composer from Ankara, İlhan Usmanbaş, whom I thought very gifted in a poetic way. (Presser eventually published some of his piano music.)

I was bursting with excitement to play the first eight bagatelles for Dallapiccola. I wanted more than anything to get his reaction, because I trusted his judgment and taste and still had warm memories of our first meeting in Florence two years before when I had played my Second Piano Sonata for him. I remembered his inviting me back to play it for him the next day because, as he said, if he were a critic he could have told me immediately what he thought of my sonata but, as he was "only a poor composer," he had to hear it at least one more time. I recalled, too, his lightly veiled barbs and sarcasms aimed at his "friends in Rome" (as he called them) who were completely out of sympathy with his having taken up composing dodecaphonic music—and were quite vocal about it. It is not hard to imagine official musical circles in the fascist Italy of Mussolini, before and during the Second World War, looking with undisguised distaste and disfavor on a composer like Luigi Dallapiccola, not so much because he had married an Italian Jewess, but far more because he had gone against the essence and spirit of Italian music and tradition to traffic in an entirely alien attitude and aesthetic as embodied in twelve-tone music.

I played the bagatelles for Luigi on an old, beat-up upright piano in a corner of a barn on the Tanglewood grounds. Luigi's reaction was immediate and strong. He liked them enormously and expressed great enthusiasm. His response, which meant so much to me, confirmed my own sense that I was on the right track. We went off together in a cheerful mood to find some refreshments. On the way we met Luciano Berio, whom Luigi introduced with particular warmth. We sat and I talked about writing four more bagatelles to complete the set. That was a great afternoon for me, and I was elated by Luigi's response to my work. In view of all this, it was inevitable that when the bagatelles were published in 1955 I dedicated them to Luigi Dallapiccola.

After our meeting in Tanglewood, Luigi and I began corresponding. His letters were cheerful reports—usually written on his return home from a trip—about performances of his works. In that period he had come into his own. When he taught at Queens, I would see him occasionally and saw that his enthusiasm and love for New York was boundless. I arranged for him to give a lecture at the Philadelphia Art Alliance, in those years a vital nerve center of the city's culture. The last time we saw each other was in the summer of 1963, the same year I wrote my Piano Trio no. 1, my last twelve-tone work. We were both participants in an international conference on "Music in East and West" held in Jerusalem. I attacked head-on the oppressive, radical aesthetics of the avant-garde of Europe and America and the equally oppressive (but for entirely different reasons) aesthetic of the Soviet Union known as "Socialist Realism."

What I said upset a great many people, except for Yuri Boskovich,[4] an Israeli composer whom I met and befriended at the conference. Luigi, clearly shocked at the strength of my direct attack on Western avant-gardism rather than Soviet Socialist Realism, said he didn't understand what I was talking about. The conference took us on tours of important sights in and around Jerusalem. On one of these trips Luigi and I sat together. He talked at length about his new opera, *Ulisse,* and during one of the stops I voiced my growing doubts about the continuing efficacy of twelve-tone music. I could see this upset him. "But we are here," he said. "This is our music . . . This is our language . . ." I didn't have the heart to pursue it further, so I let it drop. That was the last time we saw each other.

Suddenly, as I write, something quite strange—even remarkable in its way—springs to mind: I find it uncanny that the beginnings and endings of my adventure with twelve-tone music, from 1950–51 to 1963, coincide with and are framed by my first and last meetings with Luigi Dallapiccola.

I return now to my First Quartet, its inception in Rome, and Aaron Copland's reaction to the initial sketches I played for him. In those years, when I began a new composition I still tended to trust a kind of intuitive "dumb luck" that somehow, with some good ideas to work with, I could manage to fashion an entire work or a single movement without any prior planning of its overall design. No decisions were made in advance as to what came first, what last, and what lay between the end points, whether the work was to be made up of individual movements or become a single-movement, multisectional composition. And in the case of the latter, it was how to construct and develop convincing continuity from the opening statement through to an inevitable and satisfying concluding statement, whether an apotheosis or a gradual dying away into ultimate silence. That was how I still tended to work in 1963 when I wrote my first Piano Trio. As it turned out, I wrote the *last* section of the one movement work *first,* genuinely convinced it was the opening, but no matter how I tried, I could not push beyond it—it refused to budge, to open up to regions beyond itself. Eventually I was forced to admit that I had written the ending, not the opening. With that realization came the clear sense I needed to find how to open the work so that I could discover ways to reach the concluding statement convincingly.

The Piano Trio no. 1 was the last work where I allowed myself the blind-chance happenstance of feeling my way intuitively through the overall design of a work. Nor was what became the String Quartet no. 1 the first of a fairly large number of compositions where I had not yet completely learned to plan the large design and shape of a composition. The sketches I showed Copland were what I thought would be a first opening movement, but as the work evolved, it insisted on being the last. Eventually I learned to master design the hard way—by trial and error.

Since Copland was staying at the Villa Aurelia, across the street from the American Academy, it made sense to set up an appointment to show what I was doing. I had never met him before his residency at the Academy; nor, as far as I knew, was he familiar with any of my music, since I was not one of the many young composers who trooped through Tanglewood summer after summer. I remembered only that Theodore Lettvin, a pianist friend at Curtis in the late 1940s who was performing my First Piano Sonata, told me he had once met Copland and spoken to him about my music.

Aaron listened closely to my quartet sketches; his remarks, after I'd finished, were considered and, I must add, considerate. An older, more experienced composer listening to a younger colleague's work in progress is a special kind of situation that calls for tact, delicacy, and discretion, particularly if differences of aesthetic or style or personality are as marked as they were between myself and Aaron.

What he said came out as honest and serious criticism, not harsh or dismissive but thought-provoking: "It's not fresh." That was the core of his reaction, along with variants centering on the meanings of "fresh." This may be pure surmise, but I think what he meant was rather than sounding "American fresh," it sounded "European familiar." There was more of a sense of disappointment in his use of the phrase "not fresh" than of critical appraisal, perhaps a tinge of disapproval. As I am putting it, "American fresh" would be fairly close in a descriptive way to Aaron's aesthetic.

By 1950–51 he had become famous for his American "vernacular" ballets, especially *Appalachian Spring,* which did have a "fresh" sound in the context of the old repertoire of classical and romantic music, as well as more recent modern European and American music. However he had arrived at it, after years of pursuing an astringent, dissonant rhetorical style of utterance, it was what he meant, I'm sure. Something to do with being newborn, or newly minted, perhaps even inspired in a distant way by Pound's earlier modernist battle cry "Make It New," a slogan that still reverberates in every generationally new radical "cutting-edge" movement.[5] But to give Aaron his full due, even though I was not drawn to his music, he was no sloganeer, and probably not an avant-gardist, either, though he seemed to have leaned in that direction before he evolved into a populist composer.

But if the quartet sketches were not "American fresh," did that mean they necessarily sounded "European familiar"? And if that is how they were to be interpreted, did they show the influence of Bartók or Schoenberg or even Stravinsky? The answer has to be "yes," because at the time Bartók was the strongest influence on me—more as spiritual-artistic than stylistic example. For most of my generation who were powerfully drawn to quartet composing as the purest, most ideal form of music, the route back to Beethoven and the string quartet led through Bartók. But I didn't learn Beethoven through Bartók. The way for me led directly through an intensive study of Beethoven that began years before I found Bartók, in 1936 or 1937.

Simon Sadoff, the only other serious musician at Montclair State Teachers. College, asked me one day if I would like to try his transcriptions of Beethoven quartets for four hands, one piano. Like myself, besides studying the piano, he was also composing. (Years later he became conductor of the American Ballet Company's orchestra.) He evidently had an enlightened and demanding teacher who had suggested the best way to learn the Beethoven quartets was by writing them out as four-hand piano duets.

When Simon and I met to play, he opened a large loose-leaf notebook with the *primo* parts written out on the right, the *secondo* parts on the left. How many quartets were in that notebook I don't remember; but whatever we read through that first day, my memory seems fixed on the whirlwind scherzo in E major of the C♯ Minor Quartet, op. 131, fifth movement. It came as a revelation to me. Did we play it up to tempo? I doubt it. But we played it! It was an extraordinarily exhilarating experience—infinitely better than sitting passively listening to a recording, score in hand. For any musician, and especially a composer, there is no better way to get inside the heart and soul of a piece of music than to make it come to life at the piano.

In those early prewar years (and much later), it became inevitable that my every attempt to produce quartet music bore the strong imprint of Beethoven. It was from him I learned the importance of ensuring that no part got stuck permanently in the rut of its conventionally bound register or tessitura—a lesson neither Brahms nor Shostakovich seem ever to have understood. Just as important, even more so, I learned from Beethoven that by mixing the registers, that is, by allowing the viola and cello to be free to make frequent flights across the rigid borders that conventionally kept them *below* the registers of the first and second violins, the inner musical and textural design resulted in a released, self-renewing, and fluid aerated quality of ensemble, a constant refreshment to the ears of both players and listeners. Bartók, the great disciple of these Beethovenian lessons, applied them liberally and according to his own needs and interests. That his musical ideas from the First to the Sixth quartet are capital ones only make his quartets the more miraculous in the context of twentieth-century music.

The sketches I showed Aaron Copland were still evolving ideas for what turned out to be the last movement of my first string quartet, an allegro energico with a strong three-pulse. It wasn't until many years later, when the work was performed at the Eastman School of Music, that one of the music historians on the faculty pointed out with special pleasure, because he delighted in such connections, that the initial four-note motto that came back some bars later in inverted form bore a close family resemblance to the main motto of Beethoven's op. 127 third-movement scherzo. To tell the truth, while I had never remarked the resemblance, I was intrigued by it—particularly since my use of the shape of the motive had been wholly unconscious. Was this an instance where an idea—regardless of the source—affects one deeply, drops into the depths of the unconscious to rise again in related form years later, only this time with such different intent that the original image—the parent source—is forgotten and the "new" image comes to life as though it had no ancestor? Copland's remark was insightful. He had heard something without being able to identify what it was, whether it was the Beethoven at the source of my sketches or something unnameable but clearly "European." That particular movement came hard and was not completed until 1952 when I was back in Philadelphia.

I seriously doubt that any work I ever produced caused me as much trouble and went through as many revisions as the First Quartet. Between the time I returned from Italy in 1951 until its first performance at McMillin in 1953 it seems there were at least five different versions before I finally arrived at the one that satisfied me.[6]

When I had written out the individual parts of the "completed" quartet I arranged with a friend in New York to put together an impromptu quartet to read it through. At this far remove all I remember is an overall dissatisfaction with too many "soft spots," and especially with the part writing. The *insides* of the ensemble didn't meet my sense of the Beethovenian ideal sufficiently, that free, constantly aerating interchange of register between the instruments. After I'd worked to overcome what I saw as serious deficiencies, I had another impromptu quartet read it through in Philadelphia. Happily, some things seemed to work better this time. But I remained dissatisfied. This process of revision, then reading through the latest revision, was repeated at least two more times—until I felt the quartet represented what I wanted it to say and how I wanted to say it, coming as close as possible to the perfection I sought. This experience of many revisions in search of the most perfect possible form taught me one of the more important lessons I needed to learn: not to let a work out of my hands until I was as certain as is humanly possible that it was what I wanted and how I wanted it.

The last reading of the First Quartet prior to its first performance at McMillin was with the Curtis String Quartet. All of its founding members had been students at Curtis and were of the generation contemporaneous with Sam Barber. This may be pure speculation, but I believe it was Max Aronoff who was the organizing and guiding spirit of the Curtis Quartet. His personality was larger, more dynamic, his energy more vital than that of the other members—judging especially from the fact that it was he who founded and ran the New School of Music, where they all taught. In 1946, a year after we arrived in Philadelphia, he hired me to teach theory at his school.

Max was a well-known character in musical circles, more than somewhat bluff, even a bit crude. He loved off-color jokes and was something of a raconteur. Still, he was good-hearted and had an abiding love of music. When I organized a "Contemporary Music Reading Group" in 1948, Max allowed us the use of one of the school's larger studios. But when Efrem Zimbalist[7] offered me a teaching position at Curtis after I graduated in 1948—at a salary ridiculously low even in those days—it was with the express condition that I teach only at Curtis and nowhere else. Max was understandably riled when I told him I'd have to resign from the New School because of Zimbalist's condition, and he delivered himself of a few choice phrases revealing all too well his feelings about the director of the institute.

Although I knew Max was not exactly an enthusiast of new music—whatever its stripe—I asked him if he would consider giving my now-completed quartet a reading with the Curtis. The members of the quartet then were violinists Jascha Brodsky and Louis Berman, violist Max Aronoff, and cellist Orlando Cole. This would be the acid test. I had revised the work to the highest polish I could achieve.

I was already writing twelve-tone music, exploring the ordered chromaticism of its expressionistic world, completely unself-conscious, yet fully aware of what I was doing and simply assumed that if the Curtis Quartet had agreed to read my new quartet they would give it their best—which is what happened. All fluent sight-readers, they gave their energies and concentration to matters of tempo, gesture, ensemble dialogue. From the opening measures it was evident this was not a tonal work in the conventional, accepted sense but rather highly chromatic, often dense in harmonic texture without being twelve-tone per se. Max, I could see, was becoming less than enthusiastic, whereas Landy Cole was warming to the work; and, in a few exchanges with Max over how a particular passage might be done more effectively, Landy defended the music against Max's barely concealed irritation and hostility. It became clear that it was Landy who knew how to keep Max within sensible bounds. That Max Aronoff didn't care much for the music was balanced by Landy Cole's defense of it. I knew full well I would have to learn to live with the knowledge that my music would have its detractors and defenders, its doubters and supporters. For whatever reasons—ignorance, taste, or personal animosity—there were those who hated it, but there were also those who loved it. Rarely was it received with simple indifference.

In those years when I began working in publishing, everything happening in the music world, particularly as it pertained to new music, streamed through my office in an unending flow of reports on what was being composed, performed, and said about the one and the other. I saw a constant flood of journals and magazines devoted to musicological reports and studies (the *Journal of the American Musicological Society*), polemic, analytic, and aesthetic discussions of contemporary music (the British *Score,* the Viennese *Die Reihe,* the American *New Music*), record reviews (*High-Fidelity*), reviews of published new music and new books on music (*Musical Quarterly* and *Notes*), accounts of professional musical activities (*Musical America*). All these, plus innumerable other print vehicles long since forgotten, came across my desk in a torrent of information. With my innate critical skepticism of the human propensity to self-promotion, self-advertisement, and glib professional gossip, it was fascinating to observe close-up this worldwide three-ringed circus of musical events and happenings— live, recorded, published—and how all the reports seemed to take on a general homogeneity and sameness of treatment. Very little of this discursive and reportorial plethora of printed matter lifted itself to my special attention, despite the momentousness often attributed to the appearance of this new work or that new composer or performer.

Yet, looking back to the early to middle 1950s, I see I was being "educated," getting a crash course in what was then called "the contemporary" but was, in actuality, simply another—and the latest—variety of ongoing modernism. Had I spent those years in protective isolation from the world at large, shielded by a private income or trying to accommodate my natural, dissident nonconformism to the narrow straits of an academic teaching job, I doubt I would have developed as keen an awareness, as sharp a sense of the pitfalls and problems of modernism in any of its guises, particularly in music, but also—because they share common values, properties, and outlooks via ethos and thought culture—in the visual arts and in literature as I did.

What I had struggled with for years before and during my time in Rome grew clearer as a result of this "education" that I underwent in the university of life concomitant with the tough realities of being an editor and publication director for a leading publishing house. It is no exaggeration to say it profoundly affected how I thought about my own work, especially as I began to see it in the broader context of a musical world subjected to the increasing pressures of Euro-American radical avant-gardism consumed by nonsensical notions of treating random, ambient sounds as though they were music and not mere noise, and loudly trumpeted theories and proclamations of newly discovered dimensions and parameters that, so it was said, would expand the old limits of acoustic music and eventually make possible, therefore viable, a music based on electronics. It did indeed lead to synthesized and computerized forms of so-called musical composition, but not, to my admittedly prejudiced ear, with particularly noteworthy results; nor did electronic music replace acoustic music as had been loudly proclaimed by its boosters.

It is quite impossible to go into all the questions and problems that have arisen since the midpoint of the last century and that affected my work and outlook. Nonetheless, I turn my attention to a major question that has exercised me concurrent with and since the time of my String Quartet no. 1 and Twelve Bagatelles and the major shift that they bracketed. Each emerged as first entries into new worlds after long years of effort and search, finally issuing in arrived-at, clear outcomes and achieved first maturity.

Virtually all my early efforts at composition were for piano, although I wrote a tonal violin-piano sonata that hovered somewhere between Beethoven and Brahms. I also wrote songs for voice and piano to romantic poetry by Shelley,

Byron, Sara Teasdale, Housman, and others. There were tentative efforts toward music for string quartet but not yet toward writing a string quartet; that came later when I felt more secure in technique and understanding. In fact, my first "major" attempt at a quartet took the form of an abortive, giant-size fugue modeled very roughly on Beethoven's *Grosse Fuge,* op. 133. All the while—as I was sending out probes in all directions, including awkward attempts at orchestral music—I was gravely dissatisfied with my tonal efforts, chiefly because I was painfully aware that what I was writing lacked the sheer size, richness of indelible ideas, and power of realization of the masters of the nineteenth and eighteenth centuries. This gnawing dissatisfaction itself became entwined with a growing awareness, just before 1942, of the music of Stravinsky, Bartók, Schoenberg, and Mahler.

When the war came I was just beginning to penetrate the outer rings of their works and the modernist departures from the old tonal music they represented. Mostly I lived in a state of unease and dissatisfaction with the style of the music I was writing and uneasy tentativeness vis-à-vis the world that had already bypassed it, the modern, with its abandonment of what I was still struggling to master and its brusque replacement with forms of musical speech that were mostly beyond my aural comprehension. I remember saying to Szell once that no matter how much I'd tried to understand what Hindemith was doing, especially harmonically, I still could not "hear" it. Given that, I would continue writing only what I could hear internally.

Stravinsky's music had its appeal, but I was not drawn to his world of outward brilliance and empty show. On the other hand, Bartók's searching innerness spoke to me; I felt drawn to his quartets even though I was often put off by his impenetrably dense chromaticism. Mahler exerted his magic on me via the Adagietto of his Fifth Symphony and his first two symphonies. Thus I lived suspended between two worlds, more at home in the old romanticism and the classicism out of which the newer world had grown, and much less at home, in fact, often at sea, in the best music of my own century. The dilemma required resolution.

Until the time I was inducted into the army I had written only a few works that gave me any satisfaction at all—and even there I felt they were more "on the way" than that they had "arrived." But strong patterns had been established: an abiding love of piano music, an ability to write for the voice, a powerful urge toward chamber music, more specifically the string quartet, an ambition to master orchestral writing. After the war and my work with Scalero on counterpoint, I intensified my relationship with twentieth-century music. I went deeper into Bartók; I absorbed Stravinsky's rhythmic asymmetry, his hard-edged juxtapositions of gestures and colors; I tried very hard to penetrate the opaque, steel wall of Schoenberg's twelve-tone music; I pored over Alban Berg's *Lyric Suite* for string quartet, which cast a spell over me; I immersed myself more and more in the symphonies of Mahler, enchanted as often as I was repelled.

By 1947 I felt I had to master Schoenberg's ordered chromaticism. The work through which I chose to conquer his abstruse technique was his Fourth String Quartet. I listened endless times to the recording of the Kolisch Quartet[8] and tried endless more times to make it come to life at the piano. I read René Liebowitz, Josef Rufer, Ernst Krenek, whatever articles and attempts at twelve-tone theory and analysis I could find.[9] Nothing I read had the key to what remained impenetrable *as music*. Theory and theoretical analyses of row structure and manipulation were as far from an actual understanding of the music heard *qua* music as to prove utterly useless to someone who, like myself, needs and is convinced only by experience itself, its concreteness, its direct perception and the doors they open to both mental and emotional comprehension.

It is pure delusion to believe that genuine understanding of music is revealed by theoretical analysis, nor does emotional attachment by itself bring understanding of what produces the affect of the music. In the case of Schoenberg's Fourth Quartet it was the deep ambivalence of love–hate that drove me on. I was simultaneously repelled by and drawn to it. My comprehension of his row practice via partition into small units of pitch combinations grew, as did my grasp of his melodic/polyphonic constructions via his penchant for inventing new textures of melody and accompaniment. Even as I gradually came to understand how he arrived at what was on the pages of the score, I still found that his overwrought expressionist emotional palette, often combined with emotionally desiccated sensibilities, rubbed my nerves the wrong way. The music sounded ugly and unbeautiful to my ears. Yet I was driven to keep at Schoenberg's "secrets" in order to forge for myself a language with which to say, in terms of my own time and experience, those things I wanted and needed to say, and to express them as consummately well as I could according to my lights. That was the essence and core of my search in that year in Italy, even while often I would break off to practice favorite preludes and fugues of J. S. Bach's second volume of the *Well-Tempered Clavier* to clean out my ears, to return to what constituted for me the ultimate measure of serious music.

The only piano music of Schoenberg's I felt close to for its emotional depth and convincing harmony—still atonal in the free sense, not yet ordered according to twelve-tone practice—was his *Drei Klavierstücke*, op. 11. The *Sechs kleine Klavierstücke*, op. 19, interested me for its colors and its brevity; perhaps its succinctness suggested the small forms I used in the bagatelles; but, as to that, so did Couperin's rondeau couplets, brief pieces for harpsichord, as much as did Scarlatti's short sonatas. Except for the measures I came to quote later in my *Sonata-Fantasia*, Schoenberg's *Fünf Klavierstücke*, op. 23, did not speak to me. Even less did the Suite, op. 25, which I found dry and inexpressive, without either motivic or harmonic interest. The *Klavierstücke,* op. 33, never reached me on any level.

My efforts to acquaint myself with Stravinsky's solo piano music left me stone cold, but I found Bartók's early piano music of immense interest and often quite beautiful, especially his Suite, op. 14, and *Improvisations,* op. 20. I mention all these as probable sources, on which I drew symbolically more than actually, of the harmonic worlds of the bagatelles and the quartet, harmony having for me a particular power, a collective power of pitch combination that moves between effects of opaqueness and ringing clarity and has or lacks a pungency to the ear that may be as much physiological as it is psychological. It is this set of personal preferences in the *sound* of harmony that makes me choose Chopin over Schumann, Brahms over Reger, Bartók over Schoenberg, Messiaen over Boulez. As the twentieth century closed I found it strange, even sad, that, with all too few exceptions, composers seemed to have little interest in harmony—whether we speak of it as a physiological phenomenon that in my own experience can be described as a special physical ringing resonance in the ear and in the head or as a texturally ordered, continuous, direction-seeking unfolding of musical thought.

I doubt at the time of the 1952 tectonic shift in my work that I was able to comprehend fully the enormous differences that separate *tonal thinking* from *twelve-tone thinking.* The only things they had in common were pitch names: C remained C, C♯ remained C♯, etc., under any and all circumstances, and the staff: five lines and four spaces, and the ties and slurs (phrase marks) as well as the whole paraphernalia of Western metric notation. Despite these commonalities, tonal music and twelve-tone music looked very different from each other when written down. Tonal thinking was open, always en route to completing itself, to closure. Twelve-tone thinking was self-consciously circular: the rate at which the twelve notes consumed themselves was dizzying at times. Where melodic thinking in tonal music was capable of producing long, extended lines, twelve-tone melodic thought had the opposite tendency, toward brief statements or, at best, length of line achieved through metrics rather than melodic extension per se.

The greatest difference that existed between the two ways of thinking music was the presence of the cadence, a harmonic reflection of the temporary or completed closure—cessation—of a phrase in the emerging line of tonal melodic thought as against the absence of cadential nodal points in twelve-tone due primarily to the nature of twelve-tone harmony, which has no inherent points of rest. A composer wanting to simulate a cadence in twelve-tone music must *invent* a surrogate way to pause, to come to a momentary rest or arrive at a point of full closure. In this regard it was years before I discovered one day that Schoenberg "cadenced" internally, that is, while the piece was still in progress, by the simple device of *slowing down* the music by calling for a *ritardando.* The process of breathing, inhaling and exhaling, without which music cannot exist, is more "natural" to tonal thinking than it is to twelve-tone thinking. The cadence is built into tonal harmony, virtually a given, but not into twelve-tone harmony. That may be one of the reasons—but certainly not the only one—why twelve-tone music tends away from melodic thinking per se and more toward textural and timbral environments that favor the kinds of chords and chord complexes available through combining twelve equal semitones that recognize no controlling single pitch.

It was out of this long struggle with uncertainties and intensely felt longings for clarities that 1952 proved to be my watershed year. The demands of craft seemed to require exactly the same unwavering dedication to realizing fully on all levels possible that which was inherent in the new language as had been inherent and realized in the old language; for, regardless of outward differences, both remain humanly expressive musical speech, whatever their apparent oppositions show. Though at first I willingly accepted these differences and apparent oppositions, subterraneously, in some less fully conscious part of myself, something nagged at me, gave me little or no rest. The sense, half-formed, that tonal music and twelve-tone music were not negations of each other, that they did not cancel each other out as many thought, but were dynamic polar opposites, a new tension in human music and ways of thinking music, a heightened spiritual or psychological dissonance, and, as such, could therefore be thought of as two worlds potentially resolvable through new forms of juxtaposition and combination, either simultaneous or successive.

CHAPTER 5

"Let the Other George Do It"
Symphony no. 1 and Eugene Ormandy

If, according to Kierkegaard, the trouble with existence is that it can be lived only forward and judged and evaluated backward, then the possibility arises that in order to recollect portions of the past for purposes of judgment and evaluation, we run into the danger of having to live simultaneously forward and backward, and of getting entangled in two currents of temporality moving in opposite directions. The present can no more be held back for the sake of studying the past in perfect tranquility than a stream can by the randomly placed rocks and boulders that lie in its path as it flows. Nor can we ask the present to "stay"—as Goethe did for a wholly different reason—so that we can view the imperfectly remembered personal past more "steadily" and "whole." Add to that the further complication that in the act of recalling the past the recollection itself becomes cinematic and again is seen as running forward in time. The difficulty is that this act of looking backward must often be reconstructed from fragments and shards of images, mere wisps and shadows of things said and done in a far-distant time inescapably distorted by memory and perspective.

This weighs heavily as I contemplate the story of my twenty-year relationship with Eugene Ormandy—from the time of the premiere of my First Symphony until his performance with Isaac Stern of my Violin Concerto. For the most part it was a difficult relationship fraught with tensions, real and imagined—Ormandy supplying most of the histrionics. The story has three interwoven strands. First, the performance period from 1958 to December 1967; second, a long look backward to the time I wrote the symphony, 1948–49; and last, linking up to the public fracas that broke out in print in September 1969 and its immediate fallout. A later

chapter describes the melodramatic scene backstage in the conductor's room following the 1978 Philadelphia performance of the Violin Concerto that brought to
an explosive climax the fracas that first surfaced in 1969.

The premiere of my First Symphony took place March 28, 1958. Ormandy,
clearly enthusiastic about the work, gave it thorough preparation through intense study of the score and serious, conscientious rehearsal. The practice of the
Philadelphia Orchestra when rehearsing a work by a living composer was to set
up, about two-thirds of the way back in the hall, a small table with a lamp where
the composer could spread out his score and make notes about large and small
matters to call to the conductor's attention when time permitted. Yet it was not
so far from the stage that, if need be, the conductor could call out a remark or
question to the composer to deal with on the spot. Though a bit awkward, such
an arrangement tended to work fairly well. It freed the orchestra and conductor
from the immediacy of the composer's presence while they struggled to master
the initial difficulties any unfamiliar score is bound to present. It gave me a much
better aural perspective on the orchestral sound that poured from the stage into
the hall than if I'd been too far forward, up too close. In fact, it is the best way
to measure the success or failure of realizing your musical intent, its accumulat-
ing successive growth of details, phrases, sections, and, ultimately, its overall
design. Even more, it is the best and only way to judge how you have handled
the orchestra: the colors and textures of orchestration, its interior weights and
balances, timbres and gestures as apportioned between solo lines and their supporting contexts (accompaniments, environments) of shifting small parts of the
orchestra, juxtapositions of winds, brasses, strings, percussion against each other,
as well as orchestral *tuttis,* at moments of maximum intensity. It also serves a
vital, if different but essential purpose in hearing for oneself whether or not the
music literally lifts off the stage and projects across the proscenium as physical sound into every nook and cranny of the hall, or whether it fails to project
past the proscenium and dies right there on the stage. I have heard twentieth-
century works that may have had strong "presence" in recording literally fail to
"sound" in a live space. The physical reasons for this unintended failure are far
too complex to unravel readily, but it does point up even more dramatically the
acoustical marvel and wonder that is the classical repertoire of Haydn, Mozart,
and Beethoven, usually composed for smaller ensembles than the full panoply
of the modern orchestra: their music never fails to fill a live hall with acoustical
fullness and total presence.

As rehearsals proceeded, Ormandy, feeling confident that my work was shaping up, invited me to sit near him on stage. Which changed the initial formality to a warmer and more personal give and take between us. It also brought me into closer touch with the members of the orchestra, especially the principal players, where there quickly developed an easy, collegial, friendly bantering. Ormandy's geniality could be appealing, but when any sign of resistance to his will showed itself, his geniality gave way to immediately vocalized hurt, annoyance, and irritation. I caught a glimpse of this other, darker, less affable side when, just before dress rehearsal, he suggested that I consider writing a different ending for the last movement, one that would bring the work to a more satisfying, more definitive close—as he saw it. As it was, he didn't think audiences would know the work had actually ended because it rushed so precipitously to the last notes of the last measure, ending "up in the air." He felt it needed to be grounded more firmly, something more in the spirit of the nineteenth-century *fortissimo tutti* unison on the final note that said "finis" in no uncertain terms. I said I would mull it over carefully and see whether his suggestion was a viable possibility or not. When next we met I told him I'd given serious thought to his idea and tried to imagine a different close in keeping with his concerns . . . but I couldn't hear it . . . nothing had come . . . A complete change came over Ormandy. In a sharp, biting, arch tone of voice he shot out, "Far be it from me, a mere *conductor,* to tell a *composer* how he should write his music"—and walked off. That was the first cloud over our relationship.

Immediately following the weekend trio of first performances in Philadelphia, Ormandy took my symphony to New York and performed it in Carnegie Hall to enthusiastic responses from both audience and press. Shortly afterward he told me he wanted to record the symphony for Columbia Records. All that was needed as far as the recording budget was concerned was an additional three thousand dollars, and if I could raise the money, he would go ahead and set up a recording date. The prospect was immensely exciting; it would mean a major recording of my First Symphony with a great orchestra and a world-class conductor, by one of the important recording houses. But my wife and I were faced with a serious dilemma: in those years three thousand dollars was a huge sum, and we were not worldly enough to know how to deal with such exigencies. Why I didn't go straight to the Presser management, explain the circumstances, and ask for an advance against future royalties or some other viable arrangement agreeable to us both, I still do not know—particularly as the symphony was in the Presser catalog and would have ensured some income once it was recorded. Instead, the only thing I could think of was to approach the Curtis Institute, hoping that the Zimbal-

ists, especially Mary Curtis Bok Zimbalist, the founder of the school, would be
sympathetic and help with a subsidy. When they refused, our disappointment
was devastating and discouraged us from making any further efforts. We simply
let it drop. Had we been more worldly or luckier, would life have changed that
much? Who can say? In any case, when I informed Ormandy I wasn't able to
find the money, his disappointment was no less than mine. I had lost a golden
opportunity.

In the years that followed, the contretemps over the ending of the First Symphony a thing of the past, the missed opportunity of its recording a still-lingering
regret, Ormandy and I were once again on a good footing, and a warmer, more
personal relationship grew. In October 1961 he programmed *Night Music.* Those
performances live in my memory for Lorne Monroe's wonderfully passionate
playing of the solo cello centerpiece of the work. Ormandy, who was justly famous
for his great skill in providing sensitive support of repertoire concertos, showed
in *Night Music* why this reputation was fully justified. Not too long afterward, in
1963, Robert Whitney, true to his word in the conversation we had had in Louisville back in 1957, recorded my Symphony no. 1 in the same three-movement
version Ormandy had premiered in 1958.

Even as I wrestled with the question of how to go on after disentangling myself
from the twelve-tone method I had embraced so enthusiastically some ten years
earlier, I decided to transcribe for large orchestra the Twelve Bagatelles for Piano that
had begun the series of my twelve-tone works. I needed, however, a different title.
Somehow "Bagatelles for Orchestra" sounded too much like a musical oxymoron. I
finally settled on *Zodiac.* Besides its primary astronomical/astrological meaning as
a twelve-part division of the circular heavens, the term *Zodiac* carried the secondary meaning of a cycle, which was precisely the sense in which I wanted to use it.
Coincident with the period in which *Zodiac* was completed, 1965, I was invited to
take part in a New Music Symposium sponsored by the Rockefeller Foundation
in Cincinnati, Ohio. My participation in that event took two forms: first, a paper
I called "Aural Fact or Fiction; or Composing at the Seashore," which mounted a
poetically designed argument against indeterminate, impersonal, aleatoric (chance)
composition, which had by then, in my view, achieved an unwarranted ascen-
dant position in the new music world; second, on May 8, 1965, Max Rudolph, the
music director of the Cincinnati Symphony, gave the first performance of *Zodiac*
with his orchestra. Considering the brevity of rehearsal time—even under normal
subscription-concert circumstances—Rudolph produced an excellent reading of
the work. Truly first-class performances followed two years later in Philadelphia

when Ormandy scheduled *Zodiac* on five consecutive concerts between December 14 and 19, 1967.

During the fall of 1961, the time of the Philadelphia Orchestra's preparations of the *Night Music* performances, Ormandy showed genuine warmth and friendship toward me. In part, I believe it was because he wanted to show he was aware of our son Paul's illness and what our family was going through. A number of times, at his invitation, I visited him in his commodious hotel suite in the old Bellevue-Strafford on Broad Street, about a block north of the Academy of Music. On one of these visits I recall Anshel Brusilow, the concertmaster of the orchestra, being there. Ormandy, very relaxed and cordial, obviously enjoyed his role as elder colleague extending a warm hand in friendship to two younger colleagues with whom he had developed close professional relations. Years later, Brusilow, who had his own ambitions as a conductor, founded a chamber orchestra large enough to perform classical symphonies. This, however, did not seem to sit well with Ormandy. In any case, Brusilow's orchestra foundered after only one or two seasons of trying valiantly to provide a repertoire wholly different from the offerings of the Philadelphia Orchestra.

Over the stretch of time embracing the *Night Music* and *Zodiac* performances, there were a number of moments that illustrate graphically Ormandy's characteristic reactions to situations that, in themselves, were either trivial or serious. Whichever they were, they invariably received the same treatment: on-the-spot, flippant remarks intended to wound, typical responses that showed the metallic glints of his peculiar personality. The one occasion that stays with me came after Szell had taken my Second Symphony to New York and I tried to interest Ormandy in performing it, as well. Without dropping a beat he immediately let go with a quick shaft, perhaps aimed more at Szell than at me, "Let the other George do it!" Something vitriolic circulated in Ormandy's bloodstream where Szell was concerned.

The long years before 1948–49 when I wrote the original five-movement version of my Symphony no. 1 were the dark years out of which came the gigantic catastrophe we call the Second World War. If you were young then, there was no way to escape the slow, gathering buildup of tensions and ominous undercurrents shadowing and stalking our world. We became aware of strange, odd-sounding names of men troubling an already unhappy world—Lenin, Stalin, Hitler, Mussolini, Franco. Names from hell. We had grown up hearing talk about "the Great War," the first major catastrophe of the twentieth century, the war in whose last months I was born. In Germany, a race of brute men, Nazi Storm Troopers (also from hell), went about beating up, harassing, and persecuting Jews in the name of Aryan superiority and turned Nietzsche inside-out and upside-down. The world struggled through the Great Depression. Soup kitchens thrived in America. The man next door committed suicide by jumping off the bridge over the Passaic River. All of it soaked into our still-unformed minds, still-awakening souls. Without being told, we knew that the world out there was a dangerous place, a boiling cauldron of still bigger troubles to come.

And all during this time I practiced the piano and desperately wanted to learn how to write music. Some of us born in America between 1900 and 1920 felt another, opposite world stirring, a barely coherent, inner world of longings and yearnings to say something serious in one of the art forms; to leave our own stamp on the time; to leave behind, if we could, a touch of beauty, in sound, in paint, in words, and, if not beauty per se, something that mysteriously leaves its healing mark and residual trace on the human soul. These urges, old as the universe itself, were couched in idiosyncratic Americanese. By the time I was in my late teens, there was a whole vocabulary of symbolic phrases expressing these wildly powerful desires and urges to write "the Great American Novel," "the Great American Play," "the Great American Symphony." The spiritual size of these mad ambitions matched the sheer physical size of the country itself. Maybe everyone suspected or had a hunch that these ambitions were illusory, the stuff of dreams, but they inspired the artists who believed in them. We looked at Europe and thought, hadn't the impossible already happened there? It could happen here.

And in 1948, three years after the war ended, I felt ready to make the mighty effort. That was the very summer Otto Luening declaimed against writing "masterpieces" anymore. I was already full of a large and ambitious plan with which to scale the orchestral heights, still vague where specific ideas were concerned, but nonetheless, laid out in my mind as two great pillars for outer movements and two inside slow movements of differing structure and character enclosing a big scherzo of constant capricious changes that I decided to call *Capriccio*. There were historical models aplenty—especially Beethoven, Berlioz, Brahms, and Mahler. There were American composers of an older generation already actively tilling the field: Roger Sessions, Aaron Copland, William Schuman, Walter Piston, Roy Harris. Stravinsky and Schoenberg were the two stylistic poles between which the contemporary world of music was pushed, pulled, defined, and polarized. I drew on both for the largest palette possible as I sketched and wrote: Stravinsky for his rhythmic *esprit* and metric asymmetry, Schoenberg for the ache of his atonal harmony; Stravinsky for his high saturation with a kind of perverse dissonantal tonality, Schoenberg for his wide interval stretching of expressive line; Stravinsky for his outward gestural angularity, Schoenberg for his inward, expressionistic gestures. I worked feverishly all fall into the spring of 1949. Never far from my thoughts were Beethoven's "Eroica" and Ninth symphonies, Berlioz's *Symphonie fantastique*. Somehow, miraculously I had written a score of almost two thousand measures. To hear it, parts had to be extracted, multiple copies of string parts reproduced. Everything needed to be meticulously proofread so as not to waste valuable rehearsal time. I became impatient for the sound of it, to find out if it was worth the paper on which I had written it.

Once I had completed the score of my First Symphony on onionskin (large translucent sheets of manuscript paper) I brought it to my copyist, Al Boss, to discuss costs of reproducing the score and extracting orchestral parts. Fortunately, there was no deadline to meet, so that removed one major headache, but the costs of extraction and reproduction, especially of multiple string parts, were going to be out of my immediate reach. Al Boss, steady as ever, allayed my anxiety by pointing out that first he would need time to estimate how much work and what costs would be involved. "We'll work something out," he said. "Let's not worry about it now." Al's solution turned out to be a lifesaver. When he had finally arrived at a rough estimate, which came to approximately $1,500—by today's standards something in the neighborhood of $15,000—Al said, and very simply, he would treat it as a debt to be paid out over time, at my convenience, and as I could afford. The gesture was magnanimity itself. We both agreed that whenever it was that the entire sum was about to be paid in full, I would withhold, as a gesture to "lady luck," a very small "unpaid balance" of $.25 that would remain as a sign and reminder of our trust in each other.

Miraculously, one day Al informed me the parts of my First Symphony were ready. Eager to hear the work as soon as a reading could be arranged, I approached Alexander Hilsberg, who conducted the Curtis Institute student orchestra. Hilsberg was concertmaster of the Philadelphia Orchestra and harbored powerful ambitions toward being a conductor himself. I spoke with Hilsberg about the possibility of devoting one full rehearsal period to a reading of my work, describing it in outline so he would not be surprised at its length.

Not long after our first meeting, Hilsberg called to say he would do it . . . could I send him the score so he could study it? Elated but nervous, I immediately arranged for him to have the score and for the institute to get the parts to the orchestra. Then there came a second phone call from Hilsberg: he was very sorry . . . but he was terribly busy and didn't have the time to absorb such a big score . . . perhaps I should conduct the reading myself? I had to make an immediate decision. Despite my shock at the impact of his remarks and the confusions in my mind caused by my old ambivalences about doing any kind of "performance"— even though this reading would be strictly private, an in-house matter, I quickly recovered my balance and told Hilsberg yes, I would do it. He set a date only a few weeks away. Then began a difficult time. It became necessary to devote myself exclusively to studying my own score in ways a conductor would. Suddenly gears shift and the score becomes a seemingly endless mountain range of details that must be understood and dealt with in terms of organizing gestures, rhythms, expressive rises and falls, and a host of other less-easy-to-describe matters. This parallels the decisions that I had to make when the work was being composed, but in a totally different way. Composing the work takes place from the inside out; thought/feelings and feeling/thoughts establish patterns of notation on pages intended for other eyes; conducting the identical work written with great labor, love, and effort is to approach it now from the outside with the hope it will emerge clear and alive in both the performers', and the listeners', insides. I kept reminding myself that other composers—past and present—had done and were doing the same thing: Mendelssohn, Wagner, Berlioz, Strauss, Mahler, Stravinsky, and some not so well, or even poorly, such as Beethoven, Schumann, and Brahms. In any case, this was a reading, not a public performance. The actual rehearsal period with the student orchestra arrived, and I was as ready as I would ever be. Hilsberg had come, too, and this strengthened my resolve to carry the session off as professionally as possible. What was at stake, after all, was *hearing my music*, not whether I was a conductor or not.

We worked hard and concentratedly that evening. Somehow we played through the entire work without any serious mishaps. Though somewhat rough around the edges, it was a good reading. The full-blown, big-boned character and size of the symphony's musical ideas came through; the two end movements readily revealed their large-spanned lines and propulsive, rhythmic energy; the slow movements came off, as well, although they would require considerably more work to make them speak as subtly and expressively as I wanted them to; the *Capriccio* was the most problematic because of its constant shifts in tempo and fast-changing, quixotic characters—now grim and serious, now lyric and slightly unstable, now light-hearted, ironic, even sardonic. It is an understatement to say I felt happy: a sense of incredible release filled me. At the same time I was exhausted; but a *good* exhaustion, the kind that follows a mighty effort that has realized its purpose to the full. It was in that state that I suddenly became aware Hilsberg was in front of me saying, "*You* should be a conductor" with a kind of emphasis and genuineness that clearly indicated he really meant it . . . But not a word about the music itself . . . A fact which to this day still puzzles me . . . and for which I can find no satisfactory reason . . . How is it possible for a professional musician to have listened to an hourlong, passionate work and have nothing more to say to its composer than, "*You* should be a conductor"? Had he even heard the music? Or didn't it matter?

In 1968, when I stepped down as the chair of Penn's music department, I did have an opportunity to conduct. Melvin Strauss, who had developed a solid, universitywide orchestra of students and faculty, was invited to become associate conductor of the Buffalo Philharmonic. The question arose, who would conduct the orchestra during Mel's leave of absence? After casting about unsuccessfully, I decided to do it. Truth to tell, I looked forward to the prospect of conducting Mozart, Haydn, Brahms, Verdi, and Mahler. The grandest production I undertook was Handel's *Israel in Egypt,* the oratorio that I have always considered a close second to his *Messiah.* Besides the university orchestra, the performance required the large university chorus of mixed voices and four professional solo singers. However lacking in professional polish it may have been, nonetheless it was a full-out, energetic, vital projection of an inherently powerful score.

Our friend William Bolcom was visiting us just then. I had met Bill—still in his twenties—three years earlier when we made our first trip to the West Coast, where I gave lectures at various schools—UCLA, Pomona College, and the University of Washington in Seattle, among others. Bill was one of the freest, most gifted young American composers I had come across. Besides being remarkably musical, Bill also had a gift for drawing. Since his visit coincided with my performance of Handel's oratorio, he was present; and when it was over, he gave me a small set of drawings he called "George at the Forge," a series of quick on-the-spot sketches he made spontaneously during the performance. They caught in a lighthearted way the size and excitement of the evening's production. This small treasure now resides among the George Rochberg Papers in the Music Division of the New York Public Library of the Performing Arts.

It was after the Curtis reading of the First Symphony that I foolishly acceded to the bad counsel of my friends and colleagues to shorten the work. Why I didn't dig in my heels and stand my ground I still do not fully understand. I was, by nature, against any form of expediency. In this case, expediency was the core of the poor advice I was getting. It meant paring down the work to a more "practical" size—the three-movement version that Ormandy premiered in 1958.

My discontent with the state of the symphony grew to the point where finally, in 1971, I began to work at the job of restoration. By June 1972, I completed restoring the score of the first three movements. New works occupied my attention in the ensuing years and made further work on the restoration impossible. Finally, in May–June 1977 I took it up again, completing the last two movements. The gestural character and musical style of the symphony remained unchanged. What had changed, however, were details of orchestration. In brief, the essential spirit of the work was identical with what I composed in 1948–49, but it was projected through a richer, more varied physical voice. Whatever its fate may be and whatever imperfections still remain, I am content; the work exists again in the form in which I originally conceived it.

I have saved for the end of this chapter the story of the interview Ormandy gave Daniel Webster, the music critic of the *Philadelphia Inquirer,* which appeared in the Sunday edition, September 21, 1969. Ordinarily, such beginning-of-the-season interviews with conductors of major orchestras have little or no intrinsic interest except for an announcement of a projected special event. This interview, however, was quite different, for in it, Ormandy delivered some astonishingly obtuse remarks:

> "What am I to do?" [Ormandy] asked last week. "Last year I consciously tried to play more new music, and you should read the letters I received. Audiences did not like the new works. In New York, after we played some of the programs, we had letters threatening to cancel and many which did cancel their subscriptions. This year we are doing less, and the box office tells me we are doing much better in New York and here. . . .
> "This is the problem I face. First, where is the important orchestral music of our time? Who is writing it? We used money for five commissions; two of the composers returned the money because they couldn't think of a work. I think the composers are not giving us music that is worth the problems it raises.
> "The new music is so difficult to prepare. You know, they say that Pierre Boulez is the only man who can conduct Boulez's music. In Cleveland, he programmed one of his pieces. After the first rehearsal, he changed his program. There was no time to prepare the work, so he substituted another composer. He did that in New York too. There it is."

To give Ormandy his due, he was struggling with a very difficult situation not necessarily of his or any other conductor's making. By 1969, modernism had run its course, and while it was eminently successful in other arts—painting, sculpture, and architecture, for example—it was a woeful failure where twentieth-century music was concerned. Early on in that century, while there were some notable exceptions, including Stravinsky's early ballet scores, new music—itself deeply divided as to method, aesthetic, direction—appealed largely and only to loyalists and aficionados. In Ormandy's statements regarding his situation vis-à-vis new music, audiences, and the problems of programming, we catch reflections of the cultural dilemmas to which he was evidently very sensitive but that simultaneously utterly bewildered him.

All this is in retrospect, of course; but at the time of Webster's article, I was too involved in what I am now trying to describe and took personal umbrage at particular remarks Ormandy made, which I singled out in my letter to Webster, September 23, 1969, and which appeared in the *Philadelphia Inquirer* the following week under the headline *Ormandy Challenged:*

Dear Mr. Webster,

The implications of Eugene Ormandy's remarks as reported in your article in Sunday's *Inquirer* are so far-reaching, they require extensive comment. That is what I propose to do here.

    The confusion in Mr. Ormandy's point of view, and to my mind undoubtedly the very reason why he cannot see the problem for what it is, is that he, like so many performing concert musicians of this day, fails to appreciate fully the fundamental distinctions between music as a creative force—something brought into existence by one human being—and music as a repertoire for performance by many human beings, individually or collectively. The guardians of the established repertoire are by nature and disposition resistant, if not actually hostile, to the presence of the living composer. It appears that the living composer has become an interloper in the community of today's performers—granting always as exceptions those few who, young in years or in spirit, respond to their own time—freely and openly. Certainly the composer and the performer are both musicians; but they are made of different stuff, they are different breeds. Composers will do well to become their own performers again, like their counterparts in the 18th and 19th centuries: Bach, Handel, Mozart, Haydn, Beethoven, Berlioz, Wagner, Mahler, Strauss. But this advice will remain purely gratuitous until the present system of concert life is transformed into something vibrant and alive and stops pandering to box-office mentality and taste. If in the process of this transformation the orchestra can survive the crisis of changing its present conductorial-managerial set-up to something more appropriate and fitting to the conditions of the time, the composer may yet regain his rightful position of leadership in the musical culture. . . .

    The dynamic of culture requires that Mr. Ormandy, like the composers themselves of the new works he does occasionally perform and the audiences for whom he performs them, suffer the uncertainty of their ultimate value, take the risk involved in offering them, exercise his responsibilities as a leading performer of his time. The process requires time and involves many links in a progression of events, only one of which might be a performance by Mr. Ormandy. The process is admittedly a mysterious one. I cannot imagine it otherwise; and to suggest that it is otherwise, that you can tell in advance of the unfolding of the future what opinions men will hold of this work or that is to be either clairvoyant or foolishly naïve.

Mr. Ormandy complains that the "new music is so difficult to prepare." Difficult for whom? It is the glory of American instrumentalists that they can play anything put on their stands. So long as it is "on the instrument." Should the contemporary composer demand less of the performer than composers of the last century? Difficulty is transformed into challenge by devotion and the degree to which a performer is willing to dedicate himself to the task he has to accomplish. In that regard it is no different today than it was when Wagner or Brahms were around. The endless repetitions of their music have by now resolved most of the technical difficulties which their first performers had to face and overcome.

It is sad and depressing that Mr. Ormandy expresses such a lack of faith in the possibilities that anything worthwhile is being produced by composers either in this city or any other American city. I cannot agree with him—obviously.

Sincerely,
George Rochberg

From friends in the orchestra, I learned that Ormandy had gone into an absolutely ulcerous rage, apparently a common reaction for him when something seriously angered or displeased him. To all intents and purposes my public riposte initially brought to an end my professional and personal relationship with Ormandy for almost a full decade—from 1969 to 1978.

I recently reread Webster's report on the Ormandy interview made at the beginning of the 1969–70 season as well as my response to it, which had serious repercussions for me personally, but effected no change at all in the situation at large, with a sense of Yogi Berra's "it's déjà-vu all over again." For, in fact, the larger societal problems and the cultural instabilities of that time already clearly visible are still with us and, if anything, a great deal more exacerbated.

Where music is concerned, the making, unmaking, and remaking of reputations is the rule. Yesterday's bête noire can become today's hero. The stock market of taste and opinion rises and falls like a fever chart. No one can force fame or reputation into existence or prolong it beyond its inherent shelf life. Even Beethoven may someday assume a purely mythic status like Orpheus. His music and the public's taste for it could be lost along the way, not even a distant echo remaining in the empty silence.

Rilke's Angels

String Quartet no. 2 with Soprano

Even if the outward stimulus was a commission from the Contemporary Chamber Music Society of Philadelphia, it still doesn't explain where the Second String Quartet with Voice came from—its essence, its dense, dark, fiery substance. Equally unexplainable is why I decided to work into this new quartet the idea of four different tempos, sometimes sounding simultaneously, sometimes not. For years I had been fascinated with the psychology of pitting slow music against fast, fast music against slow. Something of the weight of this new work called for a technique of intensifying emotional expression through tightly controlled metronomic tempo (speed) relationships. Adding a voice to the second half of the quartet a year after the first purely instrumental part had been written was the only—and necessary— way I could have completed the work, because it made possible opening, therefore enlarging, the inner life of the music to profoundly moving lines of poetry from Rainer Maria Rilke's *Duino Elegies,* which center on the inescapable and unanswerable questions of human existence: Why are we here? Why *this* life on *this* earth, and why *only* once? As Rilke asks at the very beginning of the First Elegy, "Wer, wenn ich schriee, hörte mich denn aus der Engel Ordnungen?" (Who, if I should cry out, would hear me among the orders of Angels?).

Initially, the quartet was to be entirely instrumental. There was no thought to introduce a voice. Parallel with the genesis of the ideas and feelings that provided the motive power for the work itself was my complete absorption in Rilke's *Duino Elegies,* particularly the Ninth Elegy. His poetic grasp of the fundamental human experience of life and death and the inextricably interwoven fate of human beings with the processes of nature rang true for me. I loved his unflinching perceptions of how things are, his ability to penetrate to psychic regions without relapsing into solipsism or the false and easy vulgarities of twentieth-century psychologizing. After an interruption of a whole year, I was able to resume work on the quartet in the summer of 1961. This time I had an overpowering feeling that to go on with a purely instrumental continuation and conclusion would be all wrong, that concrete things having to do directly with life experience had to be said. Then and only then did I decide to add the soprano voice and to project it through a setting of the opening and closing portions of Rilke's Ninth Elegy.

At first, I was going to call the work *Fantasies and Arabesques,* terms that I still feel capture best the manner of the main gestural characteristics of the music. But that was before necessity demanded I introduce the voice singing Rilke's opening and closing stanzas, which had the same questioning experience of existence. As passionate an utterance as the purely instrumental part of the quartet was, I felt it was too abstract, too detached and distanced in essence. It needed to be translated to another plane through which that very same questioning experience of existence would be revealed by passing it through equally passionate levels of poetry and singing and, in so doing, make the work more humanly immediate, more concrete and direct. Rilke's outcry permeates all ten elegies and is, as William Gass so eloquently puts it in his *Reading Rilke,* "(. . . everybody's elemental outcry); and although addressed to the Angels, it is as if the Angels spoke them, because their meaning is not common, small, or mean—earthbound—as most of our fears and worries are, most of our thoughts, hopelessly human as we are. . . ."[1]

The twelve-month hiatus that passed between the writing of these two parts of the work was more than an ordinary chronological separator. It marked a fundamental change in my external life and how I was to make my living. I left publishing and entered the groves of academe to take on the chairmanship of the Music Department at the University of Pennsylvania and, with that, simultaneously began my teaching career at a level more meaningful than any I'd experienced previously.

In the summer of 1959 I first began work on the quartet. By summer's end I had the entire first part down on paper—and left hanging one melodic fragment that, as I thought then, would be the link, the thread connecting to the continuation whenever I could resume work again. I could not have foreseen the life changes that lay ahead in the following months, and especially not the way in which, when the time did come at the beginning of the summer of 1961, I would continue the quartet as a vocal work, turning it into a quintet for soprano and string quartet. During the fall of 1959 and winter of 1960 there were meetings and talks with university people who were trying to interest me in taking on the administrative task of rebuilding the Department of Music, which was desperately in need of radical surgery if it was to survive at all. I grew more and more interested but, at the same time, apprehensive about my chances of succeeding in an area about which I knew practically nothing. This is the classic case so well captured in the phrase "between a rock and a hard place," the *rock* here being the security of something well known—publishing—that I had long since mastered but had wearied of, the *hard place* being the completely unknown, the challenge of building a new department on the ruins of a former one gone moribund. By April 1960 I had accepted the university's offer and given notice to Presser, and I spent the rest of that year beginning the process of reconstructing the Music Department's faculty and curriculum—and writing a major-sized prospectus in which I laid out a five-year-and-beyond plan for the new department. It was not until the summer months of 1961 that I felt secure enough about the state of things in the department to resume work on the quartet.

By the time I was ready to work again I had become thoroughly saturated with the Ninth Elegy. It spoke worlds to me. I had found an English translation by Harry Behn[2] that seemed magical in itself as pure verbal expression and just right for musical setting. Behn's translation is one of fifteen that William Gass discusses in *Reading Rilke;* there he spells out in critically painful yet always thoroughly honest ways the hazards of trying to make poetic sense of Rilke's German in English translation. As he says, "dozens of translators have blunted their skills against his obdurate, complex, and compacted poems."[3] When I was ready to take up the quartet again, my conception of it had metamorphosed radically—and I am convinced this fundamental change in conception was the fruit of steeping myself in Rilke's *Duino Elegies* all the while I was outwardly absorbed, sometimes even eaten up by the demands of my new duties at the university.

When the summer came and I was able to return to composing, my one thought was how to make use of the melodic thread I had left hanging. Could I use it as the starting point for the next and concluding part of the quartet? One day I discovered that the prosody of the opening words of the Ninth Elegy, "Why do we treasure," fit perfectly with the motion and curve of the single melodic thread that had been waiting those two years for its poetic mate, its spiritual partner. It was one of those gifts that the gods (the angels?) occasionally confer on someone who, through unyielding patience and long yearning for such magical moments, never knowing if one will ever come, is nonetheless ready to recognize when it does. That mysteriously serendipitous mating of word and music opened up a whole new prospect in how to treat the soprano in relation to the quartet. First and foremost, the singer had to be an absolutely equal partner with the string quartet—sharing in the life of the work as natural organs would in a living body, identifiably individual, distinct, and separate, yet finding completion, therefore meaning, only in the other. Treating the voice as "soloist" and the quartet as "accompaniment" would have made impossible the cooperating, crucial role each had to play in turning the work as a whole into a passionate musical expression of the unfathomable puzzle of human existence—and what's more, through Rilke's stranger-than-strange poetic vision of life whose mysteries are known to the angels . . . but not to us who must live them.

One of my most important decisions was to compose the vocal line as a great obbligato to already existing instrumental ideas, melodic figures, passages—which, given the new musical environment, had to be reworked to make the space around the vocal obbligato open enough for it to move unhampered. Though the soprano's lines are newly conceived, the quartet first draws on the early part of the work and later on the vocal part itself for its share in the vocal–instrumental partnership. In this way I arrived at a structure in which the voice is independent of the quartet and vice versa. This made possible writing instrumental passages in their own terms without sacrificing them to the voice. It also made possible an open situation in which soprano and instruments could go together; or one could drop out while the other continued; or one entered freely after the other had begun, thus dispensing entirely with the old baggage of introductions, interludes, bridges, and transitions.

In this way I divided the larger structure of part two, the vocal–instrumental part, into two ariosos for soprano and quartet separated by a "quasi-cadenza" for the string quartet that emerges from the end of the first arioso and leads directly into the second arioso. In this "quasi-cadenza" section, the four different tempi are presented together.[4] Each tempo, whether fast or slow, is understood as a metronomic speed equivalent, per beat, to the quarter note. For example, the fastest speed is $\quarternote = 144$; the next speed but less fast is $\quarternote = 108$; the next, still less fast, $\quarternote = 72$; and the slowest speed of all, $\quarternote = 54$. The 144 and 108 each has its slower double in 72 and 54, respectively; thus each pair is related by a ratio of 2:1 in which 72 is half the speed of 144, 54 half the speed of 108. When these four speeds appear simultaneously as they do in the "quasi-cadenza" section they produce charged emotional tensions through the friction of their opposing tendencies. Numerically this is represented in the following ratio proportions where (a) 144:54 = 8:3; (b) 144:108 = 4:3; (c) 108:72 = 3:2; (d) 72:54 = 4:3.

It seems there was never a time when Veda Reynolds, Irwin Eisenberg, Alan Iglitzin, Charlie Brennand, and I did not know each other. It's as though we had simply grown together through the Philadelphia Orchestra's performances of my music (they were all members of the orchestra) and through the Contemporary Chamber Music Society they had formed. They began a concert series at Penn, and shortly after I became head of the Music Department they were engaged as string-quartet-in-residence. It was then they changed their name from the too-provincial-sounding Stringart Quartet to the sturdier, more professional-sounding Philadelphia String Quartet. Considering these were the early 1960s and modernism still rode high in the saddle, their programs at the university offered quite advanced fare. I took part, playing the piano in Webern's op. 7 (Irv Eisenberg played violin) and op. 11 (Charlie Brennand played cello). The quartet gave all six of the Bartók string quartets spread over one season. The initial impact of this music was strong and attracted large audiences of students, faculty, and people from the community.

Private musical patronage of new music may not have played much of a role in mid-twentieth-century America generally, but in Philadelphia, it made one of its rarer appearances in the person of Mrs. Herbert C. Morris, otherwise known as "Billie." It was she who helped fund the Contemporary Chamber Music Society of Philadelphia, which functioned mainly through the activities of the Philadelphia String Quartet, and it was she who provided the commission for me to write my Second Quartet. Mrs. Morris was a charming, highly intelligent, and lively woman who clearly loved music and musicians. Normally shy of the pretensions of Main Line matrons who clustered about the cultural scene, I took to Billie right away. I found her direct manner and warm and open personality immediately appealing. One of her genuine passions was modern painting. I recall the time Gene and I visited her in her I. M. Pei house in the Society Hill section of Philadelphia, close to the Delaware River. She was then in her late eighties—perhaps already in her nineties—and could no longer walk the stairs to the upper floors of her house. The elevator she had installed had a glass window facing the inside wall. As you ascended or descended, you could see canvasses of Picasso, Matisse, and other twentieth-century masters. It was an astonishing sight by any account.

The first performance of my Second Quartet was a private one, given at Billie Morris's suburban home in Bryn Mawr, on Friday, March 23, 1962. The performance took place around a large indoor swimming pool—unquestionably the most unusual physical setting of any performances of my music. The string quartet sat at one end of the pool with Janice Harsanyi, the rich-voiced soprano. The listeners were at the far end of the pool and the room that extended beyond. At this late date I can only imagine that the blue, blue water across which the sound of the music traveled acted as a resonator and perhaps even an amplifier. My five colleagues and friends had spent endless hours, many with me present, working to overcome the purely technical problems and difficulties the work presented. It was a joy to work with such dedicated, serious musicians. Janice had virtual perfect pitch and negotiated the vocal line—with its extended range in both directions—with skill and amazing vocal control. The complexities they had to overcome ranged from the row structure of the work in which was embedded the multiple-tempos scheme I had devised, to the fact that it was a single-movement work of approximately twenty-five to thirty minutes in duration, to the visual format of the work, which necessitated each musician performing from full score. Perhaps the pool did have something to do with it, adding a dimension of actually heard or imagined sound quality. But after the performance, something seemed to have been released into the air, some special excitement and energy. Whatever it was, everyone present wanted to hear it again. The repeat performance of the quartet was received even more warmly than the first one.

I doubt there were many listeners there who knew that Arnold Schoenberg had composed his Second String Quartet in 1907–8 with voice appearing in two of its movements and thus could have made any association between his and mine based simply on the obvious fact that both quartets included voice. The conductor Erich Leinsdorf—who was there that day—did, and he excitedly, even joyfully, told me how much he liked my quartet and called it a "first cousin to Schoenberg's Second Quartet." A distant cousin perhaps, but hardly first cousin. It's true, of course, that a work such as my Second Quartet owes its twelve-tone origins to steps initiated by Schoenberg's Second Quartet that led him to abandon tonality for atonality, then to discover/invent a tightly ordered chromatic system of twelve tones. But I find the texts of Stefan George's poetry that Schoenberg used for his third and fourth movements' vocal settings move in an entirely different realm from Rilke's. George's poems are soft, verging on the sentimental; Rilke's *Duino Elegies* remain fully human—toughened because freed of illusory hopefulness.

Exactly one week later, March 30, 1962, the Philadelphia Quartet and Janice Harsanyi gave the first public performance of the Second Quartet to a full house in the Harrison Auditorium of the University of Pennsylvania's Museum of Archaeology and Anthropology. There was a sense of occasion rarely present at musical events. The Philadelphia Quartet and Janice picked up on the electricity in the air and gave an intense, concentrated performance. They exceeded themselves. Among the reactions I remember best is Harry Powers's. Harry, who had joined the music faculty early in its reorganization, was a brilliant young scholar, mainly interested in theory, with a passionate interest in new music. All the more reason why I liked to chide him gently when he would announce mournfully that "music was dead, George. I don't see any hope for it the way it's going." I often thought Harry might, in fact, be right; certainly my own reactions to almost everything being written in those days tended toward the same conclusion. On this particular occasion, after the performance and at the peak of the excitement it produced, Harry approached me almost apologetically and said something like, "Well, George, maybe things aren't as bad as I thought. . . . Maybe there's some hope, after all."

<hr />

The 1971–72 season was the time of my beginning relationship with the just-born Concord String Quartet. When I take up a full discussion of my Third String Quartet I will go into greater detail. The only reason for mentioning the Third String Quartet now is to trace the skein of entangling events that involved the recording of both the Second and Third quartets in the same time frame by the Concord for two distinctly different record companies.

Early in 1971, four astonishing young players formed a new string quartet and commissioned me to write a work for them. Mark Sokol, the first violinist, and I had already met and spent some time together in New York. I accepted their commission and almost immediately set to work. Shortly afterward, the cellist, Norman Fischer, and his wife, Jeanne, a gifted pianist, came to visit us. This was our first meeting—a very lively and enjoyable one it was. Norm tells me that I insisted on playing for them a piano work I had recently written, my *Carnival Music*. He and his wife were completely surprised. Knowing only my Second Quartet, the *Carnival Music* "was not," as Norm told me, "what we'd expected," and, it turned out, neither was the Third String Quartet.

Immediately after the premiere performance of the Third Quartet, on May 15, 1972, at Tully Hall in New York, Teresa Sterne asked the Concord to record my new work for Nonesuch Records, to which they happily agreed. Prior to the premiere they had been recording avant-garde American quartets for the Vox label.[5] Because they felt indebted to Vox's founder, George Mendelssohn (who claimed direct descent from Felix Mendelssohn-Bartholdy) for his support, the Concord asked Mendelssohn, as a courtesy, if it was all right to record my Third for Nonesuch, inasmuch as Teresa Sterne had asked them first. Mendelssohn, because of the excitement generated by the Third, had apparently expected they would record it for Vox. According to Norm, Mendelssohn said in effect, "Okay. Provided you record Rochberg's Second Quartet for me *before* you record his Third for Nonesuch." A strange tale that linked the recordings of the Second and Third quartets.

The Concord rehearsed with soprano Phyllis Bryn-Julson, October 25 and 26, 1972, played for me on Saturday, October 28, 1972, and recorded for Vox October 30 and 31, 1972.[6] Four weeks later during November 20–22, 1972, we recorded the Third Quartet for Nonesuch,[7] finishing at 6:00 A.M. Thursday, Thanksgiving Day, November 23, 1972—exhausted but elated. If one asks how was it possible for these four remarkable young men to perform such Herculean feats, if in nothing else but sheer physical tenacity and energy, the answer lies *inside* their collective musical being: they were on fire with the love of making quartet music, intense in focus and concentration to a degree one finds only in the greatest performers. This may seem pure hyperbole, but all one needs for confirmation is to listen to both of their by-now "ancient" recordings for the living proof.

A failed recording session of the Second String Quartet must have taken place sometime *before,* yet close to the time of the Concord Quartet's recording for Vox, and obviously has a link to why Mendelssohn wanted the Concord to record it. This "before" period has to be the time prior to October 1972 during which Vox recorded my Piano Trio no. 1 (1963) with violinist Kees Kooper, cellist Fred Sherry, and pianist Mary Louise Boehm on the Turnabout label[8] and made its first attempt to record my Second Quartet. Kees Kooper was probably asked by Mendelssohn to find a singer and put together a quartet. Knowing neither the singer nor any of the players except for Kees Kooper, I came to the session quite apprehensive, but since I hadn't known the people who recorded the piano trio, either, before I met them at rehearsals I hoped against hope that this new group of musicians would prove to be up to what lay ahead. Unhappily, my hopes were in vain. The singer could not negotiate her part at all. Was she even a "singer," let alone a musician? I doubt she had the faintest inkling of the text or its meaning. She could neither sing on pitch nor follow the notes of her own line. The quartet, though possibly individually decent players, seemed unable to get itself together. How long I endured the situation, the numberless "takes" trying to get individual passages right, at least mechanically, I don't remember. I was in increasing agony—and I imagine so were the musicians. The moment had to come when I knew it was futile to go on, and it did. I pushed the intercom button and said I would be coming out to talk to them . . . What I did had to be done, though it was very difficult, perhaps one of the most difficult situations I'd ever faced with musicians trying to play my music. In essence what I said was quite simple and direct: "We can't go on with this recording session . . . It's not fair to my work or to you . . . Whatever the reasons, you are not prepared. You have no sense of the work . . . or what I intend by it . . . I think it best we cancel the recording session . . . I wish you all luck." There was no anger in me, only the dismal sense of failure, of something that had been wrong from the first. In any case, I'm almost certain that the cancellation of the disastrous attempt at a recording session was the catalyst that pushed George Mendelssohn into asking the Concord Quartet to make the recording of my Second Quartet with Phyllis Bryn-Julson and thereby saved the day.

Lewis Kaplan produced what turned out to be the most fantastic live public performance of the Second Quartet of any I remember. It took place in the auditorium of the Museum of Modern Art in New York on May 10, 1962. Lewis put together a string quartet, lined up soprano Janice Harsanyi—and *four page turners!* Why *four?* Because that was the number needed for the quartet players. Each of them was playing from full score, and there would have been too many downright dangerous page turns for any of them to deal with comfortably and keep going without mishap, or having to leave something out, or, far worse, for the score itself to be knocked off the stand in the heat of battle. There was certainly something quite out of the ordinary having nine people onstage where normally you need only five. Oddly enough, the very look of it created an air of momentousness, of something unusual taking place. Lewis and his musicians brought it off with great élan, brio, and sensitivity.

CHAPTER 6

Breaking with Modernism

Third String Quartet and the Concord String Quartet

> "How does it feel to have your own quartet?"
> —Harold Schonberg, *New York Times*
> music critic, ca. 1982, Santa Fe

The saga of my long and happy professional and personal relationship with the four young musicians who became the Concord String Quartet began in November 1971 with the phone call from Mark Sokol asking me if I would write a string quartet for them. Before the call was over I had agreed. In fact I was eager to try my hand at another quartet and reconnect with a medium and world of thought and feeling I had not lived and breathed for ten years—not since I finished the Second String Quartet in 1961.

In order to establish the special feel and texture of the circumstances that led to the initial impulse for how to proceed with the Third String Quartet, I go back to March 16, 1971, at the University of Illinois, where the premiere of my *Songs in Praise of Krishna* took place. I wrote the cycle for the soprano Neva Pilgrim and accompanied her at the piano. It was as thoroughly unorthodox a program as I can ever remember being involved in. During the first part I read a long, no-holds-barred paper I had written two years earlier on "The Avant-Garde and the Aesthetics of Survival."[1] There I argued against a thoughtless and wayward modernist dismissal of the very premises of the thousand-year history of the composition of music preceding the twentieth century and for a new understanding of tonal music and its long past in order to find solid ground again for the survival of music as an art of high craft and perceptible beauty.

What I had not anticipated was the solid wall of hostility that rose like a black cloud from the large audience of students and faculty in the form of stinging, angry denunciations and questions. I felt engulfed in an electrical storm of rejection. Only later did I learn that I had entered John Cage country. He'd been in residence at Illinois for two years prior and had evidently won over the greater majority of students and faculty in the school of music to his radical notions of indeterminacy, chance, randomness based on sounds—environmental and man-made—freed of the taint of "the human stain," freed of human identity and ego. This was the background of the virulence of the response to my ideas advocating a rapprochement with tradition and the past.

After this ideological skirmish, there was a brief intermission, hardly long enough to serve as a cooling-off period, and I returned to the stage with Neva Pilgrim to give the first performance of the *Krishna* cycle. It benefited in its way, I think, from the charged atmosphere still pervading the hall. A passionate telling of an all-consuming love of an earthly woman for the god Krishna, *Songs in Praise of Krishna* is an intensely sensual mask for a symbolically tragic revelation of the impossibility of commingling the human and the divine.

The determining impulse for the Third Quartet was a fall 1971 concert that took place at the University of Pennsylvania, again with Neva Pilgrim and myself performing the *Krishna Songs,* followed by George Crumb's *Black Angels* for electrified string quartet performed by the rambunctious Concord String Quartet. This concert and performance of Crumb's work, which I'd not heard before, helped produce the seed for my Third Quartet. I remember with absolute clarity that the moment *Black Angels* ended and I was leaving the hall I said to myself, "Now I know what *not* to do." That precise formulation of the negative arose, first, from my strong visceral rejection of "sound designs" with intense levels of piercingly painful electrified decibels of volume resulting in sheer noise for a medium—the string quartet—I felt was off-limits to senseless, technological, modernist manipulation, and, second, because I had already agreed to write something for the Concord. So in that mental temper and state, cogitating and mulling over what I would write for that astonishing foursome, I heard Crumb's piece and reacted as I did by clearing the inner space of my mind and soul of what I considered nonessential and thus could say, "Now I know what I *want* to do."

The major part of the story of my relation to the Concord has to be delayed until I can clear away acres of underbrush to describe my inner state and why I reacted as I did to a work like Crumb's.

During those crucial years—from the middle 1960s into the early 1970s—when I wrestled with myself over the question of modernism and what direction to take to get back to more solid ground, to terra firma, I was immersed in reading the

American poet Robinson Jeffers. I went over and over in my mind, almost like an extended mantra, what he had said in 1914, what he called his "bitter meditation" on the problem of modernism, then still in its heroic stage—urgent, expanding, gathering energy in all directions, and unrelentingly on the march:

> This originality . . . is there any way to attain it? The more advanced con-
> temporary poets were attaining it by going farther and farther along the way
> that perhaps Mallarmé's aging dream had shown them, divorcing poetry from
> reason and ideas, bringing it nearer to music, finally to astonish the world with
> what would look like pure nonsense and would be pure poetry. No doubt these
> lucky writers were imitating each other, instead of imitating Shelley and Milton
> as I had done. . . . Their successors could only make further renunciations; ideas
> had gone, now meter had gone, imagery would have to go; then recognizable
> emotions would have to go; perhaps at last even words might have to go or give
> up their meaning, nothing be left but musical syllables. Every advance required
> the elimination of some aspect of reality, and what could it profit me to know
> the direction of modern poetry if I did not like the direction? It was too much
> like putting out your eyes to cultivate the sense of hearing, or cutting off the
> right hand to develop the left. These austerities were not for me; originality
> by amputation was too painful for me. . . . [A]nd I was standing there like a
> poor God-forsaken man-of-letters, making my final decision not to become a
> "modern."[2]

Jeffers was twenty-seven at the time he wrote these black thoughts. I was in my early fifties in 1970–72, had been a "modernist" but also had been abandoning it by slow, painful stages since about 1961. Jeffers had looked hard at the "there" of the modern staring him in the face, determined to keep to what he knew and loved. I had plunged into the "heart of darkness" of my own free, if reluctant, will—and without a map. Therein lay the difference—which only served to increase the urgency of my situation a hundredfold, its necessity a thousandfold. The resolution I worked out through the writing of the Third Quartet opted against the time-honored habit of replacing a previous way of working with a "better" or "newer" way, long institutionalized in the notion of "progress" that both Western art and music history endorsed, even celebrated as "truth." What motivated me most strongly was the clear and exhilarating sense that all that modernism had brusquely bulldozed aside and the modern itself could now finally be brought together. Composing now would depend only on craft, techni-cal command, knowledge, taste, judgment—above all, on the sense of rightness, of the inevitability of choices made and the contexts they created.

Writing the Third Quartet was a joy. It came without impediment between December 1971 and February 1972. I mixed freely the atonal and the tonal; jux-taposed the intense and sometimes harsh chromatic with the gentler diatonic;

treated tonality, normally asymmetric, symmetrically, and atonality, which leans heavily toward the symmetric, asymmetrically. I was determined to put together every possible opposite in music I could command—and rejoiced in doing so. The opening movement was totally imagistic and freewheeling in its design. Diverse gestures followed one another without preparation. Styles and ideas with clearly discernible historic precedents emerged in unapologetically helter-skelter fashion, whether in rapid succession or layered in simultaneities. Emotional states associated with these clashing styles and ideas confronted each other as hard-edge colors do in abstract painting. Since there could be no expectations, nothing could be anticipated. It was in its way a kind of collage—except that in this instance the "found" forms were all newly invented. I wanted the opening to have the air of being utterly spontaneous, self-generating, as though it were happening for the first time—but that sense of spontaneity had to be composed, nothing left to chance. I was declaring my freedom from all previous single, history-bound styles, if not ideas, by making a new style of multiplicities and their potential mixtures.

One of the happiest ideas for what became the first of two interrelated marches enclosing the heart of the quartet, a set of variations in A major, came to me right after seeing Charlie Chaplin's film *Modern Times,* which lampoons in inimitable ways the self-conscious efficiencies of the use of newfangled gadgets and shiny steel machinery so characteristic of the technological maelstrom that was industrial modernism. Chaplinesque ideas acted as a quirky, out-of-balance backdrop against and through which canonic and other kinds of passages move rapidly in and out. The concluding fifth-movement Finale is designed as a set of alternating Scherzos and Serenades that move freely from the atonal to the tonal, the tonal to the atonal. While the Serenades are consistently tonal, the Scherzos are not-so-obvious variants of each other cast in either atonal or tonal terms to show that both pitch worlds, while different from each other, are, at the same time, related.

Having behind me the two chamber collage works of 1965—*Contra Mortem et Tempus* and *Music for the Magic Theater*—as well as my Third Symphony of 1966–69, all of which were full of "found forms," borrowed material, and having only recently written the *Caprice Variations,* also full of "borrowed" stuff, I could write the Third Quartet as though it were a giant collage/assemblage of everything I considered germane to my purpose and also as though it were a "concert of music" of sharply diverse kinds bridging the modern and the premodern worlds with no particular emphasis on either but as aspects of an enlarged palette of expression embracing the living past and present as I felt and understood them.

With my Third Quartet in hand, I drove to Binghamton, New York, where the Concord String Quartet lived. They were part of a young string quartet program directed and coached by Robert Mann, the leader and sustaining spirit of the

Juilliard String Quartet. This would be our first rehearsal with my new quartet and our first meeting. I had already met Mark Sokol, who played first violin and was the charismatic, high-powered founder of the Concord; Norman Fischer, the irrepressibly enthusiastic cellist and youngest of the ensemble; and Norm's equally young, gifted pianist-wife, Jeanne. When I walked into the little house it was like walking into a super-alive, loving commune. All four members of the quartet were there—Mark, Norman, Andrew Jennings, and John Kochanowski—with their wives, except for John, who was not married. Never before and not since have I met such a company of infectious, youthful, musical spirits: they had the look of being caught up in the wonder of living a kind of unmarred waking dream where life and music were completely open to them, all the joys and beauty one could imagine in that joining of music and love. Without realizing it, they were consummate romantics, and basically, so was I.

At the outset of our first rehearsal they confessed that they were utterly baffled by the opening movement . . . What did I mean by all those sudden and startling shifts of gesture, style, language? . . . They could make no sense of it . . . couldn't find its "center." "Not to worry," I assured them. "I'll show you how it goes," and I proceeded to sing it to them; and where it couldn't be sung, I vocalized its motion, its gestural arc by phrases. I was careful to avoid lengthy explanations, knowing that musicians—young and old, inexperienced and experienced—don't relish having music "explained" to them. However articulate the composer, however rich his explanatory images, verbal language cannot convey the shape of a musical phrase, nor how it is to be inflected dynamically and rhythmically, that is, where emphasis falls. A few well-chosen words sometimes convey the essence, but beyond that, it is always best to go directly to the heart of the musical matter—and sing it.

They quickly made musical sense of my deliberately disconnected series of multigestural projections, paradoxically preserving its spontaneity and feeling of first-timeness, even as they controlled every nuance, shaped every phrase. By the end of our intensely concentrated rehearsal sessions, which often carried over into the next day, they had a firm grip on the overall shape and design of the work and its three-part grouping of the five movements—Part A (I. Introduction: Fantasia, II. March); Part B (III. Variations); Part C (IV. March, V. Finale: Scherzos and Serenades). They showed an innately astute sense of pacing, setting off the A-major variations—the spiritual heart of the work—in perfect bas-relief against the rougher-hued, far more rambunctious music of the marches on either side.

The impact of the premiere of the Third at Alice Tully Hall in New York City under the sponsorship of the Naumburg Foundation on May 15, 1972, was stunning and electric. Shockwaves went through the audience, the critics, and eventually beyond. The critical furor it raised on all sides spread out from the performance itself in ever-widening concentric circles well past the release of the Nonesuch recording the following year.[3] On the positive side it catapulted the Concord String Quartet into sudden recognition as a superb ensemble of master performers of new music. But where the work itself was concerned I was totally unprepared for the tempest it caused. The eye of the storm centered directly over the tonal third movement, the unabashedly romantic A-major theme and variations. I was excoriated by modernist supporters and loyalists for having betrayed serialism, for defecting from the ranks of the serialists. Widely expressed in the press—and certainly news to me—was the sentiment that I, who had once been one of "America's leading serialists," had now, because of "a change of heart," taken to the highly dubious practice of writing "retrogressive" music that sounded like Beethoven, Brahms, Mahler, even Bartók.

Especially in the last quarter of the twentieth century, academic circles were devoted to a firm faith in the reality of a constant and unbroken chain of "progress" in the steady march of art and music, of which modernism, in the forms of cubism and abstraction in art, and twelve-tone and serialism in music, represented the highest Hegelian peaks, historically speaking. Consternation, even anger and fear, ruled. How, indeed, could such things as the Third Quartet stood for *be?* The aesthetic debate quickly degenerated into personal attacks on the defector who had dared to challenge the formerly unassailable musical bastions of the modern as the only true way to make art. I read or heard that I was "a traitor," "a reactionary"; worse still, "a counterfeiter," "a forger." My quartet represented an act of "shameless retrogression," "a cop-out," sheer indulgence in "nostalgia," a reversion to "orthodox old-school romanticism in the Schubert–Schumann–Mahler tradition." I was accused of making "pastiche," slavishly "copying" earlier and better composers while simultaneously practicing "tongue-in-cheek" and "sly irony," even producing "travesty."

One of the more inventive epithets that came my way declared me "a ventriloquist." Another critic, reviewing the recording, referred to the Third as a "work for soapbox and string quartet"—the "soapbox" being the program notes on the LP jacket. What was it about those notes that brought forth this particular epithet with its overtones suggesting some self-serving propagandistic or polemic purpose on my part? I was using the recording as a platform for launching a personal apologia. Teresa Sterne, Nonesuch's keen-eared director of recording projects, objected strongly to my notes when she first read them because, she said, they were too "personal," that I was exposing myself needlessly. I, on the other hand, felt (even more strongly) that what they said needed to be said, and in precisely the way I'd said them. As far as I understood that particular juncture in the aesthetic life and fortunes of that particular time, certain fundamental is-

sues needed to be confronted directly. After two generalized opening paragraphs
I referred to the fact that since my last serial work written in 1963, I had been
engaged in an effort to rediscover the larger and more sweeping gestures of the
past, to reconcile my love for that past and its traditions with my relation to the
present and its often-destructive pressures . . . my search had led to an ongoing
reconsideration of what the "past" (musical or otherwise) means . . . we bear the
past in us. We do not, cannot begin all over again in each generation (biologically
speaking), because the past is indelibly printed on our central nervous systems.
Each of us is part of a vast physical–mental–spiritual web of previous lives, ex-
istences, modes of thought, behavior, and perception; of actions and feelings
reaching much farther back than what we call "history" . . . The shockwave of
this enlargement of vision was to alter my whole attitude toward what was musically possible today . . . the inclusion of tonality in a multigestural music such as
the Third Quartet made possible the combination and juxtaposition of a variety
of means that denies neither the past nor the present . . . in this open ambience
tonal and atonal can live side by side . . . In this way, the inner spectrum of the
music is enlarged and expanded; many musical languages are spoken in order
to make the larger statement convincing.

Fortunately, it was not all brickbats and barbs. There was also support from
sympathetic quarters for having broken the stranglehold of serialism on composition, on the one hand, and on the other, for having succeeded in making
something genuinely beautiful. Calmer, more sober voices entered the discussion.
John Rockwell, writing in the January 1974 issue of *High Fidelity and Musical
America* magazine,[4] referred to the Third's "immediate impact . . . as a catalyst
for thought among the American musical community. Rarely has a recording
. . . occasioned such a spate of soul-searching reviews." Rockwell grasped fully
the curious paradox of the deeply rooted conservatism inherent in modernism's
"progressively ongoing compositional tradition," which, as he pointed out, was
"likely to provoke the wrath of the musical community if" a composer deviated
"from the expected norm." He went on to say: "At present we are witnessing the
gradual erosion of the serialist bulk-head in this country . . . The trouble is that
when a composer comes along who really falls outside . . . these orthodoxies . . .
the musical world still finds it hard to accept [him]." Still feeling his way among
these aesthetic quicksands, Rockwell suggested that "composers like Rochberg
. . . become increasingly tempted to dip back into the inviting repository of the
past." He finally reached the heart of the matter when he noted that Robert P.
Morgan, in a review in the November 1973 issue of *High Fidelity,*[5] "points out . . .
we can never approach Rochberg's 'Beethoven' in the same way that we listen to
Beethoven's own Beethoven." He registered his essential reservation that "the past

. . . can probably never live again in quite the way he [Rochberg] would like it to." One step further and Rockwell would have joined the company of those who are (or were) convinced that I was suffering from a terminal case of nostalgia; but fortunately his very thoughtfulness saves him from falling into this quagmire of unthinking sentimentalism.

Linda Hutcheon, in her book *A Theory of Parody,* goes even deeper when she discusses this very point. She writes:

> It is not a matter of nostalgic imitation of past models; it is a stylistic confrontation, a modern recoding which establishes difference at the heart of similarity. No integration into a new context can avoid altering meaning, and perhaps even value. George Rochberg's Third String Quartet appropriates the conventions of an earlier period and gives them a new meaning. The third movement sounds like a set of variations by Beethoven, but we cannot analyze it as such. Its real significance lies in how it does not sound like Beethoven, because we know it was written in the 1970s.[6]

One of the more partisan voices in this ongoing discussion was that of Michael Walsh. Writing in the *San Francisco Examiner,* Walsh declared:

> If any piece can claim to be the litmus test of contemporary music—and I mean *real* contemporary music, written within the last decade—it is the Third String Quartet of George Rochberg . . . Not the opening shot across the bow of academic serialism (Rochberg's own *Contra Mortem et Tempus* of 1965 has that honor), it was instead the first shot that hit the ship of serialism squarely, holing it below the water line. For the Third Quartet had the effrontery to suggest that it was time for a rapprochement with tonality and the music of the past . . . In time, Rochberg's Third Quartet may come to be seen as the work that defined the attitudes of a generation of composers . . . What is important about it was that it represented a way out of a maze.[7]

Still echoing in Walsh's 1980s piece is Rockwell's 1974 comment, "when a composer comes along who really falls outside . . . these orthodoxies . . . the musical world still finds it hard to accept [him]."[8] Walsh puts it more simply: "Rochberg . . . has never been forgiven by some of his colleagues in academia."

Two stories convey something of the texture and feel of the aftermath of the Third's premiere. On the surface, one appears to be more immediately personal, yet has far-reaching implications beyond the purely personal. The other turns on more obviously professional, practical sides of a composer's life. Both, taken together, lend more of a real sense of what actually happened in the Cubist world of mid-twentieth-century music in America.

Gene and I, out of a sense of obligation rather than pleasure, went to New York to attend a farewell party for Hugo Weisgall, the outgoing director of the American Music Center. We hardly expected this occasion to be any different from others that organizations and institutions tend to put on year in, year out. This party turned out like no other. For as we entered the large, jam-packed room, the party already in full swing with the inevitable aggregate din, I heard, shouted from across the room and in a voice I can only describe as a triumphant C-major trumpet blast: "*GEORGE!! YOU TURNED AMERICA AROUND ON ITS ASS!!!*" I'm not even sure that at first I recognized the voice that sent out that astonishing pronouncement, a big basso—sonorous and gravelly. Turning in the direction it had come from, I saw, making his way through the crowd, beaming from ear to ear, Arthur Cohn, conductor and writer on music. He was an old friend from Philadelphia days when I used to escape from the suffocating summer heat of our one-and-a-half-room apartment to the quiet coolness of the Free Library's reading rooms to work on counterpoint. Arthur had seen us come in and evidently couldn't restrain his spontaneous outburst. Needless to say, we were startled by its grandiloquence, couched in a kind of straight-out language that had a real wallop.

Arthur told us he was on his way uptown and, to save time, decided to take the subway. Once on the train he opened the score of my Third Quartet and became so absorbed that he lost all awareness of where he was. Suddenly he found himself at the end of the line, virtually at the tip of Manhattan. He'd overshot the mark, missed his stop completely. He told the story with the greatest relish and couldn't get over the fact that his total absorption in the score of the Third had made him forget where he was.

What did Arthur mean? My Third Quartet? What was happening in America that *needed* so desperately to be turned around? Starting with the broadest terms first, postwar American music until at least 1965–70 (and possibly well into the 1980s) was suffering the aesthetic death grip, the domination and intimidation of serialism—whether the homegrown variety or the European. In more immediate and direct terms, American music was being terrorized by, according to Joseph N. Straus, "The Myth of Serial 'Tyranny' in the 1950s and 1960s," his title for an artful dodge of an article that appeared in the *Musical Quarterly* in 1999.[9] There he attempted—with charts, facts, and figures offered in number-crunching, pseudosociological fashion—to prove that "the idea of serial domination is essentially false."[10]

Leon Botstein, in his "Notes from the Editor" for the same issue, points out that "What Straus has done is not so much create a counterfactual argument as use descriptive sociology to eliminate any empirical foundation for the commonplace perception that serialism was in the ascendancy in post–World War

II America." Botstein wonders, "What was all the angst about if serialism was as marginal as Straus' data suggest?" Then he clinches his point by asking, "After all, if there was no 'tyranny,' then how does one explain . . . the feeling of liberation and revolt associated with the minimalism and so-called neo-romanticism of the late seventies and early eighties?"[11] Straus sums up his position—from which Botstein is clearly demurring—in the last paragraph of his article:

> Serialism emerged as a viable compositional alternative in this period, but only one among many. Serialism and serial composers had no power to coerce or to compel. What they did have the power to do was to offer an alternative, to suggest new ways of thinking about basic musical material. But suggestion is not the same as coercion. It is time to put simplistic notions of a serial tyranny behind us in order to regain a more nuanced sense of what this music, and this crucial period in our musical history, [is] all about.[12]

Straus's effort to remove the onus from serialism and serialists by insisting that neither had the "power to coerce and compel" (*therefore,* there could have been no "tyranny" except as "myth") misses the crucial point: the real, lived-and-experienced atmosphere of the 1950s and 1960s was dominated psychologically, aesthetically, and intellectually and riven by the earlier emergence of a powerhouse of artistic presence in the persons of Arnold Schoenberg and his two satellite, equally strong artist-composers, Alban Berg and Anton Webern. After Schoenberg's *Pierrot lunaire* of 1912, nothing could be the same in Western music, any more than after Stravinsky's *Le sacre* of 1913. Two invisible capitols of aesthetic loyalty, adherence, and belief came to dominate Europe and America: The Paris-based Russian–French orbit versus the Vienna-based Central European orbit. No one escaped their attractions or repulsions. Composers defined themselves by how near or how far they would allow themselves to be drawn to either. Strong feelings and thoughts—in forms of aesthetic convictions, loyalties, fears, hatreds, and rejections—swirled around these polar opposites for the rest of the century. No, there may or may not be overt politics *qua* politics where art is concerned, but the same passions that drive political beliefs, especially of the variety of violent extremes we have witnessed in the twentieth century, also drive artistic convictions and beliefs to violent extremes. In fact, we have had a name for it all along—modernism. And when these are played out among real people as they were in the postwar era, the guileless, benign picture Straus tries to sell us fades before the reality he strives so hard and ineffectually to displace and deny. His tactics of detoxifying serialism and serialists reminded me of efforts to de-Nazify Hitler's Germany or de-Bolshevize Stalin's Russia.

Had he paid more attention to the palpable presence of the twelve-tone, serialist-dominated journals that set the tone of the period, and understood that

American academic composers took readily to serialism, its logics, methodologies, magic squares, set theories because it now gave them something solid and intellectual that offered certainties where previously none had existed, then he would have been better able to comprehend why undergraduates and graduate students in particular felt frozen and intimidated—why they resented and feared their teachers and the ideas they promulgated, which disclaimed any value attaching to works produced in any way other than the serial, and why anathema fell on my head with the appearance of my Third Quartet, which seemed to liberate those who needed the assurance that serious art music could be composed in the face of serialist dominance.

Above all, Straus failed to comprehend that primarily the greater majority of the American and European post–World War II generations of serialists found in serialism an escape from the necessity to be artists and make art, and a way to continue calling themselves composers—even though what they produced were more demonstrations or illustrations of theoretical-analytical thought processes or thought experiments than they were attempts to say anything artistically meaningful in persuasive human terms. Which is to say, they categorically rejected the nonmodernist idea that a composer carved out of uncertainties a particular, peculiarly personal form of certainty whose entire raison d'être was whatever beauty it might possess in its effort to express existentially a stance toward what we call "reality."

It would be merely mechanical to take a straight-line, chronological approach to discussing the six other works I wrote for the Concord quartet. Instead, I will group together the four numerically successive quartets—the Fourth, Fifth, Sixth, and Seventh—and follow with the Quintet for Piano and String Quartet and the Quintet for Two Violins, Viola, and Two Cellos. This allows me to deal with the *Concord Quartets* (nos. 4, 5, and 6), which I see as a composite whole named in honor of my friends, and then to treat entirely separately the Seventh Quartet for baritone and string quartet.

The multiple sources for the impulse to do a set of three quartets were quite diverse. It was another way to try to realize my old idea of "a concert of music": an entire program of stylistically varied, yet related, pieces, such as, for example, the 1970 solo violin *Caprice Variations* or a series of interconnected chamber works of similar or diverse instrumentation. It was partly a desire to mark off in a special way my approaching sixtieth birthday; and, just as surely because of my continuing awe and wonderment at Beethoven's multiple-work opp. 18 and 59, for instance—awe at the sheer energy to pour out so generously and unimpeded a set of six quartets for op. 18 and three for op. 59, or as G. F. Handel did in the month of October 1739, twelve Concerti Grossi, op. 6; sheer wonderment at the continuously fresh flow of ideas that seem never to run out. The richness and diversity of characters, qualities, and emotional levels I associate with the best baroque and classical music are what I wanted to achieve in my *Concord String Quartets.* But where Handel's and Beethoven's language was tonal, spoken through the textures and designs of their times, I wanted to speak through a broader, more inclusive language, one that embraced my predecessors as well as the more astringent, harsher, atonal values of my own day.

During the middle to late 1970s, when the Concord was preparing what every professional quartet sooner or later feels it must do to prove itself to the musical world, that is, play a cycle of all the Beethoven quartets convincingly, Mark told me of a great discovery he had made—astonishing for its simplicity of state-ment and depth of insight and observation: in all twenty-four movements that constitute the six quartets of Beethoven's op. 18, not a single ensemble texture or accompanimental pattern is repeated; everything is newly invented for each situation—thematic ideas, harmonic progressions, even contrapuntal/polyphonic textures, not to mention those hair-raising obbligato outbursts in the slow move-ment of op. 18, no. 1. At the first opportunity I checked the scores of the op. 18 quartets to see if what Mark had discovered was, in fact, the case. He was right, absolutely. This fresh understanding of Beethoven gave me the added impetus to make the effort to follow his example and match, if possible, his incredible feat.

I began by gathering ideas of all kinds, not for any quartet in particular, but for what I envisioned as the entire set—as though it were a giant-sized work rather than divisible into three distinct units. Simultaneously, I projected at least four movements per quartet, more if warranted by the design, all the while guided by a sense that I would need about fifteen movements in all. Actually I ended with fourteen: four for Quartet no. 4, five for Quartet no. 5, and five again for Quartet no. 6. Various possibilities for where my growing body of material would work and fit best presented themselves to me. There was a good deal of shuffling orders around on paper and in my head until the overall shape began to materialize. These potentially final orders had to meet a number of important criteria: maxi-mum variety of gesture and texture within each quartet, as well as across the set viewed as a totality; the broadest spectrum possible, from the purest diatonicism to the most complex chromaticism—and at that, the two obviously different kinds of chromaticism associated with tonal and atonal contexts; finally, the tightest emotional projection couched in the tightest construction manageable. Whatever else may have entered into the writing, the classical ideal constantly stood before me as goal and model.

It becomes necessary to distinguish further the two kinds of chromaticism, associated, on the one hand, with tonality, and, on the other, with atonality. The former is evocative of kinds of harmonic progressions guided by principles of tonal direction intuitively recognized as characteristic of what I think of as "*soft romanticism*," what we hear when we listen to Chopin, Schumann, Brahms, Liszt, Wagner. In individual ways, all give voice to forms of deepest yearning and longing, heart-and-soul sickness impossible of satisfaction in any known earthly form. The only refuge for the artist of "soft romanticism" lies in realizing to the fullest an aesthetic of the beautiful in which the ache of living finds its most perfect expression. "Soft romanticism" longs for what can never be. The latter form of chromaticism, that which derives from and, in turn, is expressive of the atonal palette of pitches freed of known, guided, harmonic principles rooted in tonal progression, makes possible what I call "*hard* romanticism," also a form of romantic outlook but now put through the wringer of the "century of hell," the spastic, horrific twentieth century. That century, now passed into the twenty-first, suffered inordinately and violently from naively held beliefs that "utopia"—in its many vain hopes and variant forms of socially and politically reordered governance, misguided dream projections of eighteenth- and nineteenth-century philosophers and thinkers—was not only possible, but could be realized here on earth, only to end badly. "Hard romanticism" knows this; and because it does, it suffers "out loud," expressing itself in harsh, violent outbursts of anger, anguish, despair—even at times, ecstasies of destructive apocalyptic vision. Both varieties of soft and hard romanticism make their appearance in the *Concord Quartets.*

Quartet no. 4 was completed December 18, 1977; no. 5, March 25, 1978; and no. 6, August 14, 1978. No. 4 is the most concentrated of the three, although its Serenade is loose-jointed and rhythmically elastic, a "rubato" piece. No. 5 is emotionally more open than no. 4, less chromatic while more heavily diatonic/tonal. No. 6 is perhaps the most open of the three, also the most tonal, though not exclusively, and with the widest range of gestures, certainly the longest. At the height of the public craze for Pachelbel's Canon in D, Mark Sokol one day made the offhand, casual suggestion that I consider doing a variation set on its "theme." I took him at his word and produced a movement, the third of no. 6's five, which uses for its theme so-called, the bare outline of the harmony only of the baroque chaconne-canon. This facilitated a chain of evolving variations whose harmonic progressions become more and more chromatic and emotionally charged, in the mode of mid- to late nineteenth-century soft romanticism, only to diminish its intensity slowly and return to the bare scaffolding of the baroque harmonic outline.

As a warm-up for what was to come, the Concord took the new quartets to

Bard College on November 5, 1978. Exactly three weeks later they gave a private reading for some two hundred invited guests at the home of friends, Marvin and Marian Garfinkel—a grand mansion in one of the handsomer suburbs of Philadelphia. This reading, greeted very warmly, was prelude to a set of three concerts the University of Pennsylvania gave to celebrate my sixtieth birthday—still seven months off—on January 15, 18, and 20, 1979, the last of which was devoted to the new *Concord String Quartets*. Two days later they were performed in New York at Tully Hall to a standing ovation from an audience that had visibly and audibly reacted to every gestural and harmonic turn that caught their fancy. The Concord, always at its nerved-up best when they played to a New York audience, gave an electrically charged performance.

I first met Tom Shepard in 1962 when Columbia Records recorded my Second Symphony.[13] Tom was one of the producers. In 1974, he moved to RCA, becoming division vice president of RCA Red Seal. As the time for the New York performances of the *Concord Quartets* approached I invited Tom to join Gene and me at Tully Hall. During the Fourth Quartet, which stirred the audience to its first signs of strong response, I sensed Tom's growing enthusiasm for what he was hearing. After the opening measures of the Fifth Quartet, unabashedly tonal and lighthearted in spirit, began to evoke sounds of delight all around the hall and continued unabated as the quartet went on, Tom leaned over and said in a low, clear whisper, "I'm going to record these."

Later, the heady excitement of the performance over, I had a chance to tell the Concord backstage the news that RCA was going to record the entire set of three quartets. Undeniably, this was a real bonanza for both the Concord and me. In those days it was no ordinary, everyday occurrence for a major record company to take on a new, major work by a living American composer and have it recorded by a still very young but increasingly visible string quartet, bringing the three *Concord Quartets* out in style in a two-record set.[14] What has stayed with me since is the remark by one of the recording engineers whose entire professional life had been spent working with pop singers of jazz and country music: "I can't wait to take the cellophane off the box when these come out!"

When the University of Michigan commissioned me to write a quartet for the Concord quartet and the baritone Leslie Guinn, head of its voice department, immediately I knew this Seventh Quartet would be based on poems by my son, Paul, and be a loving tribute to him. From Paul's "Black Book," in which he collected the poems he had given the most attention, I chose four from among my favorites with the idea of making each one the basis for an extended, separate movement: I. "The beast of night"; II. "Floating in a dream"; III. "Cavalry"; IV. "And when the dream had faded." The role of the string quartet was to establish the feeling context, to supply the atmosphere and texture within which the range of Paul's verbal images would have ample space to come to life through the voice, where his often taut, despairing, dark poetic lines, his lyric outbursts of unbearable fears and longings, his wildly surreal war scene "Cavalry," and his almost Taoist "Floating in a dream" would have the room necessary to reveal their deepest meanings. The form of each movement took its shape directly from the emotional intensities inherent in the nonuniform and stanzaic groupings of the lines of each poem. Which explains—but only in part—why "Floating in a dream" is the closest in design and character to the old lieder, art-song tradition; why the marchlike "Cavalry" leans heavily toward rondo form, with melodic ideas and rhythmic figures returning frequently in refrain fashion; why "The beast of night" and "And when the dream had faded" are treated in arioso style with heavy emphasis on *recitando* and *parlando* to convey the dramatic and narrative aspects both poems contain. To each of the opening and closing movements I appended two telling lines from an unfinished poem with two variants Paul called "Pieces of the Sea":

> And I cast no shadow
> On waves, or sand.

An expanded coda on this chilling expression of nothingness brings the Seventh Quartet to a close.

Compressed imagery was Paul's way. He mastered the difficult art of saying much with very little. Modified forms of refrain mark all the poems I chose. "The beast of night / Dark furred" returns later in the poem compressed into "of the dark furred night." "Floating in a dream," repeated twice, binds the poem together, opening out transcendentally into "Floating / Beyond unreality," which in turn blooms into "Swimming in this life / I am" at the poem's end. In similar fashion Paul begins each of the two major subdivisions of the last movement's text with variant versions, "And when the dream had faded / Into a yellow green cloud" and "And when the dream was red / I was a dragon." A heightened sense of the surreality of human experience and existence, lived or imagined, saturates the chaotic war imagery of "Cavalry."

This last of my string quartets and the last of the five quartets I wrote for the Concord was given its first performance in Ann Arbor, Michigan, on January 27, 1980, by the Concord with Leslie Guinn. It was followed a year later on January 11, 1981, by a performance in New York at the Ninety-second Street Y. Nonesuch recorded it in 1983.[15]

Of the works I wrote for the Concord quartet, the Quintet for Piano and String Quartet had the most unexpected and unorthodox beginning. In 1973 Robert Sherman, well-known for his live radio interviews with musicians on WQXR, invited the Concord quartet, pianist Jerome Lowenthal, and myself to a joint session during which the Concord performed a part of my Third Quartet and Lowenthal played a section of *Carnival Music* for piano solo. We conversed with Sherman about contemporary music and the inevitable associated problems of composition and performance: modernism versus tradition, atonality versus tonality. It was in every way a lively, stimulating give-and-take, the kind of charged discussion that energizes and enlivens one. From seemingly out of nowhere I began hearing "piano quintet music" in my head. In fact, the sudden rush of that sound apparition eventually crystallized into the second movement Fantasia opening piano flourish that later found its way, transformed, into one of the major ideas for the sixth movement, Molto allegro con spirito. As we were leaving the studio, in high spirits, laughing and talking, I announced: "I'm going to write a piano quintet for the five of you." There was an instantaneous outburst—of pleasure, of incredulity and "When did you decide that?"—followed by, "When will it be ready for us to play?" As it turned out, I couldn't get to it until the second half of 1975, writing it between July and December, because I was working literally day and night during the spring and summer of 1974 on my Violin Concerto for Isaac Stern in order to have the piano reduction and orchestration ready for its premiere in April 1975.

By the time the quintet was completed in December 1975, it had grown to seven movements according to an overall emotional scenario that moves from dark to light and back to dark. Troubled, haunted states alternate with serene and exuberant ones; the atonal sections, movements I, IV, and VII, tend toward free, unconventional shapes; the tonal ones, III and V, are highly controlled structures, respectively a large-spanned *brio* fugue interrupted by a tuneful scherzo, and a set of variations on a seven-bar theme, more overtly harmonic than melodic. Movement II is a fantasia, one of the mixed forms that plays back and forth between near-atonality and tonality and incorporates the very idea that came to me during the WQXR show; while VI is a sonata form, though far from strict, with moments of fantasia breaking in, movement IV, lying at the center of the work, is a dark, mournful, tolling piano solo—the spiritual heart of the music.

At the core of existence is always the inescapable dark of the unknown and the unknowable. While writing the Piano Quintet I had in mind not "portraits," but the indefinable sense of the special qualities, human and musical, I associated with

Jerry Lowenthal and the Concord boys: their unending fund of physical energy, high seriousness, capacity for the lyric line, intensity of projection. By one of those lovely quirks or timing of fate—coincidence?—Norman and Jeanne Fischer's first child, Rebecca, was born the morning of the day of the first public performance Jerry and the Concord gave at Hopkins Center, Dartmouth College, February 21, 1976. March 15 marked another performance at New York's Tully Hall. When Nonesuch recorded the quintet in 1981, the Concord chose Alan Marks to be the pianist.[16] Alan had a distinct gift for chamber ensemble playing and brought a winning clarity and depth of feeling to the recording.

My last work for the Concord was the Quintet for Two Violins, Viola, and Two Cellos. It was their tenth anniversary, and they wanted something new to help celebrate their first decade. Being in the last stages of completing *The Confidence Man,* an opera that Gene and I had been working on for three years, the pressure was mounting to work up the piano-vocal score and orchestrate the music I'd written to Gene's libretto based on Herman Melville's novel in time for the rehearsals and performances scheduled for the summer of 1982 by the Santa Fe Opera. Given these pressures, it was inevitable that I would help myself liberally to thematic ideas from the opera in order to compose the quintet as quickly as I could manage.

The first performance of the quintet took place at the Curtis Institute on January 6, 1982, with Bonnie Thron playing the second cello part. As was the custom with string quartets, if they undertook to perform a quintet with two cellos (or, as in the instance of the great Mozart quintets, two violas), it was understood that the invited guest player always did the second cello part—which, in the case of my quintet, was a juicy part, no pushover, just as I'd planned. There were a fair number of performances between 1982 and 1985. The guest cellists invited to perform the quintet with the Concord were—besides Bonnie Thron—Anthony Elliott, Nathaniel (Nick) Rosen, and Sharon Robinson.

While the five movements that make up the quintet in no way follow the course of events the opera unfolds, they do convey some of its most pungent, essential, emotional qualities. As might be expected, there were bound to be major differences between the chamber work and the opera, not least because of the total difference of genres, the one purely instrumental, the other a staged, dramatic vocal work. But in a larger sense both works share the same palette—from tonal to heavily chromatic atonal, from the gentler aspects of the former to the harsher, tougher aspects of the latter.

The first movement, Overtura, has the quick-spirited effervescence of much of act 1. For instance, in the Overtura there are ways of working far more congenial to the medium of a chamber work for five instruments than to a dramatic vocal work—though not entirely out of the question if the action of the opera were to demand it. I am referring specifically to the quintuple counterpoint passage (mm. 94–118 of the score),[17] which would be too complex and involved and, therefore, pointless to analyze here. Nevertheless, things can be said that bear on how I think and feel about traditional contrapuntal devices and their continuing place in contemporary (and future) music. For one, the principle of registral invertibility, which lies at the root of double, triple, and quintuple counterpoint, is neither old nor new. It is an age-old way of thinking music within a mental space that uses the identical motivic ideas but in constantly changing vertical orders. A simple example would be $\frac{1}{2}$ inverted to $\frac{1}{1}$, or $\frac{2}{3}$ inverted to $\frac{3}{1}$ or $\frac{2}{3}$.

As parts are added, it grows more complex and simultaneously more hazardous, chiefly because, if the context is tonal, one must ensure that inversion of the five parts in whatever arrangement of vertical order they appear always sounds right to the ear. It cannot be merely mechanical.

The reason is clear: some vertical orders simply do not work *as music* because they destroy harmonic balance, especially in a clearly tonal context. In an important sense, it becomes axiomatic that quintuple counterpoint and an atonal context are largely incompatible harmonically, because the conditions for a harmonic match hardly exist in an atonal world where no governing laws of harmony determine a musically satisfying outcome of positioning identical parts in ever-changing vertical arrangements. The great pleasure, of course, is to be able to accomplish the desired contrapuntal design through a musical projection that justifies its use. The great single marvel of the classical use of quintuple counterpoint remains the passage in the finale of Mozart's Symphony no. 41 ("Jupiter"), measures 380–402. Every one of the five principal motifs in the last movement is gathered up and sounded in the same mental–aural space in ever-changing registral placements. The degree to whether I succeeded or not in my own effort to achieve a prime use of this device is less important to comment on than the fact that I was inspired by Mozart's fantastic accomplishment to try to match it. That desire, that hunger, lies at the heart of the whole artistic enterprise.

Aria, the second movement of the Cello Quintet, draws on the heartbreak music of China Aster, the simple but tragic figure of *The Confidence Man*—too innocent, trusting, and naive for his own good—who falls prey to impossible dreams and false hopes and expectations. Some critics of Melville's work have suggested that the story of China Aster, which is only one of many odd tales woven into his unorthodox, picaresque novel, is symbolically his own. Whether right or not, it does appear that both the author and his starry-eyed character are victims of external forces ranged against them and, simultaneously, of their inherent inability to deal with the devious twists and turns of personal fate. Cellos 1 and 2 carry much of the melodic burden of this movement.

The movement that follows the crunching chromaticism of the tonal Aria—much closer to the hard romanticism I described earlier than to its softer, nineteenth-century variety—is a headlong Scherzo that takes ideas from various scenes in the opera, including the more comic ones and those devoted to the appearance of "the Angel of Bright Future," Melville's dream embodiment of China's impossible-to-realize hopes for rising above grinding poverty and failure to ultimate success and riches, a not-unreal American form of age-old fairy tales. "Bright Future" is a sexual, sinuous temptress who appears to China in his dreams, offering him "Gold, Gold, Gold" as she dances seductively around him, unstringing him. This music for "the Angel of Bright Future" is the centerpiece of the Scherzo (from mm. 150–207 inclusive).

The fourth movement, a kind of "intermezzo" in both the opera and the quintet, I call Notturno. It is an aria China sings just before circumstances close in on him, a song of the mystery and beauty of the world, a direct instrumental transcription that absorbs China's vocal line into the quintet.

The last movement, Burletta, brings into juxtaposition three different gestures: the first rapidly shifting, atonal figures; the second a refrainlike, brief, tonal stasis; and the third a rapid-fire, harmonically chromatic passage, each repetition of which is like another twirl of the wheel of a kaleidoscope.

From the beginning of this chapter it was inevitable that I would have to write about the sad end of the Concord String Quartet. Perhaps to most onlookers what appeared to be the Concord's sudden and unexpected demise came as a shock for which there was no preparation. Nor could there have been. On the surface, the Concord had made what appeared to be a remarkably secure place for itself in the musical life of America in a relatively short time. It was actively engaged in concertizing the length and breadth of the States, often to great acclaim, performing the standard repertoire as well as twentieth-century composers. It had established itself as the quartet-in-residence at the Hopkins Center at Dartmouth College. But below the surface of this appearance of rock-solid stability and success were deep fissures and fault lines beginning to show themselves—but only to those closest to the quartet, whether family, personal friends, or perhaps a few professional colleagues, or, as in my case, virtually all three plus the occasional role of spiritual and musical father-confessor. The Concord boys were part of Gene's and my extended family, as we were of theirs. We had shared a decade and a half of musical adventures together—rehearsals, performances, aftermaths, often enough a kind of mutual high-wire act. When the situation required, they had practiced individually for hours, each in his own space somewhere in our house, together as an ensemble gathered in our living room, ready for whatever risks might be involved musically, slept and taken meals with us in our "hotel" on Aronimink Drive. I had had long and serious conversations with Mark Sokol, sometimes into the late-night hours. So when the disbanding, the breakup of the quartet actually happened, it came as a great shock and trauma for all of us, however much we may have been aware of impending problems. The quartet went through great soul-disturbing turmoil, trying to save the situation, but to no avail: it had to play itself out to its inevitable conclusion. Finally the end came. The quartet had agreed among themselves to call it quits.

Institutions and individuals have their life span. It is nature's and culture's way. In rare instances only does a trace remain long after they are gone. The Concord String Quartet—its vibrant, youthful, passionate dedication to music and music making—lives on in memory, and that memory will be sustained by the recordings that are its legacy.

To answer Harold Schonberg's question quoted as the epigraph to this chapter, I need only say, like all things human, we never possess or have anything permanently, but to have lived my middle years so intensely and vividly with such fresh, vital spirits as the Concord is unforgettably etched into my soul. The greater loss of their breakup was to America's musical life. String quartets come and go—whatever else happens in this great throbbing carnival of life that is America—but there will never again be another Concord String Quartet.

CHAPTER 7

"It's Only a Small, Little, Wooden Box"
Violin Concerto and Isaac Stern

"So . . . you're the man who's been keeping us up nights!" I had rung the bell to Isaac Stern's apartment across from Central Park. His wife, Vera, opened the door. When I told her who I was, she looked at me appraisingly and, with that mildly accusatory statement, invited me in . . . Isaac was expecting me.

Not since we'd first met at dinner with William Steinberg, conductor of the Pittsburgh Symphony, had Stern and I gotten together to discuss the Violin Concerto. The work was taking shape, and I wanted his reaction to the sketches piling up. Before that dinner I'd never met either Stern or Steinberg and had a certain awe of each of these formidable musicians. They were performers of solid accomplishment, masters in their respective fields, and I was testing my mettle in a genre with a long and glorious past reaching back to the time of the concerted solo violin and orchestra works by Vivaldi and J. S. Bach, which stood at the head of a repertoire that included, besides the five concertos of Mozart, the almost impossible marvels of Beethoven, Brahms, and Bartók.

"Why me?" I had asked, looking from one to the other. Coming out of the blue, this blunt question seemed to catch them off guard. Perhaps it was too direct, too personal a note to inject suddenly into a conversation between people who had only just met. If anything, the question had much less to do with *why* I was chosen to write a concerto for Stern than it did with a deep undercurrent of apprehensiveness: Could I bring it off? Could I make something that would stand, that I would still believe in years down the road? The few violin concertos I knew by American composers were not particularly impressive. Even such monoliths as Stravinsky and Schoenberg had tried their hands at the genre. Stravinsky's neoclassical concerto of 1931[1] is a dry affair where the solo violin is often lost in the intricate polyphonic weave of not especially distinguished lines. And Schoenberg's 1936 twelve-tone, full-scale effort[2]—major in size and carrying heavy emotional freight—often loses its way in the thickets and briar patches of spastic projections of thin-wired wind and string accompanimental patterns whose constant harmonic hiccuping robs the solo part of solid sustenance and the support of orchestral underpinning. If anything saves the Schoenberg concerto from self-annihilation, it is the power and individuality of its melodic ideas and daemonic use of the solo violin—particularly in the cadenzas.

Isaac and I had a good first working session. And when at one point he said, "I feel emboldened," his round face aglow, wreathed in a warm smile, his voice full of conviction, I knew I was on the right track. We had just played through a passage in the fourth movement Intermezzo (in the score,[3] mm. 250 to 271), a variant form for solo violin and orchestra of a *tutti* orchestral outburst that first occurs in the opening movement Introduction (from the m. 52 upbeat to mm. 53–59). That day in Isaac's studio was crucial; it not only gave him a clear and growing sense of the nature and size of the work-to-be, it also helped erase any lingering apprehension I may have felt that I could produce a *true* concerto, a performance vehicle of emotional size and fervor fit for the medium of solo violin and large orchestra and worthy of a violinist of Stern's stature.

Isaac's "I feel emboldened" encouraged me greatly. It confirmed my own sense of being right. I remember being obsessed with finishing the orchestration early enough to allow sufficient time for the copying of parts and the preparation of the piano reduction, which I put in the hands of Steve Hartke, a gifted student of mine at Penn—the piano reduction being an essential tool for Isaac's preparation. By Christmas 1974 the orchestration was complete and I was exhausted, unable to do anything but rest and sleep. It took the entire holiday period past the New Year to recover sufficiently and to gradually resume anything resembling normal functioning.

After the New Year a phone call came from William Steinberg, who had been studying the score in preparation for the first performances, scheduled for April 1975 in Pittsburgh. What concerned him chiefly was his fear that the weight of the large orchestra for which I'd written would cover and drown out the violin. "After all," he said, "it's only a small, little, wooden box." Never before had I heard it put quite that way: this most singing, stringed voice, aside from the human voice itself, one of music's most passionate vehicles of expression, may be only a small, little, wooden box, but it is a beautifully made small, little, wooden box, and, in the right hands, makes magic.

Steinberg's trepidations were fed by the presence in the score of three of each woodwind—flutes, clarinets, oboes, bassoons—plus the full complement of horns, trumpets, trombones, and tuba—not to mention two harps, which provide Intermezzo (B) with its principal, characteristic color, plus percussion and string orchestra. I assured him I was fully aware of the problem and felt we could make whatever adjustments might be necessary in rehearsal should problematic spots arise . . . but I didn't think there would be any . . . There was really no cause for alarm . . . certainly not at this early stage . . . This didn't seem to mollify Steinberg, but he agreed we should wait until we were in actual rehearsal.

There are two unspoken traditions—"practices" might be a better word—in the performance of concerted works for soloists and orchestra. Granting that the violin has less sheer physical power of projection than the viola, the viola less than the still larger cello, there is also the question of whether we are dealing with the classical, the romantic, or the twentieth-century—and now the twenty-first-century—repertoires, in which, as the historically later musics show, greater and greater expressive demands are placed on both soloists and orchestras. One of the chief signs of those developments became audible in the increase of pairs of winds, horns, and trumpets to more winds, added brass, and percussion.

The first of these two practices or traditions is best exemplified in the kinds of concerns Steinberg expressed, in which instance the conductor balances the sound of the orchestra so as *never* to allow the sound of the soloist to be obscured. In such a view the soloist is the supreme voice, and the orchestra is obedient, humble, and always accompanying as a respectful servant. This is not necessarily always the case with romantic-era violin concerti in Mendelssohn, Brahms, Tchaikovsky, and even Sibelius. Quite often the soloist is performing an *accompagnando* role, playing figures, phrases, obbligati that have their importance in the overall configuration but are not primary in the compositional design. In such cases a thoroughly musical conductor will make sure that whatever instrument (or instruments) is responsible for carrying the principal melodic line is clearly heard, and the soloist will be expected to step gracefully into the middleground (or background) and modestly await the cue for returning to the musical center of things. Here we are on the threshold of the second of the two ways of viewing this delicately balanced situation, which, as I've heard often enough in concerti by Prokofiev, Bartók, Berg, Schoenberg, and younger-generation composers, pits the solo violin against the orchestra so that what the orchestra is doing musically is of such importance *it must not be held down—eviscerated—under any circumstances* simply to accommodate the soloist. From such levels of intense engagement there is one further stage to "the battle scenario," where the two—soloist and orchestra—contend *against* each other for dominance, both pushed to supreme levels of intensity and power of projection. In Gubaidulina's *Offertorium* violin concerto, as in Schnittke's Viola Concerto and Cello Concerto no. 1, one can hear such "battle scenarios" being enacted at peak levels where emotional expression borders on chaos.

In the main there was no cause for Steinberg's initial cautionary remarks: his "small, little, wooden box" of a violin was neither drowned out nor lost in the general, musical melee. I knew Isaac was unhappy with the Tempo II: Allegro assai passage (mm. 38–65) in Intermezzo (A) where soloist and orchestra are asked to play at their maximum simultaneously. This was even more true in the Intermezzo (B) Alla marcia (particularly mm. 177–92), where the horns carry the principal melodic idea over a walking bass line punched out *pesante,* and the solo violin, against this orchestral complex, has strident, nonmelodic passages arpeggiating rapidly from lower to higher registers. These degrees of solo/orchestral balance surely approach a symbolic equivalent of the entire possible range of the relationship of individual to society, reflected in forms of political absolutism all the way over to their breakdown in forms of social/political chaos and anarchy to, hopefully, more frequent appearances of democratic give and take somewhere between the two extremes.

Unhappily, I never did have the chance to work with Steinberg. Before rehearsals had even begun he was taken seriously ill and died later in 1978. Donald Johanos, the associate conductor of the Pittsburgh, a thoroughly professional and capable conductor, took over. He handled all the preliminary rehearsals and the premiere performances, which took place April 4, 5, and 6, 1975, in Heinz Hall, Pittsburgh, followed by a warmup for New York at the University of Connecticut at Storrs, April 14, and capped by the Carnegie Hall performance on April 15.

Before discussing further the events and personalities that filled the years between 1975 and October 1978 with some forty-seven performances by Isaac Stern of the Violin Concerto, I must double back and take up the composition of the work itself, as well as its revision, which I made in a Chicago hotel room between the time of Sir Georg Solti's April 10–12 performances with the Chicago Symphony and the New York premiere at Carnegie Hall with Johanos and the Pittsburgh, April 15.

There are two principal matters to describe: first, the main determinants that led me to a new way of combining the tonal and atonal languages in which the concerto was written; and second, why I chose a five-movement design divided into two parts:

Part I:
  I. Introduction (pause)
  II. Intermezzo (A) (segue)
  III. Fantasia (pause)

Part II:
  IV. Intermezzo (B) (pause)
  V. Epilogue

What I call *ars combinatoria* opens up an incredibly expanded range of dialects, kaleidoscopic in nature. Taken all together, it makes possible the widest musical language based on the half and whole tone, from which one may literally join in combination precise musical dialects as the chosen basis for either an individual work or a series of works. As a result, the composer is no longer bound by the strictures of stylistic consistency for its own sake. This may not have been exactly what Ralph Waldo Emerson had in mind when he wrote "a foolish consistency is the hobgoblin of little minds,"[4] but the fanatic modernist insistence on "stylistic consistency" that characterized the last quarter of the twentieth century surely came too close for comfort not to be entirely free of calling up Emerson's deprecating aphorism.

If one were to identify the language of the concerto, it would have to be called a refracted form of tonality filtered through the more complex dissonant prism of the atonal. Rather than attempt a full-scale analysis of its harmonic methodology—wholly inappropriate here—a few signposts should suffice to show my meaning when I refer to its tonal cast being refracted and filtered through the dissonant prism of the atonal. A good deal of the harmonic fabric underlying the melodic thought of the concerto is guided by circular (or symmetrical) harmonic sets, grounded in the developing nondominant harmonic motions discoverable in the music of classical and romantic composers, certainly Beethoven and Schubert, Chopin, Brahms, Liszt, and Wagner.

In their ears there developed harmonic devices that rotate, slowly or rapidly as the case may be, through third-related motions both major and minor and serve as large-scale nodal points defining phrase as well as section structures. For example, in the Fantasia, the center movement of the concerto and conclusion of Part I, there are local, small-scale symmetrical motions through minor-third root motions, and large-scale symmetrical motions through major-third root motions. In the latter, mixed B♭ minor/major, D minor/major, F♯ minor/major motions define significant circular nodal points. These minor/major mixtures derive primarily from a widely used motivic cell built into the harmonic fabric of twentieth-century music; but interestingly, the root of these twentieth-century mixtures can readily be found in the obvious pleasure Beethoven took in working *successive* mixtures of major- and minor-third motions. Inevitably his successors took up the device, carrying it well into the late nineteenth century. This eventually led to *simultaneity* of the major/minor mixture in a vertical array that became a "signature" chord of early atonal and twelve-tone music. In Dallapiccola's opera *Il prigionero* we find, for example, a prominent melodic use of the mixture in the "Fratello" motive F#–F♮–D. Verticalized, its three pitches reading from the top down, F♮–D–F#, become the *signature* chord characteristically employed by numerous composers. This was certainly a favorite of Webern's and readily identified in Ives's First Piano Sonata. My own *Dialogues* (1957) for clarinet and piano treats this signature chord as coin of the twelve-tone realm.

In the Fantasia of the concerto, the three-note melodic figure heard in the orchestra gathers itself into the sustained signature harmony over which the solo violin goes its own improvisatory, ruminating way each time the chromatic motive initiates a new phrase. As the phrases slowly accumulate, the symmetrical, large-scale structure based on the motion from B♭ to D to F#, all in mixed minor/major thirds, reveals itself.

Normally, the practice, even into the twentieth century, of the design of concerti most often resulted in three movements, fast–slow–fast, with cadenzas for the solo instrument placed close to the end of the opening and closing movements. I wanted to avoid that particular customary straitjacket. Rather than write a long, weighty first movement, I decided to split the old idea in two, thus arriving at the opening and closing of the concerto in the form of an Introduction and an Epilogue, both relatively short—and not necessarily "fast." While they share a number of ideas in common, neither has a cadenza. It is in the two inside Intermezzos, (*A*) alternating moderate and fast tempos, and (*B*) moving at an andante, that I placed a single cadenza in the first Intermezzo (mm. 151–205) and a double cadenza in the second Intermezzo, each coming off a brief orchestral interpolation. That entire double cadenza covers measures 76–136, with orchestral interpolations at measures 75–81 and 110–14. The center movement, Fantasia, needs no cadenza, inasmuch as it is already a free, rubato-style music.

Revising an already completed work immediately after its first performances is hardly idle or arbitrary. Deep dissatisfaction with the first form of the work starts eating away and demands that you discover the cause of the discontent and set it to rights. This was particularly urgent in the case of the concerto, because immediately following the trio of Pittsburgh performances there was another trio scheduled for Chicago with Sir Georg Solti conducting, and almost directly after those the Carnegie Hall performance. Early on, Isaac had astonished me with his remark that in his experience, he found my concerto the most demanding he had ever encountered, for both technical and musical reasons—the sole exception being Tchaikovsky's Violin Concerto. He intimated that, for one, the sheer length of the work and, for another, the fact that the soloist was called on to play an unusually large and inordinately intense role were also responsible factors. Something in Isaac's words struck home.

To tighten the original "Pittsburgh version" of the concerto, I reverted to my old practice of always going back to the beginning of the work, the movement, or the section, singing it through in my head, making sure of its continuity, and, in the process, taking note of those "soft spots" that required change. In continually returning to an important nodal point in the structure, what I was after was to ensure the flow of the music, the convincing movement from one idea to another, each gesture to the next. This was true even where there were purposeful disconnects rather than continuous, smooth flow. Regardless of which—interrupted or uninterrupted—I was trying to achieve a sense of seamlessness, of making the music move forward with a sense of naturalness. In this process of reliving the concerto from its opening gestures to its closing measures and singing it through in my head as many times as necessary to identify where it had gone lax, where there should have been muscle, I carried out the revision rapidly and sewed everything back together so that there were no gaping wounds or visible scars. The revised version dispensed with a rather big chunk—leaving the new version tighter, slimmer, trimmer. Its "premiere" took place in Carnegie Hall.

When the Pittsburgh rehearsals began, there was a feeling in the air that some great indefinable was at stake, a palpable but unspoken sense of being part of a major event about to unfold. That state of mind, I'm convinced, brought out and sustained the kind of cooperation and goodwill that prevailed throughout that entire time. And if I review in my mind the people involved and what was at stake for each, the focus sharpens measurably. For Isaac, this was a new, as-yet-unheard work by an American composer to which he had fully committed himself long in advance and expended great amounts of time and energy in preparation for presenting it, not only in Pittsburgh but in a countrywide tour of major cities well into the next season and beyond. For myself, this was my first concerto, whose fate lay entirely in how Isaac carried it off, in the art and conviction he brought to it. For Donald Johanos, suddenly it was his responsibility to take the orchestra in hand, mold it into the supportive instrument it had to be to sustain Isaac in his role, and put into motion whatever suggestions and changes resulted from our ad hoc conferences as we worked. For Sy Rosen, the stalwart manager of the Pittsburgh, he sensed something big in the air as much as anyone and kept a calm, steadying hand on the situation so that nothing interfered with bringing the concerto to readiness. And for the players of the Pittsburgh—hardworking, earnest, talented men and women who had never played any of my music before—they bore the brunt of it, because they were the physically sounding embodiment and substance of my work as they supported and helped carry Isaac to his and their mutual ultimate goal, all the while being responsive to their conductor, Isaac, and myself.

We knew we were under the gun, and it was a miracle that all went as smoothly as it did. As a result we quickly developed an easy camaraderie and kept our cool. There were no prima donnas and no temper tantrums. We conferred as often as necessary, during, before, and after rehearsals. In this way the concerto took shape. Isaac grew more and more confident, and clearly the orchestra was enjoying playing my music—in itself a source of great satisfaction to me. Though still tense, I began feeling less trepidatious about the outcome.

It's not clear when, but sometime close to the end of rehearsals, sitting in Heinz Hall with Johanos's young assistant conductor, score in hand, listening intently, I became aware of Sy Rosen pacing slowly back and forth behind us—in the break between seating sections—muttering to himself, "It's a hit . . . it's a hit . . ."

Sy's stage-whispered pronouncement-prophecy, for all I know, had its effect. Each of the three performances was greeted with tumultuous applause. The premiere itself brought the audience to its feet. Its infectious enthusiasm led Isaac, who had played brilliantly, back onstage time after time, where I joined him, sharing the wildly released response of the audience and our colleagues in the orchestra.

The Chicago performances followed only a few days later with Sir Georg Solti, one of the few truly great conductors of that time in America and Europe, and his formidable orchestra. Of all the conductors who did the concerto with Isaac, Solti was the only one who wanted a piano rehearsal. Which would have been fine if Solti had not insisted on conducting us: it became immediately apparent that he'd not yet had the chance to familiarize himself thoroughly with the speech and character of the music—which is essentially *parlando,* that is, in a speaking mode or style, led by the soloist, not the conductor. Trying though it was, we managed to convey to Solti the overall freedom with which the concerto had to be projected in order to allow the soloist the temporal and dynamic space necessary to unhampered articulation. With orchestra rehearsals to solidify this, the result rivaled what had taken place in Pittsburgh.

The New York premiere of the revised version on April 15 was a true homecoming for Isaac. Of the early performances of the concerto, that single appearance in New York was a genuine triumph, replete with an incredible standing ovation from a tumultuously noisy hall packed to the rafters. After the concert a seemingly endless line of well-wishers, beginning onstage, wound its way backstage almost to the door leading out to West Fifty-sixth Street. I found myself engulfed by the overwhelming warmth of hundreds of people.

The next port of call for the Violin Concerto was San Francisco, May 7–10, 1975. After the first San Francisco performance of the concerto, Isaac introduced me to Johnny Green and John Williams, Hollywood composers of considerable reputation whom he had invited to hear him do my concerto. Johnny Green had a marvelous lyric gift that made songs such as "Body and Soul," "Out of Nowhere," and "I Cover the Waterfront," all from the early 1930s, unique in American popular music. I was especially happy to meet him because I knew and loved his songs and took great pleasure in telling him so. He beamed when I told him that his "Body and Soul" was not only one of my all-time favorites but also one of the great treasures of American popular music, and without question the equal of any Schubert song one might mention.

Alec Wilder, author of the remarkable 1972 study *American Popular Song*,[5] considers Johnny Green one of "the Great Craftsmen," along with Hoagy Carmichael, Duke Ellington, Harry Warren—all of whom wrote unique songs that still stand among the prized standards of the popular-song repertoire that came out of the flowering in American popular culture between 1900 and 1950. These songs remain as fresh and singable as they were sixty and seventy years ago. They possess that one precious quality that Tolstoy in his strange and often maddening essay "What is Art?"[6] claimed as the *sine qua non* of musical art: melodic infectiousness. By infectiousness Tolstoy meant what one loves and wants for oneself, that which lives in the ear, the heart and the soul. With that as a dependable rule of thumb to judge by, the parallel output of works by the numerous American "classical" composers contemporaneous with the great American songwriters actively producing in the same fifty-year period hardly makes an impressive comparative showing. Except perhaps for Samuel Barber and Aaron Copland, whose works remain in frequent performance, the great majority of American composers, whether affiliated with university teaching or not, seem to have faded from public consciousness.

Speaking of infectiousness, Johnny Green and I hit it off right away. He liked the Violin Concerto, remarking generously on its constantly evolving melodic line. But nary a word from John Williams from the moment Isaac introduced us, either out of deep reserve, shyness, or simply disinterest. After the well-wishers were gone, Green, Williams, and I left the hall with Isaac and drove to a Chinese restaurant for a dinner he hosted. On the way, Isaac, who had grown up in San Francisco, couldn't help pointing out favorite spots in a city he clearly loved. At the restaurant we were joined by Karl Haas,[7] whom I knew only by reputation as a radio personality. He talked about music and composers to unseen audiences who enjoyed being enlightened by such media savants. For my part, I was happy to talk to Johnny Green and learn about his early years in an America that wasn't very different from the one I entered more than a decade later in 1918. That was the best part of the evening for me, listening to Johnny's endless stories. No conversation took place between Williams and me. I even wonder if he was at all interested in what Johnny Green had to say. Truth is, had I more regard for the genre of movie music and been impressed by something Williams had written, my own attitude might have been entirely different. But after a lifetime of seeing films, American and foreign, only two film-score composers have consistently "spoken" to me: Nino Rota, whose comedic jazz satires and wonderful marching clown music give an energy and color to Fellini's films far out of the ordinary, and Bernard Herrmann, whose scores for Alfred Hitchcock keep the right kind of screwed-up tension and musical environment for films like *Vertigo,* with its inexorable, shocking twists and turns.

Before returning home after the San Francisco performances, I flew to Iowa City to spend some days at the University of Iowa, where I'd been invited to talk about my music with the students. In American universities of that period, the greater majority of the general run of graduate composition students showed few or no observable skills, nor enough of a rudimentary knowledge of harmony and counterpoint to satisfy the lowest degree of expectation of craftsmanship. Many of the people who taught seemed themselves without passion for the art of music, its making, and the intellectual grit to convey their insistence on maintaining high critical standards of judgment and taste. Composing remains still, despite the temper of things, a daunting and demanding art. In America—especially since the advent of serialism, Schenkerian analysis, metatheories, electronics, and the computer—this once-noble art has suffered from pseudointellectualism, scientism, and an openly declared devotion to noise, sensation, and innovation.

After I had played one of the San Francisco tapes for a large gathering of faculty and students, one of the younger members of the faculty asked a question I have been pondering ever since, because it has come to symbolize the great divide between mid-twentieth-century contemporary music, its premises and theses, and the past itself. "Why is the music so hot?" he wanted to know. On the surface, this seemed a simple enough question. I understood the reason for his question when I recalled some pieces he had shown me the previous day with titles stressing "coolness"—a code word among the young denoting an overly sophisticated attitude, strongly tinged with solipsism and tending more toward detached or distanced uninvolvement with life, at the same time suggesting low physical temperature. Translated, his question was also asking why was I so passionately involved with life and music, why did it have to be so intense? I forget how I responded, but in the ensuing years I have reached what I consider some tenable conclusions that suggest the dimensions of an answer, if not *the* answer to a query that goes to the root of where art comes from in the life of mankind.

In life as in art, emotional involvement begets intensity, intensity begets energy, energy begets heat. In every instance where either is concerned, actions reaching beyond self must be fully engaged to bring about the desired transformation of other selves or, in the case of art, of recalcitrant matter such as sounds, paints, words, wood, stone, marble, clay, metal, plastic.

A prime example of this is easily Richard Wagner, who is reputed to have excused himself from receiving a group of visitors once by saying, "Gentlemen, I am in heat." Another appears in Mary McCarthy's 1946 review of *The Iceman Cometh*. She says, "It appears to have been written at some extreme temperature of the mind."[8] And finally, according to Elizabeth Hardwick, Melville was the "madly driven man, forever at his desk. . . . It is very hard to live with one so desperately stretched, pummeled, weary, frazzled and fractious, but more dreadful to live *in* such a state than to live *with* it."[9]

"Forever at his desk"—that describes every great painter, sculptor, poet, composer, novelist forever at shaping the world to reflect a "madly driven vision." Van Gogh, Cézanne, Picasso; Michelangelo, Rodin; Wordsworth, Shelley, Yeats; Bach, Beethoven; Dickens, Balzac, Dostoyevsky. Obsession doesn't determine the aesthetic of style any more than style determines degree in intensity. But whatever the style, for an absolute certainty it can't be made to reveal its essence and dimensions except through the great energy and inherent heat that drives obsessed vision. Even Stravinsky's early works—*Firebird, Petrouchka,* and *Le sacre*—are all possessed of intensity and energy, therefore, heat—despite his inexplicable belief that music was not an "expressive" art. Webern's highly centripetal, intellectual twelve-tone art is the very paragon of precision in musical thinking; it is paradoxically passionately and intensely made. All the more reason to cherish music as one of the high-intensity forms of energy and heat that, as Berlioz writes in his *Evenings with the Orchestra*, "concentrates . . . all its powers on the sense of hearing . . . on the nervous system which it excites, the circulation of the blood which it accelerates, the brain which it sets on fire."[10]

In surveying the performances of the Violin Concerto—in December 1975, the spring and fall of 1976, then fanning out to include European performances (in

Paris and London) in March 1977, and ending by bracketing 1978 with the Columbia recording with the Pittsburgh in January[11] and the Philadelphia performances in October—it is astonishing that, including the time of writing the work in 1974, they filled the better part of five years. My astonishment only increases with the realization of the devotion, care, and constant effort Isaac lavished upon the work during those years. How much more vivid when seen at this distance in time is the whole picture. In truth, the revision aside, the concerto had only to be written once, whereas Isaac had to rehearse and perform the music many times over. The inevitable and constant traveling, the many hotels to settle into for, at most, only a few days and then move on, the many orchestras and different conductors to adjust and relate to in order to prepare for two—more often three—successive performances, rarely only one—Isaac took it all in stride. In fact, after "touring" with him for short periods, it was clear that he was in his element, enjoying it thoroughly. This was his métier; and his ever-cheerful, upbeat, equable nature and manner, salted and peppered with his own brand of wit and humor, prevailed no matter where he went. He was comfortable and easy with himself and the world he moved in—and that world responded to him in full measure.

We couldn't have been more different from each other, Isaac and I. At first, I felt great excitement living through and experiencing the Pittsburgh, New York, Chicago, and San Francisco performances and rounding off 1975 with those in New Orleans, St. Louis, and Cincinnati, but it became increasingly clear with each new change of scene, hotel, orchestra, and conductor I was not cut out for the quick shifts and rigors of the performer's life. It wasn't long before it began to pall, and I longed to escape to the quiet and relative calm of my own life and work where I could think without the immediate noise of the world riding in on me, where I would inevitably suffer the uncertainty of what I was trying to bring to clarity, where I could probe the contradictions of existence itself and brood over hatching them in the shape and form of musical thoughts. In that period, besides the Violin Concerto, I was writing the mezzo-soprano monodrama *Phaedra*, the Fourth Symphony, the *Concord String Quartets*, the *Transcendental Variations* for string orchestra, the *Partita-Variations* for piano solo, and the alto cycle *Songs of Inanna and Dumuzi*.

Even while I was living on the skin of things traveling with Isaac and often feeling enough like a misfit to want to escape, I couldn't help but marvel at how he blossomed in those very same circumstances that wearied me. From time to time I sensed that he was aware of this, but neither of us ever spoke of it. He must have recognized that our marked personal differences stemmed, in part at least, from the difference between being a composer and being a performer and how that difference drives each in diametrically opposite ways. What astonishes me is that I was totally unaware of the remarkable nature of the entire picture as it unfolded in time; and, only now, after so many years, am I able to see how unusual, indeed how unique in my own life and times was the unmistakable fact of Isaac Stern's firm belief in my concerto and the lengths to which he had gone to champion it.

One of my clearest memories is walking into Isaac's hotel suite in Detroit and finding him watching a football game on TV—with the sound turned off—while he practiced passages from the concerto. In a million years I would never have guessed he was such an avid sports fan, nor was he in the least aware of the incongruous picture he made. Here was America's premier virtuoso violinist—*fiddler* he often called himself when he would telephone and begin by saying, "Hello, Composer, this is Fiddler"—behaving like any ordinary run-of-the-mill American "Joe." In disbelieving shock and wonderment at the contradictory ways of man, I stood there hearing scraps and bits of my music being played to the visual accompaniment of a random ballet of galumphing burly figures filling the silent TV screen in senseless, pointless patterns. There was more to Isaac and his boundless worldly interests than the confines of the concert hall and making music would have us believe.

I recall the time I invited him to visit us in Newtown Square. He arrived in a chartered private plane at the small-craft landing field of the Philadelphia International Airport, where I met him and then drove to our "hotel" in what we used to call "the Tulgy Wood." On the way he kept commenting on the beautifully groomed countryside, which an English friend once likened to the area around Sussex, England. After an animated but relaxed visit—replete with stories and talk about ourselves and families, mostly—I drove him back to the airport. His pilot was waiting, the plane ready to take off, and I wished him a fond adieu and safe trip. As the small plane rose into the air, I stood there wondering about this man who combined such musical gifts with the largesse of a generous nature and the worldliness and consummate ease with which he carried it all off.

At the beginning of Chapter 5, which deals with my relationship with Eugene Ormandy, I indicated I was saving for a later chapter the melodramatic scene backstage in the conductor's room following the 1978 Philadelphia performances of the Violin Concerto, which brought to an explosive climax the fracas that first surfaced in 1969. The time has come to tell that story—and to tell it in calm reflection.

The fact that Isaac was a man possessed of considerable tact and discretion explains why—even though he was ignorant of what had brought about the rift between Ormandy and me—he evidently was proceeding quietly behind the scenes trying to persuade Ormandy to program the concerto. Finally, after a number of years, he succeeded. I was enormously pleased at the good news, but not without a gnawing sense of apprehension. I soon came to recognize that even if it should, unfortunately, turn out not to be possible to repair the breach between us, Ormandy's conscientiousness, his seriousness as a musician and conductor, would ultimately win out over any bad feelings he might still harbor toward me. Besides, he and Isaac were not only old and good friends, they were also close colleagues and had had their own battles. Still energetic and resilient despite his advancing years—he was then almost seventy-nine—Ormandy allowed himself to be guided by Isaac's experience with the work, his intimate knowledge of its every detail. Once again, he proved to be the perfect concerto partner, giving Isaac plenty of headroom, letting him lead, supporting him at every turn with precisely the right balance of orchestral sound, and, when it was called for, coming forward with full presence in orchestral *tuttis*. No wonder the performances went as well as they did.

It was that—and the heady audience responses to each performance—which helped thaw my reserve and lingering sense of apprehensiveness to the point where I wanted to express freely and openly my feelings of renewed warmth and admiration for Ormandy for his share in the réclame that greeted the concerto and, if at all possible, to heal the rupture between us. Suffused with such feelings, after the last performance I went backstage to Ormandy's room, where I found Isaac, his wife, Vera, and Ormandy's wife, Gretel, already there. After greeting everyone, telling Isaac he'd done the concerto proud and had given one of his very best, most sterling performances, I turned directly to Ormandy and began to speak to him of my desire for a rapprochement, my hope that we could put the past behind us. It was clear from his unmistakable reserve and distance that his guard was up, the past still rankling him. It was not going to be easy to bridge the gap, now almost ten years old, but I genuinely wanted to assuage his wounded sensibilities, not with flattery and empty praise but by showing renewed warmth and affection for him, feelings inseparable from my admiration for his unique musicianship and especially for how he had brought my music to life.

I began to speak in an unbroken stream of words riding on the flush of good feeling, but quick as lightning, when I called him by his first name, "Gene," that single syllable, that unguarded familiarity on my part brought on a sudden and violent change in the man . . . he flew into a paroxysm of rage . . . his face purpled with overpowering anger . . . he began to thrash about, his movements abrupt and uncontrollable . . . words, staccato phrases broke from him . . . "how dare you call me by my first name . . . you're not my friend . . . "only my friends can call me Gene" . . . his pitch rose . . . he began to rave . . . "you told all your friends to call me, to write me letters . . . letters . . . asking why I didn't play your concerto . . . they never left me alone . . . you attacked me . . . in public . . . in the newspaper . . . unforgivable . . . who are you to attack me before the whole world?" I was dumbfounded . . . rooted to one spot . . . stock-still . . . not more than an arm's length from his erratic, wild movements directly in front of me . . . now this way, now that. Suddenly he seemed struck by remorse. "But I love your concerto . . . it's beautiful . . . I love it." And just as suddenly, he erupted again, raging at me . . . at my brazen assault on his opinions, his good name, his feelings, his very person . . . by now I was frozen in place . . . unable to say anything . . . nothing I could have said would have placated him, nothing would have mollified him . . . again he softened and said how much he loved the concerto . . . again he returned to his raging tirade . . . I was only dimly aware that Isaac and Vera and Gretel Ormandy were in total shock . . . no one said a word . . . how long Ormandy carried on in this unhinged way, giving vent to his long-pent-up feelings, is impossible to say . . . suddenly, Isaac stepped forward calmly and approached Ormandy . . . "Look at George, look at him, Gene . . . does he look like the kind of man who would set out to harm anyone?" That broke the spell . . . Isaac's manner and words had the right effect . . . took the tension out of the room just as suddenly as it had entered with Ormandy's frenzied outpouring of the incredible and unnecessary hurt he'd carried all those years. I came to and, as gently as possible, said to Ormandy, "I'm terribly sorry . . . I must leave . . . but I want you to know how much it means to me that you played my music the way you did." With that I excused myself, saying there were people waiting for Isaac and me at a friend's house. I left to get my car, then drove with Isaac to the Wolfgangs,' not far from the university, where my Gene was waiting for us . . . my last clear memory of that unforgettable night is sitting around the kitchen table with Isaac, Matt Moore, Marvin Wolfgang, and other friends while we talked animatedly, ate and drank, and acted as though nothing but the performance had taken place back at the Academy of Music only a few hours earlier. Isaac never mentioned the scene he had witnessed in Ormandy's studio. Nor did I.

Stravinsky's Caveat

Circles of Fire and the
Hirsch–Pinkas Piano Duo

The single most significant impulse that led to the 1996–97 *Circles of Fire* for two pianos was my long-held obsession with the properties of symmetry in music, which traces back to Bach's *Art of Fugue*—an inexhaustible well. Pinpointing it further leads unerringly to Bach's use of the principle of mirror symmetry, the very essence of the fugue theme itself that underlies the never-completed *Art of Fugue* and, more particularly, the expanded elaboration of the properties of mirror (reflective) symmetry in the four-part fugue of Contrapunctus XII and the three-part fugue of Contrapunctus XIII. By Bach's own time, contrapuntal devices rooted in reflective symmetry already had a long and stable tradition in the practice of invertible counterpoint. It is entirely relevant to my story of *Circles of Fire* and the sources on which it fed to add quickly that those same devices continued to appear prominently in the music of Mozart, Haydn, Beethoven, and Brahms—and then took on new life in the works of Schoenberg, Berg, and Webern in the first half of the twentieth century.

Mirror symmetry makes possible reflecting the original form of a thematic or motivic idea—or a texture—simultaneously or successively with its inverted (reflected) form. In *Art of Fugue,* Bach calls the original and its reflected inversion respectively *rectus* and *inversus.* One of my favorite passages in Lewis Thomas's *The Medusa and the Snail* is where he describes the act of listening to Bach's music as a direct experience of "listening to a human mind."[1] His profound insight presented as metaphor. Though I'm convinced he means it as literal fact, it is readily corroborated in the negative empirical evidence of our inability to tie symmetrical forms of thinking in music to any particular time, place, or individual as to origins.

———————————————

When I first met the gifted Israeli-born pianist Sally Pinkas and, not long afterward, her husband, Evan Hirsch, the intellectual anchor of the two, none of us could have foreseen that within a few years the reality of *Circles of Fire* for two pianos would absorb the greater part of my life in its composition and Sally and Evan's in rehearsals, performances, and recording.

Feeding into *Circles of Fire* and virtually parallel with my work on it, I found myself caught up in the idea of the refrain as a powerful structural element in poetry and music. At the root of its power lies the binding force of repetition of pungent, striking musical and verbal images. Such repetitive imagery satisfies all the more precisely because we seem to take great sensuous and intellectual pleasure in structured returns, which serve to increase their infectiousness.

In the earliest stages of thinking about the work I wanted to write for Sally and Evan, what direction its overall form should take, I found myself obsessed by the refrain idea as structural binder for the entire work. Other thoughts rose that simultaneously had to do with designing the new work on the polarities of symmetry and asymmetry expressed through maximum variety of different musics of diverse character; in other words, once again to take up my old idea of a single work being "a concert of music." I decided that the refrain idea could serve both as structural binder and unifier, providing it defined itself through recognizable emotional character. No matter how different from each other successive variants might be, identity of surface character would have to indicate fundamental connection, and all variants would express an underlying symmetrical organization.

My personal response to the profound spiritual ethos of baroque music, its *Empfindsamkeit,* its soberness, solemnity, and gravitas, took shape in the idea for concentrated but relatively brief "Solemn Refrains" to appear at five strategic symmetrical points, thus establishing the frame of the fifteen numbered sections I had decided on. Each of the five refrains derives from the identical internal symmetry of pitch organization to be found in Bach's *Art of Fugue,* itself based on the Dorian mode, whose two tetrachords $\overline{\text{DEFG}}$: $\overline{\text{ABCD}}$ are symmetrical to each other (and are hinged on the unheard enharmonic axis G#/A♭). Two musically different "Solemn Refrains," I and V, open and close the work yet express the same symmetrical melodic and harmonic conditions. The three remaining interior "Solemn Refrains" are all variants of one another: in the succession of sections, Solemn Refrain II appears as no. 5, III as no. 8, and IV as no. 11.

II is *rectus* (or original) to IV as *inversus* (or symmetrical inversion). III provides the axial harmonic symmetry on which II and IV rest. All the remaining ten sections arrange themselves on a broad-ranging spectrum, from various kinds of symmetry (tonal and atonal) to various kinds of asymmetry (again tonal and atonal). For example, no. 3 ("Canonic Variations") explores atonally whole-tone rising and falling motions; no. 6 ("Gargoyles"), severely dissonant, explores *rectus/inversus* forms of twelve-tone orders between the two pianos; no. 9 ("Sognando") explores tonal circular harmonic order; no. 13 ("Fuga a sei voci"), my version of Bach's Contrapunctus XIII, is tonal, to be sure, but pits the two pianos against each other, periodically going in and out of harmonic phase, yet always in rigorous symmetrical relation to each other. Asymmetry—while not always the *sole* basis of another group of four sections—chiefly characterizes no. 2 ("Chiaroscuro") and its variant form, no. 14, no. 4 ("Gioco del fuoco"), no. 7 ("Nebulae"), and no. 12 ("Caprichos"). And finally, no. 10 ("Infinite Ricercar") is a four-part symmetrical canon (or round) that passes through a whole-tone hexachord (six notes) theoretically forever.

When I told Sally and Evan I was thinking of writing a large-scale work for them, they responded with great enthusiasm. Being of an eminently practical turn of mind, they immediately suggested developing a co-commissioning plan with a number of participating academic institutions countrywide where premiere performances could eventually take place. This seemed a perfectly natural approach—so I agreed. Sally, a strong-willed, quick-thinking young woman, took it upon herself to set the plan in motion and ultimately bring it to fruition. During the process, requiring a great deal of time and effort, I marveled that she was able to carry on her full schedule as artist-in-residence at Dartmouth and also prepare for innumerable concerts—whether with Evan, or solo, or with chamber ensembles and occasionally orchestras.

At the same time, she was working to record a substantial number of my solo piano works, a project for which she had received a prestigious grant. She came to Newtown Square to work with me as often as her hectic schedule permitted. In the midst of everything else, she recorded for the Gasparo label a technically brilliant, deeply felt double-CD set of over two hours of piano music, which included *Partita-Variations* (1976), *Nach Bach* (1966), *Sonata-Fantasia* (1956), *Carnival Music* (1971), *Four Short Sonatas* (1984), and *Variations on an Original Theme* (1941).[2] Simultaneously, Evan was teaching his piano students at Brandeis, giving solo concerts and four-hand, one piano and duo-piano concerts with Sally and—amazingly and singlehandedly—slowly renovating the old house they had bought in one of the Boston suburbs.

As I completed each of the fifteen sections of *Circles of Fire,* I had it photo-copied and mailed to Sally and Evan. How long it was between that protracted process and the day we met early in 1998 for our first rehearsal of the work I can't say. That afternoon in Edi Rieber's piano-filled music room—three Steinways, to be exact—still retains a special aura. The sound of two pianos mixing registers and sonorities has an indescribable flavor. Orchestration for two pianos has as different a meaning from orchestration for chamber ensembles as it does from orchestration for the full-size modern orchestra. The primary difference between the three lies in the homogeneous timbre of two pianos as compared with the mixed timbres of heterogeneous chamber ensembles and/or the full palette of timbral mixtures of the large symphony orchestra.

The true joy of that first rehearsal lay in its erasing any initial doubts—particu-larly in regard to those sections where I had taken a risk—that things would work out as I wanted, no. 9 ("Sognando") being a case in point. A kind of dreaming music, *sognando* being Italian for "dreaming." Aside from how it came about as a serendipitous combination of two entirely different and separate pieces of music by Brahms (discussed in detail later), its very delicacy and overall dynamic range (*piano* to *pianissimo* to *pianississimo*) left me wondering whether it would be substantial enough as physical sound to be recognizably what I consider a two-piano sound. In Evan and Sally's hands it proved itself *as orchestration* of subtly shaded hues—exactly what I was after.

Another instance—and quite opposite—was no. 4 ("Gioco del Fuoco" [Play of Fire]), particularly those passages (for example, mm. 103–40) where piano I plays an asymmetric rhythmic tune (*pp*) against Piano II, which splashes cluster-filled groups of figurations (*pp*), later the two pianos reversing roles. Still later, both pianos (mm. 141–80), playing in rhythmic unison, exchanging roles frequently, spread their combined registers over a three- and four-octave span in which the upper and lower registers—whether played by I or II—almost always remain free of any mixture while the great middle register is in constant mixtures of the two. This produces the acoustic effect of *increasing* the sense of the physical scope of the sound of the music. I have no rational explanation for this effect and wonder if acousticians could offer a reasonable explanation of this phenomenon that in no way depends on the dynamic that remains *fortissimo* for quite long stretches.

Five institutions agreed to join the co-commissioning plan plus a schedule of "premieres" that Sally and Evan would perform. I attended the premiere "pre-miere" at Duke University in Durham, North Carolina, out of affection and regard for Steve Jaffe, one of my earlier Penn students, who was now teaching composi-tion at Duke; also, of course, to be with Sally and Evan at the start of what they had worked so hard to achieve. It was immediately after that very first performance of *Circles of Fire,* March 3, 1998, that Evan delivered himself of what remains the most memorable spoken line to come out of the *Circles of Fire* experiences we shared. Backstage, to friends and admirers who gathered 'round, he remarked: "This is the first time I sat down to play a concert and did not get up until over an hour later." This latest "concert of music" took place for me in what Henry Corbin calls "the imaginal world" lying somewhere between the perceptual world of the senses and the paradoxically insubstantial (because suprasensory) world of the transcendental.[3] In that imaginal middle world Evan's playing the piano for over an hour was one kind of experience for him, but for me, it was a suspended world out of time and out of space, a kind of dream state.

A few weeks later, on March 31, Sally and Evan gave the second premiere at Curtis under an arrangement with the Penn Contemporary Players at the University of Pennsylvania. Again less than a week later, they played *Circles of Fire* on Sally's home ground, at Hopkins Center, Dartmouth College, April 4, 1998, and the next day at the University of Vermont in Burlington. The last of the premieres took them to Arizona State University in Tempe, May 1. Following these performances they appeared with me June 21, 1998, at a young composers conference sponsored by the Cincinnati Conservatory of the University of Cincinnati, where, besides the public performance they gave, we did a master class together on the structure and orchestration of *Circles of Fire.* From July 1998 to November 2000, Sally and Evan played the work in Israel, Russia, Nigeria, and back again in the United States at Washington University in St. Louis and Rice University in Houston. I rejoined them in Houston, where again we gave a demonstration-lecture to students and faculty that explored technical aspects of *Circles of Fire.* In the midst of all this traveling and performing, they took time in December 1998 to record the work for Gasparo.[4]

Since all the American performances of *Circles of Fire* were sponsored by one form or another of academic institutions—university-associated conservatories of music, university schools of music, and departments of music, this provides the perfect lead-in to a discussion of my almost twenty-five-year affiliation with the academic world through my relation to the University of Pennsylvania from 1960 to 1983.

The most exacting and difficult years were the earliest. These were the years when our son Paul's illness was first diagnosed as cancer and, from 1961, paralleled my efforts to build a new Department of Music with a new faculty and curriculum. Paul's death in November 1964 was an earthquake in our lives. Those early years at Penn appear to me now as surreal, the rebuilding of the Music Department disconnected, light-years apart from what Paul and our family suffered. My office in the old Hare Hall was directly across the street from the University of Pennsylvania Hospital, where Paul was treated during one of his many periods there. In memory it is as though those early years of fearful anxiety for Paul and the identical real-time period during which I was so heavily involved in university and departmental life were taking place on two different planets in different universes, a dreaded and shattering ending coinciding with a hope-invested beginning. Life goes on in spite of everything, and nothing balances out personal loss and tragedy. Shortly afterward, Vartan Gregorian, provost of the university in the last years of my tenure there, decided to appoint me as the first to occupy the newly created Annenberg Professor of Humanities chair. (Vartan was master of the apt aphorism. My favorite—which helped me through a particularly difficult moment—was one I had occasion to remind him of in one of his supremely difficult times: "Eagles don't eat worms.") I continued to teach, as I had from the beginning of my appointment to the Penn faculty, a composition seminar, an advanced harmony course in which I tested my findings in tonal circular harmonic sets in nineteenth- and early twentieth-century music, that is, late romantic and early modern, and occasionally guided a PhD candidate through a dissertation.

These densely packed experiences of university life helped me develop a powerful sense of the currents and undercurrents of the contrary atmospherics of the academic world, its narrow passageways through its over-self-conscious immersion in its self-created myth of "rational thought," its constant ritualistic repetitions of overidealized verbal formulas, and ultimately a profound sense of the glaring difference between the seemingly clear aims of scientific study and research and, outwardly, the far less clear *purposes* of art—if, indeed, it is even possible to claim such utilitarian ends for artistic endeavor.

In my first two years as a new chairman I sat as a regular member of the College of Arts and Sciences curriculum committee, an education in itself. Fired by a kind of missionary zeal to convert my more rational-minded colleagues to seeing things from another point of view, I took every occasion to speak for the necessity of recognizing the world of the nonverbal as a world of images and imagination whose "language" employed configurations equal in power and force of conviction in human experience to logical formulation, the so-called objective, rational world of thinking expressed verbally in contradistinction to the so-called subjective, irrational world of feeling expressed nonverbally. Evidently my mini-lectures had their most powerful effect on the dean of the college, a scholar himself whose field was the etymology of Old Icelandic and a man I was very fond of. At the tail end of one of my impassioned speeches he interrupted and shouted, in totally undisguised tones of exasperation, his usual mildly ironic manner and look totally shattered, "George if you say 'non-verbal' one more time I am going to *scream!!*"

The struggle in me between the avowed rational goals of academia and the impossible-to-pin-down artistic urge that I had reduced, for purely expedient ends, to the contention between the verbal and the nonverbal never abated. Sometimes it would break out in sudden, sharp outbursts—especially in composition seminars, to the puzzlement, perhaps even consternation, of my graduate students, all of them hungering to become composers who would achieve recognized works worthy of the great line preceding them. My mildly berating diatribes were intended to warn them against tying their fates to the unwarmed and unwarming atmosphere of a bland, routinized academic existence. Their only protection against this creeping form of spiritual atrophy lay in developing and maintaining an outward skeptical eye joined to an inward self-critical view—in sum, a starchy, subversive attitude that serves as the immune system guarding the inviolability of the artistic instinct.

I delighted in taking sharp gibes at what I called "this Temple of Rationality," which, as I told my students, was " concerned only with why things are as they are . . . your concern is to bring a new world into being . . . transformed into music that reverberates, first, in your own souls, then in others'. Ask yourselves, 'what am I doing here . . . how am I going to live . . . and what is the price of trying to make art?'"

As a composer I was now leading a double life, one as an "academic" composer, seen from the viewpoint of those to whom such distinctions seemed to matter, the other as a free agent whose work possessed a certain currency in the larger world outside academia. By the time I was airing my ad hoc homiletics I had apparently attained, by some mysterious process of guild identification, status as an "academic composer." Which, in itself, constituted mere appearance and at the furthest remove possible from how I felt about university life generally: in it, but not of it. My barely disguised role as dissident and my frequent lapses into subversive homilies delivered for my students' benefit lead directly to two interlocking stories, the first revolving about what I call Stravinsky's "caveat," the other a recounting of a chance meeting on a train from New York to Philadelphia with Edward T. Cone,[5] a member of the Princeton music faculty.

It is not clear what reasons or circumstances led Stravinsky—by then a longtime resident of the United States—to issue his "caveat" to American composers. But his meaning couldn't have been clearer or more direct. He warned against teaching in an academic institution or identifying as composers with teaching composition in such an environment. From Stravinsky's point of view, they were placing themselves in grave danger, artistically speaking, and should do anything *but* teach to keep themselves afloat economically, anything else *but* identify with an academic world antithetical to the world of art and its creation. This was the sum and substance of Stravinsky's statement. At the time it was given wide circulation by the College Music Society, with an accompanying request to me and other "academic composers" to respond to his position for publication in an upcoming issue of their journal.[6]

In this particular instance I took an equivocal stance, because Stravinsky left no room for the anomaly, the paradox, the peculiar nature and position of art in America. Yes, I said, in principle Stravinsky is right; the philosophical, aesthetic side of his caveat is unarguable. The anomaly was that trying to make art and being an artist-composer in America was itself the paradox. For that reason, I had to disagree and say, "No, Stravinsky is wrong *if* the individual composer has no other means of economic survival." That this was so seemed clear enough. Most composers lacked professional performance skills; there was, therefore, no way they could function in the performance world. Even if they could perform as soloists or conductors, a serious performance career could be as much an obstacle to developing as a composer as a career devoted to teaching full-time at a college or university. It was a dilemma any way one looked at it; either career, taken seriously, swallowed up the time and energy, emotional and psychic resources needed to produce artworks. My only suggestion, strongly advanced, was to remain wary of the academic life and not allow it to divorce the composer from what should be his/her primary goal—to compose music of quality, against all odds. Under whatever conditions, throughout the long history of music in Western culture, has that not been the perennial challenge?

I am even more in agreement with Stravinsky's caveat *now* than I was formerly. Too many composers have already tilled the rocky soil of American academia with little result, and still newer generations continue the fruitless task of trying to make art out of meager circumstance. As always, art music still remains in short supply, and no one can say from where or whence it may, if at all, emerge to surprise and renew stale tastes.

The story of my conversation with Ed Cone fits right in with the tale of Stravinsky's caveat. So tight a fit that if composers who teach in American colleges and universities had not existed in such numbers sufficient to form the membership of the American Society of University Composers (ASUC), the question Ed raised at the outset of our conversation need never have been broached. A relatively short time before our chance meeting I had received an invitation from ASUC to become one of its charter, or founding, members. (ASUC is the inevitable acronym of the particular words arranged in that particular order. It was a thoughtless and unfortunate result, considering the unintended vocables to which the four letters constituting the acronym give voice when spoken aloud, not to mention the too-evident hint of self-mockery and self-ridicule that sounds in the acronym.) Put off by the implications I sensed in this new organization's title, I declined—and never gave it a second thought.

When we met on the train quite by chance, Ed Cone seemed eager to talk. He came right to the point: "Would you mind telling me frankly why you turned down our invitation to join ASUC?" (From the way Ed put it, I gathered he was one of the guiding spirits and initial organizers of the society.) "There were only two people who refused to join us," he continued, "you and Roger Sessions." I confess to being secretly delighted by this news. Roger, of whom I was enormously fond, and for whom I had great regard and respect as a fine and serious composer, was basically a loner. Or in Herman Melville's thesaurus, an *isolato.* My basic instinct always led me back to the plain fact that every artist who is dead serious about his work is a loner, an isolato, "a group of one." (History, personal feeling, and observation continually bear me out.) Roger and I had never even communicated on the subject of this new society, which, as Ed Cone explained to me, had been formed as a lobbying means to help strengthen and foster the status and position of composers on campuses generally. In short, to gain greater recognition in practical ways from university and college administrators in order to benefit the lot of academic composers. My own half-formed guess was that ASUC hoped by banding together they would overcome the sense of lesser academic standing for its members, individually and collectively, than was felt in a community of colleagues who were the acknowledged boyars and princes, cardinals, and prelates of the rational disciplines of mathematics, physics, bio-medical research, and so on.

All this emerged after I explained, as simply and directly as I could, my basic reason for not joining: that I couldn't remember a time when I didn't view writing music as a purely private, a deeply personal act, a way of expressing what I felt about existence itself. From this it followed that my affiliation with an academic institution such as Penn was, lacking a private income, hardly a matter of idle choice but of sheer economic necessity. It was, therefore, no contradiction in terms, as I saw and felt it, to reject out of hand the idea of identifying myself *as a composer* with where I taught for a living. Even though I was fully aware of the difficult position of many individual composers in academic settings, I saw no way in which the private pursuit of artistic ends could (or should) be hitched to political ends—however worthy they might appear to others. I was not persuaded that the quality and level of the music being composed in academic circles would suddenly be altered for the better by the existence of such a society. It was clear to me that Ed Cone was not in accord with my position. Nonetheless we parted amicably at Princeton, and I continued on to Philadelphia.

It is not possible to go into every aspect of a work such as *Circles of Fire* and stay within the self-imposed limitations of the *least* technical possible format I've chosen as a point of departure for discussion of three sections—no. 9 ("Sognando"), no. 10 ("Caprichos"), and no. 13 ("Fuga a sei voci")—because of some special condition or circumstance bearing on either sources or compositional approach or both. "Sognando" partakes of a dreamlike set of circumstances that led to its composition and inclusion in the work. The story begins with a concert given by the pianist Marcantonio Barone[7] and a visiting Russian clarinetist (principal of the Bolshoi Ballet orchestra) and his twenty-year-old son, a remarkable French hornist. All three collaborated in performing my *Horn Trio* for clarinet, horn, and piano (1948, revised 1980). Tony Barone and his Russian colleague then played the Brahms Sonata for Clarinet and Piano, op. 120, no. 1, the slow movement of which I have always found particularly moving in a reflective, melancholic way, dreamlike in its atmosphere. For days afterward I kept hearing the second movement's opening clarinet melody. It simply would not go away. Somewhere in this obsessive inward hearing/listening there began to sound the harmonies of the middle section of Brahms's Intermezzo, op. 118, no. 4, for piano solo, another longtime favorite that I loved for its seamless, magical harmonic progression through three seemingly unrelated keys.

At first I wondered why these two Brahms pieces were activating each other—with no conscious effort on my part, calling each other up continually. Then, of their own "will," one day they literally "joined" together in my head as though they belonged together; and, even though the "join" was out of metric sync with how each existed in its original form, I was astonished—and not a little baffled—that they fit as well as they did despite the oddly off-kilter way they arranged themselves metrically. "Can't be," I kept saying to myself. It had about it a touch of the surreal that we see in de Chirico and, even more successfully realized, in Magritte. "Something very strange going on here." And with that, I went to the piano and began improvising on the "join" I had heard in my head—and to my utter delight, what my inner, intuitive process had *worked out for itself* and then *presented* to my conscious awareness was true. It worked perfectly—so long as I allowed for untying the original metric structure of the clarinet melody to fit the considerably slowed-down-in-tempo motion of the purely harmonic progressions of the middle portion of the piano intermezzo. There was indeed a marriage between the two, magical in its new unity and unexpected melodic and harmonic match. From that "join" I fashioned "Sognando"—retaining a great deal of the original clarinet sonata movement but always with changes determined essentially by my decision to symmetrize the new "piece."

No. 12 ("Caprichos") takes its title from Goya's biting set of graphic commentaries on the follies of man's overweening pride and ever-renewing propensity for self-congratulation. Himself part of the generation that lived during the so-called Enlightenment in the eighteenth century, Goya titled plate 43 in his series of etchings and aquatints "El sueño de la razon produce monstrous" (The Dream [or Sleep] of Reason Produces Monsters). After the political chaos and murderous horrors of the twentieth century that humankind perpetrated upon itself as it slept/dreamt its false ideologies, each proclaimed as everlasting truth, Goya's intuition—the acid of his vision as it bites its way into the metallic substance that is human folly—grows in strength and leaves behind the smoking ruins of Enlightenment "truths" that erected the one-dimensional, flat, stage-set facades of the perfectibility of man and the illusory ideals of one form of utopia after another.

The use of "Caprichos" as a title borrowed from Goya's set of etchings has its own history, which leads back to 1948–49, the time of my First Symphony. The third movement of that work was originally called "Capriccio," a more traditional musical title to designate mere *capriciousness*. At the time the "Capriccio" movement was withdrawn, I made a two-piano transcription of it. It was this transcription I decided to rework, because I discovered in it copious elements of symmetrical harmonic relationships that, at the time I wrote the symphony, were purely intuitive—but not accidental; and the fact of the strong presence of those elements determined my decision to include it in *Circles of Fire*. I decided, too, on the new, tougher title—"Caprichos"—to emphasize the inherent satire and irony that provides a link with the newly composed "Gargoyles," no. 6. Without changing the basic design of the original music, I made many detailed changes in the inner textures of this final version, recomposing a number of places, adding new phrases where necessary, altering places rhythmically to sharpen their point and enhance their structural impact. Thus "Caprichos" is the fourth and final form of (1) the original orchestral symphony movement, which (2) I transcribed as a literal two-piano version, followed in turn by (3) the completely rewritten, restored orchestral version.

Inevitably, Contrapunctus XIII from Bach's *Art of Fugue* found its place as no. 13 in *Circles of Fire*. This monumental work had planted itself in 1939–40 when Hans Weisse gave me the Breitkopf and Härtel edition, and I began working my way through it slowly, painstakingly, baffled by its mysteries, seeking to grasp its code, returning to it over and over again to grapple with its secrets, to draw strength from its unchanging core of spiritually grounded musical wisdom.

Two three-voice fugues in score, one sitting on top of the other measure for measure, each a note-for-note mirror image of the other: that is the physical appearance of Contrapunctus XIII on the printed page. The first three-voice fugue (A), which Bach designates as *rectus* is inverted note for note with the voices in different registral relations to each other in the second three-voice fugue (B), designated as *inversus*. The means by which Bach accomplishes this contrapuntal feat is symmetrical inversion: in Fugue A a motion of a fourth *down* followed by a motion an octave *up* is simultaneously inverted (mirrored, reflected) by a motion of a fourth *up* followed by a motion an octave *down* in Fugue B, and so on. It is clear that Bach did not intend *Art of Fugue* for performance per se, because nowhere in the work does he designate any instrumentation. Even so, innumerable performance versions do exist and keep cropping up. I'm not sure how Bach would have felt about joining what I call Fugues A and B into a single six-voice fugue so that they are heard as one simultaneity. He might have objected on the grounds that harmonic clashes frequently occur when sounding the *rectus* together with the *inversus;* for example, E-minor and C-minor "tonalities" clash against each other, or F major against B minor, and so on. Then again, he might not. In fact, he might have found it intriguing to bring Fugues A and B together as a single six-voice fugue *because* the harmonic frictions throw a strangely dissonant mist over those places where they occur, only to be cleared away in an instant by consonant harmonic agreement again in the principal D-minor key. The aural effect of going out of tonal phase, touching briefly on a suggestion of the kind of mildly sour dissonance identified with what used to be called the "wrong note" school (pantonal music) in the 1920s and 1930s, bears a very close relation to the music of the "Back-to-Bach" movement largely attributed to Stravinsky's neoclassicism.

My transcription for two pianos in *Circles of Fire* is not literal. I edited Bach's original first, to make it feasible for two keyboards; second, in the process I expanded—in fact exaggerated—the use of the occasional trill that appears in Bach to become a major gestural characteristic of my version; and third, I took the liberty of extending two cadences, particularly the final one, because they seemed too cursory and abrupt in their original forms, and I wanted to let the energy of the music round itself off in a more stately, unhurried fashion. The extension of the final cadence I worked in precise accord with the symmetrical principles that govern Bach's Contrapunctus XIII.

Rochberg (right) at the age of fifteen with teacher Julius Koehl, Passaic, New Jersey, 1933. The two performed piano duets on WOR-AM, New York City (courtesy of the New York Public Library).

Rochberg and wife Gene, soon after their marriage on August 18, 1941 (courtesy of the University of Pennsylvania).

Dmitri Mitropoulos (center) with Rochberg (right) accepting the Gershwin Prize for *Night Music*, 1953 (courtesy of the New York Public Library).

Rochberg and his parents outside Carnegie Hall following the premiere of *Night Music* by the New York Philharmonic, April 23, 1953 (courtesy of the New York Public Library).

Rochberg's children, Paul and Francesca ("Chessie"), at home in Newtown Square, Pennsylvania, ca. 1956 (from the collection of Gene Rochberg).

Paul Rochberg
at 16
sketched by his father

Rochberg's drawing of his son Paul, 1960 or 1961 (courtesy of the New York Public Library).

Panel discussion on serial composition, International Conference of Composers, Stratford, Ontario, August 1960: (left to right) John Weinzweig, Morton Feldman, Harry Freedman, John Beckwith, and Rochberg (courtesy of the New York Public Library).

Rochberg in rehearsal with the Concord String Quartet, Spaulding Auditorium, Dartmouth, 1974: (left to right) Norman Fischer, Andrew Jennings, John Kochanowski, Mark Sokol, and Rochberg (photograph by Stuart Bratesman, courtesy of the New York Public Library).

Rochberg with Isaac Stern, on tour performing the Violin Concerto, 1978 (courtesy of the Sacher Foundation).

Rochberg with the Concord Quartet and pianist Alan Marks following a performance of the Piano Quintet in Santa Fe, summer 1979: (left to right) Norman Fischer, John Kochanowski, Mark Sokol, Rochberg, Alan Marks, and Andrew Jennings (courtesy of the Sacher Foundation).

Rochberg receiving an ovation following the premiere of the Oboe Concerto, performed by Joseph Robinson, oboe, and the New York Philharmonic, Zubin Mehta, conductor, December 1984 (courtesy of the Sacher Foundation).

Rochberg with Chicago mayor Harold Washington, January 1986 (courtesy of the New York Public Library).

Rochberg with conductor Georg Solti for the premiere of the Fifth Symphony by the Chicago Symphony Orchestra, January 1986 (courtesy of the New York Public Library).

Rochberg in his study at home on Aronimink Drive, Newtown Square, Pennsylvania, in the 1980s (from the collection of Gene Rochberg).

Rochberg with conductor Lorin Maazel for a performance of the Sixth Symphony by the Pittsburgh Symphony Orchestra during its tour of the Soviet Union, 1989 (courtesy of the Sacher Foundation).

Rochberg (right) and Anthony Gigliotti, clarinetist of the Philadelphia Orchestra, for whom Rochberg composed his Clarinet Concerto, February 24, 1996 (photograph by Michael Garber).

An example of Rochberg's hand: the opening page of the *Sonata Seria* (1998) (courtesy of the Theodore Presser Company).

Rochberg and Eliot Fisk at Chamber Music Northwest, Portland, Oregon, July 1998 (courtesy of the New York Public Library).

Rochberg and wife Gene at home on Aronimink Drive in Newtown Square, late 1990s (from the collection of Gene Rochberg).

(Left to right) Rochberg, Sabine Tomek, Christopher Lyndon-Gee, and Gene Rochberg, in a restaurant near the concert hall in Saarbrücken, December 2000 (from the collection of Gene Rochberg).

George Rochberg at work in his home in Dunwoody Village, Newtown Square, Pennsylvania, ca. 2001 (from the collection of Gene Rochberg).

Rochberg with violinist Peter Sheppard Skaerved during a rehearsal of the restored version of the Violin Concerto with the Saarbrücken Radio Symphony Orchestra, March 2002 (courtesy of the New York Public Library).

Rochberg at home in Dunwoody Village, Newtown Square, Pennsylvania, April 2005 (photograph by Michael Garber, courtesy of the New York Public Library).

Rochberg and wife Gene at home in Dunwoody Village, Newtown Square, Pennsylvania, April 2005 (photograph by Michael Garber, courtesy of the New York Public Library).

CHAPTER 8

Unlocking the Past

Contra Mortem et Tempus and *Music for the Magic Theater*

From somewhere in the far folds of memory, John Keats's "All poetry is the work of One Mind" keeps surfacing—reminding me of a strange but necessary truth. Strange because it unites all individual and collective experience and difference; necessary because it is at one and the same time defense and bulwark against the constant round of ephemeral enthusiasms that have kept the art world, since the early twentieth century, in a perpetual boil of "originality." This vision of a universalizing mind limns out the farthest possible reach of a way of viewing the workings of the human imagination, which inevitably involves the individual struggle to produce art and, simultaneously, a way of perceiving each of us as an individual filament of a vast, interconnected nervous system, a single cell of a far-flung organism of suprahuman consciousness in which we mysteriously share.

Of the time in the 1960s I am writing about, holding steady this shimmering mirage-vision of an ultimate unity of historical difference, cultural and linguistic difference, aesthetic and stylistic difference, individual racial, ethnic, religious, and personality difference, made it possible to understand the variegated modern movement not as a monolithic, single, and fixed consistent mind-set, but as a randomly grouped, many-layered aspect of a great dialectic contending against the power of the past—resisting, denying, dismissing, even trying to obliterate it. But to no avail. Like everything that had come before modernism, I saw that it, too, was subject to the totality of the universal and could not escape the pull of the mysterious processes inherent in Blake's idea of Eternity, the Eternity that "is in love with the productions of time." The modern is as much a part of the eternal present as tradition itself, which it can neither replace nor supplant. Such was my train of thought as I struggled to extricate myself from the binds of serialism and atonality beginning in 1961.

No story about my music has quite the special resonance and meaning as the story of the mixed quartet *Contra Mortem et Tempus* (Against Death and Time), for flute, clarinet, violin, and piano, and the fifteen-player ensemble *Music for the Magic Theater,* made up of a wind quartet of flute, oboe, clarinet, bassoon, a brass quintet of two French horns, trumpet, trombone, and tuba, and a string quintet of two violins, viola, cello, double bass, and solo piano.

To tell the story as clearly as possible—despite its lived complexity of emotional uncertainties complicated by thorny aesthetic issues, all of it made even more difficult because there were virtually no precedents, only my own instincts and impulses to rely on—is to picture my fight to regain the lost ground of old tonal thinking, of melodic invention supported by genuinely heard harmony, in contradistinction to arbitrarily throwing together abstract conglomerates of pitches, an indefensible practice that had been used since the early twentieth century. On the one side that picture is bounded by the last twelve-tone work I wrote in 1963, the First Piano Trio, and on the other by the breakthrough works of 1965, *Contra Mortem et Tempus* and *Music for the Magic Theater,* and the last of the breakthrough works, the Third Symphony of 1966–69, and finally to come into the clear in 1970 with the solo violin *Caprice Variations,* my first consciously designated "concert of music," and a year later the Third String Quartet. Inside those bracketing works and years, I struggled and despaired over the problem of how to grow enough solid ground under my feet so I could stand and move around musically—which meant also intellectually and psychologically. What the coming-into-the-clear allowed me is expressed best in the following excerpt from a letter I wrote to Peter Sheppard Skaerved, the young British violinist, in August 2000:

> Throughout I've managed to give modernism and modernists a real hard time, especially over the ever-rising-from-the- ashes-like proverbial issue, of the thing that really bugs the hell out of them: erasing all walls and borders based on historicity and aesthetic purities—declaring an all-at-once world within which all that matters once again is craftsmanship of the ancient kind, taste of the kind Mozart and Haydn possessed; judgment of the kind Bach and Beethoven and Brahms and Bartók applied to every major decision they made; s'far as I'm concerned it's back to basics, nothing to hide behind, not even so-called talent.

Born at the same time in the first months of 1965, like fraternal twins, outwardly the *Contra* and *Magic Theater* are as unlike as any two anythings can be. Yet they are made of the same stuff, spawned by the same impulses and feelings, generated and projected by the same urgent need to shed the limitations of any prior way of working that blocked my path back to the tonal past. The problem was how to regain that past, how to reconnect with its language, its speech, its different internal pace, how to make its ethos come alive again while combining it with my sense of the twentieth century, the vital time of my life and experience—and yet speak unself-consciously.

Writing the *Contra* and the *Magic Theater* almost simultaneously required that I plunge still deeper into a wider modernism than I had practiced before. Therein lay the paradox: in order to break out of and away from a narrow, restrictive—too abstract on the one hand while too expressionistic on the other—way of hearing and thinking music, the world of those two twin-like works took me into the very core of my still-unresolved struggle to overcome modernism's radical rejection of virtually everything that had come before. Out of them I was able to forge the key that opened the door to a new understanding of music, mind, human culture—and, above all, what we call time, lived time. Their differences include not only those that determine the more intimate, chamber character of *Contra Mortem et Tempus,* in direct contrast to the larger, more public, small-orchestra aspects of the *Music for the Magic Theater,* but also their respective durations and gestural proportions. The *Contra,* with its approximately twelve-minute duration, cast in an indeterminate unfolding of seemingly unrelated images, is far more modest in its overall proportions than the *Magic Theater,* which fills out its three "acts" of approximately thirty minutes in multilingual, layered combinations of indeterminate/determinate, atonal/tonal, measured/unmeasured images and gestures.

Common to both works is the technique—though in a sense that is something of a misnomer, which I can explain—of collage and assemblage, related terms borrowed from the painters' and sculptors' worlds, which bring together in unpredictable combination "found" or "borrowed" forms. That is, already existing artifacts of human culture: in the case of painting and sculpture, objects of the "real" or "art" worlds, or in the case of music, already composed musical ideas, passages, motifs, rhythmic patterns and references, harmonic progressions or identities literally borrowed for reuse in new works. When I say it is a misnomer to call the use of these devices "technique," I mean that both works came to me in a somewhat somnambulistic state of mind, the one emerging directly on the heels of the other. There was no effort in the usual sense when composition is the result of slow, conscious, deliberate making. There was no awareness of using "techniques" or "devices"; these works simply came to life—they were already *there* and needed only to be written down. They came in a sure-footed, quasi-dreamlike state from which I "awoke" only after I had finished putting them on paper.

The hard work had been done. I had made decisions that laid out the basic directions of the music to come. What guided me and kept me on course was the hard-won conviction that Keats was right: not only was "all poetry . . . the work of One Mind," so was "all music" the work of the same One Mind. I could now see clearly that history was the consensual chronological storyline of the shifting surfaces of human existence streaming on in continual variations. What were preserved as significant markers, crucial nodal points, changes of direction in the movements of culture, rested firmly on the unchanging source invisible to the physical eye, inaudible to the physical ear, and unintelligible to the pathways of cognition but transparently clear to intuitive awareness of the unalterable core of a universalizing suprahuman mind. Understood this way, all ideas became common property. "Borrowing," what did it mean if not borrowing from one's larger Self? Being influenced, if not being drawn to, affected by, in love with aspects of that larger Self? How else should one understand J. S. Bach ingesting whole works of Vivaldi; Mozart the child imbibing J. C. Bach and later, the man absorbing J .S. Bach; Beethoven drinking the pure waters of Haydn and the wines of Mozart; and Brahms drawing breath and life from Schubert, brawn and strength from Beethoven, heart and wounded soul from Schumann? Could one find a better way to understand the continuation and weaving of baroque counterpoint and choral tradition through the classical and romantic, the post-romantic and modern— Haydn and Mozart; Beethoven, Brahms, and Mahler; Stravinsky, Schoenberg, and Bartók? And in the heart of the baroque do we not find the Renaissance and in the Renaissance the medieval? Even if "all music is the work of One Mind" were true only *metaphorically,* understanding it as metaphor leads to freeing human culture of the divisive, internecine, ideological warfare fraught with the binds and manacles bred by aesthetic zealotry.

All this bore fruit. In two widely different, overlapping ways that came intuitively, by feel and an immediacy of knowing, I discovered what fit, what was right, what was needed in every situation. Of prime value in this new stage were certain clarifying realizations that had dawned on me years before: I had found that twentieth-century American and European composers of the serialist persuasion sounded much more like each other than did eighteenth- and nineteenth-century tonal composers, who differed widely from each other in temperament, emotional temperature, and, above all, in capacity for melodic/harmonic invention. As a result they sound much less like each other than one might have expected. Identity seemed to have lost out under the press of avant-gardism, while it had flourished freely in traditional soil. By a process of "boiling out" whatever distinguishing stylistic idiosyncrasies may have been present in the original contexts from which

I borrowed, I arrived at a common denominator of pitch groups and aggregates that I shaped to my own purposes.

Thus the bits and pieces I borrowed from some seven contemporary composers (including myself) became the raw stuff out of which I produced the *Contra,* my first collage/assemblage of "found forms." This "boiling out" and reducing-to-common-denominator process served very well for working atonal music because it allowed the formation of new images and gestures, singly and in combination, of compatible elements of the same language. But in writing the *Magic Theater* I discovered that using tonal music as a source of "found forms" necessitated an essentially opposite approach to the circumscribed one I took with *Contra,* that of retaining stylistic identities as I did in the case of Mozart's Divertimento in B♭ Major, K. 287, and motivic materials and passages (at times barely disguised, other times quoted virtually unchanged) from Mahler's Symphony no. 9. These clear identities, rich in readily identifiable characteristics, were juxtaposed in combinations of opposites, pitting them directly against atonal passages of my own composition or against purposely near-chaotic assemblages of atonal "found forms" from twentieth-century composers. The methods in which such combinations of opposites could be projected seemed at the time endlessly variable, allowing the imagination to roam freely without impediment in making fresh textures and contexts. Both ways of working this range of old and new borrowed material were a living affirmation of the idea of One Mind as source of all music sounding together to evoke new atmospheres and qualities of expression made possible by the simultaneities of *ars combinatoria.* Even more than *Contra,* the *Magic Theater* became an all-at-once world, a music without walls or visible borders.

How did I come by the titles of these works? In each instance, while I had strong feelings about what each should be *as music,* I had no clear ideas about what to call these strange new pieces that so urgently needed to be born. Only after each was completed did a title come to me—and in ways that reflected my deepest experience.

November 22, 1964: one year to the very day that John Fitzgerald Kennedy's tragic assassination shook the soul of America to its roots, our son Paul's death shattered the foundation of our lives. We were shaken to the core, traumatized, bewildered by the enormity of his loss. Uncomprehending that it should be at all. Dazed, benumbed by the terrible reality of not just Death—but *his* particular death. That the dreaded end that must come to all living things had come to Paul so early, had cut him off from the years he needed to become the poet that was in him to become. And left us bereft, utterly so—Gene, me, and our beautiful young Francesca ("Chessie"), too young at twelve to understand the cold terror that took her brother.

Wild feelings tore through me. I was wracked by grief, misery, especially by searing anger at everything we humans have no control over . . . I raged and railed inwardly. . . . I was consumed . . . and angry in a way I never would have believed possible . . . at Life because there was also Death . . . at Death because it was beyond all knowing. . . . In my journal I poured out my pain, my anguish . . . day after day . . . floods of words of heartache, soul-sickness, incomprehension. . . . I talked to Paul as though he were still here. . . . At night I dreamed of him . . . night after night he came to me and we embraced and talked. . . . I carried those dream images with me for years . . . they became precious, living-again memories . . . the sense of them still comes to me in these late years . . . a kind of bittersweet balm that does not heal. . . .

After the New Year of 1965, exhausted into a sleepwalking state, going through the motions of everyday existence, resuming teaching and whatever else constituted the quotidian of my work at the university, the need to write music came over me again, enveloping me in a half-in, half-out state of consciousness. In that half-lit, somnambulist condition the first of the fraternal twins dreamed itself into existence—fragmented, tenuous, tentative, yet made of steel. The title of this music against death translated the English into the Latin phrase *Contra Mortem*. One day, like the music, it was suddenly in my head. The rest of the title followed—in English—"and Time." I knew *tempus* was "time," but I wanted the title to have the ring of authentic Latin. My good colleague Norman Smith, whose musicological specialty was medieval music, came to my rescue and gave me the final Latin form: *Contra Mortem et Tempus*. It now had the distanced, covered, if alien, sense of what in English sounded to my ear too naked, harsh, even aggressive: *Against Death and Time*. Despite its softer, more distanced, alien sound, the Latin still expresses exactly what I felt: deep, inconsolable grief, rage, and defiant anger against those implacable realities from which no living thing escapes. Time and Death work hand in glove. Time colludes with Death. Time, the picador on horseback, keeps pricking the bull with his lance and breaks him down, his strength, his will, and prepares the way for Death, the too-proud matador who delivers the final sword thrust.

After Paul died, the reality of my still being alive caused a guilt that goaded me into wanting to live for both of us, to keep him alive—in another dimension—through my music. Impossible, but true: it was that overwhelming need that led me to grasp that, whatever else the pursuit of art may be in the ordinary round of human existence, whether for self-realization or the pursuit of personal fame and fortune or simply for the pleasure of others, ultimately art was a way of defying the brutal depredations and diminishments of Time and Death and fighting to live *against* their crushing forces. The immortality of the great works of the past is itself—illusion or not—the measure of humankind's ceaseless fight to live against Death and Time.

How many poets have defied Death outright? Paul, in his poems, like the bodhisattva he was, quietly, bravely faced "the beast of night" that lapped "at the light" he carried. Yeats in "A Prayer for Old Age" says: "That I may seem, though I die old / A foolish, passionate man." And he ends his last poem of September 4, 1938, "Under Ben Bulben," with this epitaph: "Cast a cold eye / on life, on death. / Horseman, pass by!"

Dante writes a sonnet in which he grieves a lady's death—and then in *Vita nuova* explains it coolly: "This sonnet is divided into four parts. In the first part I address Death by certain appropriate names; in the second I tell why I curse it; in the third I revile it; in the fourth I turn to speaking to an apparently indefinite person, yet very definite to my mind."[1]

John Donne dares to face Death down with his "Death, Be Not Proud." And Hamlet—or is it Shakespeare?—says, "Not a whit, we defy augury; there's a special providence in the fall of a sparrow. If it be now, 'tis not to come; if it be not to come, it will be now; if it be not now, yet it will come: the readiness is all."

"The readiness is all." Defiant? More patient, accepting. Perhaps better than the posture of Don Quixote battling the windmills of the inevitable. Still, I must live against Death and Time. I shall go down one day still *Contra Mortem et Tempus.*

What if, in the face of a particular human being, one discerned *in* or *behind* that face the fainter image of another face, and in or behind that second face a third, and in or behind the third still another, and so on, continuing the process in an endless series of ever-shifting, uniquely particular features, transparent to each other—as though each superimposed image of a face could be extracted and by itself be reminiscent or familiar in ways impossible to describe or define? Imagine these layers of mirroring facial images superimposed on each other as melodic images set transparently on top of each other so that one becomes dizzied and amazed by how much *alike* they are, how much they share shapes and turns of phrase, curvatures of an up-down-and-around figure, or a down-up-and-around figure so that there is no longer any true distinction between the means, the historical times represented, the attributable styles, the many individualities of the composers who gave them existence. What is lost or what gained in boiling out difference in order to discover sameness of feature, family relationship among and between types? Is an atonal chord a disturbed condition of a tonal one, a tonal chord not yet the distorted condition that becomes atonal to the ear, the psychology of hearing? Are they interchangeable conditions of each other, or is there possibly even a third condition that we begin to intuit exists somewhere in the ether and underlies the configuration of each and both? Would this not be acceptable as dream; and if so, then why not as the illusion of physical reality, another form of the dream?

These metaphors are preamble and prelude to entering the world of *Music for the Magic Theater*. What was still embryonic in the *Contra* emerged in full bloom in *Magic Theater*, leaving behind the narrow confines of the modernist sources of the former, and, by breaking through the walls of historical and stylistic reference in the latter, allowed to exist side by side at the same time in an all-at-once context of unsuspected similarities—even while clear difference continued—among diverse sources, making possible a new vocabulary of musical expression through collage and assemblage. I associate a sense of passing freely through rooms of expression while working "found forms."

What made it possible to combine such widely differing sources was the recognition of a three-note, downward chromatic half-step motif appearing prominently in each of the specific historical references I chose as major elements of the *Magic Theater* collage/assemblage. That motif is the exact opposite in direction from the one that links together many of the source referents in the *Contra*. Each chromatic motif (or figure) is the retrograde of the other. Does awareness of it make a serious difference to the perception of both works? That is, does knowing the presence of a common binding motto-motif retrograde to itself alter how one hears these two works? Inasmuch as it made a great difference in the writing of them, it seems inevitable that knowing the nature of the binding retrograde device could affect one's hearing to a marked degree by enhancing perception of what is at work. On the other hand, it is entirely possible to derive great pleasure from hearing, say, the Third Symphony of Brahms without being able to identify and follow his unique practice of transforming melodic motives through variation. Among the extensive sources which comprise the "found forms" I used in writing *Magic Theater*, there are five in which the dominant chromatic motif appears prominently: Mahler, Symphony no. 9; Varèse, *Déserts*; Mozart, Divertimento, K. 287, Adagio; Beethoven, String Quartet, op. 130, Cavatina; Rochberg, *Sonata-Fantasia* for piano. Inasmuch as the title for the work came after the music was composed, there are no overt "programmatic" intentions to be discovered in the "library" of sources I made use of—beyond the general temporal scheme of mixing references to and combinations of past and present, present and past.

In the long life we have shared since 1939, Gene and I have always discussed everything important to us. Where the music I was writing was concerned, she has been my first listener and best critic. With remarkably unerring and keen aesthetic judgment about painting and sculpture, literature and music, she always has astute things to say about what works, what doesn't, and why. Her sharp insights have their own innate strength born of unself-conscious honesty, and, therefore, I took them seriously. It became my habit from early on to play what I was working on for her and to get her reaction to passages I felt were problematic for one reason or another, certainly when the work was completed (or I thought it was) but not yet in its final, fixed form. So it was with the final sketches for what became the *Music for the Magic Theater.* When I'd finished playing them for her, Gene unhesitatingly said, "Why, that's the music for the Magic Theater"—and I knew immediately she was right. She had voiced in words what I had unconsciously sought for in my music: an evocation of Hermann Hesse's *Steppenwolf,* a novel of a time—the 1920s, between the two world wars—that had lost its bearings in Europe in ways characteristic of war-weary, disillusioned Europeans and in America in ways characteristic of pre-1929-Crash, overly optimistic Americans. In Hesse's novel his "Magic Theater" appears, accompanied by strange atmospheres and circumstances, to Harry Haller, a lost, disaffected, suicidal German intellectual who wanders the night-dark streets of unnamed cities. On one of these nights he sees on an old stone wall "bright letters dancing and then disappearing, returning and vanishing once more." These on- and off-again spluttering letters spell out:

MAGIC THEATER
ENTRANCE NOT FOR EVERYBODY
FOR MADMEN ONLY![2]

On another of his night wanderings he meets a man carrying a signboard that spells out the same message with an added line:

ANARCHIST EVENING ENTERTAINMENT[3]

The signboard man hands Harry a small booklet titled "A Treatise on the Steppenwolf. Not for everybody."[4] Harry takes it to his room and reads it.

Harry meets Hermine in one of his night haunts. They become friends, and she undertakes to teach him how to dance—something his life as an arrogant, disaffected, disdainful, intellectual loner had bypassed. Hermine becomes the key to his reeducation in living: she guides him to a beautiful young woman, Maria, who instructs him in the arts of lovemaking and introduces him to a saxophone player, Pablo, the engaging leader of the café band whose music he and Hermine dance to night after night. Pablo, the master of the Magic Theater, inducts Harry into its mysteries. There in the Magic Theater, Harry is given a second chance to relive crucial early experiences he botched the first time around and to re-learn the art of living and being human. It is there Harry meets Mozart—Pablo magically metamorphosed into one of the immortals, the god of Harry's youth, whose "clear and ice-cold laughter out of a world unknown to men, a world born of sufferings, purged and divine humour"[5] rings through the theater. The same Mozart who in an earlier, earthly incarnation, wearing the mask of Sarastro, once guided Tamino through his trials in the temple, tested and rewarded him with Pamina for his patience, endurance, and moral purity. Now it is Pablo/Mozart (or Mozart/Pablo) who becomes Harry's guide, examiner, and judge through the surreal "Magic Theater" and finds him wanting, lacking in basic understanding of what life demands of us humans—and, declaring him guilty, sentences Harry "to live and to learn to laugh."[6] Harry resolves to "be a better hand at the game. One day I would learn how to laugh. Pablo was waiting for me, and Mozart too."[7]

Such is Hermann Hesse's "Magic Theater," a moral testing ground for living in a world that has lost its compass, a world that no longer knows where the cardinal points are.

My *Magic Theater* symbolically enacts the "enmity and entanglement" between the ravening wolf and the civilized human being in the conflict of the mad-for-change modern and the impossible-to-destabilize classical—in short, between the present and the past. That Mozart came to saturate my *Music for the Magic Theater* was due in no small measure to the deep imprint Hesse's vision of his essence and spirit had made on me long before I dreamed of writing the work. Not only was Mozart the perfect representation of the classical past, I was (and remain) convinced that it was he, great eclectic that he was, who had fashioned the classical out of all he had absorbed from childhood on from his great contemporaries, especially Haydn, and created what we call classicism. (I still remember my old friend Paul Mocsanyi saying: "Mozart created the eighteenth century; the eighteenth century didn't create Mozart.") No accident, then, that I chose to show Mozart's classicizing propensities for balance and proportion, his elegance of expression and purity of tonal projection through his B♭ Divertimento with its two horns and string quartet, which fit my instrumental design perfectly. It was sturdy enough to withstand any nontonal music I pitted against it and, at the same time, malleable enough to accommodate with no harm to its essence my enlargements of its orchestral frame by adding new voices. This worked miraculously well in the case of the golden-hued E♭ Adagio, which I was able to transform into a mini *duo concertante* for violin and piano obbligati, with winds (flute, oboe, clarinet, and bassoon) added to the original two horns and strings.

At the other end of this representation of the past I placed Mahler's Ninth Symphony with frequent references to passages using the downward chromatic half-step motto. Why Mahler and not Strauss or Wagner? Because Mahler's music, with its obbligato splendors of orchestral writing, was the last great tonal voice of the line that stretched from Mozart into the first decades of the twentieth century. One hundred and twenty years separate the death of Mozart in 1791 and the death of Mahler in 1911. The classical period, which Mozart dominates, saw the second and greatest flowering of the tonal integration of melody, harmony, and polyphony—the baroque being the first crowning of the efforts to discover and establish tonal expression and coherence that began in the stirrings of the medieval and developed through the Renaissance.

The music of Mahler is redolent of the soft romanticism of the middle-late nineteenth century, and by the time he died it had reached the threshold of the hard romanticism of the hyperhysteria of expressionism I associate with early twentieth-century atonality. It was against this arching spectrum/anchor symbolized in Mozart at one end and Mahler at the other I pitted everything in the *Magic Theater* that is *not* tonal, including those passages that, though rooted in tonality, nevertheless hide behind an atonal mask. In this contention of different aesthetic worlds, in this antagonism and conflict of present and past—in which the past remains calm and unperturbed—lies the "enmity and entanglement" for which there can be no peace or resolution so long as modernist aggression persists in attempting to establish its hegemony. This is what my *Music for the Magic Theater* attempts to depict.

Ever since I first laid eyes on the cubist works of Picasso and Braque and the nonobjective paintings of Kandinsky, I was taken by the strange new logic of discontinuity they offered. Given the contiguously connective syntax of tonal music and its temporal extensions through the phrase and the cadence—full close, half close, and deceptive cadences all playing a major role in classical and romantic music—it was atonality that for the first time in centuries theoretically paved the way in music for discontinuity by jettisoning cadential articulation—the logic or illogic of what followed what no longer being germane. Here was the point where painting and music parted company: in the two-dimensional surface of a Cubist or nonobjective painting—whether considered a collage or an assemblage—space was the primary dimension within which images were disposed and arranged;

but in the unfolding of motion in music—without respect to tempo, thinness or thickness of texture, and considerations of lightness or depth of expressive feeling. It was the dimension of time that bound succession and mattered most. But even with the possibilities for the indeterminate and the discontinuous that atonality now made available to composers, succession of musical images on the temporal plane could not be replaced by anything analogous to simultaneity of visual images in space. At best one might achieve the *illusion* of spatial as opposed to temporal disposition, but never the actuality. This question preoccupied me during the same years that led to producing the *Contra* and *Magic Theater*. Decisions as to how to resolve this and other related questions affected differently every work where I applied the techniques of collage and assemblage.

Given my own penchant for variations, Picasso's great series of variations on the masters hit me like a ton of bricks and served only to increase my already great admiration and love for his enormous freedom of movement as a painter. Whether I saw them on museum walls or in studies in book form, I marveled at the man's passion for taking off from the inspiration of those who had come before him, his ability to employ every style he'd ever invented or modified in bringing off these variation series. Picasso probably had a greater effect on opening me up to what I began to see possible in music—intellectually, psychologically and emotionally—than any other composer, painter, writer, or poet of the twentieth century. Above all, Picasso showed me how provincial it was to insist, as so many painters and composers of my time did, on finding a particular identifying image or voice and sticking as closely as possible to it forever—consistency of style and image having attained a kind of self-justifying status, especially among painters. Picasso remains for me the prime exemplar of the twentieth-century artist who roamed freely where his restless, pluralistic imagination took him.

The hours and hours I spent in museums in New York, Philadelphia, Boston, Washington, Chicago, London, Paris, ultimately had their reward. I drank in floods of images; pondered the ideas they represented; struggled with the ideas they stirred up in me. From this explosion and welter of color and line and ideas I learned how to translate their impact on me into ways of thinking and designing composition that could free me from the rigidity of the single-idea methodology and manner of serialism and began the transference from the old, always ongoing temporality of music to the spatial, where instead of the physical objects of cubist collage or assemblage, it seemed entirely right and possible to use preexisting music—old or new—as found forms in spatialized contexts without respect to period, style, or chronology. Instead of the spatial source of real-world objects and materials painters used, I turned to the temporal sources of past and present, put them in juxtaposition—and, when necessity demanded and opportunity permitted, spatialized them. This is precisely what happened with the *Contra* and the *Magic Theater*.

Both works emerged as though from a dream state. The one followed the other with virtually no time between. The design for each came without effort, unclouded. Were it not for the existent reality of those two works—along with some others—I would have excellent reason to doubt the truth of those feelings and thoughts that continually arise in me that, in far less poetic language, rephrase Shakespeare's "we are such stuff as dreams are made on": Our existence is a dreaming in the flesh we translate into the substance of our art. Whatever dreams us into this human form between two states we neither know nor remember in consciousness; whatever separates us from the state we leave behind at birth and the one we enter into at death; whatever it is also dreams our art into existence.

What were they, these pressures that had been building up inside me? What feeling/thoughts and thought/feelings accompanied this buildup? There was nothing orderly about them; they occurred in a free-flowing stream of consciousness, ongoing, very much in the manner of a never-ending, continuous visual video- or audiotape, repeating, always moving on, combining already seen or heard visual scenes or musical ideas, fluid in motion, multidirectional in curiously circular ways always doubling back and veering off again. Or as a constantly unfolding interior dialogue with one's self, sometimes, in fact, with others, the dialogic stream enlarging to a conversation with a disembodied, actual or imaginary, friend in whom one finds common ground, degrees of agreement when in the grip of internally trying to settle crucial matters; or, contrariwise, with an adversary who is urging a position opposite to the one you hold or are in the process of fleshing out and trying to make more solid.

Whatever its content—the course running from deeply personal and emotional to intellectual to beliefs tied to strong feelings and convictions—some form of interior dialogue expanding to inclusion of others runs deep in the human psyche in virtually all humans during the hours of waking consciousness. Still further, our dreams during sleep are another form of this internal dialoguing that never stops till death brings it to an abrupt halt. Then what of the daydream? Surely another form. And what of the act of making art? An externally searching form of dreaming into which we invite others to enter by seeing, hearing, reading, perceiving, internalizing the dreaming shaped. Except when there's no magic to the making. Especially composing by predetermined methodologies, mechanics, designing sounds by some kind of applied technology—electronic or otherwise. These kill the dreaming consciousness.

From the beginning my plan was for a pair of works opposite in tone, opposite in "voice": *Contra*—intimate, personal, more homogeneous in its sources; *Magic Theater*—not only more heterogeneous in its historic spread of source materials, but also longer and projected in a "voice" far more public than *Contra*.

The Bowdoin Contemporary Music Festival asked me to write a piece for the recently formed Aeolian Chamber Players, a mixed quartet founded by violinist Lewis Kaplan, with flutist Thomas Nyfenger, clarinetist Lloyd Greenberg, and pianist Gilbert Kalish. They gave the first performance of the *Contra* at the Summer Music Festival, Bowdoin College, August 18, 1965.

Some years later—in August 1972—I wrote an entirely different kind of music for the Aeolian Chamber Players, who had added a cello to their ensemble: the five-movement *Electrikaleidoscope* for flute, clarinet, violin, cello, piano (acoustic and electric). Except for its dark center, the tonal third-movement Adagio—which I dedicated to the eleven Israeli athletes murdered in cold blood September 5–6, 1972, at the Olympic Games in Munich, Germany—the work is essentially light in spirit, a divertimento. This shows itself in the two "blues-rock" movements that flank the Adagio in the full-fledged rhythmic style of the popular music of the day. By then, I had already turned from collage/assemblage to writing tonal music or combining tonal movements with freely atonal ones. The *Electrikaleidoscope* (1972) followed *Caprice Variations* (1970), Third String Quartet (1971), and *Songs in Praise of Krishna* (1970) and *Fantasies* (1971), song cycles for voice and piano—both of them freed of the "mind-forg'd manacles" of dodecaphony.

In selecting sources for *Contra* I was guided more by the available instruments that made up the Aeolian Chamber Players than any other single consideration. Everything I used would surrender some part of its original form and identity to a totally new set of relations determined by association—direct or indirect—with wholly other ideas, sometimes confirming its inherent quality, sometimes confronted and challenged by an opposite one. Intuitively, I knew that the process of what I referred to earlier as "boiling out" would make whatever I used more malleable to my purposes. Regardless of whether a source had the strength to retain its initial identity, its very quality as expression would necessarily alter under the pressure of a new context determined by other material, other sources, or even my own invention. The sources I chose were:

Varèse, *Density 21.5* for flute solo
Ives, Largo for violin, clarinet, piano
Boulez, *Sonatine* for flute and piano
Berio, *Sequenza* for flute solo

Berg, Four Pieces for clarinet and piano
Webern, Four Pieces, op. 7, for violin and piano
Rochberg, *Dialogues* for clarinet and piano

Neither *Contra* nor *Magic Theater* needs to be subjected to thoroughgoing analysis; however, certain points will be helpful to describe—for example, the piano harmonics I invented for *Contra.*

Every vibrating substance—a violin string or air column—is capable of producing a composite series of notes (pitches) that make up the "harmonic series." Thus, the open C string of the cello—its lowest note—will activate, when bowed, the entire series of sixteen upper partials (or harmonics). To produce any given partial on the open C string, the player places a finger on that part of the string that will produce, for example, middle C—the fourth partial sounding two octaves above the fundamental note—when the bow is lightly drawn across the string. To apply this same principle to the piano's low strings, one needs to go *inside* the instrument in order to produce harmonics. The resulting sound is that of a clear, ringing bell tone—miniaturized as compared with orchestral tubular bells or church bells. At the very opening of *Contra,* the pianist is asked to produce a bell tone two octaves above the fundamental C♯—which is C♯'s fourth partial. Simultaneously, the violinist plays the harmonic D, two octaves and a half step above the piano middle C♯; seconds later, the clarinet enters playing its lowest E♭. These three pitches—C♯–D♮–E♭—constitute the upward-rising chromatic half-step motto of *Contra.* Their registral disposition, however, has been altered by octave displacements that produce the atonal chord E♭–C♯–D♮. With the entrance of the flute some seconds later on its low E♭, the music is under way. After *Contra* was published, a few composers began to avail themselves of the use of this new technique of piano harmonics—a sign of the readiness with which composers tend to adopt or appropriate or take up any new usable device that appeals to them.

Taking over, appropriating, or borrowing—all are related, whether in the realm of newly invented, usable techniques (the Bartók pizzicato, piano harmonics, new notational symbols) or appealing, for whatever reason, preexisting music. But when it comes to the art of combining borrowed materials, that is an entirely different matter: it is *how* one combines as much as *what* one combines that counts. As has always been the case, where no precedent exists, there is no right or wrong way: only instinct, judgment, and taste. A few examples from *Contra* will illustrate my point. On the oblong spread of pages 14 and 15 of the score of *Contra* I combined a quiet, tonal piano figure from Ives's Largo with a long, already sounding high-register pedal tone (C♯) played by the violin, and fragments of phrases for flute from Berio's *Sequenza* for flute solo, which, though chromatic in essence, I treated as though they were in the same key (of G) as the Ives. This quasitonal feint is quickly dissipated when the third phrase of the flute leaves behind the held, cloudy G-major chord mixed with E♭ and F♮ in a burst of animated flurries of atonal figures—the violin C dropping out before the flute passage has been completed and is interrupted by the clarinet, on page 16 of the score, which takes over the same violin note. The passage comes out of a highly chromatic passage only to dissolve back into another one.

Perhaps the single longest continuously consistent passage in all of *Contra*— page 32 through page 37—is the one in which I combine explosive atonal figures for piano from Boulez's flute and piano *Sonatine* with a flute–clarinet–violin texture I composed as a discontinuous wall of dissonant, atonal chromaticism. Only with the last, fragmented, low-register piano passages that grow in intensity and density of sound does the flute explode into a frenzied dash to its top register, where it is joined by clarinet and violin.

In *Magic Theater* I paraphrased the same *Contra* mixture, this time enlarging the range and density of the backdrop against which the piano figures (renotated in open, proportional notation) move frantically. The sheer volume of sound made by the nine instruments other than the piano instead of the three in the *Contra* version (compare pp. 84–88 inclusive in score of *Magic Theater*) changes everything.

For one more example of different ways of combining different gestures, I turn to pages 23 and 24 of *Contra,* where the music of a piano passage from Webern— calm, vaguely tonal in its chromaticized harmonic vocabulary—enters into an essentially expressive trio of flute, clarinet, and violin music, already in progress, in which the violin leads melodically. As the violin reaches a high point in speed and volume, the flute breaks in with a mad rush of rapid-fire notes played very fast and loud. The piano, silent until just before the flute riff ends, acts as a calm- ing, braking, cadential resting point. A new phrase from the violin leads to the sounding of the upward-rising three-note motto produced by piano harmonics as the music goes off in a new direction.

From the outset I thought of the *Music for the Magic Theater* as a drama of the cultural clash of temporal divisions. The struggle embodied in the work is between aspects of a reality refracted through the remembered *past,* the imme- diately suffered *present,* the often nervously anticipated, anxious-making *future.* When trying to make art, you are constantly confronted by the inescapable fact that your life and your decisions are interwoven with multiple cultural pasts, actual presents, and possible futures; and no effort to wish them away or to conceptual-ize a simple resolution of their inherent anomalies will help lead you out of the labyrinth that is time. Hence the uncertainty that hangs over us individually and collectively; hence the unresolvability that marks the last half of the twentieth century and the first years of the twenty-first. Is there only one eternal, unchang-ing "present" experienced by succession after succession of those of us who have lived any identifiable portion of it? But then, what of "past" and "future"? Are they mere metaphors for convenient tabulation and record keeping? Or is "reality" a perpetual overlapping of different pasts, presents, and futures where each possible zeitgeist is made definably distinct by virtue of textural difference and identity of events—natural, individually human, culturally collective?

All this purposeful irresoluteness and questioning determined my decision to divide *Magic Theater* into the three "acts" that play out musically the dilemmas and confrontational shifts and changes that had overcome music by the middle of the last century. Each act is described simply at the major dividing points of the work. Act I stands at its head and reads: "in which the present and the past are all mixed-up . . . and it is difficult to decide or to know where reality is . . ." With the reworking/recomposition of Mozart's Adagio from the B♭ Divertimento, K. 287, Act II begins (see rehearsal number 34 in full score[8]): "in which the past haunts us with its nostalgic beauty . . . and calls to us from the deeps of inner spaces of heart and mind . . . but the past is all shadow and dream—insubstantial . . . and we can't hold on to it because the present is too pressing . . ." Act III follows the dissolution of the Mozart music into chaos and clashing noises (see page 79 of score): "in which we realize that only the present is really real . . . because it is all we have . . . but in the end it too is shadow and dream . . . and disappears . . . into what? . . ." The disappearance referred to is the long, slow denouement (see pp. 108–12 of score) that ends with four chromatic half steps vertically redistributed by octave displacements over a five-octave range: C♮–B♭–B♮–A♮. The first three half steps—C♮–B♮–B♭—form the downward chromatic motto of the *Magic Theater*.

It was the Fromm Foundation that commissioned the *Magic Theater* for the University of Chicago's seventy-fifth anniversary. The first performance was given by the University of Chicago Contemporary Chamber Players on January 24, 1967, with Ralph Shapey conducting. The version I wrote later for small orchestra was premiered by the Buffalo Philharmonic, January 19, 1969, and conducted by Melvin Strauss.

Between the first performance of the fifteen-player chamber-ensemble version of *Magic Theater,* January 24, 1967, and the first performance of its small-orchestra version, January 19, 1969, Act II, the reworked Mozart Adagio, developed a prob-lem serious enough to demand that I do something about it. People whose taste and judgment I valued and trusted were visibly disturbed—some spoke of being shocked—at so blatant a use of tonal music in the overall context of the work; they said it was too long and even suggested that the Mozart would be more acceptable (tolerable?) if it were only shortened, its six minutes cut down. Anyway, what was Mozart doing in it? The raw juxtaposition of tonal music—and Mozart's at that, even if it was "reworked"—in a collage/assemblage where atonal ideas darted in every direction possible, producing constant psychological uncertainty and unrest—and suddenly the quiet, ineffably serene, yet melancholy-tinged E♭ Adagio . . . what did it all mean, and how was the listener supposed to take it? I mulled it over, not really convinced that anything needed "fixing" but wondering if there was a "solution" at all.

Whatever the objections from others, combining Mozart with the atonal wildernesses of the 1960s was precisely what I meant: it was what ensured—as I saw it—the possible continuation of writing music against the prevailing opaqueness that hobbled a grasp of the cultural conflict over temporal divisions and the strange anomalies they harbor. The presence of Mozart's Adagio established the right of a composer to enlarge his linguistic palette to include any part of the past that interested him, the only criterion being, as far as I was concerned, that a convincing music resulted.

Instead of subtracting from Mozart's original scoring for two French horns and string orchestra, I added. The recomposition I had in mind required the very important obbligato voice and color of the piano as soloist and partner with a violin solo in a *duo concertante*. At the same time I augmented the size of the ensemble, simultaneously expanding its timbral palette with a flute, an oboe, a clarinet, and a bassoon in order to lend their contrasting color emphasis to Mozart's melodic lines. I retained the initial purpose of the pair of horns as harmonic support while extending their use as soloists. In the piano/violin duo I added obbligato polyphony in the tonal language of Mozart so not to disturb in any way the purity of his musical speech.

I altered one other aspect of Mozart's score: to take the sense of serenity at the core of his music one step further into a realm of detachment from the contingent physicality of our outer world by lifting the first violin part an octave higher than Mozart called for. The urge to do so has its sources for me—besides my own natural inclination to write for solo violin in its highest tessitura—in passages in Mozart's own violin concerti; more particularly in the violin solo obbligato of the incredible Benedictus in Beethoven's *Missa Solemnis*. This tendency surfaced again in my Third Quartet variation movement and my Violin Concerto—always tied to an instinctive impulse to take the violin (and its music) out of the "physical" and achieve, if possible, the super-refinement I associate with old Renaissance drawings and etchings and Picasso's remarkable line drawings.

Through their sharing of essential melodic lines and obbligati counterpoints, the interplay of piano and violin solos in *Magic Theater* Act II achieved one further goal: to make of the Mozart Adagio a *concertante* music in which the same melodic lines and contrapuntal obbligati become common property of the double-soloist texture. The contrast in the colors of the winds and horns in context with the piano/violin *duo concertante* helped immeasurably to sharpen the distinctions in sound of the duo from the rest of the ensemble.

The breakthrough into a world where it was possible to write tonal music again (without inhibition or embarrassment)—or rework earlier composers', to combine either or both with my own nontonal music or a reworking of others', to move freely in whatever direction satisfied the muse or the situation—did not happen overnight. There were years between the first sighting of the possibility (in 1961) and the arrival to what seemed at first an exotic and strange new world (1965). Then followed the stages (and the works that represented them) I had to pass through before I could take off in the solo violin *Caprice Variations* and Third String Quartet. Each stage allowed me to explore further the possible forms of *ars combinatoria* (theoretically there are no limits); each new work found its own identity in a particular way unique to itself, in a particular range of combinations of the tonal and the atonal; each pushed hard against the invisible walls of collage and assemblage. I admitted only one proviso: that the result worked *as* music, that it *be* music. The serendipitous experience that became the *Caprice Variations* and opened the doors to the Third String Quartet would never have happened had I not found my way through the maze of the plethora of possibilities. To have discovered ways to reconnect the various musics of the tonal past with the various musics of the nontonal present (atonal, for certain; but also de–key centered by virtue of new chromatic subdivisions of pitch gamuts and associated harmonic possibilities) was to experience a new sense of inner freedom.

Central to the current of ideas that fed the breakthrough works and the stages that followed were jolting infusions of deep skepticism about what I saw and heard in the musical world around me. For one, I was appalled at the sharp drop in temperature in what was being composed and what was being written and said about this new music. Both gave off the cold breath of a passionless scientism. The music sounded tasteless, bereft of any perceivable musical sense, utterly lifeless. To talk or write about these simulacra, an obscurantist pseudolanguage, spelled like English, generally followed—if stiffly uncomfortable and self-conscious—the syntax of English but escaped completely any meaningful sense. In America, these nonsense productions came largely from the academic world; in Europe, they emanated from journals (the *Score, Die Reihe*), composer conclaves such as Darmstadt in Germany, and "research" installations, IRCAM in Paris being the prime example. All had winter in their souls. For another, paralleling these unwarmed sounds and words there was apparent a posture of assumed certainty from both the serialists and the chance (aleatory) composers—but for totally different reasons. In the case of the serialists it was the iron-clad logic of the total control they thought they were exerting over what they considered the "parameters" of measurable functions (in their view *all* dimensions of music were subject to such controls) that gave them the security of certitude. The chance composers' certitude was, paradoxically, born of Eastern/Zen Buddhist tenets of philosophy—not logical but metaphysical and rooted in uncertainty.

Regardless of the programmatic/ideological differences between them, both held their separate bundles of convictions with the faith and fervor of fanatic religious believers. As I interpreted it, the perceptible drop in temperature signaled an almost complete shift from heart to head while the serial–aleatory dichotomy settled into an aesthetic divide between a determination to achieve total control over every possible parameter of music—in short, total order—and a no-holds-barred belief in the wonders of randomness, a complete giving over to the unpredictables of chance. Amazing how "laws" of the universe and mind still escape human comprehension—yet both ended in an identical fall into indeterminateness: that is, both produced arrays of sound events, whether planned or unplanned, ordered or random, of indiscriminate shapes lacking all perceptible profiles of identity, therefore outside memorability, mere successions of audible sensations below the level of emotional and musical meaning.

The stubborn unwillingness of human beings to accept that existence—as lived, felt, thought—is an entirely uncertain enterprise was what undid twentieth-century music. The search for certainty underlies human efforts in all directions imaginable to establish the physical, emotional, and intellectual security of certitude. The problem, of course, is that there are too many different "certitudes" side by side contending with each other everywhere we turn. Long before religious monotheism and an obsessive belief in *one* god (however addressed) repeated in variant forms several times over, there was pantheism and a relaxed tolerance for whole pantheons of gods, goddesses, and lesser spirits animating the world. And before the development of modern science, which periodically revises its paradigms according to what it thinks is *more* "true" of the universe, superstition and ignorance set the standard for what was "true" about the world and, therefore, to be believed. Ironically, the very uncertainty that provided the driving force in human affairs, by virtue of the negative energies it produced, was exactly what was needed for the arts to flourish—and flourish they did. *Homo faber* struggled endlessly with the refractoriness of the materials out of which came the arts. No good or great artist is not also a fine craftsman.

Where music is concerned, along with the long and arduous development of the basically stable language we call tonality, there eventually arose the false illusion of aesthetic certainty. This became the undoing of twentieth-century musical thought and the illusions of the avant-garde: that it could replace the old, traditional certainty with a more precise, therefore, more dependable, certainty.

My own conviction is that it is precisely out of uncertainty—the primary condition of human existence—that art is made possible, not by resolving anything—whether those questions or dilemmas that intellect and rationality or religious belief of whatever kind are ill equipped to deal with—but by wresting from uncertainty (that arouses confusions and doubts) a pattern, a design, a shape, a totality that is convincing *musically*. Whatever it is or may be, art is neither science nor religion nor philosophy—and certainly not politics. It is at its best (given the grace of luck) when not driven by any of these things, and certainly not by an obsessive, single-minded faith in some form or other of a system or method, nor when made subject to outside demands and pressures (whatever they are) that do not come from the necessity of the making itself. That is my meaning when I say that uncertainty drives the artwork, is the seedbed of the composer's search for clarity as he makes specific choices within his overall command of craft. And if that craft falls short of what he needs to bring his work to full realization, then uncertainty drives his courage to continue the search.

When it became clear that I needed to restore to myself the discarded clarities of tonal thinking in whatever guise they had surfaced historically—baroque, classical, romantic, post-romantic—I took the necessary step to balance things out, for a language of expression that served the entire gamut of human emotions, the entire 360-degree complex of them. After the imbalances of modernism had run their course, it was not only essential to restore the cadence and the harmonic world in which it served to mark off the stream of ongoing musical thought in sensible periods for the sake of clear articulation, it was even more essential to position that articulated stream of tonal musical thinking as the polar opposite to the indeterminate structures of the atonal world born in the twentieth century.

That restoration made a whole range of polarities equally available to musical thinking. Translated this means various intensities—according to expressive demands—of dissonant, chromatic atonality juxtaposed against consonant, diatonic tonality. Beethoven already knew or intimated this possible state of polar opposition when, after the stormy, almost discontinuous instrumental gestures of the opening of the choral movement of his Ninth, he addresses the universe with the unexpectedly strange words of the baritone solo recitative, "O Freunde, nicht diese Töne!" (Oh, friends, not these sounds!), and then launches into the most joyous paean of all to the brotherhood of man ever composed. *Nicht diese Töne.* Not these sounds. What sounds is he talking about? The sounds that destroy peace and harmony, the sounds that bring disruption, pain, unhappiness, sadness, depression? Was this a prophetic insight into the darkness yet to break loose in the twentieth century and wreak havoc in music? Was this a foretelling, however shadowy and vague, of serialism's and aleatory's sinking into the wastes of indeterminateness? Then there's Beethoven's other strangely prophetic question-and-answer polarity, "Muss es sein? Es muss sein!" (Must it be? It must be!), which we find in his last quartet, op. 135: The Negative of Fear—of what, the future?—juxtaposed with the Positive of Resolve—to act despite risks and pitfalls.

I could continue spelling out other significant combinations of polar opposites. But mere accretion will not make my point any stronger. It is sufficient to have laid out the large blueprint of how I arrived at the necessity to make *Contra Mortem et Tempus* and *Music for the Magic Theater* as I did. This is the raison d'être for the language, the form of expression, and the content of that expression—in those works and the ones that came after. Without the presence of the past there is no balance in the present. The one stabilizes and anchors the other, and while they can do nothing to alleviate the heavy uncertainty that surrounds us, with a keen awareness of the past and its profound relation to the present in our consciousness, we can negotiate the hazards uncertainty lays in our paths—existentially *and* aesthetically. Together they can help remove the shackles of absolutes and free us from the false dreams of purity that marred and almost destroyed the twentieth century—and now threatens the twenty-first.

PART II

CHAPTER 9

A Passion According to the Twentieth Century

Third Symphony and the Juilliard Orchestra and Chorus

"Muddying the waters of the present with the clear waters of the past . . ." This phrase came to me while talking to a nonmusician friend of a young American composer who had to defend his dissertation to the faculty of a British university where he was pursuing an advanced degree. The question put to him was: how did he justify his desire to combine past tonal practice with twentieth/twenty-first-century nontonal practice? However pointedly ironic my phrase, it conveys my sense that such a question is—considering what has happened over the past thirty-five years—wholly irrelevant. What's more, it misses the crucial point that the view of art as a progressive motion from one stylistic consistency to another has given way to a more open, pluralistic view that allows for bringing together all manner of disparate gestures and languages. It spells out the paradigm shift from the long-standing insistence on a basic consistency of style, idea, and language to the conviction that a pluralism of means—a veritable *inconsistency* of styles, ideas, and languages (what some call "polystylism")—opens the door to a whole new range of possibilities. Simultaneously, it increases the risks of composition itself, because greater taste and judgment as well as historical knowledge now become essential to dealing convincingly with the difficulties inherent in handling *un*likeness and *dis*similarity. This question of likeness/unlikeness, similarity/dissimilarity was already active during the time of the formation of aesthetic attitudes that shaped the high baroque—the time of Handel and Bach. Preferences in how to treat the range of musical emotions and characters, particularly in multimovement instrumental works—suites, partitas, concertos—leaned heavily in the direction of one essential feeling and one gestural character per movement.

Thus, while each single movement may have maintained consistency, the work as a whole did not. With the establishment of classicism and the sonata-allegro form, however, an entirely different view came to prevail. The exposition of the sonata form, in which the composer stated his ideas (to be developed later and, finally, confirmed in the recapitulation), came to allow for the mixture of different emotional states and variations in the character of gestures. With Mozart and Beethoven, the exposition established two main thematic ideas or groups and a full-scale closing cadential section. It would not be difficult to imagine that musicians whose lives spanned the transitional shift from the high-baroque view of the aesthetics of formal content to that of the classical view were sharply divided in their loyalties.

All of which opens the way to how I fulfilled the commission for a large work offered me by the Juilliard School of Music in 1966. Peter Mennin, head of Juilliard, whom I'd known since the time of the *Night Music* performances with Dimitri Mitropoulos, called to ask if I would be interested in writing a large work for the school orchestra and, if I wanted, for the school's excellent chorus. He was offering to put at my disposal exactly the kinds of forces I had been dreaming about for some years. I leapt at the chance, because it renewed in me the sense of a conception I had been nurturing since 1959. It was a conception for a choral work with large orchestra whose texts would allow me to deal with the enormity of the human tragedy that had overtaken the twentieth century, without falling into the obvious clichés and pathetic sentimentalism that marred virtually every attempt I know, with one significant exception: Primo Levi's *Se questo è un uomo*.[1]

Here was a chance to tackle head-on what I had conceived years before but till then had eluded me. The work I brought to completion in 1969—large though it was—never could have approached the full dimensions of the original conception, but it did capture and convey its core, its essence. I called the new symphony—my third—*A Passion According to the Twentieth Century,* modeling the form of its phraseology on the New Testament's Gospel according to Mark and borrowing the term "passion" from its profound association with the sufferings of Jesus Christ immortalized in J. S. Bach's *St. Matthew Passion*. What I intended by calling the Third Symphony "A Passion According to the Twentieth Century" was to open the widest possible reach—without specifying historically real events—the sense of the impossibility of conveying the sufferings of millions upon millions of human beings at the hands of an anthropomorphized "Twentieth Century" whose collective, evil physiognomy one had to turn away from for fear of being turned to stone.

What emerged was a work of symphonic proportions that was structurally a giant collage/assemblage for double mixed choruses, chamber chorus, a quartet of soprano, alto, tenor, and bass soloists, and a considerably expanded orchestra. The tradition of the great choral works of Bach and Handel, which continued in the religious and secular monuments of Haydn, Mozart, and Beethoven and climaxed in Mahler's Eighth Symphony, held an endless fascination for me, especially their sheer grandeur rooted in the contrapuntal art and polyphony of the baroque. This, too, acted as a basic source and form of expression of the Third but conveyed a stark difference because of its collage/assemblage aspects. The first performance took place in the Juilliard Theater in Lincoln Center on November 24, 1970, with the Juilliard Orchestra and Chorus, the Collegiate Chorale, soprano Joyce Mathis, alto Joy Blakett, tenor John Russell, and bass Robert Shiesley, all under the direction of Abraham Kaplan.

Kaplan's reputation rested largely on his being considered a particularly good choral conductor. Unfortunately, there was far more to the Third Symphony than just choruses. There was also a very much enlarged orchestra with six flutes, six oboes, five clarinets plus bass clarinet and contrabass clarinet, five bassoons plus contrabassoon, six horns, eight trumpets, four trombones with two bass trombones and contrabass trombone, three tubas with contrabass tuba, piano, pipe organ, electronic organ, glockenspiel, celesta, vibraphone, timpani, assorted percussion, and strings. This massive, Berlioz-sized orchestra was a natural outgrowth of the necessity to be able to project the heightened, spiritual intensities of the emotional drama I wanted to depict through the soloists and massed voices of the several choruses. The collage/assemblage nature of the work required a conductor who knew how to coordinate multiple choral and soloists' parts with an instrumental body not always in metric synchronicity with the voices—a taxing job for any conductor.

To his credit, Kaplan came through with a coherent, if not always totally satisfying, performance. It seemed to me that his chief concerns never went beyond merely managing the flow and movement of the music in purely mechanical terms. From beginning to end of rehearsals and that single performance of the Third, he never seemed to grow, nor show any interest or curiosity about what lay behind my choice of texts or my use of past and present in joining my musical thoughts to those of Heinrich Schütz, J. S. Bach, Beethoven, Mahler, and Charles Ives—neither their raison d'être nor their possible meanings. What saved the day was the total commitment and dedication of the almost three hundred Juilliard students who sang the solo and choral parts and played in the orchestra. Combined with the strength and professionalism of the Collegiate Chorale, they sang and played with fervent belief in the music and made my Third Symphony come alive.

The texts I chose, three in number—two in German and one in Latin—unify themselves around my idea of twentieth-century man's "passion": the terrible drama of his unending struggle with his own nature and the radical, extreme forms of behavior to which he resorts in his too-often-overheated frantic efforts to wrest *certainty* from *uncertainty*.

Each of the texts comes from a work of the living past. The source of the principal text that dominates the *Passion* is the cantata "Saul, Saul, was verfolgst du mich" (SWV 415) by the baroque composer Heinrich Schütz (1585–1672):

> Saul, Saul, was verfolgst du mich?
> Es wird dir schwer werden
> Wider den Stachel zu löcken

Its King James translation is:

> Saul, Saul, why do you persecute me?
> It will be hard for you to kick against the pricks[2]

The line "Was verfolgst du mich?" (Why do you persecute me?) reverberates throughout the work. It saturates the very body and soul of it. Its emotional/spiritual essence centers on this human outcry, its never-ending questioning. The after statement, "Es wird dir schwer werden / Wider den Stachel zu löcken" suggests other possible meanings besides the New Testament one, "it will be hard for you to kick against the pricks." The phrase "to kick against the pricks" is the sticking point I can't get past. It suggests "pricks of conscience." I can't imagine anyone with obsessively held beliefs suffering "pricks of conscience" as they go about the unrelenting business of hunting down, pursuing, and persecuting heretics, doubters, apostates, unbelievers. The potential for such fanaticism exists in the human genome. Were it not so, human typology would not produce over and over again the religious zealot, the political ideologue, the doctrinaire intellectual, the hidebound aesthetic zealot. The records and history of our afflicted species are replete with endless examples, documentation, and proofs—early and late—that bear out the reprehensible behavior of those who have and continue to demand "purity" or "loyalty" or "consistency" in matters of race, religion, politics, ideas, art.

Next in prominence in the *Passion* is "Durch Adams Fall ist Ganz Verderbt" (Through Adam's fall all is lost), the title of two organ preludes by J. S. Bach based on the Lutheran chorale tune of the same name.[3] If we understand "Adam's Fall" as "the fall of man" and the phrase "all is lost" as "the loss of Paradise," we are at the doorstep of the title's eschatological meaning: the death and ultimate destiny of man brought upon himself by his faithlessness and disloyalty while still in the Garden of Eden. However, there are other ways of unlocking the meanings that lie in the notion that "through the fall of man everything was lost." Far more compatible to my understanding, for example, is the interpretation that "through the fall of man into consciousness [i.e., self-awareness], man entered into uncertainty," or the Blakean coloration "through the fall from Innocence man entered into Experience." In each case, including the literal meaning of the title itself, "man is doomed to uncertainty and all its painful quandaries and dilemmas."

Finally, the third text is drawn from the Catholic mass, and its musical source from Beethoven's *Missa Solemnis:* "Agnus Dei, qui tollis peccata mundi, miserere nobis" (O Lamb of God, who takest away the sins of the world, have mercy on us).

It's not likely that I chose the texts and their musical sources with any conscious foreknowledge of their possible interrelated meanings and combinations, but more than likely, I proceeded by an intuitive sense of what fit, what felt right, what worked in any given situation. This would have been the case in developing an especially large collage/assemblage that depended on action-reaction continuity and structural buildup rather than working out in advance a more consciously formal design. It is in reflection that a number of striking interconnections have presented themselves, and they are what I describe before approaching the purely musical aspects of the *Passion*.

The interpenetrations of "Was verfolgst du mich," "Durch Adams Fall," and the Agnus Dei set going profound psychological, spiritual, philosophical resonances that I tried to capture in special kinds of inferential ways in the combinations only music makes possible: for example, by combining in polyphony the texts and musics of the fugue subject I wrote on "Was verfolgst du mich" in the same context with one of the Bach organ chorale preludes, now set for chorus, on "Durch Adams Fall" (starting at m. 344 and ending at m. 371, where it joins an extended, climactic elaboration of elements of the fugue subject). In another example of polyphonic combination (mm. 461–75), the quartet of soloists sings the text "Was verfolgst du mich" within overlapping pairs (bass/tenor, tenor/alto, alto/soprano) accompanied by Choruses I and II singing the crucial part of the Agnus Dei, the Miserere nobis. Between these two instances, there is another example, this time of two different fugue subjects brought together as a double fugue: the F-minor fugue of the *Marcia funèbre* of Beethoven's "Eroica" Symphony, where I have parts of the two choruses singing the text of "Durch Adams Fall" while other parts sing the fugue tune I wrote to "Was verfolgst du mich" (mm. 417–36).

Besides the three text sources and their associated musics there are, additionally, purely instrumental sources that play major roles in the totality of the work. There are instances where the fit between two works composed hundreds of years apart defies rational explanation. All one can do is marvel that such strange phenomena occur at all. This is exactly the case as the work approaches its conclusion: the coda of the first movement of Beethoven's Ninth Symphony and my last reference to Schütz's cantata come together in an astonishingly perfect harmonic match. The Schütz fits *inside* the grandeur of the Beethoven as though it had always been there and needed only to be called forth. The only immediate clues as to why these two passages from different times and musical cultures seem to belong to each other is that both are enfolded in a huge D-minor harmonic envelope, both evoke an identical ethos, both give off the same spiritual overtones. I will return to this unexpectedly synchronous fit between the two works by Schütz and Beethoven produced roughly two hundred years apart.

The Beethoven references, in addition to the F-minor fugue from the "Eroica" I set to "Durch Adams Fall," the enclosure of Schütz by the *basso ostinato* coda of the Ninth Symphony first movement, and the Agnus Dei from the *Missa Solemnis,* also include two powerful passages from the Fifth Symphony that occur toward the end of the opening movement. These I set to "Was verfolgst du mich." From Mahler's First and Second symphonies I borrowed far-off (*lontano*) fanfares that enter the fabric of the orchestral music as intrusive, troublesome-sounding commentary.

Finally, the "question" (asked by solo trumpet) and one of the "answers" (given by winds) of Ives's *Unanswered Question* of 1903 are incorporated in vocal and instrumental form. Which of the unanswerable questions that plague human beings Ives may have had in mind when he wrote this remarkable music no one knows. I chose to include Ives's "question" because in its sound I heard the same quality and the same spirit of the primary question my *Passion According to the Twentieth Century* asks over and over again, has asked in every generation of man since the beginning and doubtless will never be stilled.

Returning to the more immediate issue of the strange, echoing reverberations across the centuries between the Schütz cantata and the first-movement coda of Beethoven's Ninth, it's fair to say that dialogue between different times and different cultures is a fundamental premise of my collage/assemblage works. It is what grants to such compositions as *Music for the Magic Theater* and my Third Symphony an almost "natural" sense of a strangely familiar musical speech even when the elements being worked come from other times and other composers.

The same holds true to a marked degree in my later noncollage works, structured in more traditionally formal fashion, where different elements from widely separated cultures and composers appear. The premise itself that a dialogue is possible between and among disparate elements from disparate times and cultural climes is not so strange once one grasps the still deeper, underlying premise that change itself, issuing in seemingly unrelated and unrelatable changes in expression, impulse, and substance, rests on an unchanging core. An enlargement of perspective of how we view time and how that affects human culture and its endlessly shifting and changing surface manifestations becomes the key to intuiting the commonality of suddenly seeing or hearing the dialogue taking place between dissimilar-seeming surfaces.

In the West we have so inured our minds to the idea of time as an arrow moving only in one direction—always to the future—that we have handcuffed ourselves to the rational habit of viewing the arrow of time as a material substance by which we live out our candle-brief existence. We measure in precise units of time the length of that existence and all the events—actual and imagined—that make up its duration.

I used to introduce the "uncertainty principle" of the perception of temporal duration to my composition students by playing for them complete (because relatively brief) movements of the music of the twentieth-century composer Anton Webern, asking them to gauge the duration of the movements in seconds or minutes. In a class of roughly a dozen people, answers would range from ten or fifteen seconds to a minute or a minute and a half. When I read them the printed timing of the particular recorded example, mildly embarrassed smiles mingled with visible expressions of shock.

I confess to a marked preference for the notion of time as felt, experienced, perceived motion through patterns and configurations of change. Only within the limitations of our own capacities can we lay claim to "knowledge" of such changes within ourselves and to a far lesser degree in the natural environs around us. We can claim experience—subjective knowledge—of life cycles, felt and observed, but we cannot claim the same for solar cycles or galactic cycles, where processes involving changes of enormous proportions lie far outside the range of our sensory capacities, our perceptions—even though they may probably be observable, but in ways very limited to the astronomical instruments, including satellites, available to professional astronomers and cosmologists.

Alternately, I am suggesting that what we call motion through time is the passage of energy forms and forces through cycles of change which have no Hegelian future in their sights. Music, then, becomes an almost perfect metaphor for this passage of energy forms and forces shaped by human beings through cycles of patterned change in the best of all possible worlds. In music, only the present is present because it is the only experientially felt, therefore real, time. Which may prove to be, on the closest examination, why different musics from different times and cultures can talk to each other, can dialogue, without discomfort or self-consciousness.

I invoke one last argument: such a dialogue is possible because "All music is the work of One Mind." The Eternal Present in which the One Mind exists is the "present" I referred to earlier as the only temporal division possible to music. Even double bar repeats, da capo returns to repetitions of earlier sections, recapitulations of previous thematic ideas in sonata form—none of them recovers a "past" recalled, because all of them continue to live only in the "present," which is the temporal condition of music. Strangely, this is corroborated by an experience characteristic of the composer's mind in the very act of working out his/her ideas—their progression, succession, and repetition: even though live *performance* of music takes place in clock time (for example, a Mahler symphony might last eighty minutes), the composer's mind is capable of encompassing not only an inward hearing of the work as it unfolds, thus imagining the successive condition of live performance, but more importantly, figuratively, to "see"—as though in spatial arrangements—the positions various ideas take up in the design of the work imagined. Thus crucial decisions are arrived at that determine whether a reappearance of an idea is to be condensed, enlarged, or varied in ways that retain identifying characteristics while changing them significantly to suggest connections to other ideas. By this spatializing process of seeing the work all-at-once, important decisions affecting disposition of placement and, particularly, comparisons between appearances of the same or similar ideas can be "seen" while, simultaneously, "heard."

The sources out of which the *Passion* is fashioned come more from premodern than modern repertoire, relying heavily, as they do, on the baroque and classical: Heinrich Schütz and J. S. Bach; Beethoven's "Marcia funèbre" fugue, itself somewhat anomalous because while its thematic spirit is baroque, its scalar counterpoint is not—especially in its thematic sequences; Beethoven's Agnus Dei from the *Missa Solemnis;* and the coda to the first movement of Beethoven's Ninth Symphony. Despite the atonality at the beginning and end of the work, despite frequent intensification through atonal, expressionistic chromaticism that clearly identifies it as music of the mid-twentieth century, despite the giant eggbeater, chaotic climax produced by the sheer noise of choral and instrumental fragments and figures clashing with each other in randomly frenetic fashion—despite all of its use of modernist devices, modernist frenzy, and modernist language, when all is said and done, the overall sense and impression of the *Passion* is of a work whose essence is steeped in the baroque, whose spirit and sound are redolent of the baroque. Whether it is character, ethos, or indelibility of musical profile, it is the baroque that subsumes all the other musics and leaves its unmistakable stamp.

Even a collage/assemblage, which tends to be loose and free in its successive associations and unfoldings, still needs an audible coherence of procedure beneath its mask of spontaneity. I am convinced that it was my initial choice of the three texts and the clusters of combinations of texts and musical sources that grew out of their mixtures that became the determining factors in the ultimate, emerging organization of the Third Symphony. As with all collages and assemblages, the resulting form is a growth toward a whole rather than predetermined. It is what defines the spirit of the collage/assemblage as a freely evolving concatenation of diverse, often contentious, elements and tendencies.

Recently a friend sent me this passage from the prose writings of Czesław Milosz, the great Polish poet:

> . . . what occurred in Poland was an encounter of an European poet with the hell of the twentieth century, not hell's first circle, but a much deeper one. . . . [4] [In that environment] people's attitude toward the language also changes. It recovers its simplest function and is again an instrument serving a purpose; no one doubts that the language must name reality, which exists objectively, massive, tangible, and terrifying in its concreteness.[5]

Naming the "reality, which exists objectively," was what I attempted to do in my *Passion According to the Twentieth Century*. I knew it could be done only indirectly, because the means of human expression are insufficient and inadequate to "name" the horrors that constitute the depths of the hell of human actions in the twentieth century. Terms like *holocaust, ethnic cleansing, killing fields, gulags,* and *concentration camps* are only symbolic cues—arrows pointing to something still unnamable. Monstrous, monumental evil cannot be shown entire, neither grasped nor comprehended through the meager symbols and language we have. I'm not even sure they are adequate to our feelings.

Until the twentieth century, mankind went through contortions of soul and mind to avoid confronting the simple but dreadful truth that evil was not some malevolent force or power that emanated from external agencies let loose on the world—often with God's express permission to chasten and test His creation so that some "good" might result; in this regard the prologue to the biblical story of Job becomes a ludicrous parody on the whole question of "good and evil"—but for which mankind itself is solely responsible. No matter that as respected and admired an intellectual as Hannah Arendt tried to downsize evil by calling it "banal." Evil remains intractably intrinsic to human nature. It is, as Milosz put it, "massive, tangible and terrifying in its concreteness." *We* are the objective reality simply by being here and being what we are.

"O for a Muse of Fire"

Eliot Fisk and Works for Guitar— Solo, Duo, and Ensemble

In the fall of 1989 my publisher called saying Carnegie Hall wanted to know if I would consider a commission for a work for Eliot Fisk, the brilliant young virtuoso guitarist. While we'd never met, I had heard some Fisk recordings and was particularly impressed by the consummate art and sensitivity he and Paula Robison, his flutist partner, had brought to their recording of Robert Beaser's *Mountain Songs*.[1] The 1990–91 season would be Carnegie Hall's centennial, and the hall's management wanted to present a number of outstanding performers in concert, playing works written especially for them by composers of their choice. I was Fisk's—but what did he have in mind? Something for guitar and string quartet, my publisher said. "Guitar and string quartet? I'm sorry, but that doesn't interest me at all. Please tell Carnegie I'm happy to know Fisk wants a work from me, but the combination he proposes leaves me cold."

Unspoken but running through my mind was the objection that, in purely musical terms, the guitar's inherent limitations of power of acoustical projection would act to inhibit the quartet's full expressive range—especially its ability to flare out in passion. Then again, in order for the voice of the guitar to be heard at all—considerations of the lack of sufficient differentiation in color contrasts aside—the quartet would have to take a more modest, inevitably secondary role. Even though I thought I had shut the door on the whole idea, something kept nagging at me. What if Fisk would agree to my writing a flute/guitar duo for him and Paula Robison—a piece with plenty of room for contrasts of color and expression? The combination intrigued me first for its idiomatic possibilities, and second because it removed any qualms about their individual voices being heard.

Fired by the idea, I called my publisher, told him I had reconsidered and would be happy to accept the commission if Fisk would agree to a duo for himself and his partner. After a few more calls it was settled to everyone's satisfaction, and I looked forward to a first meeting with Fisk in New York.

The impact of Eliot's playing still rings clear and fresh as though I'd only just heard it. There was a vitality and musical intelligence in his playing one finds in only the very best performers. The emotional intensity and intellectual conviction of his passion for music won me over completely. It had everything to do with my willingness to keep struggling against what I felt were the hurdles in the way of writing for so idiosyncratic an instrument as the guitar—and struggle I did for almost a decade to produce, along with other more congenial things, not one but four substantial works for Eliot: either solo, duo, or ensemble. With each one he was my sure guide through the knots and tangles of how to bring to life the infinitely subtle shades and nuances of the many *voices* of the guitar. Even more he showed me how to write out in clear notation the esoterica of the surprisingly large vocabulary of sound qualities and their corresponding registral positions only a master guitarist would command and know how to produce and notate. Eliot demonstrated the seemingly numberless ways of producing one specific pitch, one single note, each with a slightly different timbral quality and resonance. After all my years of composing, suddenly I had become a student again, working diligently to overcome a major gap in my education and experience.

With no to-do or awkward formality, Eliot launched into his magical introduction to the glories of his instrument. He played his own astonishing transcription of the still-amazing chaconne from the solo violin D-Minor Partita of J. S. Bach. It bowled me over. I could not have been more than six feet from where Eliot was playing. Like great waves the music poured over me. It was no longer an object of perception outside of me; it was a force that swept over and included me. I became an element in its surging, singing melodic/harmonic sweep of fantastic variations tumbling one after another out of the womb of the world.

I wanted to write something that would fit Eliot's large, expansive nature and his and Paula's consummately expressive music making. Before I could begin work on such a piece I needed to pave the way by writing something smaller, something less ambitious in scale, a flute/guitar duo where I could try my hand at writing idiomatically *for* the guitar as opposed to merely producing a neuter-gender part lacking personality. In the past I had steeped myself in the spiritually saturated slow movement of J. S. Bach's *Italian Concerto* for solo harpsichord. When the need came over me I would play it over and over at the piano. Its meditative beauty was the perfect antidote to having to contend with a world that "is too much with us: late and soon, getting and spending," where "we lay waste our powers."[2] I never tired of its purity of line, its perfection of harmony. It seemed only right that its endless melody be the cantilena of the flute and the harmonic figures of the harpsichord accompaniment be the basis for a reworking for guitar. Keeping always in mind Bach's essential musical thought, I recomposed his accompanimental pattern without altering its original harmonic function. To suit the guitar I changed the key from D minor to E minor; and again for the sake of the guitar and its newly invented accompanimental pattern, I enlarged the metric structure by an additional beat, which necessitated changing the time signature from 3/4 to 4/4 and accommodating the melodic flute line to the different metric structure. In carrying out this reworking I opened up the two large phrases that constitute the movement's form in order to allow the guitar to echo the melodic closures, first stated by the flute, and their harmonic cadences at the end of both phrases, and also to make room for a fairly extensive cadenza for solo guitar before the flute rejoins its partner for the final cadence. Times being what they were in the last years of the twentieth century, I decided to call the piece *Ora Pro Nobis* (Pray for Us). It was completed in February 1990. Eliot and Paula gave its first performance January 25, 1991, in Zanesville, Ohio.

It seems humans are always in conflict, always at war. What we euphemistically call "peace" is merely the *absence* of war. Eliot's program note to the CD that contains his and Paula's recording of *Muse of Fire*,[3] the Carnegie commission I wrote for them, is a reminder that in the period in which I wrote *Ora Pro Nobis* and *Muse of Fire*. America had gone to war to free Kuwait from the aggressive grasp of the Iraqi dictator Saddam Hussein. The Israelis and Palestinians were at each other's throats, locked in daily mortal combat, and Russia—close to the end of its historically brief guise as the Soviet Union—was beaten badly and driven out of Afghanistan while at the same time it made bitter war on Chechnya, one of its Muslim states.

Our culture—does it even deserve to be called "civilization"?—is such now that regardless of whether actual war is happening somewhere, anywhere on this globe or not, an ever-avid public appetite for the vicarious is being fed a steady stream of war movies old and new, endlessly repeated reports of real conflicts fill the TV screen, and enactments of the devastations of war thrive in live theater. The British actor-director Kenneth Branagh took Shakespeare's most brutal portrayal of war, *Henry V,* from the stage to the film screen[4] and gave to it what Shakespeare alone could limn: searing visual realism. Branagh's cinema version appeared in the same period as I began work on my conception of the *Muse.* What is absolutely clear is that the title came to me because of Branagh's compelling film and the opening lines of *Henry V*: "O for a muse of fire, that would ascend / The brightest heaven of invention." Shakespeare reminded me in this potently striking figure what it is every composer longs for: to be able to "ascend the brightest heaven of invention" guided by "a muse of fire."

Muse of Fire, begun in 1989, was completed in Italy in April 1990 during a five-week stay at the Rockefeller Foundation Bellagio Study and Conference Center, which sits high up on the Bellagio promontory overlooking Lake Como. From our room in the spaciously large and gracious Villa Serbelloni we could see, directly below, the landings where the boats docked, letting people off, taking on new passengers as they ferried back and forth, crisscross, to the towns that dotted the lake's shores. At any time of the day this made for a lively, colorful scene, heightened by the sound of church bells from the tower of a nearby cathedral. In the distance on the far side of the lake loomed the Alps, made even grander by seeing their lofty peaks beyond the often choppy waters of Lake Como. After a cold or rainy night, in the morning we could see the peaks capped with fresh snow in the warming sun. And if we looked left out our bathroom window we could see Lake Lecco on the other side of the promontory that divided it from Lake Como.

The studio for composers—wisely, there was never more than one composer in residence at any given time—was built into the solid rock of a hill deep in the woods at some distance from the Villa. We dubbed it "the Bunker." Work on the *Muse* was far enough along when we arrived that I was able to finish it without difficulty or delay. This allowed us time to explore the grounds of the Villa Serbelloni, which led up by stages to the top of the promontory through beautifully kept gardens and wooded areas. The very peak of the promontory offered a view of both sun-drenched lakes glistening far below with millions of diamond flecks of reflected light, the boats tiny in the distance. A golden haze lay over the glowing stillness . . . nothing moved . . . time stopped . . . It was then that I experienced the hidden essence of *serenissima*—the unearthly, serene beauty of the world behind the scrim of its space—and timebound *maya*, its surface reality. Not until years later—1994–95—was I able to come even close, in the final section of my Concerto for Clarinet and Orchestra, to evoking a sense of what *serenissima* had come to mean to me. Like all the impalpables of existence, the sense of the ineffable eludes direct translation into the too-precise language of music.

Writing *Ora Pro Nobis* had helped me over initial inhibitions where the guitar was concerned. With the *Muse* I felt that any possible kinks had been dispensed with and I proceeded with a newly gained feeling of freedom, able to turn in whatever direction the piece itself seemed to want to go. There are those undeniable times when a work exhibits a will of its own that must be obeyed. In this instance, its "will" and my own were in perfect accord. It had to be a *fantasia,* a one-movement work with a released, high-spirited play of gestures and ideas that would give both instruments full opportunity to exhibit their individually idiomatic selves. At the same time, it should coordinate different functions of motivic interplay through utterance and response and contain long melodic lines for the flute and energetic accompanying harmonic support from the guitar, with frequent, if brief, contrapuntal intersections of figures between the two. It had to be a *fantasia* with a high temperature, at times even overheated. With what? Desperation, or ecstatic release? Some form of high tension—which in music is unnameable. Certainly passionate in explosive utterances for both instruments, dropping to strange echoes, drumbeats—*tambour* on the guitar suggests the sound of distant drums—intimating what? War? Strange mixtures of motives of fragmented lyricism for flute, echoes in guitar—extroverted bursts of animation relapsing into introverted withdrawals—guitar mutterings, aborted lyric figures.

There is one long, continuous tune in which both join in the traditional pattern of flute carrying the ecstatic melodic release and guitar accompanying with running arpeggiated harmonic figures progressing through tonal motions that verge on a kind of "south of the border" pop tune. (Inspired perhaps by distant associations with Villa-Lobos's *Brasilieras,* of which I was once very fond?) The first statement of the tune, marked "Allegro con brio" begins at measure 196 and continues to measure 272. The line never cadences into closure but breaks into a duo cadenza for both players, then picks up again for its balancing second long phrase at measure 339, breaks off at measure 393—and after a pause begins a new section with new motives and figurations, again with *tambour* drumbeats echoing in the distance. When the *Muse* ends it is in a burst of tempestuous nervous energy that takes it to the very edge of controlled chaos.

Oddly, I have no memory of the first performance of *Muse of Fire,* which took place February 1, 1991, in Carnegie Hall. What I do remember, however, is a rehearsal in Paula Robison's apartment, where we polished everything to a fine point. It was clear that Eliot and Paula had a firm grasp of the shape of the work and responded to its *brio,* its way of dropping into quietnesses and suddenly erupting again into fiery flashes of high temperature. By the time they recorded the *Muse* they were in full command—they played as though they "owned" it.

Several sources fed into the seven-section collection of "versions" of American popular music to which I gave the title *American Bouquet:* first and foremost, my lifelong love for the best of that vast ocean of songs from the 1920s into the

1950s that caught the buoyant spirit of wit, hope, and energy that helped carry America through the Great Depression and past World War II. Secondly, my great admiration for the magical alchemy of Bartók's transformations of Central European folk music to a wholly different level of composition, which suggested something of a similar nature might be accomplished with American popular music if approached in an analogous spirit; and finally, the very real possibility that Eliot may well be right when he reminds me that the night he and Paula premiered the *Muse,* he had played some solo guitar pieces of Villa-Lobos whose "impassioned romanticism" gave me the direct impetus to set about writing the *Bouquet.*

Here are the seven sections—with titles, composers, and dates of composition—of the versions I made of five songs by some of the best composers of those early years plus the two pieces I wrote for the set:

1. "My Heart Stood Still" (Richard Rodgers) (unknown date)
2. "I Only Have Eyes for You" (Harry Warren) (May 29, 1991)
3. "Two Sleepy People" (Hoagy Carmichael) (May 13, 1991)
4. "Liza" (George Gershwin) (May 30–June 2, 1991)
5. "How to Explain" (Rochberg) (May 13, 1991)
6. "Deep Purple" (Peter DeRose) (May 12, 1991)
7. "Notre Dame Blues" (Rochberg) (May 23, 1991)

Eliot premiered the entire set of seven at the Manhattan School of Music in New York City on February 13, 1997. At one time or another he would program a small group of two or three along with more conventional fare to find out how audiences reacted. Gradually, over time, Eliot grew more comfortable with the style of this music, its inherent looseness of shape and phrase, its harmonies reflective of the harmonic world of late nineteenth-century romanticism mixed with incipient impressionism and, not least, its range of feelings from the romantic to the raw sensuality of blues to the more complex, borderline atonal idiom of 1950s bebop—best characterized by Thelonious Monk's search for the "thirteenth tone."

At first Eliot didn't have the faintest inkling of what this music was about. He knew it existed, but only in some distant, parallel universe to the one he inhabited musically. But he learned, and eventually I believe it had something to do with helping to expand his musical horizons. He told me he had been in touch with jazz guitarists and even branched out in the direction of learning about flamenco guitar playing—which, from even the little I know, is a completely different world, extraordinarily vivid, intense, and rhythmically complex beyond description. With the release of the recording in 2000,[5] Eliot demonstrated complete mastery of the

American Bouquet. There he sounds completely at home, as though he had been born to the musical worlds represented.

───

Eden: Out of Time and Out of Space was planned as a chamber concerto for a mixed ensemble of winds and strings and is the largest of the four works I wrote for Eliot Fisk. So as not to overwhelm the sound of the guitar, I purposely kept the size of the ensemble to a sextet of flute, clarinet, French horn, violin, viola, and cello. In part this decision resulted from my reaction to having previously heard in live concert overly ambitious ensemble works in which the guitar was intended to be the soloist but, instead, had to struggle to be heard against over-powering numbers of instruments. It was crucial to frame a context in which the guitar would never be overwhelmed—musically or acoustically. Most important was my desire to produce as delicate and quietly intimate-sounding a piece of music as I could. *Eden: Out of Time and Out of Space* was written in 1997, co-commissioned by Chamber Music Northwest (Portland, Oregon) and the Chamber Music Society of Lincoln Center (New York City). The first performances took place in Portland on July 2 and 3, 1998, with subsequent performances in Alice Tully Hall, New York City, on November 15 and 17, 1998.

I wanted my work to sound hushed, withdrawn, intimate, distant, and, above all, delicate and full of tracery. This coincided with how I understood a brief passage in one of the dedicatory poems William Butler Yeats wrote for his verse play *The Shadowy Waters* (1905), in which he asks:

> Is Eden far away, . . . ?
> . . . Do our woods
> And winds and ponds cover more quiet woods,
> More shining winds, more star-glimmering ponds?
> Is Eden out of time and out of space?[6]

The title of the chamber concerto arose from my feeling that, *if there were an-swers to such unanswerable questions,* Eden, the heaven of our longing and desire for release from pain and suffering, was where Yeats conjectured that paradise might be: out of time and out of space . . . in another realm of different dimensions . . . but closed to us in the form in which we live out our lives and breathe . . . here on earth.

In its performances in Tully Hall, *Eden* sounded exactly as I hoped it would, as though heard through a scrim—distant, hushed, intimate, yet somehow close up. Serendipitously, the acoustical properties of the hall, combined with the atmosphere *Eden* covered itself with, produced just the right mix of veiled, magical sound. This had not been the case in the hall in Reed College earlier that summer. Not only were the hall's acoustics too hard and cold, the players, including Eliot as soloist, had not yet found their way into the superdelicate world of *Eden,* and the mix was not yet propitious for what I wanted. It awaited the performance in Tully Hall to arrive at that special magic—and arrive it did.

When I heard the Arabesque recording for the first time, the *Muse* and *Bouquet* sounded completely right: "upfront" with full presence and clarity, exactly what I wanted for them; but I was sorely disappointed in and puzzled by the recorded sound of *Eden.*[7] It had lost its *lontano,* its far-awayness, the magic of its hushed intimacy that had spread its invisible yet palpable atmospheric presence through Tully Hall. I began to puzzle out why this should be so.

I don't know where and under what conditions *Eden* was recorded, but I infer from the result that the recording studio itself must have had a dry and cold atmosphere; in other words, it was acoustically sterile. Perhaps, too, the microphone placements were not conducive to lending the sense of distance needed to approach the character of the work. It was, so I surmise, an extreme case of the inevitable divide between the manipulable/manipulated sound of electronically recorded music and the warm, live sound of music played and heard in a live hall full of people. Unhappily, the recording process itself had stripped *Eden* of its protective cover and left it completely uncovered—unwarmed and cold to the ear.

These thoughts are preface and prologue to considering a strangely elusive yet very real sense of a characteristic of virtually all music—regardless of language, style, or historical period of composition: the indefinable, immeasurable connections and relations between the quality of mind and spirit of the composer who in inexpressible ways unconsciously imparts to his/her music that inherent condition of being *covered* or its offputting condition of being *uncovered.* I can think of no way to describe in concrete terms, or explain in rational terms, what set of inherently musical states goes to make up the mysterious crystallization into one particular work being *covered* and another being *uncovered.*

It is impossible to say when and under what circumstances the idea that music could be covered or uncovered came to me. But if there is a single, external source, it has to be the cogent four-page essay I read decades ago by Lewis Thomas, which closes his remarkable *The Lives of a Cell.*

In "The World's Biggest Membrane"[8] Thomas describes, in poetic language, the singularly delicate process by which the earth grew the membrane we call "the sky." "Viewed from the distance of the moon," he writes, "the astonishing thing about the earth, catching the breath, is that it is alive." By contrast, the moon, battered and pounded for eons by meteorites, is "dead as an old bone."

Aloft, floating free beneath the moist, gleaming membrane of bright blue sky, is the rising earth, the only exuberant thing in this part of the cosmos. . . . It has the organized, self-contained look of a live creature full of information, marvelously skilled in handling the sun.[9]

Thomas outlines the stages by which "the earth came alive" and "began constructing its own membrane, for the general purpose of editing the sun." Editing the sun entailed the essential development of sufficient quantities of oxygen in order for the rays of the sun to penetrate the atmosphere—the sky-membrane it was growing—and, at the same time, to filter out

> the very bands of ultraviolet light that are most devastating for nucleic acids and proteins, while allowing full penetration of the visible light needed for photosynthesis. If it had not been for this semipermeability, we could never have come along. . . . Now we are protected against lethal ultraviolet rays by a narrow rim of ozone, thirty miles out.[10]

Besides breathing for us so that we can breathe, the earth's "biggest membrane"— what Thomas calls the "miraculous achievement" which is our sky—protects us every minute of every day against "millions of meteorites [that] fall against the outer limits of the membrane and are burned to nothing by the friction. Without this shelter, our surface would long since have become the pounded powder of the moon."[11]

Thomas provided me with the analogy of the aliveness of the earth, which produces out of its organized self its own protective covering—the atmosphere of the bright blue sky, magical in the light of the sun it lets shine through while suffused by it at the same time. This is what I mean by music being covered: like the earth, such music grows its own covering atmosphere, alive and breathing in its organic structure so that through its radiant sound it simultaneously reflects its living human source and origin. But like the unfortunate moon, which, having no self-grown, protective, covering atmosphere, is dead, uncovered music gives off no organic radiance of aliveness—it doesn't breathe, it has no atmosphere, nor is it organized for producing radiance and life. It remains the dead matter of the mere sounds of which it is compounded.

CHAPTER 10

Pictures of the Floating World

Ukiyo-E, Slow Fires of Autumn, Between Two Worlds, and *Imago Mundi*

Three weeks is hardly long enough to absorb the unique country and culture of Japan. Yet it was those three weeks Gene and I spent in the Land of the Rising Sun in the early summer of 1973 that translated directly into music for me. No people and no culture ever had remotely comparable the effect upon me as did the Japanese, their music, their art and theater. No travel experience beyond the borders of America had anywhere near the memorable effect of that Japanese experience. Not the trip to Australia in 1986, though I loved its earth colors, landscapes of high rolling hills and grazing sheep, its songbirds and exotic animals, its people and their easy ways. En route to Australia we had stopped at Tahiti, where astonishingly the people looked exactly as Gauguin had painted them, and on the return home we saw Fiji with its handsome, strong-featured, statuesque men and women and peaceful landscape.

Not even the five-month stay in 1957 in Mexico, with its strange admixture of Spanish genes, customs, and Catholicism coupled with indigenous Aztec Indian physiognomies and culture, the exotic colors, the bullfights, mariachi bands, earthquakes, and bad food. Not the Russia of the Soviet Union in October 1989 (where we traveled for performances of my Sixth Symphony) just before the great implosion that crumbled into dust and ruination an ill-starred social experiment. Not any of the three times I spent weeks and months in Israel, where I conducted and taught—the early summer of 1963, across the end of 1969 into the beginning of 1970, and the fall of 1982. The three world monotheisms were all still very much alive in the postage-stamp area that was once ancient Israel, with their inevitable tensions and wars. Each of these travel experiences left strong memories and impressions. But it was the exotic Japanese experience that most fascinated me and drew out of me music unlike any I'd previously composed, unlike because of its marked differences in color, texture, form, expression, emotional source, and range.

What took me to Japan was an invitation to participate in a conference of the International Society for the Study of Time, to be held at a hotel near Lake Yamanaka at the foot of Mount Fuji, the enormous, cone-shaped pile of rock and earth that looms over that part of Japan and, so they say, once was visible from as far away as old Edo, now Tokyo. Unfortunately, we never saw Fuji entire: its upper part and crater peak were shrouded in clouds and mists the whole time we were there. Its massive presence was palpable and extraordinarily oppressive, and I felt its ever-present, overbearing bulk constantly.

The invitation to participate in the "study of time" conference came from J. T. Fraser, the founder of the society. A brilliant man of restless energy, Fraser had the idea to treat the wide-ranging meanings and interpretations of time in a thoroughly interdisciplinary fashion by bringing together in conferences held in countries other than the U.S. an international group of men and women with strong professional interests in time and its endlessly ramifying paths—whether in the sciences or the humanities. My contribution to the 1973 Lake Yamanaka conference was a paper on "The Structure of Time in Music," where I traced the beginnings of rhythmic notation and temporal motion in medieval music through its evolution in the expanding forms of tonal music of the eighteenth and nineteenth centuries to the radical break that came with the atonal adventure in the twentieth.[1] With the advent of modernism and radically new thinking about pitch and time, music underwent a complete transformation in its profile and character. It adopted discontinuity, embraced the suspension of the beat, sacrificed the teleology of goal-directedness. All of these, together with a marked propensity for motionless motion and stasis, displaced time and its traditional sense of movement toward structural goals in favor of spatial imagery and its vibratory gestures of free-floating sounds and sound complexes.

The conference was stimulating for the ideas put forth, but also because of two totally unexpected events impossible to forget. Someone among the representatives of the Japanese university hosting the proceedings had the happy idea of inviting the "Yonin No Kai"—literally the "Group of Four"—ensemble of traditional instrument performers who established themselves in 1957 and by 1973 had become a Japanese national treasure. Their instruments included the *shakuhachi,* a vertical flute made of bamboo wood, and three different-sized *kotos.* Hearing the *shakuhachi* as played by Kozan Kitahara was strangely moving—as much for the incredible range of the subtle inflections of expression possible on it, which make the instrument sound almost human, as for its incredibly dark, rich, woody timbre in its lowest register and piercing poignancy in its upper register.

Before leaving Japan, we became friendly with the "Group of Four" and were invited—a rare experience for Western visitors—to the home of one of the *koto* players. What struck us was the stark contrast between the almost ascetic spareness of the Japanese part of the house, rooms in dark woods, virtually no furnishings or decorations other than the ubiquitous Japanese *tatami* mats on the polished wood floors—except for the niche holding a beautiful flower arrangement—and the "Western" room to which our hostess led us and her colleagues in her delightfully shy way. The sheer heaviness of the look of the overstuffed sofa and armchairs that sat there became heavier still against the clean spareness of the rest of the house. Oddly enough, I felt immediately at home because I'd grown up in rooms with just such furniture.

Kitahara kept urging me to write a piece for Yonin No Kai, even writing out the *koto* tuning, its scale or mode, and the respective ranges of the different sizes of the *koto,* whose timbre and resonance I became increasingly fond of. Unfortunately, I never took him up on his urgings: on the one hand, I was not sufficiently comfortable with the intriguing strangeness of the *shakahachi/koto* combination and its musical idioms and possibilities, yet on the other, I was drawn to the poetic expressiveness of the vertical flute and the reverberating strength of the attack timbre of the generic *koto.* Whether large or small, its pitches could be bent microtonally by pressure from the fingers of the left hand on the resonating string or strings. What I realize now, many years later, is that in a deeply subconscious way Kitahara's urgings and my still very fresh auditory memory of the *shakuhachi* and *koto* had a profound and lasting effect on me and the music I wrote after I returned to the States. For example, in my first *Ukiyo-E* for harp solo, I treated the harp more like a Japanese *koto,* finding ways to give the harp a wider spectrum of timbral variety in order to release the different colors and distinct resonances of the upper, middle, and lower registers. Without giving up the idiomatic harp glissandi, which can be extremely effective if used sparingly and in the right places, I wanted above all to get away from the hackneyed, mellifluous arpeggiation I associated with French harp music of the late nineteenth and early twentieth centuries.

The pleasantly odd coincidence of the farewell banquet dinner coming on July 5 produced the second event. I had paid no attention to the fact that that particular day was also my fifty-fifth birthday, but Gene had quietly arranged that it become part of the dinner festivities. When the chefs appeared, bearing a large, sculpted ice cream replica of Mount Fuji, the whole dining room burst into a rousing rendition of "Happy Birthday" pointed straight at me. What with the shouted pleasantries from my colleagues and friends, it made a joyful noise!

A special guest at dinner was a Japanese doctor who sat near Gene and me. He was an unusually impressive man with gaunt, craggy features, taller than most Japanese of the prewar generation. In excellent English, the doctor told us about Japanese music and especially of his love for Noh drama and its highly stylized singing—more, as we learned, a kind of intoned, bone-sad chanting projected in a tightly pinched, high-placed nasal tone of voice. He never mentioned the extreme *slowness* of Noh, something we experienced ourselves toward the end of our stay. That dreamlike slowness cast a spell over me: far more than mechanical slow motion, it is closer to an otherworldly pace, a form of floating, motionless motion, than any form of Western acting or theater I know of. That almost surreal, ritualized slowness, combined with the mournful, white-painted faces of the ghost characters telling their tragic tales costumed in ornately rich, traditional kimonos was mesmerizing. By some kind of intuitive understanding below the level of language, we heard, saw, and felt what was happening onstage. That slowness—which still haunts and grips me—reaches into the core of existence itself.

After the excitement of the birthday greeting, the doctor, addressing me directly, announced he was going to sing a Noh "song" in my honor. The room settled into rapt silence—and he began. His voice rose and fell with the emotions and meaning of the text; he became transformed by the authenticity of what he was vocalizing in the ritual intonations of Noh. It was magical. Not a professional Noh actor, yet he performed like one. Even though the listener may lack any knowledge of the "story" being told, nonetheless the dark pain of it, caught in the strangulated vocal sounds, is unmistakably conveyed. In those few moments he had opened the world of Noh to me. Turning to me, he asked, "Now, would you sing us an American song?"

Truth to tell, his request came as an even greater surprise—and shock—than the suddenness of the birthday greeting. With only a split second to decide what would suit the occasion—and knowing there was nothing of my own that fit the bill—I broke into a song by Cole Porter, one of my favorites, "You'd Be So Easy to Love." Even as I sang it I wondered if I could manage to put it across, knowing I had little memory for song lyrics. (Gene, on the other hand, is a living repository of all the old songs of American popular music—words *and* music.) I launched into it, giving as much shape as I could to Porter's beautiful line. The doctor seemed quite pleased and smiled his appreciation as the room broke into noise again.

I brought two musical souvenirs back from our trip, never dreaming each would become stimulus and source for music I would write. The first, a recorded set of ceremonial Gagaku court music played on traditional Japanese wind and percussion instruments, had a strong emotional appeal for me. From it I took the courage to try to write a work for large orchestra in which clear elements of Japanese music—and particularly Gagaku music—played a powerful role. *Imago Mundi* was the result. The second souvenir was a Japanese music box we found in a small shop—a beautiful, largish, light blue ball that looked like a Christmas tree ornament. When you pulled the chain that hung from it, it chimed a sadly sweet tune, which I learned from our pianist friend Etsko Tazaki was a very old traditional Japanese folk lullaby. It was that very affecting, melancholy, simple tune, with its irregular phrase shapes, that triggered my imagination when, some six years later, in 1978–79, I wrote *Slow Fires of Autumn* for flute and harp. Both works—different from each other in every possible regard—embraced completely the imagery and feel, the melodic and rhythmic characteristics, of their Japanese sources.

As soon as I had settled in after returning from Japan I began casting about for ideas for an orchestral work I had been commissioned to write for the Baltimore Symphony and had promised for performance in the spring of 1974. I had long had the habit of stirring the pot into action by plowing through all kinds of music, provoking myself into a state of irritated, critical tension—testing, judging, probing works that interested me for one reason or another. It was how I had trained myself. Instinctively I knew that without a strong critical apparatus it was not possible to develop the taste and judgment a composer needed. This time, however, was different. I had not yet had the chance to listen carefully to the Gagaku recordings I'd brought back; so I began, absolutely fascinated by what I was hearing. Gagaku was a music of powerful presence. Not simply exotic sounds, but a music of chiseled melodic lines and vivid colors. I was intrigued by the elegantly shaped phrases that intertwined in a kind of oddly familiar, yet not familiar, polyphony that joined parallel lines without locking them into harmonic agreement the way Western polyphony does.

I listened day after day to one piece after another until I fixed on a particularly gripping Gagaku piece that had a riveting intensity about it—a slow, ceremonial, harsh, chantlike processional. Like all the Gagaku music in this set of recordings, this particular piece had a strange wisdom of feeling about it beyond any other Western or Asian music I knew—something uncanny, remote and ancient, impersonal and unnameable sounded through the piercing flutes and oboelike reed instruments, the pentatonic panpipe *sho* and the ever-present small and large percussion instruments marking off movement and shape. Among these and other things, what drew me so strongly was its very anonymity counterpoised against our Western passion for ego identity and personal expression. Yet for all that, it simultaneously contained what seemed to me pre-echoes of Western implied harmony, musical phraseology, and incipient polyphony.

I began by jotting down what I heard on the recording. This developed into a set of sketches out of which came extended elaborations and freely evolving variants of the core Gagaku ideas. To these Gagaku-inspired possibilities I juxtaposed my own music—yet keeping the gestures, the melodic/harmonic ideas, and rhythmic figures I found well within the dark, emotional spirit generated by Gagaku. Different; yet the same. The same; yet different. This was crucial to having a dialogue with this ancient Japanese world. I wanted to open my world still further, having already made a conscious aesthetic composite of everything that had happened in premodern Western music that held serious interest for me. Now I wanted to open it to the music of the Far East, in this case to a particular Asian music that had captured both my love and my fancy. The urge on my part was toward a fusion that could be taken seriously—on its own terms. If the fusion worked, there would be no need to know its sources.

Since I like simple ideas to appear in complex settings and complex ideas to give the appearance of simplicity, *Imago Mundi,* despite all its inner contradictions in terms of gesture, image, sources, and so forth, is built on large, clear lines of structural articulation and has no "program" as such, regardless of the larger circumference and intention suggested by the title. The first and last sections are intimately related largely through their use of Gagaku and other gestures. The second section subdivides into Alla Marcia, Fantasia, and Fanfares. In the last section, all the ideas presented previously are summed up and brought together in new combinations, some of them developments or extensions of music stated more directly and simply earlier.

The dark, gritty sound of the orchestra in *Imago* is due largely to the predominance of the oboe, the treble double-reed of the winds. In the first performance of the *Imago* by the Baltimore Symphony Orchestra on May 8, 1974, two oboes plus an English horn delivered the pungent, nasal voice of the principal Gagaku motive and melodic line. To amplify the sheer reediness of the oboe/English horn complex, when Sir Georg Solti performed *Imago* with the Chicago Symphony, I requested another oboe be added. In the recording Christopher Lyndon-Gee made with the Saarbrücken Radio Orchestra in December 2001,[2] he continued the use of three oboes plus English horn to excellent effect. That extra oboe tips the balance of the color to exactly the right sound.

The predominant sound of winds, brass, and percussion in *Imago Mundi* is the inevitable result of the combination in my mind and ear of both the Japanese sources and my own music inspired by my reaction to Gagaku. A large assortment of percussion instruments in addition to timpani constitutes a small "orchestra" inside the larger orchestra, some of them taking a prominent solo role: specific-pitch, high bell sounds of celesta and glockenspiel, and nonpitch instruments such as guiros, tambourine, cymbals, deep gong, log drum, and bass drum. The role of the string orchestra is crucial for two qualities only strings can produce: first, for the very quiet and slow canonic passages toward the end of the work that, because they are symmetrical in structure, drift slowly downward or push gently upward as though in response to each other; second, the giant, deep *koto*-like effects in the last major section of the work produced by the slap pizzicatos from cellos and double basses that punctuate the slow, inexorable march to the end.

Imago Mundi. Image of the World. *Ukiyo-E.* Pictures of the Floating World. These two intersect at the axis of imaging. Which suggests the highly personal nature of our individual perceptions of the world and our lives in it. All three Japanese-influenced works—*Imago Mundi, Ukiyo-E (Pictures of the Floating World)*, and *Slow Fires of Autumn (Ukiyo-E II)*—as well as the flute and piano *Between Two Worlds (Ukiyo-E III)*, whose brief five movements I wrote in the fall of 1982 in Israel, are imagistic: personal, subjective evocations, each in its own way a dreaming consciousness's internal picturing through musical images (obeying no necessary logic of association or succession) moving freely in a fluid space (rather than time) unanchored from gravity; and, in the case of the Japanese-influenced *Ukiyo-E* chamber pieces, the sense of motion is, more often than not, closer to floating than anything else imaginable.

Well before our trip to Japan I was familiar with the traditional school of Japanese painting known as Ukiyo-E, having seen the vividly colored wood-block and engraved prints of the two Ukiyo-E masters Hokusai (1760–1849) and Hiroshige (1797–1858). Hokusai, the older of the two, lived into the mid-nineteenth century—at the time of his death, more than double the average age of most Japanese of that time. By then he was known as "the sage of painting." In *The Great Wave off Kanagawa*, one of his *Thirty-six Views of Mount Fuji*, the superrefinement and clarity of his drawing show him at his best and help me understand the fascination Hokusai's Ukiyo-E paintings had for his contemporaries. There he pictures the dramatic power of the huge wave's held tension at its highest cresting peak against the far distant view of a seemingly much smaller Mount Fuji in the background off to the right. This indelible image is one of awesome beauty. However representational Ukiyo-E may be, the appeal of its "pictures of the floating world" lies in its precise delineation of a world we recognize but is not necessarily "real" in the purely mundane sense. A special sensibility of greatly refined craft of the highest order wedded to artistic vision seems to converge in producing a level of visual magic that converts the natural world and people into a sense of what may lie behind reality.

Part of that magic that I have tried in my own way to translate into musical imagery has to do with the sense of suspension of gravity, the weightlessness of objects and people in space. Musically, this translates into a way of moving seamlessly from image to image, gesture to gesture, idea to idea without the necessity of connecting links binding too closely the succession of motion, figuratively letting the music float in a space that does not confine it to movement in any predesignated direction or order. The piercing charm of Ukiyo-E lies in its power to image the world not as static, fixed forms of "reality" but as floating pictures of radiant qualities ranging from states of melancholic forlornness and emptiness to quiet or ecstatic joy. D. H. Lawrence writes in his *Apocalypse*—an uncanny book that mounts a powerful diatribe against the Book of Revelation—a passage that is virtually a description of the necessary mental condition for composing Ukiyo-E whether in sound, color or word: "allow the mind to move in cycles, or to flit here and there over a cluster of images. . . . One cycle finished, we can drop or rise to another level and be in a new world at once."[3]

In essence, the passage is a prescription of "how to be modern" written in the 1920s, when being modern seemed to carry everything before it, so great was its energy, enthusiastic release from the "old" and elation at the "new" in Europe and America. If only on the basis of what is clearly evident in Hokusai's work, the Japanese were surely modern long before the West. One might even speculate that elements of what we in the West think of as aspects of modernism were already long present in theatrical and musical traditions and practices of Japanese Noh plays.

As I sat with Gene from eleven o'clock in the morning until five o'clock that summer afternoon in a Noh theater on the outskirts of Tokyo and took in the acting, singing, costumes, stripped-down stage scenery, and especially the music being made as a kind of parallel commentary on the dramatic proceedings provided by a small "chamber" ensemble of traditional instruments—flutes, plucked stringed instruments like the *biwa* and various small percussion—I kept marveling at the unself-conscious modernity, as seen and heard by a Westerner, of what I was experiencing.

On our return trip from Japan via Hawaii we flew to San Francisco, where we were to meet our daughter Chessie and her husband and join up with the Concord String Quartet, in town to give a concert. It was there that they gave one of their blazing performances of my Third Quartet at the Legion of Honor Hall. During that brief but full stay in San Francisco, Marcella de Cray, former harpist of the Philadelphia Orchestra, invited me to visit her in her studio. She wanted me to write a solo harp piece for her and thought this was the best way to introduce me to the changes in harp technique reflected in the new and recent music being composed for her instrument. Without question, composers were taking the harp a far distance from its traditional ways and uses. After playing a number of avant-garde passages demonstrating devices that to my ears sounded more like noise effects than music—all the while explaining in detail how these sounds were made—Marcella than invited me to "play" the harp. It was an oddly scary moment for someone who didn't even know how to hold the instrument. She saw my dilemma immediately, sat me down comfortably in front of the harp, and slowly lowered it against the inside of my right shoulder, where it rested against my body. Then she encouraged me to move my hands across the strings and to try other effects—just to get the "feel" of making the harp actually sound. To say the least, it sounded awful—but I did get the hang of it and then suddenly felt at ease. My one "lesson" on the harp turned out to be most important.

When I actually began writing not too many months later, the memory of that "lesson" stood me in more than good stead: I "saw" Marcella's harp in front of me as I sat in my study, slowly "pulled" it toward me until it "rested" in the crook of my neck and right shoulder—and began to "hear" the quality of the music I wanted. Ruminative, half-whispered, sad-edged, slowly unfolding melodic figures that never complete themselves . . . but trail off, only now and then a harsh, unhappy sound, a fragment of a soft, sometimes hard, glissando, a shadowy, not quite tonal motive . . . subsiding into a suggestion of a new possibility . . . but never completing itself. It's as though I dreamed this first *Ukiyo-E* (*Pictures of the Floating World*) into existence. Its very nature of tentativeness fit perfectly that aspect of the aesthetic of the painting tradition of Ukiyo-E, which suggests rather than states, does not becloud the impersonal world of nature with the demanding presence of the human ego. At best, it lets into its almost neutral world only whiffs of human yearnings, human longings, the bewilderments of human existence. For all this the harp is wondrously suited, with its incredibly separate and separable colors in its low, middle, and high registers. Its deep lower-register notes seem to ring forever, sounding through whatever lies above them, whether in the form of gently ringing, bell-like harmonics in the middle register or near-melodic figurations, chords, arpeggiations in the upper. Treated rightly, the harp can whisper almost to inaudibility, sting sharply with hard-plucked fingernail notes, make glissandi with the delicacy of breezes passing through outdoor windchimes, or ring out nobly with full, strong, resonant chords. Writing the solo harp *Ukiyo-E* renewed and refreshed the instrument for me.

Marcella gave its premiere at a San Francisco Contemporary Music Players concert in San Francisco on April 28, 1975, and later recorded it for Grenadilla Records.[4] In 1998, Yolanda Kondonassis, a harpist with exceptional refinement as a performer, recorded it for Telarc as one of a varied program of works under the general title *Pictures of the Floating World.*[5]

When I turned my attention to the harp again, it was the fall of 1978. November, the sad time for us. I don't know whether it was the annual turn of the clock to the anniversary of Paul's leaving us that accounted for the depth of my melancholy that November. Perhaps it was the sense that had settled over me with that summer's end and the first signs of autumn that the fires that had flared up in the spring and summer months were dying out—slowly, very slowly but surely. An all-pervasive ache settled in me and lasted all through the time when, in January 1979, I finished the work I'd undertaken for flute and harp. While driving one day, the words of the title for the music that had filled me until early winter suddenly formed themselves, *Slow Fires of Autumn*—the slow burning out of the life in nature. The music became a bone-deep meditation on what comes before the final sleep, the inexorable slow dying away, the wilting, shriveling, shrinking, and curling of all the greens of summer turning to all the browns of fall and winter. The music grew out of the Japanese music-box lullaby, its flavor almost F minor, its Japanese modality floating in its own weight of years.

Those were still the years when private American foundations such as the Walter W. Naumburg Foundation maintained an actively generous and enlightened annual program of selecting highly gifted young soloists and chamber groups (such as string quartets) to present in New York debuts and commissioned composers to supply new works for such occasions. It was for Carol Wincenc, an extraordinarily gifted young flutist, being sponsored that year by the Naumburg for her Alice Tully Hall debut concert on April 23, 1979, with her equally gifted partner, the harpist Nancy Allen, that I wrote *Slow Fires of Autumn*. Since it borrows some harp figures from the first *Ukiyo-E* of 1973, I decided to add the subtitle "Ukiyo-E II." In this way I locked it into the series of imagistic Japanese-inspired works that I saw as "pictures of the floating world."

Like the solo harp *Ukiyo-E* written in unmeasured, open score, *Slow Fires* is also in open score, except at the very end, when bar lines mark off the odd-shaped, ten-measure phrases of the Japanese lullaby. In the four side-by-side repetitions of the lullaby that constitute the last section, the roles of flute and harp are reversed: from the outset of *Slow Fires,* the flute is the principal voice, while the harp provides support and commentary, only occasionally taking the lead. At the very end the harp takes over as principal voice, the flute commenting—until the last few measures.

I enjoyed working closely with Carol Wincenc and Nancy Allen and tried to lead them by indirection and suggestion into the heart of *Slow Fires of Autumn,* what it meant musically and emotionally. Both highly proficient, gifted young musicians, they were willing to work hard to grasp the essence of a contemporary, if not exactly orthodox, piece. In another sense, it was exceedingly hard work for me, because I saw that it was not so much the Japanese flavor of the atmosphere that seemed to elude them as much as it was the darkness of the work, its heavy-laden, grieving sense that spread in all directions.

It was at the recording of *Slow Fires* I discovered how demanding of themselves Carol and Nancy could be. We had spent most of the morning on roughly half the work, piling up many "takes." After a lunch break, I learned that they were unhappy and dissatisfied with the results of the morning's work. The sense of *performance,* which a recording must convey in order to be convincing, was missing. It would result only in too self-conscious a sense of projection, too careful and controlled; it had to be looser, freer, and more spontaneous. They wanted to scrap what they had done and start all over again. The CRI people and I agreed it was an excellent idea, so Carol and Nancy, freed of their initial inhibitions, began to *perform* the work, and the music simply flowed out of them.

The year 1994 saw the release of an Australian recording of *Slow Fires of Autumn,* by Tall Poppies Records with two superb performers, flutist Geoffrey Collins and harpist Alice Giles, neither of whom I knew.[6] Remarkably, they had grasped the Japanese inspiration of the music, understood its nuances and sensibilities perfectly. I delighted in the poetry of the Aussies' reading. Collins clearly understood the now vertical *shakuhachi* role, the now Western transverse flute role of his instrument. Matching Collins's understanding, Giles grasped those places where the harp is required to sound like a *koto* and the clear contrast with the Western tradition of her instrument. Together they were unafraid of the dark emotional resonances of *Slow Fires of Autumn.*

Even though it was written in Jerusalem in 1982, something about the flute and piano work I call *Between Two Worlds,* its five miniature movements replete with imagistic gestures and atmospheres, prompted me to include it in the more directly Japanese-influenced chamber series as *Ukiyo-E III*. The *Five Images*, as the subtitle indicates, are:

Fantasia
Scherzoso (Fast Dance)
Night Scene (A)
Sarabande (Slow Dance)
Night Scene (B)

Clearly the impulses that had brought the earlier *Ukiyo-E* pieces into being were still at work in me. The work was given its first performance by my friends, flutist Sue Ann Kahn and pianist Vladimir Sokoloff, at the National Flute Convention held in Philadelphia on August 19, 1983. Later Sue Ann recorded it with pianist Andrew Willis for CRI.[7] *Between Two Worlds* was written for a young amateur flutist, Karen Wolfgang, the daughter of two close family friends, Marvin and Lennie Wolfgang.

The title of the work suggests not only the separate realms of nature and culture between which we find ourselves so tenuously suspended, but also the sense of living—often with the tensions of unresolvable uncertainty—an interior, personal existence simultaneously with exterior demands on our capacities and energies coming from a world outside of us. At the time of actual work on the piece, I was living in Jerusalem, in the center of the strife-torn Middle East, ever worsening.

Distance may lend clarity. And it was the psychic and geographic distance I felt so keenly, between a faraway America, superficially peaceful, but in the grip of Reaganism and the Cold War with the Soviet Union, and being, if only briefly, in the center of an area where hot war and terrorism had been going on for a long time between Israel and the Arabs, that I tried to gather into the title of this seemingly unreal-world music as a suggestion of its emotional sources.

In 1992, *Between Two Worlds* was sensitively recorded on a Koch International CD by the flutist Alexa Still, a New Zealander, and pianist Susan DeWitt Smith[8]— neither of whom I knew, and again, without any help from me. Which speaks to the point I made earlier about performers finding their own way into the heart of a work from the music itself. The unidentified author of the program notes for Still's recording states: "To the listener, Rochberg's use of the flute . . . is inescapably similar to the sounds of the *shakuhachi* . . . and it is interesting to note that ancient solo literature for the *shakuhachi* provided a means of meditation for the player and listener." His or her observations are keen and to the point, grasping the shadow of the Japanese inspiration particularly over the last three movements.

Returning to the four works at hand, *Imago Mundi* is a large-scale work for orchestra by any standard of measure, while each of the three *Ukiyo-E* pieces is intentionally a small-scale chamber work. Their relatively different structural proportions, reflected in their timings, can't help but reflect the differences in the size of gestures and musical ideas that make up the primary stuff of these various imagistic works.

Imago Mundi pictures the external world—but only insofar as our pictures of the world outside ourselves are imaginings, mental fictions, shadowed reflections of the "reality" of past as well as present times. Gagaku ceremonial court music, even if experienced only through recordings, evokes a sense of largeness of scale and gesture. It was the initiating stimulus for discovering or inventing similarly large-sized, therefore compatible, gestures and ideas to flesh out the sense of designing a set of theatrical panels—tapestries might be appropriate in some places—crowded with ceremony and event. At the same time, however, these staged or theatrical projections are mixed with an ominous sense of internal distress—feelings and sensations of impending doom and disaster rising from the bowels of an unsettled and unsettling world around us.

Compared with these resonances of large-scale gestures and ideas that are the substance of *Imago Mundi,* the works for one and two instruments that consti-tute the *Ukiyo-E* series are entirely subjective and relatively small in scale as to duration, gesture, and ideas. *Ukiyo-E* for solo harp is without any reference I am aware of to an external world. And even though *Slow Fires of Autumn* for flute and harp is redolent with an intensely felt response to the dying out of the fires of summer, it is a deeply subjective picturing of an inner human landscape. *Between Two Worlds* for flute and piano hovers between picturing external and internal worlds. Its last three movements tilt the work finally toward the inner.

Whichever world—outer or inner—is the source ultimately of these four works, they have one primary condition in common: they are wrought of nameless and nameable images, far more of the former than the latter. And even when those that are nameable seem most evident to the ear, they, too, remain—exactly like the nameless images—"pictures of the floating world."

CHAPTER 11

A Trio of Symphonies
Four, Five, and Six

Taken together, the three hefty, large-scale orchestral works discussed in this chapter cover roughly a decade, from 1976 to 1987. They represent attempts to demarcate separate worlds—in the same sense we describe to ourselves the three major planets of our solar system: the living Earth on which we stubbornly persist; Venus, so hot at 800° Fahrenheit it is inimical to life in any form as we know it; and Mars, the red, dead, cold planet whose surface striations were once taken for canals. Each symphony has its own design, temperature, interior emotional scenario, duration related to size and scale of gestures and ideas, and orchestral flavor and resonance. What cannot be inferred, however, from these separate musical worlds are the vastly different circumstances and sources that brought them to life in the first place. These have far greater weight in determining their whys and wherefores than almost anything else I can think of. Except perhaps for a lifelong desire *not* to consciously repeat what I've already done—what I call "self-replicating," a kind of aesthetic self-cloning, a particularly crippling modernist insistence on the "brand name," "trademark," or "fingerprint" confining it to an extraordinarily narrow range, usually a single, abstract idea or gesture by which artists *always* will be recognized as their individual unique selves and never mistaken for anyone else.

Since our essence as individuals is a given, physically characterized by body and facial gestures, sound of voice, and other externally recognizable, determinative features and qualities, I take it that the same essence translates into differences of the interior aesthetic level for the composer, the painter, the writer, and so on. That being the case, there's no need to worry about the identity of one's artistic personality. What does concern me, however, is seeking new levels and paths of expression, by which I mean *utterance,* how what needs saying is projected to the fullest degree possible.

When Vilem Sokol, music director of the Seattle Youth Symphony Orchestra, contacted me to ask if I would write a large-scale work for his orchestra—made up of, as I found out at the first rehearsal, an astonishing group of brilliantly gifted, well-schooled young musicians, ages eleven to twenty—as part of the celebration of the 1976 Bicentennial, I agreed without hesitation. I had met Vilem through his son Mark Sokol, my close colleague and friend during those fabulous years when I worked so intensely with the Concord String Quartet. The whole Sokol clan included nine children, all professional musicians. Agatha, Mark's mother, was a pianist; Mark's siblings, older and younger, were mainly string players with positions in major and regional orchestras all over the country. He used to describe with particular delight and pride how when the family gathered for the Christmas holidays, one of the works they invariably played was the string octet of Mendelssohn. The Sokols represent the triumphant proof of the power of biology to generate musical talent wrapped in the need and love of making music and how this nature-borne reality breaks through any and all obstacles and material encrustations of man-made cultural conditions.

To write about the Fourth Symphony necessitates a long look backward to the middle 1930s, a two-decade jump ahead into the late 1950s, and then on to putting everything together for the Seattle Youth Symphony in 1976. The reasons are simple: a particularly important idea for the last movement, "Introduction and Finale," has directly traceable roots to what I was doing in the mid-1930s; the second movement, "Serenade-Scherzo," is a complete reworking of a 1956 or 1957 orchestral piece I then called *Waltz Serenade;* finally, everything—including existing sketches for ideas made around 1974—had to be rethought, put through the critical wringer to achieve unification of orchestral essence and flavor in order to bind together a considerable range of readily recognizable disparate musical styles, classical, romantic, and twelve-tone atonality, which yielded tonal results.

This mélange of styles began to take root when in the fall of 1935 I entered Montclair State Teacher's College, even though what I hungered for was a musical education, one that would lay the groundwork for my life as a composer. But that was to come some years later and in a totally unexpected way. Meanwhile I did those things the situation allowed, the most important becoming pianist for the college Dance Club in my sophomore year. Unknowingly, this was an experience that planted the seed for my Fourth Symphony.

The Dance Club was run by Maggie Sherwin, a youngish woman who had grown up in the then-burgeoning modern dance movement in America. She had trained and danced with Doris Humphreys, a prominent dancer and choreographer of those early years. Though basically ignorant of dance matters, I thoroughly enjoyed working with Maggie Sherwin and her troupe of a dozen or more lithe, healthy, good-looking female dancers—among them my Gene, and all of them classmates. In those years, modern dance tended to be freely athletic: bodies were supremely active, in motion and unpostured, quite the opposite of ballet and its dependence on fixed traditions. Maggie taught the dancers how to run, leap into the air, and fall into a graceful slide on the floor miraculously without harming themselves—and making it look both perfectly natural and beautiful at the same time.

My job was to provide support for choreography and a stimulating musical environment. In the three years I worked closely with them, each ended with a full-evening public recital of a variety of short dances and a long narrative, dramatically told through dance and music. Especially vivid was the *Tristan and Isolde* of the spring 1938 program, for which I composed a group of musical ideas on which I improvised during rehearsals and performance. I sat at the piano, following the dancers' movements closely. Somehow it became instinctive on both sides: they knew they could trust me to stay with them at every major turn in the telling of the danced story; I knew the overall shape of the narrative as they had worked it out in dance form and could anticipate every "scene" shift, ready to support them musically. Not a Wagnerian by choice or taste, I have to confess Wagner's way of weaving his melodic/harmonic motifs and ideas intrigued me, so it was "natural" to work out ways of improvising on the chief ideas I felt were worth writing down. A crucial factor was that the ideas be readily recognizable so that the dancers knew where they were musically and I knew where they were scenically: there was no fixed time limit for the dance narrative or the music. Somehow everything fit, everything felt secure.

Of the primary ideas I used for *Tristan and Isolde,* one in particular had rooted itself in my soul. Admittedly Wagnerian in its harmonic and melodic motion, it stayed with me for all the years that followed. When I began to contemplate the shape of the third and last movement of the Fourth Symphony, I decided on an "Introduction and Finale" cast roughly in the frame of the old classical sonata form. The difference, however, between the generalized idea of the sonata form and the actual structure I arrived at depended on interruptions drawn from principal ideas taken from both the "Introduction" and the first movement. What I took from the "Introduction" and varied each of the two times it broke into the forward rush of the Presto of the "Finale" was a reworked/recomposed form of the most Wagnerian, romantic-sounding musical idea from the old 1938 Dance Club *Tristan and Isolde* music. It suited the character of the opening "Introduction"— expansive, moving restlessly through various keys, emotionally malleable—and acted as a perfect foil to the classical-sounding, Haydnesque Presto, music that was playful, energetic, and robust.

Working backward, the second-movement "Serenade-Scherzo" has its roots in an earlier separate orchestral piece that I reworked almost entirely: all that remains of the first version are the essential melodic ideas, each of them another variant—melodic and harmonic—of a twelve-tone row. The atonality inherent (usually) in such a row (or series) I turned inside-out so it becomes essentially tonal, that is, key-centered and directional, with the inevitable resurrection of the cadence as marking points of arrival and defining articulation of musical speech. Once again, I dealt with the problem of reconciling opposites that seem to contradict each other but are, in reality, simply different faces of the same primary features.

The reworking of the old *Waltz Serenade* was strongly affected by the great Scherzo of Mahler's Fifth Symphony, which I had conducted in 1968 with the University of Pennsylvania orchestra. Something of his handling of the orchestration for that movement, its instrumental gestures, overall color palette, lodged itself in my ears and powerfully affected my treatment of the orchestra in the new version of the "Serenade-Scherzo." Rather than attempt to suppress it, I gave it free rein and let its presence operate uninhibited.

The different tempos called for by the nature of the music—whether twelve-tone or tonal—were bound to produce a generally loose, if not free, overall sense of motion, perhaps best described as *quixotic*. One additional aspect needs to be emphasized: inasmuch as every idea expressed is unmistakably melodic, clear articulation demanded the use of cadence. The use of cadence to show pauses, breathing places, full or partial closing through completed or purposely incompleted musical thought, is not only a necessary condition of tonal thinking, it is a prime characteristic of establishing direction, clear aural signs to the ear and listening mind of where the music is going and how it is getting there. The erasure of cadence and direction in twentieth-century music, particularly of the twelve-tone or serial variety, robbed the performer, as well as the listener, of where they were, how they got there, and where they were going. Something of this had already plagued Wagner's music (later Richard Strauss's, but never Gustav Mahler's) and produced an aggravated awareness on the part of musical analysts, who invented the term *wandering* (or *roving*) *chords* to designate and account for the perceptual–

psychological uncertainty of not quite knowing where they were or where the music was headed.

The utter loss of a sense of direction ultimately put its stamp on totally chromaticized music—even if the music were organized according to certain "laws" or ideas of order. In that sense—but in that sense only—I see a curious parallelism and perceptual kinship between the two-dimensionality of the loss of articulated perspective represented in the American abstract-expressionist way of painting, and of the heavily abstract nature of what used to be called the "international style" of serialism: modern music stripped of the cadence and an articulated sense of direction. In the inverse, where the three-dimensionality of perspective and articulation through the cadence and a clear sense of direction are reinvoked, we see and hear again the glories of the greatest representational painting and the glories of tonal music.

The first incarnation as *Waltz Serenade* of what some twenty years later became the "Serenade-Scherzo" second movement of the Fourth Symphony, received its premiere performance by the Cincinnati Symphony led by Thor Johnson in the late 1950s. The difference between the two versions lies more in their orchestration and probably what I felt later were necessary editorial changes. The basic materials and structure of the two remain clearly related.

The mixed "style" of the 1976 Fourth Symphony—even though it leans heavily toward the tonal side—is something of a reaction to the more consistent internal "style" of the 1974 Violin Concerto, where everything is freshly composed and does not specifically relate to earlier ideas, compositions, or attempts at composition. In one sense the Fourth Symphony was *zusammengenommen*, gathered together from widely differing sources and times of my life. Even one of the main ideas for the first movement came from a time when Gene and I used to relax basking at the Jersey Shore. It was also the time of the rented white piano that wouldn't "sound" when the weather turned wet, cold, and damp. On days when the sun shone strongly, I loved to walk "on the strand," where the ocean water wet the sand and then cooled it off.

The almost Schubertian tune that dominates the first major section of the opening movement and derives from the spirit and essence of nineteenth-century romantic-era music came to me on one of those slow, calming walks by the edge of the sea. Simple and straightforward, it was just right for what I wanted and eminently malleable.

The emotional weight of the inherent drama of this roughly forty-five-minute symphony is carried by its first movement, which alternates between two tempi: Adagio and Andante con moto. The soft romanticism of this first movement is inescapable; its character sets itself against the harder variety of the romantic tendency of the second-movement "Serenade-Scherzo" and returns to put its stamp again on the music of the "Introduction"—but not the "Finale" Presto—of the third and last movement.

———

Not long afterward, in the early months of 1983, John Edwards, the likable, old-style manager of the Chicago Symphony Orchestra, called to ask if I would be interested in writing a work for them. It seemed there was a patron who hoped I would consider doing a "concerto for brass." Not only was John very mysterious about the identity of the patron, I couldn't get a single word out of him as to why this person was so keen on such a work. I could only conjecture that, whoever it was, the patron was in love with the power, polish, and sheer gorgeous sound of the justly famous CSO brass section, or perhaps they had heard my *Imago Mundi*, which places heavy stress on the brasses, or perhaps even the Violin Concerto, where they are sporadically prominent—luminous or dark with foreboding. The incomparable Sir Georg Solti had previously performed both with the CSO.

I told John I would be happy to write a work but preferred to try my hand at another symphony, which, in this case, would be my Fifth. I wanted the freedom to make use of a wider palette but, as I assured him, without neglecting the brasses. Finally, after a number of calls, we settled on the terms of the commission. The patron—so I gathered from John—was very pleased I had accepted and was sympathetic to my need for greater latitude.

The year 1983 was mostly taken up with writing the Oboe Concerto for the New York Philharmonic and preparing it for performance and recording.[1] In the early spring of 1984 I had to be in Chicago and decided to see Solti if possible. In one sense there was still plenty of time. The symphony wasn't due until 1986, the year of the sesquicentennial celebration of the city of Chicago—the "official" reason for the commission in the first place. But in another sense, I had come to appreciate that time, which, for all we know, given the limitations of our perceptions and understandings of the world we find ourselves in, may be but a man-made thing, another one of those universal concepts that we allow to dominate our lives and dictate our behavior and actions. What we call "time" does not flow by at all, certainly not in a regulated, easily predictable speed, but consumes itself fiercely and, before we know it, has already fled, become mere memory, the past. For these reasons I was eager to see Solti and have a chance to discuss what was on my mind, particularly as it bore on matters of instrumentation. So it was arranged.

I arrived at his spacious apartment on one of the upper floors of a fashionable Lakeshore Drive high-rise and was led into the living room by Mrs. Solti, a charming young woman. The purpose of my last visit had been to go over the score of

Imago Mundi with Solti. This would have been some years after his performance of my Violin Concerto with Isaac Stern. During the session with the *Imago* score I came to see how thoroughly Solti concerned himself with every last detail of a piece of music. It was far more than just being a perfectionist—it became crystal clear he had a commanding intelligence that understood the sweep of the whole and its relation to the smallest detail. He saw crucial connections between musical expression and musical design, overlooking nothing in his search for the right gesture, the right color, the right tempo. He asked penetrating questions in order to identify the character of the music—without which it would have been, at best, a mere concatenation of meaningless sounds.

The weather that wintry, early April day in the Windy City was wildly volatile. I could see its rapid changes as I stood in Solti's living room, taking in the scene through the large picture window overlooking Lake Michigan. Heavy, looming, dark clouds were being pushed hard and fast across the dull gray sky by strong winds. Nasty-looking, choppy, short waves covered the surface of the lake. I was enjoying the drama of the scene when, behind me, I heard a door open and Solti walked in—but very slowly. He looked so worn and weary I was overcome with guilt that I should be imposing on this remarkable man in his present state. Solti smiled wanly as we shook hands, and to cover the awkwardness of the moment I half turned back to the window and said something about the magnificent view of the turbulence nature was making with the lake and sky.

I can still see Solti's totally dismissive reaction. He averted his head from the window and where I was standing and, with a weak wave of his hand, brushed the whole wild scene away as though it were an offense to his sight. Then we sat down and began our talk. Solti explained he had only just returned from a tour abroad and mentioned something about playing Handel. His face brightened when I said how much I admired Handel's music, and we quickly turned to what had brought me. I told him about John Edwards's phone calls and the mystery of the anonymous patron who wanted me to consider writing a "concerto for brass." A clear smile slowly spread across Solti's face, and, with his index finger pointing to himself, he said, "That was me!"

The simplicity and openness of his pleased admission took my breath away; it was the last thing I would have expected. The tension of his tiredness vanished as we laughed together. His "That was me" still reverberates. It became coupled with another indelible phrase that Solti voiced when we were saying our goodbyes a little later: "Don't wait too long . . ." I sensed what was on his mind. He wasn't getting any younger. In point of fact, neither was I, but he was already in his seventies, on his way to his eighties; I was still in my middle sixties.

Questions surrounding thoughts of our individual mortality grow stronger,

not weaker, as we add another year, yet another, and still another to our increasing age . . . That night I had dinner with the novelist Saul Bellow. Before his wife
joined us, he was in a blue funk and could talk about nothing else but how that
morning he'd gone to see his older brother, who was in the hospital . . . and not
doing too well. That day in Chicago was no ordinary day for me: dark, portentous with the strange mingling of uncontrollable nature roused toward violent
turbulence and the unquiet, private thoughts of impending endings in human
life just barely voiced. I am reminded of Shakespeare's Prospero, who says upon
leaving his magical island realm to reclaim his dukedom:

> And thence retire to my Milan, where
> Every third thought shall be my grave.
> (*The Tempest,* act 5, scene 1)

Performances of the Fifth Symphony were scheduled for January 1986. The
score was in Solti's hands well beforehand so he would have sufficient time to
acquaint himself with it. As the fall 1985–86 season was exhaustingly full for Solti,
there was no time for us to get together to go over the score leisurely. But his
natural propensity for the pursuit of perfection demonstrated itself in a forty-five-
minute phone call from London (where he was then conducting) to my home in
Newtown Square. I sat at our dining-room table, the full score of the Fifth spread
out before me while Sir Georg, in London, peppered me with more questions
than there were notes in the score. He wanted to make sure of every last detail
and nuance possible. The new symphony was totally unlike anything else of mine
he'd previously done in musical substance, emotional intensity, harmonic and
melodic and motivic language, not to speak of orchestral sound.

Shortly after we arrived in Chicago for the rehearsals and the January 30, 1986,
premiere of the Fifth Symphony, I was informed by the orchestra staff that an
appointment had been made to pay our respects to His Honor Harold Washington, the mayor of Chicago. When the time came—Solti begged off because
of the pressure of work—we were driven to City Hall and led to the mayor's
office. Unhappily, weeks before the trip to Chicago, Gene had broken her right
arm, which was in a cast up to her elbow. Undeterred by the discomfort of the
cast, she was remarkably cheerful. As we entered the outer part of the office,
facing us was a metal detector, the kind familiar enough in airports but, where
it stood, distinctly out of place I thought. The woman who ran the office for the
mayor greeted us with great aplomb and was now inviting us to step through
the detector. As Gene passed through the frame, whatever alarm bells that were
part of its system went off clanging and banging, making a fearful racket in such
close quarters. Consternation ruled on all sides; but Gene, who immediately

understood the situation, laughingly explained that a steel pin in her arm under the cast was the culprit. This seemed to satisfy the office manager and, much relieved, she led us into the inner sanctum. There stood Harold Washington, an imposing figure of a man, an African American, his broad, welcoming smile and laughing eyes taking us all in. Introductions were made all around, and we began to talk. Suddenly a photographer appeared as though from nowhere and began taking shots of me, the mayor, and the orchestra staff members. I had brought my score with me, and, opening it, I asked the mayor if he could read music. The ice had been broken, and he laughingly admitted he couldn't. My own mood was relaxed and open. Just as I said to him, "That's all right, I'll sing it for you"—general laughter broke out, goodwill on all sides. The photographer took the photo, which caught precisely that moment of joviality.

In medias res. In the middle of things. That was how I wanted the opening of the multisectioned Fifth Symphony to begin. As though it had already begun—somewhere out of hearing, in a fury of violent emotions—suddenly it surrounds the listener, it is present, at its peak, and takes the audience into its world with insistent calling that cuts through the tumult of the strings with high horns and trumpets.

The "Opening Statement" consists of interlocking panels of weavings of constantly changing motivic patterns, all relatively short, characteristic, many of them lyrical in essence, with another large group suggesting fanfare figures, martial in tone. "Episodes" and "Developments" constitute the big middle of the overall shape of the symphony, which draws to a deliberately precipitous close in its abrupt "Finale." The overall shape schematically looks like this:

I. Opening Statement
II. Episode 1
III. Development 1
IV. Episode 2
V. Development 2
VI. Episode 3
.VII. Finale

Plunging into the middle of things at the very outset, I dove straight down into the hot core of hard romanticism. There is something unrelenting about the Fifth Symphony, something unforgiving that will not be appeased, something that refuses to be mollified. Regardless of the frequent moments of showing or *trying* to show a softer side, an incessant pressure is at work. There is no letup, no possibility of relaxation of pressure or slackening of the tensions that hold the emotional life of this music in a vise and will not let go.

It is wholly unmitigated, refusing to be milder, or softer, or less intense, or less severe for long. All efforts to do so cannot hold, because there is an insistence on returning always to its overwrought, agitated condition despite all efforts to soften its essential nature. Anxiety lurks at its edges, waiting for a chance to break through, take over, and dominate again. Even those times when it lapses or falls into a state close to dream or fantasy, the darkness closes in, and violence erupts—or threatens to. The almost longing love song of the cello solo is never unblemished. Shadows eat away at and blur the edges of the long, slow fantasia of the four horns, which borders on strangeness and despair. The one moment when the high trumpet cries out the main motif of the horn fantasia, trying desperately to reach for some sense of approaching not peace, but perhaps possible resolution, is totally frustrated by the sudden, abrupt rush to the chaotic end, which refuses all resolutions. This is unremitting hard romanticism that could have been composed only in the twentieth century—emotionally light-years away from nineteenth-century soft romanticism.

Not long after the Fifth Symphony was launched I began work on the Sixth, which had been commissioned by the Pittsburgh Symphony Orchestra for Lorin Maazel. It was completed in January 1987. Later that year, on October 16, it received its premiere in Heinz Hall, Pittsburgh. Written for large orchestra, it includes—besides winds, brasses, and strings—two harps, two timpani, xylophone, vibraphone, tubular bells, and a wide variety of percussion instruments.

Because it is impossible to improve on the original program note I wrote for the premiere, I am quoting the most pertinent and germane passages, especially those that, now in February 2003, relate uncomfortably close to the troubling talk of war, which fills the air once again.

> The Sixth is in two parts, designated Fantasia and Marcia, respectively. Central to the Fantasia are various kinds of fanfares, evoking not only the ancient association with what we now know to be the false glories of war, but also the hidden, underlying tragic implications of making war and its inability to rid itself of a sophisticated barbarism rationalized as the military side of national defense. I find nothing glorious in death and destruction, regardless of the rhetorics overtly or covertly advanced in their cause. These fanfares come in unexpected ways and in unexpected places during the course of the Fantasia, emerging out of or interrupting or taking over other kinds of musical ideas. The core of this ensemble of other ideas is a Lento that goes below the surface of things into dark and probing regions and provides the basis for deriving different yet related motifs and melodic ideas.

Part II is made up of a series of three different marches, of which the first is the overall frame for the second and third. In the old classical tradition of character pieces such as the scherzo, march, and dance forms, contrasting parts were called "trios." In that sense, each of these two other marches can be thought of as an extended "trio." *Fanfares* again occur in these "trios"—some of them variants of fanfares from the Fantasia, others brand-new. The main tune of the third march—all three marches have clearly defined melodies of different character and attitude—was the principal tune of a parade march I wrote in 1943 for the 261st Infantry Regiment Band when I was briefly attached as a Special Service officer to one of the companies while it was in training in Camp Shelby, Mississippi. The tune I use in this work haunted me all during the ensuing time after World War II, and I knew someday I would make use of it. The figures in the woodwinds accompanying this tune are drawn from the second march, thus making a kind of polyphonic joining of the two. What perhaps can be called the epilogue—really an extended coda—of Part II pulls the marches back into the world of the Fantasia.

A long footnote to the march I wrote for the regimental band: I called it *March of the Halberds,* the halberd—a mean-looking, unwieldy, medieval weapon combining a spear head (or pike) and battle ax—the insignia of the arm patch worn by the men of the 261st Regiment. At the time I knew little about scoring for a military band, so I wrote it out as a piano score with, here and there, expanded short-score amplifications to indicate other parts to be played. I then approached the band director and played the march for him, and he agreed—enthusiastically, as I recall—to score it. Not long after, he called and invited me to come to hear his band play it. It sounded fine, in the grand tradition of John Philip Sousa. In short, it was the real thing, authentic.

The question as to why I wrote it in the first place is another matter entirely. Perhaps it was the immediate stimulus of the situation I found myself in. Or simply that marches have always appealed to me since childhood. My earliest vivid, "live" memory is of flags flying, bands playing, and soldiers marching in formation in what looked like endless ranks. I was four or five years old at the time, and my father held me up so I could see everything around me. Crowds of excited, eager people lined the sidewalks of Main Avenue in downtown Passaic, New Jersey, where I grew up. The crowd went wild when they saw General "Black Jack" Pershing, the leader of the American Expeditionary Forces. There he was, smiling as he waved, standing in the open back of a big black car moving slowly, at a snail's pace: the man who had led the doughboys to victory "over there" and helped bring the bloody Great War to a close. It remains one of the most vivid scenes in a long life—alive, unforgettable.

The sources for the three marches in the symphony were various and widespread. The principal march—enclosing the second and third in traditional trio form: A (March I)–Trio I (March II)–A^1–Trio II (March III)–A^2—came from a Suite for Orchestra I had written in 1947. I treated the original as a sketch from which I built up an entirely new piece. Its appearances as enclosures of Marches II and III took on the character of either an expanded development (A^1) or a coda-recapitulation (A^2). March II was an enlargement through orchestration of the opening movement of my 1971 piano solo work *Carnival Music.* Where the march from the suite was ominous in tone, this second march (and its fanfares) was both subtle and raucous-sounding by turns. After the dramatically expanded development of March I, the 1943 *March of the Halberds,* with four trumpets blaring its principal tune in unison, bursts in with a brash and bright *fortissimo.* The structural ensemble of these three marches is absorbed into what becomes an expanded coda recalling the character and ideas of the Fantasia with which the symphony begins.

Truth to tell, I have never concerned myself much with the question of what other works appear on the same program with a work of mine, new or old. With the Sixth Symphony I suddenly found myself extremely concerned. For reasons I have never fathomed, Lorin Maazel chose to couple it with Stravinsky's *Le sacre du printemps. Le sacre* is a monolith of the early twentieth century, a veritable blockbuster where Stravinsky pushed the envelope of his brand of modernism to the edge of the abyss. I wondered briefly how my new symphony would hold up cheek by jowl with *Le sacre,* the live presence of its unique neoprimitive utterance, against the late twentieth-century hard romanticism with which the Sixth gives urgent voice to a wholly different kind of modernism, a deeply personal, emotionally expressionistic indictment of the two world wars and other horrors that had come between the writing of each work—1913 in the case of Stravinsky, 1986–87 in my case.

There was a great tumult of response to the first performance of the Sixth. It was one of those times when the players of the Pittsburgh Symphony had been completely won over by the music and gave it everything they had. Maazel was much taken with the work and reveled in its emotional drama and orchestral colors. I was especially happy with the way he molded and shaped the phrasing of the lines of the strings in the first-part Fantasia. He gave those melodic shapes a super-warmth of feeling that unlocked the longing ache inherent in them. He fully grasped the play and brilliance of the three marches, and—best of all—his sense of tempo was flawless. He raised the coda of the Sixth's climactic endpoint to an unbearable pitch of emotional tension—and broke off. The audience rose to its feet in a unison *furioso* of responsive, noisy enthusiasm the like of which could only warm the heart and memory of any composer.

Two years later, when the Pittsburgh Symphony Orchestra went on its European tour that started in the Soviet Union, Gene and I traveled with them, joining them in Leningrad for their first concert, Moscow for the second, and Warsaw, Poland, for the third. The program Lorin Maazel had chosen included my Sixth Symphony, Mahler's great Seventh Symphony, Samuel Barber's Violin Concerto, and George Gershwin's *American in Paris*. The concerts in Leningrad, Moscow, and Warsaw took place during the week of October 7–11, 1989—just a few months before the total collapse of the Marxist socialist experiment that had taken the Russian people on a seventy-year-long aimless ramble down the road to nowhere. Gene and I would have continued with the orchestra for at least a part of its westward tour to Paris and other cities, but when we learned that the "presenters" had turned thumbs down to the performance of the Sixth it made no sense. Instead, we decided to go to London and, from there, home.

It was after the Moscow performance Maazel gave of the Sixth that I learned the Berlin Philharmonic had just announced its choice of a new conductor. Evidently, Maazel was on the short list of three conductors of international reputation but had lost to Claudio Abbado. Once I heard this news, I understood that the passionate energy and new depths of intensity of feeling that marked Maazel's conducting of the Sixth, after learning he had been rejected for a post he apparently craved intensely, was his way of working through his grave disappointment, by investing all the blackness and bleakness he must have felt—conditions of soul I am well acquainted with—through the darkness and blackness that belong to the Sixth. I had grown accustomed to his urbanity, a kind of cultivated suaveness of person and musical professionalism. But that Moscow performance was the best he'd ever given the work and in turn released the most amazing audience response of the three concerts I heard on that tour. As a result, I gained a new admiration and respect for Maazel the conductor and a new affection for Maazel the man.

Following the concert, we boarded a Soviet Aeroflot plane, destination Leningrad. No doubt by prearranged planning, but as far as we were concerned, pleasantly unexpected, we found ourselves sitting in the same forward row with Lorin Maazel, who was diverting company the entire flight. We talked about many things, but what I remember best was the virtuosic clarity of his incredibly detailed explanation with written notations of the formulas for converting Celsius weather temperature readings into Fahrenheit readings and back to Celsius.

Late that night we arrived at the airport, where transportation was waiting to take us to the Hotel Leningrad. All the time we were in Leningrad—not more than two days—I kept reminding myself that this was once the capital of czarist Russia, once called Saint Petersburg; that it was in St. Petersburg my maternal grandmother had a brother who was in Czar Nicholas's guard. I surmised he must have been a military man by profession; some of his children—my mother's first cousins—had studied piano, and possibly composition, at the St. Petersburg Conservatory. Unhappily, the line of direct knowledge of that side of my family breaks off; I have no way of tracing what became of them after the Bolshevik Revolution turned the world upside-down in 1917.

The Hotel Leningrad sat diagonally across the Neva River from the Naval Academy. We could see moored close to the academy the old battleship *Potemkin,* which had played a major symbolic role in the workers' and military's uprisings against the czarist government at the start of the Bolshevik Revolution. It was impossible not to think of the Nevsky Prospect, the famous boulevard where the fashionable of St. Petersburg in Tolstoy's and Dostoyevsky's novels still stroll; of Sergei Eisenstein's gripping film about the legendary Alexander Nevsky and his people, and how they turned back and utterly destroyed the arrogant German Knight Templars' invasion of Holy Mother Russia to the music of Sergei Prokofiev's inimitable score, especially for the "Battle on the Ice." And it was impossible not to remember how the young Prokofiev, after a promising career in Europe and America, had fallen for the lies and blandishments of the communists, who lured him back into their giant spider's web from which he never extricated himself until he died, ironically, the same day as Stalin in 1953.

For the next stop, it was arranged that we had a compartment to ourselves in a first-class car. The irony was, of course, that in a "classless" society as Soviet Russia called itself, there should be first-, second-, and third-class cars—but that was the irreversible reality that no ideology could explain away. There was no food on the train, only hot tea served by a peasant-looking, babushka-wearing Russian woman who tended her samovar at one end of the car we were in. The daughter of one of the orchestra members had packed crackers and cheese in his bags for just such emergencies, and he was kind enough to share them with us. I don't think Gene or I slept much that night. I sat looking out the window into a bleak, dark, and depressed-looking landscape of small, huddled buildings. The landscape was monotonously flat, with few if any trees, close up or in the farther-removed distance, and few lights. It was almost impossible to form any image of that part of Russia we were moving through except for an image of black on black: black night on still blacker sludge of endless earth swallowed in darkness. In retrospect, it was almost like an Ad Reinhardt black-on-black abstraction on canvas. It was a great relief to pull into Moscow the next morning.

We were met at the train station and taken to the Hotel Rossia, a monstrously huge affair that covered four city blocks. It was worth your life to remember where your room was, on which floor, and what number. Getting and returning the key to your room was a cumbersome arrangement: you dealt with "the key lady." These women sat at desks (day and night, it seems), keeping track of keys and occupants. Besides a very large "breakfast room" on the ground floor where, for four rubles per person, you could eat your fill of sausages that came out of huge vats of steaming water, ham, eggs, potatoes, tea, and coffee, there were also small cafés in the corners of certain floors where you could have a snack and something to drink—but you had to remember on which floor and which corner of the floor they were.

The most memorable event involving food was a great banquet given for the entire Pittsburgh Symphony Orchestra. Course after course of the most delicious dishes were served, food unavailable to average Russians: every kind of meat, poultry, fish, salads, vegetables, desserts—and vodka that flowed like water. We found ourselves at the same table with some of the principals of the woodwind section. Bernard Goldberg, the first flute of the orchestra, who had been imbibing freely of the Russian elixir that, according to Dostoyevsky, was the chief cause of the perennial enslavement of the Russian peasant, insisted over and over again on how much better a composer he thought I was than Mahler. While I found his reasoning heavily flawed even as I enjoyed hearing his conclusion, whether or not I agreed with him didn't seem to concern him in the least. He finally offered one virtually incontestable argument, which, as far as I could tell, was not inspired by the quantity of vodka he had enjoyed: Mahler went on too long, he said, which, in my own opinion, was often the case and was in fact the chief reason I had always felt that Mahler had spoiled his Seventh Symphony, with an overlong last movement whose ideas simply did not match or live up to those that made the previous four so true and convincing. To clinch his point, Bernie summed up his position with a statement that had all the weight of the full conviction of finality: "Mahler," he said, "did not know when to stop, he didn't know when to shut up! You do." I had had just enough vodka myself to appreciate his insightful critique, therefore to agree with him—an agreement we sealed with a round of laughter that both relieves tension and, simultaneously, signifies a coming together of likemindedness, and, of course, with another shot of vodka.

Whenever I think of that brief time in Moscow, what rises to mind immediately—even more strongly than the memory of Maazel's profoundly dark performance of my Sixth—was the afternoon we spent walking in and around Red Square under the walls of the Kremlin, never out of sight of the medieval, almost primitively strong and remarkably colorful Church of St. Basil, with some nine small bulbous towers circling a much larger one that commandeered the center.

It was open that day, so we decided to see what its interior was like. Its absolute bareness of ornaments and icons, amounting to an odd sensation of emptiness in the pit of one's stomach, strikingly matched its bone-chilling coldness. There were just enough people—young, dressed shabbily but decently, in couples mostly—to give Red Square not a fullness, but some motion, a sluggish sense of activity reflected in the looks on the stolid faces I saw. Those are not the kind of looks one forgets easily. Here in Red Square were hundreds of young Soviet Russians, some, like ourselves, standing, watching the special-uniformed soldiers going though their robotic, high-military polish and its choreographed, ridiculously exaggerated motions, stiffly parading back and forth as they guarded the tomb of Lenin, where the saint of the communist revolution lay embalmed. The Russians' eyes registered zero, blankness, whether they stood and watched or walked away and resumed their weary steps around the square. There was no laughter. No smiles. Nor tender looks. Their young-old faces registered the lines of bitter disappointment in life, the unhappiness of their uncertain, bleak futures. Most of all, their helplessness. This is what I saw, took away with me, and cannot forget.

In a strangely unreal way, what I foresaw in Red Square that day was the sudden collapse of the Soviet system, the debacle of its implosion because of the accumulated dead weight of the entire apparatus of mismanagement and misgovernment that occurred only a few short months after we had been there in early October 1989.

In the years leading up to America's entry into World War II, Gene and I had close friends—all university students devoted to politics as well as music, art, theater, and literature but mostly to the politics of utopian intellectual theories bearing on the fate of man, in their case, with a heavy emphasis on Marxism. I was the only musician among them; Gene was actively pursuing her dream of becoming an actress. I listened avidly to the endless and erudite discussions of the Marxian theory of communism and particularly of events in Stalinist Russia that appalled us all in those prewar years. But there were times when I suddenly lost interest in the endlessly winding twists and turns of their byzantine talk and drifted over to the piano in the room—when there was one—and began to play Brahms or Beethoven or simply improvise. Stalin's brand of carrying out Lenin's idea of the "dictatorship of the proletariat" drove our friends straight into the arms of Trotsky's idea of international communism, an idea that was anathema to Stalin and Stalinists and for which Trotsky paid with his life.

Never an adept of the tortuous process of testing the validity of argumentation and opinion known as "dialectical materialism," an intellectual derivative of Marxism, I instinctively rejected communism, its theoretical varieties as well as the Lenin–Stalin system as practiced in the Soviet Union on the grounds of only one idea. That idea was Soviet socialist realism, according to which, "freedom" of artistic practice—the right to pursue one's work in peace, to be performed, published, and so on—in all the arts was granted *only* to the artist who consistently showed allegiance to the Soviet system by producing works that praised all of its illusory, nonexistent virtues. No "bourgeois decadent" backsliding was permitted; otherwise it was curtains for the offender. Soviet socialist realism broke Prokofiev's heart and tormented Shostakovich into a near-pathologic nervous wreck, killed the poet Osip Mandelstam, and sent Alexander Solzhenitsyn to the gulags and eventually into American exile.

All of this provided the rock-solid foundation of my intuitive rejection of abstract thinking in all forms, especially in art generally and applied rationalism in music particularly. Mental straitjackets—William Blake's "mind-forg'd manacles"—kill art and artists. The inevitably narrow limits of tailored systems of human thought cannot contain the energies of life and its mysteries. Nor can the reality of what we call "life" or its ineffable qualities—uncontainable within the limits of human understanding, let alone *control*—be tailored to the petty vagaries and unceasing appetites of overheated and oversized human egos.

The next—and last—stop for us: Warsaw, Poland. The Sixth was received well but without the excitement it had generated in Moscow. Musically, Warsaw was thoroughly familiar with advanced developments in Western Europe and America, even if politically Poland was still a satellite of Soviet Russia, dominated by communist controls. This strange mix may have affected Poles much more adversely than met the visitor's eye, but my sense of Warsaw, the look of it, of its people, was one of a much cleaner, more open, freer atmosphere, a far more Western city than the third-world, down-at-the-heels look of Leningrad and especially Moscow.

It was after our return home that the Soviet Union imploded and I realized we had been witness—however briefly—to the last dying gasps of one of the worst possible experiments of the twentieth century in social and political engineering, engaged in by unbelievably misguided human beings before it passed into the dust of history and oblivion.

Gods of Wrath

Phaedra, a Monodrama for
Mezzo-Soprano and Orchestra

The story of how I came to know Robert Lowell's wondrous evocation of Phaedra's tragic fate is a perfect instance of how small things can sometimes have major consequences. The "small thing" in this case was Gene's and my desire to see our friend Miriam Philips act the role of Oenone, Phaedra's nurse, in the production of the Lowell play being presented by the Theater of the Living Arts repertory company in Philadelphia in May 1967. The major consequence of experiencing this production of Lowell's verse translation of Racine's *Phèdre*[1] has been a lifelong involvement with the mythological figure of a woman invested with proportions of tragic grandeur. What I saw on the stage that night was incredibly vivid: an actress whom I'd never seen before or since, Diana Sands, played the role of Phaedra, a woman torn apart by illicit love for her stepson, Hippolytus—son of her husband, Theseus, king of Athens—with a passion of barbaric ferocity that totally convinced. Sands became the living, larger-than-life Phaedra. She was not merely a professional actress skillfully portraying a character in a play, she was Phaedra herself—raging brilliance. She spoke Robert Lowell's lines with such a heightened passionate diction that his poetry filled the theater with a ringing power that took on the reverberating resonance of music—verbal music. It was that transformation that made me want to set Phaedra, in all her barbaric pain and ferocity, to music.

I was especially happy when Gene agreed to shape Lowell's five-act drama into a text suitable to my purpose, concentrating on the high points, the emotional peaks of Phaedra's tragedy. Only they would be sung. For the rest, the narrative aspects would be treated instrumentally, as interludes. To have treated them vocally would have necessitated writing an opera. Which would have subverted my initial impulse to write a tightly focused monodrama for a single singer and diluted the concentration on the monumental figure of Phaedra, the ill-fated wife of Theseus, legendary Greek hero, Minotaur-slayer. I read Lowell's play over and over—looking for those texts that would provide the essential emotional substance of Phaedra's story for the four arias I had in mind. Each would represent a major emotional peak in the tragic unfolding of her tale. The more I read and reread, the more I was entranced by the polished craft and rightness of Lowell's language—a unique American English, a bit old-fashioned, formal yet relaxed, with its unforced rhymes and strong images.

Lowell relates in an indirect, almost diffident, way that his play is the third in a progression from the fifth-century-B.C. Greek poet-dramatist Euripides' *Hippolytos* to the seventeenth-century French classical dramatist Jean Racine's *Phèdre*. He states, "Racine quite alters, and to my mind, even surpasses his wonderful original."[2] That alteration undoubtedly shifted the focus of the myth-based *Hippolytos* of Euripides to the Hippolytus of Lowell's Phaedra and her insane, uncontrollable love, making her the fulcrum on which the tragedy hinges. Lowell refers to his version based on Racine as "free," adding,

> nevertheless, I have used every speech in the original, and almost every line is either translated or paraphrased. Racine is said to have written prose drafts and then versed them . . . In versing Racine, I have taken the same liberty . . . I have translated as a poet, and tried to give my lines a certain dignity, speed and flare [*sic*].[3]

The order of vocal and orchestral sections of my monodrama is as follows:

ARIA: In May in Brilliant Athens
INTERLUDE: Black Sails
ARIA: You Monster!
INTERLUDE: Theseus' Homecoming
SUPPLICATION: Theseus, I Heard the Deluge of Your Voice
CABALETTA: My Last Calamity Has Come
POSTLUDE: The Death of Hippolytus

I chose for the first aria a long speech of Phaedra's in act 1, scene 3, where she describes to her nurse Oenone the very moment she laid eyes on Hippolytus, which was the day of her wedding to his father, Theseus. Gene fashioned a repetitive refrain strophic text based on Lowell's phrase "In May, / in brilliant Athens, on my marriage day."

In the background of the text from which this opening strophic aria derives lies the wrathful goddess of love Aphrodite, whose endless appetite for wreaking vengeance on every mortal who has crossed her is infamous in myth. Hence

Phaedra's bitter outcry to Oenone early in the play: "Remorseless Aphrodite drives me. I, my race's last and worst love-victim, die." The Greek scholar Edith Hamilton corroborates this when she describes how Phaedra falls in love with Hippolytus "madly and miserably, overwhelmed with shame at such a love, but unable to conquer it. Aphrodite was back of this wretched and ominous state of affairs. She was angry at Hippolytus and determined to punish him to the utmost."[4] Aphrodite kills two mortals with one stone in an unbridled love passion.

The second aria, "You Monster!," is based on a long speech of Phaedra's in act 2, scene 5. News has reached Theseus's court that "fearful tales / are circulating. Sailors saw his [Theseus's] sails, / his infamous black sails, spin round and round / in Charybdis' whirlpool; all hands were drowned." Hippolytus now confesses his love to Aricia, a princess of Athens whose six brothers have been killed by Theseus in an unsuccessful attempt to wrest the throne away from him. With her husband believed dead, Phaedra feels free to confess her mad love for Hippolytus. In the scene when she confronts Hippolytus, he rejects her protestations of love with a horrified "What are you saying, Madam? You forget / my father is your husband!" Phaedra loses all control and pours out the venom of her poisoned love. This confessional scene is a grand *recitando* for the singer in free, arioso style, all-out musically intense, in which a subtle, flexible relationship exists between the voice and the orchestra, one in which the voice remains essentially free of the beat while the orchestra recovers the beat when necessary.

From this point on, events move inexorably toward the violently tragic end. The report of Theseus's death at sea turns out to be false—a mere rumor. He returns home, utterly bewildered by the coldness that greets him. Theseus cannot comprehend what has happened in his absence. He says, "Wait, let no one stir. / Phaedra shall tell me what has troubled her." In the last scene of this act, Hippolytus has a brief monologue: "I feel the rot / of love seeping like poison through this house. / I feel the pollution. I cannot rouse / my former loyalties."

Oenone, Phaedra's nurse and companion, in act 4, scene 1, leaks the truth of Phaedra's earlier confession to her of her love for Hippolytus. Through her innuendo and veiled hints, Theseus misconstrues her meaning and rushes to the conclusion that Hippolytus, his beloved son, has seduced Phaedra against her will. Enraged, Theseus calls on Poseidon, the sea god, to avenge him, and nothing Hippolytus can say will mollify his father.

The third vocal section is a "supplication arioso" in which Phaedra, having heard that Hippolytus is banished, and fearing for his life, pleads with her husband. I cast this arioso in the ethos and language of the baroque: long, unfolding vocal lines—a quasi-passacaglia falling chromatic bass in the orchestra at the start, also appearing as interludes, accompanimental figuration, and again at the conclusion. It has a curiously distant sense of echoing the pathos and depth of the only English baroque composer whose harmonic world and richness I have long admired, Henry Purcell—especially in his "When I Am Laid in Earth" aria in *Dido and Aeneas.*

Theseus can't believe that Phaedra is pleading for his son's life, which only reinforces his conviction that Hippolytus is guilty. In act 4, scene 6, Phaedra describes to her nurse Oenone what she calls "my last calamity"—the knowledge that Hippolytus loves and wants not her, not Phaedra, but Aricia . The aria that follows derives from that text: "My Last Calamity Has Come." Of the four vocal pieces in *Phaedra,* it is the most pathologically driven, the most explosively hysterical. Also the most difficult rhythmically for the singer, depending as it does on constant offbeats, and the most complex and ornate in its inner orchestral workings.

Three orchestral interludes complete the work, acting not so much as bearers of narrative connectives between vocal sections, but as descriptive of moods and events of primary import in driving the play forward to its inexorable end. The first of them, "Black Sails," based almost entirely on interlocking fanfares— portentous, ominous—recalls the mood surrounding the unfounded, false reports of Theseus's death at sea. The second, "Theseus' Homecoming," attempts to evoke the strangeness and coldness of the mood of his return—his troubled sense that something is deeply wrong and the wild feelings that grip him as he concludes too quickly that Hippolytus has breached honor and decency. Inevitably, the last of the orchestral interludes is "The Death of Hippolytus"—brought about by wrathful Poseidon at Theseus's prayer.

Phaedra, commissioned by the New Music Ensemble of Syracuse, New York, was given its first performance by soprano Neva Pilgrim with the Syracuse Symphony, David Loebel conducting, on January 9, 1976. Neither this nor a subsequent performance with Lucy Shelton, soprano, met what I felt were the dramatic, emotional, and musical dimensions needed to bring off the role of the splendidly tragic Phaedra. To be completely convincing, Phaedra had to be sung by a singer with the artistic range and personality that encompassed the size of the character she has to portray—whether in concert or on the stage. Not until 1998 did such a singer-artist appear.

The circumstance that brought this about was Gilbert Rose's visit to Newtown Square to discuss what works to program for a retrospective concert of my music for my eightieth year. I'd met Gil a few years before, soon after he had founded and was conducting the Boston Modern Orchestra Project (BMOP) to considerable critical acclaim for adventuresome programming exploring the range of twentieth-century music, and for the panache and professionalism of his musicians and his conducting. Projected against the staid, conventional fare offered by the Boston Symphony and the long-established new music ensembles functioning on the periphery of the musical life of a city like Boston, Gil and BMOP had clearly injected a new and energetic spirit and enthusiasm into a tired, stale situation. In those earlier days, Gil had given a tremendously persuasive account of my *Music for the Magic Theater,* and that convinced me he could bring off a retrospective with style and polish. Among the works I thought would best show the wide span of my music, *Phaedra* would fit perfectly.

Not only for its representation of my large-scale vocal–orchestral music and its particularly unique uses of tonality—from early baroque to extensions through dissonant chromaticism bordering the atonal—but especially because I saw *Phaedra* as one of my most effective pieces of *hard* romanticism. Not simply what some like to call "neoromanticism"—a meaningless term at best—but a full-blown romanticism where human emotions are stretched to their most extreme breaking point. Gil took to the idea right away, and the search for just the right singer was on. It led straight to Mary Nessinger.

In the spring of 1998, Gil and Mary came to Newtown Square to begin our preparations. We worked for hours, during which I played through the "Supplication" aria, indicated what I thought were the right tempi for the quicker, more agitated movements (the opening "In May" aria and the closing "Cabaletta"), and how to treat the "You Monster!" aria as an explosive, grand *recitativo.* I urged them to read Lowell's play to get the full sense and depth of the harrowing story that had inspired the music. I wanted them to see what I saw: a Phaedra driven by passions beyond her control, a Phaedra who was both pawn and victim of the cruel whims and wiles of pagan gods and goddesses acting more out of caprice than design. If possible, to ponder the enormous divide between completely opposite sets of beliefs in the nonhuman forces that impinge on and determine the lives humans live—a pagan culture of polytheism at the root of the ancient Greek myths that animated and ruled the natural world indifferent to the creatures who inhabited it, eventually supplanted by the rise of a Judeo-Christian Western culture whose monotheism(s) claimed to offer the easy consolations—perhaps even protection—of a personal god.

It would reduce Phaedra to sheer meaninglessness to envision her as a hysterically dysfunctional, contemporary Western woman bordering on the pathological, merely another instance of human passions gone off the rails, caught in the confusions of modern life, and thereby deprive her of the grandeur of her struggles against implacable forces she is convinced are invisibly weaving her fate and willing her death. I wanted to open them to an insight into the ancient pagan view of raw and wracked passions that can only lose out against the nonhuman forces stacked against them. How else to grasp the iron-clad web of fate that brings Phaedra down—and Hippolytus with her?

The BMOP retrospective took place in Jordan Hall of the New England Conservatory of Music, October 17, 1998, followed by two days of recording.[5] The program consisted of four thoroughly diverse works: *Phaedra* (1973–74); *Cheltenham Concerto* (1958) for fifteen winds, brasses, and strings, a twelve-tone work; *Cantio Sacra* (1953), a transcription for oboe, English horn, trumpet, trombone, and string orchestra of a set of organ variations on "Warum betrübst du dich, mein Herz" by Samuel Scheidt, one of the better predecessors of J. S. Bach; and *Black Sounds* (1965) for an ensemble of seventeen players.

The surprise of the October 17 concert was the audience's response to *Black Sounds*—a strikingly colorful work and an uninhibited projection of visceral feelings. All of it is steeped in the atonal, operating at high decibel levels. Both musicians and nonmusicians were wildly enthusiastic, completely won over by it. I had looked forward to *Phaedra* capturing their hearts, hence my surprise. Which proves (once again?) that what a composer prizes most among his own works may not necessarily accord with the tastes of others.

The time of *Phaedra* is still very real and alive in my memory. What was the urge, besides Diana Sands, to write the work, and why do I place such importance on what it represents and conveys, not only as music, but as an echoing of a long-gone past, buried deep beneath layer on layer of two thousand and more years of other and totally different human cultures groping toward greater and greater freedom for human beings? Could *Phaedra* be part of the same urge to reconnect with a more ancient world, a pagan world closer in touch with the cosmos than we are today, that pagan world represented in the old Hindu poetry of Krishna and Radha, the god figure and the woman of human origins, which led to my *Songs in Praise of Krishna* (1970), and those old pagan stories and religious beliefs in the great Sumerian goddess Inanna and her human king-consort Dumuzi, which led to my *Songs of Inanna and Dumuzi* (1977)? These three works—all vocal—parallel and derive from some of the very cultures of the pagan world that D. H. Lawrence describes as "the great river civilizations of the Euphrates, the Nile and the Indus, with the lesser sea-civilization of the Aegean."[6]

What was it I wanted to (and still feel the necessity to) reconnect with? A world richer in feelings and symbols than our deadened, shallow, emptied-out world? A world that unlocks feelings and senses buried deep in our genes? These are not idle questions, nor are the questionings merely some private fancy on my part. They stem from the troubled sense that has shadowed me my entire conscious adult existence: that our time, our Western civilization, has long since reached its limit and, with the giant blows of both world wars and world upheavals that accompanied and followed from them, began the Great Unraveling.

These days since the turn to the twenty-first century have become, indeed, the "days of terror" described in story form in my 1970 essay on "Humanism versus Science"[7]—"days of terror" that have befallen America, Israel, and Europe in brutal, actualized destruction and death issuing from the vicious hatred burning deep in the bowels of barbaric Islamic terrorists. This is how D. H. Lawrence saw it back in 1929–30:

> We have lost almost entirely the great and intricately developed sensual aware-ness, or sense-awareness, and sense-knowledge of the ancients. It was a great depth of knowledge arrived at direct, by instinct and intuition, as we say, not by reason . . . And the connection was not logical but emotional.[8]

Which explains in part why Phaedra can be larger than life, and why the gods who weave the dread loom of fate about her, Hippolytus, and Theseus (Oedipus, Electra, and Orestes, as well . . .), are symbols of cosmic, nonhuman forces against which humans can only contend but never defeat or overcome.

CHAPTER 12

A Triptych of Sonatas

Sonata for Violin and Piano (1988),
Sonata for Viola and Piano (1979),
Sonata-Aria for Cello and Piano (1992)

Before I knew anything about the history and background of chamber-music literature for solo string instruments and piano, the very sound of the violin, viola, or cello in concert with the piano exerted a magnetism I found irresistible. Its intimacy of expression set it apart from the bigger-boned trio for violin, cello, and piano or the string quartet, in their separate ways far more public forms of musical expression. Beethoven's "Kreutzer" Sonata, op. 47, for violin and piano, is one of the great exceptions. It is about as large a public, musical statement as one can find in what is essentially a private, intimate form of expression for two thoroughly contrasting instruments.

There is a magic in these duos with their constantly changing patterns of color, in the subtle varieties of sound patterns as different registers and textures mix, mingle, and share in a composed design of exchange. Sometimes I experienced flashes of a synesthesia of two of our principal faculties of perception—hearing and seeing simultaneously, the one translating into the other. Very much like hearing the slowly or rapidly shifting patterns of sounds as though they were cloud shapes seen catching and losing the rays of the sun.

Only a few composers have had the luck to make this magic happen consistently—Mozart, Beethoven, and Brahms. The secret of how they managed this lay in their inordinate skill in handling the art of musical conversation—how their incomparable ideas were made to pass from one instrument to the other in an inevitable, seamless flow of dialogue. The root of the art of chamber style lies precisely in this give-and-take, back-and-forth play between equal partners carrying on a musical dialogue whose meaning cannot be construed as anything other than how thoroughly the rich nature of the composer's ideas and its design of exchange engages both players and listeners. This is as true for J. S. Bach's viola da gamba sonatas with harpsichord as it is for the duo sonatas of Mozart, Beethoven, and Brahms.

For a budding composer, making a duo for violin and piano come to life is incalculably important. That is why I look back on my friendship and association in the late 1930s with the solidly schooled violinist Ken Dean as more than ordinarily crucial to my development. How many times we played César Franck's Sonata for Violin and Piano is of far less importance than the fact that through those performances I experienced directly the making of the musical dialogue of Franck's design, his wonderfully rich chromatic harmony (with more than one hint of what I later came to call "circular harmonic progressions") and particularly the amazing freshness and flow of the felicitously natural canon that passed back and forth between the two instruments as the principal melodic idea of the last movement.

All this bore fruit in my first attempt to master the violin–piano duo in the sonata I wrote about 1939–40. Its language inevitably reflected its sources: traditional tonality as spoken by Mozart, Beethoven, and Brahms, with specially clear indications pointing to some of the more idiosyncratic approaches to the overall structural design and melodic gestures of all three. For example, in the first movement I attempted to adopt the nobility of tone and quasi-improvisatory searching of a Beethovian slow introduction leading into a Brahmsian sonata-allegro first theme. Even though I later rejected the work, at the time I threw myself with great enthusiasm into playing it with Ken Dean as often as possible.

One of those occasions left a strong residual memory, if for no other reason than that it was in the grand old tradition of a musical evening amid quite elegant surroundings. The place was in New Jersey, an unusually large living room with high ceilings, stark white walls, and numerous wrought-iron pieces of rich design plus a sophisticated company of artists, musicians, and cognoscenti of the arts gathered in the studio-home of Reginald Marsh. Marsh was already a well-known painter whose canvasses bustled energetically with crowds of people going about the business of living while enjoying being thoroughly immersed in it.

That night I was introduced to a composer who, while he had nice things to say about my sonata, took the trouble to point out in a kindly manner that some of the devices I used had long since gone by the boards—were outmoded, anachronistic: for example, the eighteenth- and nineteenth-century device of note or chord repetition in rapid succession to create a sense of animation and forward motion. It was my introduction to the critical hazards of not being up-to-date, "contemporary," and started me on the road to wrestling with the problems of the past and the present and their often bruising confrontation. Particularly, I was concerned, on the one hand, with how to reconcile them and, on the other, eventually, how to justify the ways of my own time—its deviations and abrogations—with the still-overpowering presence of the old masters.

In November 1942 my life changed drastically: I was drafted into the army. Gene went to Minneapolis to stay with our friends the McCloskys, and I went to Fort Dix, New Jersey, and from there was shipped to Fort McClellan, a camp in Anniston, Alabama, for basic training.

In the weeks before departure I was at work on a new violin–piano sonata, and when the time came to leave each other and the New York we'd both come to love, composing music ceased. Actually I had roughed out two movements in sketch, more a melodic and harmonic outlining of what I had in mind than a finished piece of work. Even so, the outlining itself marked a significant change in direction, and though at the time not fully aware of its implications, I had discovered—"stumbled on" would perhaps be an even more accurate description—the musical "hieroglyph," the harmonic pitch aggregate that symbolized the equal division into two groups of six and six half steps each of the twelve chromatic notes of Western music. This hieroglyph—I call it that to emphasize its symbolic, magical property—provided the essential melodic characteristics of the main theme of the first movement: the linked pairs of intervals, F–C and B–F♯, which outlined the fundamental tonal fifths of the two keys bound together by the tritone F–B. In retrospect I know it was my parallel study of Bartók's music and his way with chromaticizing an extended form of tonality that had opened my ears to the possibilities inherent in such tonal extensions, which spilled over into new ways of thinking and hearing melodically.

Decades passed before I took up these unfinished sketches and fashioned what in 1979 became not a sonata for violin and piano, as originally intended, but a sonata for viola and piano. However, first I need to tell the story of the Sonata for Violin and Piano (1988), a four-movement work where, finally, I was able to realize a lifelong ambition to produce a full-scale violin–piano duo with a complex emotional scenario embracing the intimate and public realms of expression.

Maria Bachmann, a superbly gifted young violinist, took first prize in the 1986 Concert Artists Guild International New York Competition. The guild, whose principal aim was to encourage and further the professional careers of unusually promising performers, approached me with the idea of writing a major work for Maria, which she would perform publicly and also record. A commission was arranged, with additional funding from the McKim Fund in the Music Division of the Library of Congress and the New York State Arts Council. Maria had studied composition privately with me while pursuing her violin studies at the Curtis

Institute. With her keen ear and refinement in musical taste and style in playing, she brought to her music making an enviable technical command combined with a wide range of subtlety and sensitivity. When I set about writing the sonata for her and her duo partner, Jon Klibonoff—a strongly talented pianist of expressive power and technical prowess—I felt free to attempt a work with no limits on what I asked of them musically. Together they made a perfectly matched duo capable of a gamut of expression that ranged from releasing torrents of searing emotionalism to the most tender passages, from the sense of a dark, haunted hopelessness to the transcendent weightlessness of being freed of gravity.

The range of what the sonata expressed spread throughout the four movements. Yet each had its individual stamp. The opening movement I called Sarabande because its general cast, following the tradition of melancholic rumination characteristic of the baroque sarabande, weaves a slowly evolving, intricate tapestry of brief figures and motives drawn from the solo violin soliloquy that begins the work and carries faint echoes of the feeling world of Bach's solo partitas. A touch of gargoylish music marks the beginning of the Scherzo Capriccioso that follows. The violin and piano are entangled in a swiftly moving will-o'-the-wisp canon that leads to unleashing the harsher, uglier side of gargoyle music—sharply punctuated percussive passages constituting the main body of the movement from measure 22 to a developmental reprise of the canon theme, which carries over to measure 202 followed by a final, hushed restatement of the canon between violin and piano.

The canon itself was first sketched during World War II, when the unit to which I was attached was holding a defensive position in the Saarland region in January 1945. Except for the heavy artillery shells that passed overhead at random times during the day—we dubbed ours "outgoing mail," the Germans' "incoming mail"—an ominous, unsettling quiet hung over the area. Whether outgoing or incoming, they sounded like huge railroad cars whooshing as they rushed through the air. The biting cold of winter and the occasional patrols on which we were sent kept us from lapsing into somnolence.

The third and fourth movements are each—in separate ways—fantasias on a wide variety of characteristic motives. The motive that dominates the final movement had already made its appearance earlier in the second movement. My favorite passages are the interior Adagio of movement three where the violin floats high up into the stratosphere on the E string—calm, tender, murmuring— and the *più grave* at the end of the fourth movement, where the piano, in a stark, almost passacaglia-like bass-register melody, brings the work to its dark close as the violin, mainly on its lower strings, mutters broken fragments of chromaticized commentary in disconnected pizzicato phrases. These are extensions of the first muttered phrase, whose pitches are E♭–D–E♮–C♯, which form an anagram of the prominent motto figure (C♯–E♮–E♭–D) that appears in every movement, whether in its original or transposed form or as still another variant anagram.

The recording Maria and Jon made for the Connoisseur Society in 1990 is a model of duo partnership.[1] I have always enjoyed the idea of their coupling my sonata with the great "Kreutzer" Sonata of Beethoven, in which they showed their grasp of one of the greatest duos for violin and piano ever composed. Each acts as a perfect foil for the other: the diatonic tonal design of Beethoven carried out on a grand scale pitted against the hard romanticism of a highly chromaticized and extended tonality of a late twentieth-century duo that attempts to open out the language of the previous century in an enlarged vocabulary expressing the contemporary psychology of musical dialogue.

How did a large sketch of what was originally intended to be a sonata for violin and piano turn into a sonata for viola and piano? That is indeed what happened to the two movements I had to abandon in 1942 because of the war and the draft, and this is how it came about.

In 1978 the "Friends of William Primrose"—the celebrated master of the viola—the American Viola Society, and Brigham Young University commissioned me to write a work in honor of his seventy-fifth birthday. That was the catalyst that led to the sonata I wrote for the occasion. In casting about for the right approach to the music I wanted to produce for the Primrose piece, I decided to dig out the old violin sonata sketches and test their possibilities. Uppermost in my mind was a series of questions that had to do primarily with the viability of the old ideas and their emotional substance. Would they lend themselves to transference to the darker timbres of the viola? Would the overall qualities of my initial ideas sound *natural* to the viola—not just larger than the violin, but also more plangent in tone? It was the dirgelike, sadly singing character of the second-movement music that ultimately decided the issue. Inevitably, a good many changes resulted in reworking the old sketches and proved the rightness of my decision to go ahead. At the same time, rewriting the piano part in order to achieve a true duo sound made the version for viola take on the kind of new life and color I wanted.

I did virtually nothing to alter the basic design of the 1942 sketch. I touched it here and there to add fluency or strength, but I did nothing to add to or take away from either of the essential structures of the original two movements. I wanted to preserve the traditional sonata form of the first and the lyric-song form of the second. Also, I wanted to maintain the initial thought-forms of the thematic content. Its very variety suited the necessities of the formal functions, therefore the continuities of melodic thinking.

I fussed a great deal over the harmony of the piano part. This was crucial, because the relation between the viola and piano parts depended on how inevitably
they meshed, how well they sounded together. The piano part blossomed under
the changes I made, especially those passages in the first movement where the
viola carries the first theme. After reworking the two movements, I played them
for Gene. I suggested she listen as though they constituted the finished work. In
effect, I was saying the sonata could stand as a two-movement statement. When
the ending of the Adagio lamentoso had faded away, she immediately said, "But
it's not finished. It needs something more to give it that sense of completion, that
feeling that everything that needed to be said has been said."

Instinctively, I knew she was right, but all along I had resisted the feeling that
something of a definitive, concluding nature needed to follow the Adagio lamentoso. The kind of last movement I knew I could not add—that in fact I detested—
was a fast, concluding movement in order to fulfill a purely perfunctory function.
If anything, it would have to speak the language and expressive character of what
preceded it. I rejected the idea of a stormy finale—a kind of "battle scenario" merely
to round off the old fast–slow–fast structural format. After days of fretting and
worrying about the problem, I settled on writing an epilogue, one that had the
sense of "remembrance of things past," a musical recollection of major idiomatic
elements that were characteristic of the opening Allegro moderato movement. To
accomplish this I knew that I needed to write a fantasia—a free, open, unhampered
musical flow that went from thought to thought without being bound into a tight
formal structure. The Fantasia: Epilogue became the shortest of the three movements, but despite its restless, constantly changing motion from idea to idea, it
ends the work with a sense of deep repose and resolution—paradoxically, because
of its last, stabbing, painful, *più forte espressivo* outburst just before the concluding
pianissimo F-major chord.

Two friends and good colleagues, Joseph de Pasquale, then principal violist
of the Philadelphia Orchestra, and pianist Vladimir ("Billy") Sokoloff, gave the
first performance on July 14, 1979, in Provo, Utah, at the Seventh International
Viola Congress.

As I approach discussing the third sonata of this triptych, the feeling has grown
stronger and stronger that I have been writing an informal—however personalized
it may be—history of twentieth-century music and its discontents. It is very much to
the point that these three sonatas are hinged at one end to 1942, the time of World
War II, and at the other to 1992, fifty years later, the time of the Gulf War.

Collectively, these discontents form a messy, even sorry, record of endlessly rising, trumpeted enthusiasms—their many frustrations and failures, their short life spans—all part of the efforts to find a new musical speech for the twentieth century, itself marred by profoundly tragic events and failed hopes for human beings. Nor did the few major successes in twentieth-century music—individual works by Stravinsky, Schoenberg, Bartók, Berg, and Varèse—add up to more than hints and clues toward a larger language for wider general use. Even the effort to reconnect with tonal tradition turned out to be an incomplete and insufficient answer to the needs of a baffling situation—baffling because it was misread, misunderstood, and misperceived, all due mainly to the strong prejudice for pseudoscientific points of view, aided and abetted by the equally strong penchant for method and rationalism sanctioned in academe.

Gradually, from 1965 on, it came to me that if there were an answer, it lay in the direction of wedding old tonal means (as practiced by the classical masters through Brahms and Mahler) seen from new points of view to whatever remained still vital from the best of the early modernist period. What was needed was an *ars combinatoria,* an art of combination, out of which could develop the widest possible range within the elastic bounds of an *all-at-once world.* That world and its potentially all-encompassing language describe not only the musical content of the *Sonata-Aria,* but its title, as well. Much earlier, I had begun inventing compound titles that joined together terms designating major design and gestural characteristics—hence, *Sonata-Fantasia* (1956) and *Partita-Variations* (1976). In the case of the *Sonata-Aria* (1992) for cello and piano, I was pointing directly to the strong presence of traditional sonata-form elements sewn into and through the long-spanned, cantabile role of the cello's Aria.

The opening of the *Sonata-Aria* through measure 66 can be taken as the first thematic group of a sonata-form exposition: in the cello, there is a line of musical thought made up of linking, consecutive motives that play important roles throughout, though not necessarily always in the same order as initially presented. Similarly, the piano part projects crucial rhythmic and harmonic sequences and patterns that also figure in later significant developmental passages. At measure 67, *molto calmo,* piano figurations prepare the way for the first appearance of the cello Aria. This half-whispered, half-spoken, cantabile line is a single melody made up of two distinct phrases—in the old terminology of traditional phrase structure, *antecedent* and *consequent*—the first, nine slow measures long, the second, ten. This first statement of the Aria, with its six-measure piano introduction establishing the harmonic and emotional atmosphere, can also be understood as the second thematic group of the exposition.

The continuing interplay of the ideas of the two thematic, exposition groups provides ample opportunity for developments of a wide range and variety of gesture and levels of intensity. There follow five separate and consecutive developmental groups, each of a different character. Is there a recapitulation? Not in any observable, usual sense of the term. There are varied references to and repetitions of significant elements of the exposition, true; but I have accounted for them as being more developmental in character than as probable hints at recapitulation. What militates against the latter is the emotional scenario of the work, which makes a recapitulation in the conventional sense unnecessary. Not only does it lack necessity, but to have forced one on the work would have been artificial and unconvincing, therefore unnatural and false. Hence its absence.

No name exists for this freeform use of sonata and aria, nor for the manner in which the various ideas and sections are deployed. Their succession is dictated by the logic of emotion and feeling: that which is necessary in an organic, morphological sense—that is, as an outgrowth of energy forms that seek realization as they move in time. Perhaps, then, the *Sonata-Aria* falls somewhere between how I tend to proceed in my imagistic music—for instance, the *Ukiyo-E* pieces—and an intuitively felt rather than formal approach to the major aspects of the principles that underpin the sonata form seen as a yet historically evolving musical structure with no final, ultimately finished form possible.

No single key defines the tonality of the overall organization of *Sonata-Aria*. Rather, the description itself must be broadened to take into account the four large nodal points that constitute the defining symmetry of its multitonal centers. These four nodes are equidistant minor thirds that form the traditional diminished chord in the earlier language of monotonality: B♭–C♯–E♮–G♮. Since all these intervals are equidistant, symmetrical rotation can occur starting from C♯ or E♮ or G♮ without altering the diminished chord itself or its identification of symmetrized multi-key-centered tonal functions. These multi-key-centered passages play significant roles in the development sections.

The gravitational pull to a single tonal center no longer holds in multi-key centers. Whichever of the metaphors fits best, whether monarchic or despotic, authoritarian or tyrannical, single-key control has been relinquished to multicenters. Centers of gravity are also dispersed. Yet structure in the overall sense, while different from diatonic monotonality, remains clear and audible. Enlarged tonality permits not only distribution of control over more than a single center, it permits also the expansion of harmonic material to include traditional triadic harmony and harmonic progressions, as well as nontraditional atonal constructions, whether clustered formations or highly chromaticized aggregates. Nevertheless there is no contradiction in suggesting that, in the aesthetic of an *all-at-once world,* composing in the diatonic, monotonal tradition remains eminently possible. Since the occasion warranted, I did not hesitate to do so in my

Ricordanza (1972) for cello and piano, *Partita-Variations* (1976) for piano solo, and individual movements in the Quintet for Piano and String Quartet (1985) and String Quintet (1982).

The *Sonata-Aria* was written in 1992 as a memorial to Norman Fischer's father, Gerald J. Fischer. Norman and his wife, Jeanne, formed the Fischer Duo (cello and piano) after the demise of the Concord String Quartet. They first performed the duo at the Shepherd School of Music, Rice University, Houston, Texas, on January 25, 1993.

Their devotion to Jerry Fischer went very deep and proved itself in the endless hours they worked on their own and with me to give everything possible to the fullest realization of the work they (and their family and friends) had commissioned from me. I had decided on a single, uninterrupted, through-composed sonata based on ruminations on the opening E-minor chord of Brahms's Sonata, op. 38, the first of his two remarkable cello–piano sonatas. What emerged, I later realized, was another "grief-eating" piece that came to mean as much to me as it did to Norman and Jeanne, and while we never discussed that aspect of it, I am convinced that the very intensity of their performances of *Sonata-Aria* reflected their awareness of its presence. No one who hears their recording can miss their profoundly personal relation to the work.[2] Their incomparable duo-playing covers the widest possible range from the most sensitively tender, melancholic contemplation of the hardest reality we know in life to the raging paroxysms and outbursts of almost-impossible-to-contain emotions verging on near chaos to a final, hard-won acceptance of the ultimate mystery that surrounds all human existence.

In 1941, I wrote a song for low voice and piano using text of Percy Bysshe Shelley's grief-laden poem that encloses in its imagery all personal loss and its private pain and the boundless cry against "the world's wrong." It is a fitting close to this chapter.

A DIRGE

Rough wind, that moanest loud
Grief too sad for song;
Wild wind, when sullen cloud
Knells all the night long;
Sad storm, whose tears are vain,
Bare woods, whose branches strain,
Deep caves and dreary main,—
Wail, for the world's wrong!

CHAPTER 13

Blown on the Wind
Oboe and Clarinet Concertos

Once I had left behind the twelve-tone world and the intensities of ordered chromaticism, I returned not only to my early love of classical tonal music, but also to my early infatuation and experience with popular song. Often—and quite unconsciously—I took full advantage of the plastic inflections and almost speech-like *parlando* delivery of the old popular songs that had long since formed a rich deposit alongside the classical sources to which they themselves were distantly related.

A clear, yet not always specific (as to sources), imprint of the generic phraseology and inflection of popular song left its mark on my two wind concertos. In each of them, the opening melodic lines unmistakably show the intermixture of *parlando*-like lines cast in the generic mold and manner of popular song and melodic types normally associated with traditional classical models. The same is true of my Violin Concerto, especially the high-on-the-fingerboard opening of the violin melody supported by clusterlike harmonies of the second Intermezzo fourth movement; also of the opening flute line of *Muse of Fire* for flute and guitar (which reappears, recast in variant form in my third trio for violin, cello, and piano, *Summer, 1990*).

The sheer infectiousness of American popular song—its immediacy of melodic appeal—brings to mind the key phrases in a letter Mozart wrote to his father, Leopold, phrases that constitute "the Mozartean aesthetic," a tradition on which rested the concept of "learnèd," very much alive in Bach's time and still vital in the generations that followed. As much a psychology as a philosophy of composition that Mozart himself adhered to as a matter of deep conviction, the essence of these few lines seems to be based on keen, lifelong observation of the music of his contemporaries, some of which—Haydn's for example—he admired greatly, most of which he dismissed out of hand. Mozart insists that the surface of music—what is immediately perceptible—be "pleasing" to the ear while what is beneath that surface should be "learnèd," the result of high craft in the realms of harmonic progression and uses of the contrapuntal art. In a letter of September 26, 1781, describing a particularly emotional and turbulent aria from his opera *Die Entfürung aus dem Serail,* he writes, "The music in the most tremorous situation [must] *never offend the ear, but . . . be pleasing, remaining as a consequence always music.*"[1]

Alfred Einstein sums up "the Mozartean aesthetic" in a "nutshell," as he calls it: "Music must not 'sweat,' it must be natural, though controlled with the highest art."[2] His paraphrase refers to an earlier letter of October 14, 1777, where Mozart describes his reaction to a concerto for two flutes of a contemporary, Friedrich Graf: "It is not at all pleasing to the ear, not a bit natural. He often plunges into a new key far too brusquely and it is all quite devoid of charm . . . The poor fellow must have taken a great deal of trouble over it and he must have studied hard enough."[3] Einstein comments that "Mozart prefers to hide his counterpoint, to conceal his 'art'; it must not appear as artificiality."[4]

I have raised the issue of Mozart's aesthetic because it points the way to its relevance to my two wind concertos. As I tell the stories of writing them, the Mozartean aesthetic's stress on an appealing surface melodic line (*il filo,* as Mozart and his father called it) combined with high craft and hidden art underneath the natural flow of the line will emerge.

My parents had generously arranged for me to have a cottage on a farm in upper New York State for the summer of 1946. It was the first real vacation Gene, Paul, and I had together since I returned from the war. I was twenty-eight and more determined than ever to make up for lost time. That summer, on a screened-in porch, I spent hours every day plowing through Paul Hindemith's harmony book, doing all the exercises in it to his quirky, idiosyncratic melodies in order to train my ear away from the piano. In any case, there was no piano to be had. As a relief from this self-imposed labor, I also began writing small two-voiced pieces—"exercises" in their way, but freer and more challenging than the hurdles Hindemith provided. From these pieces emerged a duo for oboe and bassoon with hints of Hindemithian melodic overtones—not surprising considering what I'd been doing all summer— yet, oddly enough, Stravinskian metrics and rhythmic phraseology took over in its quicker movements.

Right after the war, I was more immediately drawn to Stravinsky's music than to Schoenberg's, and I found it far easier to grasp and respond to. I took a great shine to Stravinsky's *Symphony in Three Movements,* which had real bite in its outer movements. Only a short year later I began my emotionally intense adventure with Schoenberg, which, as I look back now after many years, was exciting, yes, but also exasperating and extraordinarily disorienting, and I waxed and waned over it. Ambivalence, fascination, and repulsion were at work in me almost all the time, but I stayed stubbornly with it because I knew that way lay the road to the language I ultimately wanted and needed to express musically what was strongest in my heart and soul. I laid aside the oboe–bassoon duo as I did other works of those years, because they no longer satisfied me. Yet in 1979–80, when I showed the duo to Sol Schoenbach, principal bassoonist of the Philadelphia Orchestra, he urged me to make it available to players.[5] It was his enthusiasm that saved the duo from oblivion and kept it alive until the time I was casting about for ideas for my Oboe Concerto. It was the march movement of the duo that I decided to include.

In retrospect, I find it strange that Zubin Mehta, who conducted the concerto's premiere, had as much difficulty as he did finding his way to the right tempo for the easy, swinging rhythm and beat of the march. True, it was slower than the usual parade march, yet with enough speed for the oboe to etch out its ironically wry, sometimes sardonic phrases against the persistent *basso ostinato,* Peg-Leg-Pete figure in the orchestra (♩ ♪♫ ♩ ♪♫) with heavy emphasis marking the first and third beats of the 4/4 measure and light, very short, staccato releases on beats 2 and 4. The oboe solo rides this ostinato as though it were being carried on the back of a camel or an elephant—with a slight lurch.

Ideas—and works, too—often benefit from long years of hibernation. If they have genuine worth, they have a mysterious way of "presenting" themselves to our consciousness as though to say, "I am still here and ready for the world anytime you are." My own conviction is that such ideas and works are a sign that—even without any significant experience—we are capable of having strong ideas often long before we know what makes them substantive and ultimately of a quality that is usable.

That 1946 summer experience proved in a very important sense that we are ultimately our own teachers—autodidacts. Every real composer inevitably finds himself facing himself alone, forced by the nature of what it means to make art, to become wholly independent of others' opinions or advice. We know, for example, that when Beethoven traveled to Vienna at the age of twenty-two, with the support and help of Baron van Swieten (also a supporter of Mozart), he presumably went with the idea of studying with Haydn. But their meetings were sporadic, and when he brought Haydn his three Piano Trios, op. 1, the older composer, now a true master, recognized throughout Europe, found them strange, perhaps even crude. My guess is that Haydn was put off by their rugged strength, perhaps even disconcerted by the evidence of such early power and independence of expression.

A gifted composer obeys the law of his own being—whatever it is and in whatever direction it takes him. In that struggle for self-realization he inevitably becomes an autodidact: in the most basic sense, self-taught and self-wrought. Someone who must follow the idiosyncratic twists and turns of his nature, the bends and branchings of his artistic personality as it unfolds.

As control of my ability to hear away from the piano grew stronger and stronger, a strange and wonderful phenomenon took place. When I reached a certain stage while working on a new piece, a "radio" would switch on in my head. Even when work was done for the day and I was away from my desk doing perfectly ordinary, everyday things, it continued to "broadcast" at will, as though the music had taken on a life of its own and all I needed to do was listen closely, and remember as much as I could to write it down as soon as possible. I found, too, I could turn my "radio" on whenever I wanted to, as though it also had the capacities of a cassette, rewind it to whatever passages I needed to review, and replay them. This way it became possible to compare mentally/aurally a particular passage with its variant or variants that I planned to use at a later point. I was astonished one day after finishing a composition and having done everything I possibly could to bring it to the closest state of perfection, that the "radio" in my head automatically shut itself off. It stopped "broadcasting" with the completion of the work and remained silent until I was writing again. At which point it turned itself on and began "broadcasting" the new work in progress.

Francis Goelet, a longtime friend and patron of the New York Philharmonic, commissioned my Concerto for Oboe and Orchestra in 1983 for the Philharmonic and its principal oboist, Joseph Robinson. I met Goelet on several occasions and found his gentle shyness oddly appealing. His reticence and quiet, self-effacing manner stood in stark contrast to the heavy-laden personality and manner of Zubin Mehta, conductor of the Philharmonic at that time. My pleasure in the performances and recording that followed soon after the premiere concerts, which began on December 13, 1984, came entirely from working closely with Joe Robinson, whose vibrant, lyric intensity and rich warmth of sound projected through wonderfully alive, inflected shapes and phrases—exactly what I had in mind as I composed the work.

As we rehearsed for the premiere performances and the recording, it grew increasingly clear that there was some kind of mismatch between Mehta's musical temperament and my own. I knew from having heard him do the great staples of the romantic repertoire that he reveled in the grandiose musical gesture, the production of great gobs of orchestral sound. What should have come across as full and rich in emotional expression often sounded merely loud and bombastic. And to my ear it seemed, even while generating physical excitement, especially in climactic passages, heavy as lead. Mehta never felt at one with the world of my music or comfortable with its levels and shifts from the most delicate and refined poetry to painful outbursts of desperation. He was never at ease in the unsettled metrics of the dry play of the scherzo and the quirky sardonicism of the march or at home with the hints of underlying tragic hopelessness in the dialogue between oboe and orchestra nor with the misted-over cloud-clusters in the orchestra while the oboe keens its last intonings as the work comes to its close. I could feel his sheer impatience as he waited for Joe to complete his two quite fulsome cadenzas, not to mention those occasional brief transitional solo passages leading from one section to another.

When Joe Robinson and I began working on the concerto, he loved to talk about Marcel Tabuteau, the longtime principal oboist of the Philadelphia Orchestra who was his teacher. Tabuteau was considered one of the truly great orchestral musicians and oboists of his day. A strong person himself, Joe was clearly in awe of Tabuteau, perhaps even a little cowed by his forceful, dominant personality. Tabuteau had the reputation of being a fearsome taskmaster. Ormandy, himself a man of great ego given to famous fits of temper, allowed Tabuteau to have his way, knowing he could not be budged.

Writing about Joe Robinson's memories and experiences with Tabuteau stirs my own memories of the man, one in particular. I had just finished my 1953 *Chamber Symphony* for nine instruments, and the parts were prepared and ready for whatever might come. Tabuteau was then coach and conductor of student wind chamber ensembles and the chamber orchestra at Curtis, and since I was eager to hear the work, I approached him and asked if it might be possible to arrange for a reading of my new work, which required three winds (oboe, clarinet, bassoon); three brass (French horn, trumpet, trombone); and three strings (violin, viola, cello). I said nothing about its being a twelve-tone work.

Tabuteau was surprisingly responsive—I had prepared myself for a refusal; instead we set a date. On the day chosen, I walked into the studio where Tabuteau and the players were waiting. He was cordiality itself, and the students seemed quite eager. After I made a few remarks about the work, the reading began. All went well in the first movement, despite some of its tricky rhythmic patterns, and I had the feeling Tabuteau and the musicians were enjoying themselves. Then we began to read through the second movement Adagio. Well into the movement, at a dramatic, emotionally charged point where the oboe is called upon to play a series of rapidly tongued groups of the lowest note on the instrument, Tabuteau stopped, turned to me, and, with a sudden, sharp edge in his voice, began to instruct me on a matter where he was the unquestioned authority. "You know, Mr. Rochberg," he said, "these figures you have written for the oboe here are impossible to execute. They cannot be played." He turned to the student oboist and, directing him, said, "Al, show Mr. Rochberg what I mean."

Put on the spot, and with all eyes and ears upon him waiting for the moment of truth—Al Genovese (who later played first oboe for George Szell and the Cleveland Orchestra) readied himself, sucked on his reed for a couple of seconds, and proceeded to nail the passage. He played it with complete aplomb and assurance at the speed and *più forte* volume called for. It was as though a bolt of lightning had struck the room. Al sat there, holding his oboe, looking straight ahead, waiting for what Tabuteau would say. Tabuteau, meanwhile, had become very agitated. The student had proved his teacher wrong in a crucial professional matter and situation. In fact, painfully wrong. He had literally contradicted the acknowledged greatest master of the oboe as to what could *not* be executed properly and in the presence of the young composer who had produced the offending passage. Whatever Tabuteau felt, whether extreme annoyance or great embarrassment, he launched into a hot stream of abusive language, for which he was famous among his students. I could see Al stiffen. Everyone, including myself, steadied himself against the onslaught: "You stupid, you know-nothing . . . you dummy . . . How could you do such a thing? . . ." and so on until he ran out of steam. As suddenly as he had grown hot and flared out, he recaptured his composure and, without further ado, turned to the ensemble and continued the reading as though absolutely nothing out of the ordinary had happened.

After John de Lancie (another Tabuteau student) left the Philadelphia Orchestra to become director of the Curtis Institute, Richard Woodhams, a superb musician and oboist who had studied with John at Curtis, succeeded to his teacher's chair as principal oboist in the orchestra. Covering a very substantial part of the twentieth century and spilling over into the twenty-first, the line of succession had gone from Tabuteau to de Lancie to Woodhams—embracing the musical and dynastic succession in one of America's great orchestras from teacher to pupil. Joe Robinson stands outside that line only because he studied with Tabuteau in France after Tabuteau had retired from the Philadelphia Orchestra and Curtis.

Dick Woodhams was soloist in my Oboe Concerto on two separate occasions. The first was with the Philadelphia Orchestra in March 1992 and the second, with the Curtis Institute Orchestra in October 1993. He was scheduled to perform the Richard Strauss Oboe Concerto with Wolfgang Sawallisch and the Philadelphia, but when Sawallisch couldn't conduct because of illness, Dick elected to do my work. It was then necessary to find another conductor who was free. Herbert Blomstedt, the Swedish conductor, director of the San Francisco Orchestra, was available and agreed to do the concert. The three of us met for a piano rehearsal, which I felt was important for Blomstedt, who was totally unfamiliar with my concerto, and even more so—but for different reasons—for Dick, because, knowing his technical prowess and interpretive sensitivities, I wanted him to discover the life of the work as I felt it. Instinctively, I knew—given his solidity of sound and tone production colored by a wide range of subtle intimacies of timbre—Dick's style of playing would suit my music perfectly.

Listening to the taped performances Dick Woodhams gave with the Philadelphia Orchestra and Herbert Blomstedt on March 12 and 13, 1992, helped me recapture the sense of why I responded so strongly to his playing. It has a poetry and a fantasy of feeling and imagination that go beyond mere musical expressiveness. It seems to be fed by a larger intelligence that channels itself through music making and invests that music making with qualities that enlarge and enrich it.

Before describing the Clarinet Concerto, it is necessary to discuss the cadenzas built into the tissue of both wind concertos. Classical and romantic composers of concertos tended to prepare the cadenza by building a full orchestral *tutti* approach to a grand, solid cadential pause—the whole maneuver bordering on the melodramatic—thus setting the soloist off against the orchestra. The main argument of the music was temporarily suspended in order to allow the solo instrument to have its moment in the sun. Often, if the composer himself was the soloist (as in the case of Mozart and Beethoven, both acknowledged piano virtuosi, or Paganini, who was a spectacular violinist), he might either improvise a cadenza on the spot if he were so moved or play a variant version based on a preplanned cadenza not fully written out. The practice of writing out the cadenza as a fixed, composed part of the work was not clearly established until Beethoven's time—though this did not preclude the possibility of other (and later) composers or instrumentalists providing their own cadenzas. (The most curious instance of this ongoing practice is the cadenza for the Brahms Violin Concerto that was commissioned from Alfred Schnittke by Gidon Kremer, the virtuoso violinist—an act tantamount to pitting antimatter against matter.) Such fixed cadenzas allow the soloist to shine, to display his or her wizardry, to pull out all the stops.

The cadenzas I wrote *are* the music. They are not display pieces for the soloist. Which explains why they can occur anywhere in the course of the work. That is why it is possible to have more than one cadenza in a given concerto. By weaving into the fabric of the music those passages where the soloist alone carries the main argument of the work forward, no interruption impedes its emerging growth of ideas, gestures, and shapes.

In the Clarinet Concerto (1994–95), the treatment of the cadenza idea follows essentially the same principles and design procedures I developed in the concertos for violin (1974) and oboe (1983). Soon after the Clarinet Concerto begins, an extended accompanied solo, quasi-improvisatory passage (mm. 23–54) makes its appearance. Brief orchestral figures support, comment, and break in on the clarinet figures, making way for an emotionally charged orchestral passage. The clarinet remains silent, rejoining the orchestra at measure 63. The first, full-scale cadenza for clarinet begins with the upbeat to measure 120 and continues through measure 140. Starting with bravura passages, breaking off, then leading into an expressive, lyric line, it concludes *pianissimo* in its lowest register—the *chalumeau*. Later in the work, a long second cadenza comes out of an obbligato figuration the clarinet has been weaving through a forceful, harmonically cadential orchestral passage and continues the same figuration (mm. 380–446), which combines reminiscences of earlier ideas with new material. As the clarinet holds the final note of this second cadenza, a string quartet joins the clarinet in a variation version of one of my favorite passages from the slow movement of Mozart's Clarinet Concerto—music I have long cherished. A brief solo at measure 453, soon joined by the orchestra at 457, becomes the quiet transition to the final section of the concerto, called Serenissima.

I'm not quite sure what it was about the work that drew Anthony Gigliotti so powerfully to my Violin Concerto when Isaac Stern performed it with the Philadelphia Orchestra. Whatever it was, Tony, who was principal clarinetist of the orchestra and had lived through the rehearsals and performances of the Violin Concerto, spoke to me often during that period and later about his strong desire to have me write a clarinet concerto for him, a major work that would show every facet of his instrument to best advantage.

During the 1980s, I was writing other works, but Tony had planted the seed and I began to envision a concerto for clarinet as a companion piece, only bigger-boned than the Oboe Concerto. All I needed, I explained to Tony whenever he brought up the subject, was the assurance of a commission from the Philadelphia Orchestra, serious interest on the part of Wolfgang Sawallisch, who had recently replaced Riccardo Muti, and a commitment to a specific time of performance. Which meant setting a firm deadline. My reasons for the last were simple: I worked best under a deadline, because it gave me a goal in real time toward which I could aim, and on the basis of past experience, I could calculate the time I would need for the necessary steps to complete the score and have the parts extracted, proofread, and ready for first rehearsal. After what seemed like interminable delays, a commission from the orchestra was finally arranged, and a performance time was scheduled for February 1996.

I began work in 1994 and completed the concerto the following year. I believe 1996 was to be the year Tony retired, and the performance of the concerto would be his valedictory. Tony, born in 1922, was then in his seventies and, unfortunately, not well. Since he could not perform standing, a platform was built so he could sit comfortably raised above the stage as he played, and near the conductor. The difficulty was, as Tony explained to me, that he was unable to hold the clarinet for extended periods when he stood. This handicap alone put his playing at a considerable disadvantage during those first performances with the Philadelphia Orchestra. This may also have had its side effect on Sawallisch. It seemed to make his conducting, while professional and competent, cautious and dull to begin with. The poetry and brilliance I had hoped for from Tony and the orchestra were not there. A cloud of inhibition hung over those February 1996 performances.

After Tony retired from the orchestra, his health seemed to improve sufficiently to allow him to extend his teaching activities. With his young wife Tai-ling's connections to the Taipei Symphony Orchestra and Taiwanese culture and society, Tony made the trip to Taipei, where he performed and recorded my concerto with the TSO and its conductor, Felix Chiu-sen Chen. I saw very little of Tony during the years between 1996 and 2001, but we kept up contact via phone. That was how I learned that plans had developed for recording the Clarinet Concerto with the TSO.[6]

Like many musicians from Asia, Chen had studied in Europe and acquired great skill and proficiency as a conductor. From all I gathered from Tony, he was a highly intelligent and sensitive man. In the months after he returned home, Tony became ill again and had to be hospitalized. When he recuperated, he called me to say he was sending a copy of the final edit of the recording. Tony extolled the work of the recording engineer—a young musician named Felix Chiu-sen Chen—and the TSO in glowing terms, and because he was not given to easy praise, I took very seriously his great enthusiasm for everyone involved. Most particularly, the TSO. Several times he repeated, "Felix loves the Serenissima."

Soon after the final edit arrived in the mail, I listened to it, astonished at what Tony and his Asian colleagues had accomplished . . . but most especially Tony. He played with incredible understanding, complete control, power and strength where they were needed, and poetry and sensitivity of such refinement of feeling it took my breath away. Chen, with Tony's help and guidance, had reached into the very heart of the work. And the TSO . . . every bit as superb as Tony had said they were.

Toward the end of 2001, Tony died. I became haunted by the thought that when I wrote the concerto in 1994–95 I was writing a requiem for my friend Tony Gigliotti.

Though there are important similarities of treatment in both concertos, the Clarinet Concerto is bigger-boned than the smaller and more delicately built Oboe Concerto; it uses a larger orchestra, is longer than its companion, and has a broader and wider gamut of expression. Yet their similarities run not so much to structural design as they do to emotional spirit and ethos, which are clearly discernible in two major tendencies that move in sharply distinct and opposite directions. The first of these, heard in the opening statements of each work with their singing, lyrical lines, tends more toward the dark-tinged, melancholic, poetically softer side—a continually returning expressive characteristic; the second shows equally strong propensities toward the harder, wilder, released side projected through what I have termed "gargoyle music." Also present in both is a third tendency much more difficult to pin down: an undercurrent of emotional pressures, in the form of gestures of desperation that sometimes break out into momentary clashing chaos. This is more evident in the Clarinet Concerto than in the Oboe Concerto, though the latter bears the burden of these same pressures.

Because what I'm calling "gargoyle music" has such an unmistakably different "face" from music that is wry, ironic, or sardonic, it needs to be discussed. Gargoyle music includes or may touch on the wry, the ironic, the sardonic, but it cannot be limited or confined to any of these gestural attitudes. Quite the contrary: it pushes past all these into the demonic regions of the dark forces. That element alone raises some very thorny questions that demand attention.

It is in the Clarinet Concerto rather than the Oboe Concerto that the presence of gargoyle music is more pronounced, more self-evident. The wryness of the metrically asymmetric scherzo in the Oboe Concerto (mm. 77–110), which is raised a couple of notches tighter into the leering sardonic Alla marcia (mm. 134–76), has a certain grotesqueness, to be sure—and purposely so—but merely brushes by without entering headlong into the demonic, which would be needed if these sections were to transform into genuine gargoyle music. Beginning with the Clarinet Concerto's measure 207 and ending with measure 359—or measure 379, depending on whether one chooses a much freer interpretation of those additional passages—an entire complex of different musics, deriving from various musical sources, combines marches, scherzos, and a radically reharmonized orchestral accompaniment to the Witches' Sabbath music (originally for E♭ clarinet; now for A clarinet) in Berlioz's *Symphonie fantastique,* where all merge into an excited and chaotic hyper-scherzo of unrestrained, demonically hysterical melee to become true gargoyle music.

With this reference to Berlioz's Witches' Sabbath (in German medieval folklore a midnight orgy of demons and witches known as "Walpurgis Nacht"), we move closer to the refractory, age-old difficulty of the question of evil and its relation to the term *gargoyle*—also associated with the medieval period in the West but with still-deeper roots leading back into pre-Christian practices of paganism.

Nowhere in Western music before the time of Mahler—with the possible great exception of Berlioz—do we find any hints, originating traces, or precedents for gargoyle music. When Mahler addresses his wife, Alma, in the agonized cry found in the sketches for his Tenth Symphony, "Almschi, der Teufel tanzt mit mir" (Almschi, the devil dances with me), I hear the terrifying third-movement scherzo of his Seventh Symphony, at the head of which he wrote, "Schattenhaft." Literally, "shadowy" or "shadowlike," but in the context of this "music from hell," the meaning of the term bursts wide open and suggests both "under the shadow of evil" and "threatened by the dark shadow of evil."

Poland was still under the iron heel of the Soviet Union in October 1989 when I described to a large group of students, at the University of Warsaw, Mahler's Seventh Symphony *Schattenhaftscherzo* as a "music of terror." Since then, the world has come to know what true terror means. Whether or not the world has the slightest inkling of the existence of Mahler's *Schattenhaftscherzo,* it is still what I described: a prophetic sensing into what lay ahead, what has since arrived, and what we now must face as our collective future, no matter the form it takes. Reflecting on it, I see Mahler's scherzo as the first great mature expression of what is meant by *gargoyle music.*

Despite his agonized, personal outcry to Alma, Mahler's vision of the future—our present, a full century later—was fearful, dark, urgent, and immense. The long shadow of evil—the *Schattenhaftscherzo* of his Seventh Symphony—lay heavy and oppressive over the world he saw and now lies over our present world in the deadly grip of terror and terrorism. From visions such as Mahler's and realities such as our own, it is a short step to reenter the pre-Christian, pagan world of real and imagined fears of evil that produced stone-carved sculptures—the grotesques and gargoyles of the medieval Christian world of Gothic architecture that jut out from the facades of churches and cathedrals in huge number over Europe's old cities. These fearsome-looking creatures with monstrously distorted features—distended tongues, bulging eyes, ferocious grimaces, grossly enlarged and exposed genitalia—pictured the ugliest possible beasts, humans, mythic griffins, apelike creatures, human heads on animal bodies, all to help avert the forces of evil from approaching the houses of the Lord, to frighten them away. As a boy I was fascinated by photographs of these fearsome figures, these endlessly varied gargoyles, human and bestial. They captured my purely visual imagination without my knowing what religious or moral purpose they had once served historically.

The coming together of the imagery of the gargoyle and grotesque and the unsolvable problem of evil came to fascinate me in my mature years. Its manifestations vary from touches of gargoyle music in such early works as my Chamber Symphony (1952), to an increasingly greater presence in *Black Sounds* (1966), *Tableaux* (1968), *Imago Mundi* (1973), and *Circles of Fire* (1996–97). Gargoyle music runs like a reddish-black thread through my music. Unconsciously on the part of many composers of the twentieth century, and now the twenty-first, I suspect it is also a genuine presence. Something of its dark, threatening sound appears in Schoenberg's early atonal works (*Erwartung, Five Orchestral Pieces*), in Stravinsky's *Le sacre*, in Bartók's *Miraculous Mandarin* and *Bluebeard's Castle*, and in Alban Berg's *Wozzeck* and *Lulu*. Perhaps Varèse is the first among his twentieth-century peers to have given conscious voice to what I am calling "gargoyle music" and its potential, if not actual, association with evil in works like *Arcana* and *Déserts*. Both works are deeply personal statements that reveal the chaos sounding in modern man's soul and psyche.

CHAPTER 14

A Trio of Trios

Piano Trio no. 1 (1962–63),
Piano Trio no. 2 (1985),
Piano Trio no. 3 (*Summer,* 1990)

In 1903, Samuel Butler's novel *The Way of All Flesh* was published posthumously.[1] He had used his pen as a spiritual weapon pointed straight at the heart of Victorian cant and hypocrisy, with its religious smoke and mirrors. By the novel's end, Butler's hero, Ernest Pontifex, is

> continually studying scientific and metaphysical writers, in the hope of either finding or making for himself a philosopher's stone in the shape of a system which should go on all fours under all circumstances. . . . he told me that he concluded that *no system which should go perfectly upon all fours was possible . . . and therefore no absolutely incontrovertible first premise could ever be laid. . . .* Having found out *that no system based on absolute certainty was possible* he was contented.[2]

Unexpectedly, Samuel Butler's conclusion "that no system based on absolute certainty was possible" received its strongest corroboration from the most unlikely quarter—the scientific thinking of the 1920s in the work of Werner Heisenberg, who developed the "uncertainty principle," which put forth the premise that human subjective observation profoundly altered the results of scientific measurement.

In the postscript to his late-1990s play *Copenhagen,*[3] which concerns the relationship and work of Heisenberg and his partner Niels Bohr, British playwright Michael Frayn sums up the situation by suggesting that a deep connection exists between the anomalies inherent in the technical "uncertainty principle" and the uncertainty of human behavior, thought, and intention.

In his introduction to Heisenberg's 1958 lectures published under the title *Physics and Philosophy: The Revolution in Modern Science,*[4] F. S. C. Northrop uses "uncertainty" and "indeterminacy" interchangeably. Offering no interpretive distinction between the two, Northrop virtually makes them coequals in the sense of conditions or states subject to illogic, unclarity, disorderliness, lack of direction, and formlessness—all of these combining toward disintegrating into chaos. That very interchangeability tends to mask and obscure what I sense are finer distinctions and subtle differences between a more highly emotional psychic state (uncertainty) and potentially a more technical, cooler, mental state (indeterminacy). Uncertainty, while it may fall one way or another, is potentially resolvable, whereas indeterminacy tends more toward being an unresolvable, steady state or condition. The indeterminate state appears to contain (possibly) aspects of the uncertain, whereas the uncertain would appear not to be capable of including or containing the indeterminate. These superfine distinctions have to do with the question of resolvability or nonresolvability.

It was this shade of difference that led me to give the title "Indeterminacy in the New Music" to a paper I published in 1960 in *The Score,* devoted to problems and issues of the then contemporary music.[5] Using the word *indeterminacy* in the title helped to gather up all the confusions, questions, and doubts—yes, uncertainties—that characterized not only my own state of mind during the second half of the twentieth century, but the state of mind that was all-pervasive in the world at large after World War II ended and the Cold War between the ideologies of communism and democracy began. Even my apparent commitment to twelve-tone systematization from 1952 on was insufficient to conceal my own uncertainties and gnawing disquiet about the ultimate rightness of a sole use of twelve-tone organization and the unbalanced tendencies it produced. That was why I had to write "Indeterminacy in the New Music" and why, as the 1960s came on, I determined to employ indeterminate means to compose what, even as I wrote it, I knew would be my last twelve-tone work, the First Piano Trio of 1963. But first the paper on indeterminacy.

The overarching idea behind the "Indeterminacy" paper lies in linking the two diametrically opposite systems of postwar composition directly to the physical concept of *entropy.* Entropy, according to the second law of thermodynamics, "is the measure of the tendency of nature toward disorder, non-differentiation, and a final state of static equilibrium."[6] In other words, a tendency toward nondifferentiated sameness spreads throughout physical systems deprived, closed off from regenerating sources of new, life-giving energy.

The essential thrust of my 1960 paper was to show how total serialism and chance (or aleatoric) music—despite their opposite philosophies of approach to composition—resulted in closed, entropic systems, subject to perceptual and psychological chaos and sameness, to nondifferentiation and indeterminacy. By declaring all parameters of serial organization equivalent in quantitative value, in serialism, no *qualitative* values are discoverable because serialism theoretically disallows them. Composers and music theorists took up serialism with the passion of a faith, in this case an aesthetic faith, writing music and promulgating airy abstractions according to an "equivalence principle." In such an order based upon an identity of measured equivalents, no hierarchy of differentiated values or functions was possible, nor was any admissible or permissible. A false claim was being made for concrete reality based upon a groundless symbolism of identities: pitch, time, volume of sound, and varieties of timbre. Out of this mélange of misguided notions sprang an indeterminacy of which the practitioners of serialism and associated theories were wholly unconscious. Thus the equivalence principle tended to reduce differentiation to a minimum and, having created a kind of musical entropy, resulted in a state of indeterminacy.

A rage for order seized on each successive postwar generation of intellectuals, political and social theorists and ideologists, artists, and composers, following the twentieth-century world upheavals (1914–18 and 1939–45) and their ensuing political, economic, cultural, social, and spiritual distress and disorder. The very subject of this rage for new order coming directly on the heels of widespread disillusionment, uncertainty, and disintegration deserves a much lengthier and deeper treatment, but for the moment my concerns are the confusions to which they gave rise in the times immediately following the cessations of hostilities.

The principal symptomatic confusions that arose soon after 1918 and continued into the period past 1945 were driven by a lust for the purity of the single, uncontaminated idea. The various forms of this hunger for reducing things to a one-idea aesthetic of "purity" produced a string of approaches to composition often at odds with one another: hair-splitting microtonality, pseudotonal minimalism, no system in the form of aleatory, too much system in the form of twelve-tone and then serialism. These resulted in the imbalances of nondifferentiation, that is, sameness of sound; entropy, that is, formlessness; and indeterminacy, that is, a condition or state that resulted in a strange kind of soullessness, of aesthetic death. The emptiness of this cultural void needed desperately to be filled. And filled it was: with volumes of verbal explanation and head-splitting rationalization by applying pseudo-mathematics, pseudo-logic, and pseudo-scientific concepts to the turgid, unreadable prose that poured out, filling the pages of professional music journals, magazines, and books. The burden of this torrent of verbiage was, presumably, to justify the claims being advanced to make these new and strange phenomena acceptable, if not palatable, to all interested parties, including the public at large.

This colored my thinking in those crucial years of the 1950s, and I began to harbor serious doubts about continuing to write twelve-tone music. Not only did I question its obligatory and artificially predetermined chromaticism, I had become weary of its abstract stinginess, its asperity of language dominated by a constantly strident dissonant palette resulting in a desiccated, starved form of musical expression. A heavy cloud of uncertainty settled over me, enveloping my inner life and state of mind. As much as I felt the rightness of tonal melodic and harmonic motion, its richness of language, expression, and structural forms, instinctively I knew I could not go back to that alone.

What the tonal needed—considering the impact of twentieth-century history—was the starkness, the angular asperities, the dark emotional and spiritual world of its atonal opposite if there was to be any chance of a more complete relation to the incredible range of human existence as I had experienced and observed it. The prismatic clarities and strengths of the tonal required completion by the presence of the atonal; the restive, neurotic unclarities of the atonal were in dire need of the restorative, calming powers of the tonal. One could not do without the other. Finding a way to join tonality to forms of atonality—though not necessarily twelve-tone or serial—became my ultimate direction and goal.

I took courage from the example of Picasso's decision to leave behind his sole concentration on pure cubism in favor of enlarging his range of visual imagery where cubism as planar abstraction combined with concrete figural representation to show the human face and form in new and unexpected ways. Picasso showed me how to resolve my dilemma. What had at first seemed to be nothing but irreconcilable incompatibles gradually became a more truly expressive enlargement of possibilities: a wedding of the old tonal world to the new atonal world. The three piano trios written between 1963 and 1990 are aspects—nodal points—of the outline of stages through which I had to pass to arrive at the vocabulary of musical expression sufficiently inclusive to contain what I valued most in traditional tonal speech in its considerable varieties and in the emotionally harsher, tougher, and more forbidding atonal landscape of modernist thinking.

My First Piano Trio was composed between November 1962 and July 1963. Before beginning work on it, I talked with my dear friend Dita Mocsanyi, a professional chamber pianist with long years of performing the repertoire of the great piano trios of the classical and romantic masters. When she and her husband,

Paul Mocsanyi, immigrated to New York in 1941, Gene became Paul Mocsanyi's tutor in English, helping him to try to overcome his propensity to contort the ubiquitous English article "the" to a Central European "ze." In the process the four of us became fast friends. We found ourselves in perfect accord concerning the thoroughly unpalatable and unconvincing new music being foisted on a surprisingly uncritical world, ready to hail anything new that came down the pike. So it was quite natural to ask Dita to talk to me about which trios she admired and loved most and why. I wanted to hear from her what she thought a piano trio should be. Her choice of Schubert did not surprise me, particularly when she focused on the conversational aspect of music composed for three equal partners. I found myself in complete sympathy with her views, responding especially to her stress on the conversational nature of a three-way chamber work. All my chamber music to that point had as a basic premise designing a musical dialogue between and among the ensemble of whatever two, three, four, or more instruments were involved.

It was no accident then that the Nieuw Amsterdam Trio, which Dita had founded, commissioned the work. I arranged for them to give its premiere in Buffalo, New York, in the spring of 1964 while I was Slee Professor at the state university. When it was published in 1967 I dedicated it to Dita and her two string partners, who were completely unfazed by the non-Schubertian, thoroughly contemporary language of my trio. That it was a twelve-tone work—and purposely indeterminate at that— did not seem to bother them in the least. They treated it *as music,* bravely faced its difficulties of execution and gave it a solid, professional performance. Even if not thoroughly at ease with its inner substance, whatever the lack of understanding and penetration of its unorthodoxies, their projection of its discontinuities and elliptical discourse came through. Perfect understanding and unison with the spirit of a new piece of music can come only by living with it, studying and performing it many times, uncovering with growing insight what it has to say, finding one's way into its inner life. That is when, miraculously, musical performance glows with a radiant energy.

Into this concept I bring one of Luigi Pirandello's most moving plays, *Sei personaggi in cerca d'autore* (Six Characters in Search of an Author). Here a set of fictional characters is portrayed wandering about the backstage and stage areas during *real* rehearsals by *real* actors of a *real* play, characters with fully human traits, problems, entanglements with each other, needing, wanting desperately a live author who will bring to life before a *real* audience the tragic fate of their entwined, unhappy lives. The stage is set for the inverse in my 1963 Trio, because there the author—myself—has already predetermined the essential nature of his work: there will be no specific identifiable ideas understood in an earlier sense as melodies or motives. Instead, the "melodic" aspects will, like their "harmonic" counterparts, be indeterminate, difficult to remember or identify. They will not be allowed to develop *individuation* or *identity* as understood in the Western concept of the development of an individual human being with a distinct consciousness of self and ego. The only thing the author will allow his "characters" to do is to play their nondifferentiated parts in the overall design of a one-movement work.

Nonetheless, each of the strings is permitted a strong solo presence in the form of a cadenza; and even though the piano cadenza is less overtly demonstrative, its generally quiet surface is broken into now and then by outbursts of impatience. These cadenzas provide the major nodal points and form of the shape of the work as a whole. In between, the ensemble breaks down into seemingly random duos, usually between violin and cello, and brief soloistic responses and comments. For example, after the introductory violin cadenza (pp. 2–3), the piano breaks in briefly (p. 4) and the cello, which interrupts rudely in solo fashion, is itself interrupted by an angry piano flourish (p. 5) that calls forth fragmented responses from the violin with a comment from the cello. The piano resumes, the violin and cello as a duo interrupt for one measure, the piano reenters with a flurry as the cello completes its figure in the next measure; the entire ensemble falls silent for a very brief eighth-note rest.

This purposeful, seeming randomness of sudden entry and exit is intended to give an impression of completely free, undetermined behavior, but the score shows differently. It is fully controlled. For this very reason, a performance of the 1963 Trio requires that each player performs from score so that he can anticipate his partners' every move—very much in the same spirit as my Second String Quartet.

Duos and trios prevail—but rarely for more than brief periods. Only the last three pages (27–29), with the opening two measures acting as upbeat to this closing passage (p. 26), bring all three instruments together in a deceptively resolving, ameliorating union of the trio ensemble. All these levels of impossible-to-define degrees of indeterminacy are purposeful. Only the language of the work is "determinate"—it is twelve-tone music based on a row. But beyond the specific, predetermined identity of the row—incidentally, known only to its author—everything else is intentionally indeterminate, partaking of the condition of uncertainty, which I consider the overwhelmingly strong and affecting presence in human affairs, including our sciences.

I regard the 1963 Trio as a true representation of my state of mind at the time I wrote it, and, not incidentally, also the state of mind of the serial culture itself, touted at the time as the "International style." In bidding the twelve-tone world adieu in this fashion, I was saying without consciously knowing it: the atonal way of writing music is appropriate *only* to the expression of those conditions of thought and feeling that tend toward the dark side—the side of uncertainty and the indeterminate. That is how it fell out for me in my later works when I felt impelled to express music in the spirit of the poet Paul Celan's line "Wahr spricht, wer Schatten spricht" (He who speaks, speaks of dark things).[7]

Strangest of all, *only* in art can one strive to transform *uncertainty and indeterminacy into expressions of certainty of idea and realization*. It is one of the unspoken aspects of the magic that binds and holds us to art in all its forms. Only there is it possible occasionally to create the truth of the "illusion of certainty" and believe in its "reality" without having to prostrate oneself before idols and addle one's brains with fog-obscuring beliefs.

In 1973, Vox recorded Piano Trio no. 1 with Kees Kooper, Fred Sherry, and Mary Louise Boehm.[8] Prior to recording, I was able to help guide them through the hidden dangers and pitfalls of a work that does not reveal itself readily. It was a happy moment when, after the recording session, the three musicians unanimously expressed their feelings of deep conviction about the music.

The years between writing the First and Second piano trios—more than two decades, from 1963 to 1985—were years in which a veritable revolution took place in how I wrote and thought about music. I broke away from the obsessive single-mindedness of avant-gardism and penetrated more deeply into traditional tonal music and found new ways of expanding single-key tonality into composite, symmetrical structures based on circular multiple key centers—tonal loci—which made the old tonal forms, particularly the classical sonata, a still viable vehicle for large-scale organic musical thinking. The Piano Trio no. 2 (1985) was one of the works of that time to which I applied this open system of symmetrically organized tonal music. The most significant aural aspect of this expanded tonal approach is that every harmonic shift from one tonal locus to another is thoroughly audible. Thus there are no puzzles for the ear to unravel. Everything is clearly evident even if these shifts cannot be named—except by keen-eared, thoroughly knowledgeable professional musicians. They can be heard because they are out in the open. This way of composing tonal music shares with earlier classical and romantic tonal music the absolute necessity on the part of the composer to fill his work with memorable, identifiable ideas—melodic, harmonic, and rhythmic.

In the summer of 1982, after the critical fiasco that had overtaken our opera *The Confidence Man*, Gene and I went to Israel, where I had previously agreed to teach the fall term at the Rubin Academy of Music and Art in Jerusalem. During those few months, we lived in Mishkenot Sha'ananim, a handsome housing unit for visiting artists and intellectuals from America, Europe, and elsewhere, not far from the famous Hotel David on the "downtown" side of Jerusalem and the German Quarter in the old residential section (so-called from the time of colonial Palestine under British rule) in the other direction. Except for a particularly pesky breed of Middle Eastern mosquitoes (which we battled the whole time we were there), our apartment was roomy and very comfortable. The academy was kind enough to give me an upright piano for my use. Close by in the same complex was the Jerusalem Music Center, where various events—concerts, master classes—took place.

Quite by accident, when I happened to be in the center I saw Menachem Pressler. We greeted each other warmly and talked about what we were doing in Israel. It was then I reminded Menachem of the suggestion he had made in the States that I write a work for the Beaux Arts. "Is it still on?" I asked. Menachem's reply was immediate and positive. "By all means. Go ahead, write us a trio and when it's ready, let me know and we'll arrange for a commission and set the time of performance in the Library of Congress." A purely fortuitous chance meeting had produced a desirable outcome.

It came at a time when I was more than ready to think seriously about writing some new chamber music in the form of another piano trio. Also, I was especially eager to explore further the possibilities of working with multiple tonal loci that gave the old tonality an unexpected freshness, allowing mixtures of diatonicism and intensified chromaticism bordering on atonal tendencies when the situation demanded. This brought a new mental fluidity to composing and, with it, the breaking down of old self-imposed limitations, which released a considerably enlarged and freer harmonic palette.

The Piano Trio no. 2 was commissioned by the Elizabeth Sprague Coolidge Foundation of the Library of Congress for the Beaux Arts Trio. Its premiere took place in the Coolidge Auditorium in Washington, D.C., on February 27, 1986. The work was published in that same year. I dedicated it to the Beaux Arts Trio, long considered the finest piano trio in the world. Besides pianist Menachem Pressler, its other members at that time were violinist Isidore Cohen and cellist Bernard Greenhouse.

The Second Piano Trio stands in direct contrast to the First. Where the First is wholly indeterminate—difficult to get a handle on because its language is too homogeneous, not quite specific enough to grasp readily—the Second is essentially determinate, with only patches of clouded areas hard to unravel aurally. And where the First is in one continuous movement with discontinuities built in along the way to keep expectations of what happens next as low as possible, the Second is cast in three structured movements with virtually no surprises except possibly for the nature of some of the ideas in each, which have clear identity and make their successive appearances according to plan.

The opening movement is in sonata form, full of diverse gestures and tempo changes that emanate from and return to the initial *amabile,* moving gently, lyrically. The second, a quasi-fantasia *largo* in tripartite form, serves as transition to the lively last movement *allegro con spirito,* a modified rondo form with essentially two opposing thematic structures: the one spiky, tunefully moving angularly over rapidly falling chromatic thirds; the other essentially lyric, diatonic, with four parts acting polyphonically throughout the ensemble. A fairly extensive development on the head motive of the first rondo theme, now in inverted form, is combined with fragments from a countersubject of the lyrical second rondo theme. This leads back to the opening spiky, spirited tune, which begins a recapitulation in D♭ major, reverts to E major, detours to G major, and ends finally in a concluding animated burst in E major. All the nodal points of the rotation of the minor-third symmetry are "reviewed" for the last time—with the exception of B♭ major, which, with the other loci, earlier dominated the opening movement.

My next commission came from Tony Checchia, head of the Philadelphia Chamber Music Society, for another trio for the Beaux Arts. The fact that the personnel of the Beaux Arts had changed had no bearing on what I intended to write. The continuing presence of its pianist and founder, Menachem Pressler, who has been called "the soul" of the Beaux Arts, has ensured continuity in the trio's musical personality. A "new" Beaux Arts Trio gave the first performance of *Summer, 1990,* my Third Piano Trio, at the Port of History Museum in Philadelphia on December 16, 1991. Its members were pianist Menachem Pressler, violinist Ida Kavafian, and cellist Peter Wiley. Three years later they recorded the work for Philips.[9]

Summer, 1990 is a musical hybrid in two senses. First, it embraces both the determinism of clearly identifiable, tonal melodic and harmonic ideas and passages of indeterminism, where some of these identities are put under such severe pressure and duress of intensified chromaticism that they become, like Piano Trio no. 1, thoroughly atonal. Second, it shares with Piano Trio no. 2 the use of circular harmonic sets, that is, symmetrically related tonal loci. From a retrospective point of view, each work constitutes a major portion of a "concert of music," a fully diversified program with respect to the nature of ideas and their treatment even while sharing certain attitudes and devices in common, including emotional scenarios and structural tendencies. For example, the first and third trios are both single-movement, through-composed works but have quite unlike emotional atmospheres, temperaments, and intensities.

The set of three piano trios was recorded February 5–6, 1996, and March 18, 1996, by the Kapell Trio (named after William Kapell, a brilliant young pianist killed in a plane crash) and released by Gasparo Records two years later.[10] The members of the Kapell Trio are pianist Stephen Swedish, violinist Christopher Lee, and cellist André Emelianoff.

From my first hearing of the Kapell Trio CD through the numerous hearings since, what has impressed me most about the musicians is the naturalness, the unself-consciousness of their approach to the obviously different musical worlds of the trios. As an ensemble playing stylistically diverse musics that placed great demands on their energies, emotional sensitivities, and technical strengths, they understood that each work, regardless of its differences in language, emotional temperature, and structural layout, had to be performed *as music,* rather than as demonstrations of the multi-universe of expression that had become contemporary music in the last half of the twentieth century.

In devising their CD program, they elected to begin the set by presenting the second trio, emotionally the lightest, at the outset, juxtaposing its clear tonal language with the first trio, the most obviously modern-sounding, clouded in atonal indeterminacy from beginning to end, and ending with the third trio, which mixes the tonal and the atonal, the determinate and the indeterminate, the softer and harder sides of a more expansive contemporary romanticism—neither "new" nor "old."

Constructing with Canons

Sonata-Fantasia for Solo Piano

Of the twelve-tone music I wrote between 1952 and 1963, among the more ambitious in size and scale are the orchestral Second Symphony and the *Sonata-
Fantasia* for solo piano. Although they were written within the same twelve-
month period—the symphony in the winter of 1955 to the spring of 1956, the
piano work from July 19 to October 30, 1956—they differ totally in character,
gesture, and melodic and harmonic content. Both came on the full tide of those
years in the middle 1950s when I felt I had gained genuine understanding and
insight into the inner workings and uncharted subtleties of the twelve-tone
world—especially the esoterica of the six-note hexachord. The hexachord became the key for me. With it, I unlocked a wholly individual approach to melodic continuity and harmonic relatedness. I could put aside, once and for all,
mere adjacency, a hopelessly inadequate "harmonic principle" of twelve-tone
theory and practice based on nothing more than random proximity of mere
succession of notes in a given series.

Three large-scale piano works collectively provided the major sources that
fed the impulse and impetus to produce the *Sonata-Fantasia:* the mighty "Hammerklavier" Sonata fugue of Beethoven, the adventuresome, avant-gardish,
and at times cloudily incoherent *Concord Sonata* by Charles Ives, and a great
sprawl of a work, Stefan Wolpe's modernist *Passacaglia.* Added to this was the
influence of Scriabin's late piano sonatas and Samuel Barber's Piano Sonata,
which use three staves to accommodate an expanded sense of a many-layered
music. The expansion into three staves opened a greater sense of the interior
space of the music I wanted and, in turn, made possible textures and gestures

that led to a way of writing for the piano I had never dealt with or thought of before.

I don't remember when I first began to think of Beethoven as a *constructor*. Everything he brought to completion shows the totally awakened constructor-mind at work. Nothing escaped the scope of his incredibly powerful ear. Nothing purely abstract or narrowly rational is allowed to dry the soul of his music. His is not the world of the "problem-solver," where passion, intensity, feeling are forbidden entry. The specter of the old Descartian dualism hangs heavy over the problem-solving, mechanistic mind that knows nothing of combining intensity of clear thinking with great heat. Yet it is just such a combination that is joined in the term *intellectual passion*—always to be found in the bloodstream of all great art, old or new. More than any other influence on my approach to the *Sonata-Fantasia* was the image of Beethoven the constructor, the powerhouse mind/ ear that instinctively joined intense thought and feeling to produce a music of intellectual passion that gave me the courage to construct the canonic imitations of Sonata II and the canons of Sonata III that play such a prominent role in the *Sonata-Fantasia*. From his "Ode to Psyche," Keats's "wreath'd trellis of a working brain" best illuminates the constructor's musical thinking fired by intellectual passion.

My use of the phrase "constructing with canons" should not be wrongly construed as an indulgence in the abstract mechanics of twelve-tone manipulation rife in America and Europe from the 1950s onward. On the contrary, the hexachord came to play a uniquely flexible role in the uses of the twelve-tone row in the *Sonata-Fantasia,* which made possible a diversity of emotional projections and contrasts in the canons I wrote. For example, the first of the two-part canons in Sonata III has a marked rhetorical, declamatory character, in direct juxtaposition with the lyrical, singing, tender character of the second of these two-part canons; and when joined together the two-part canons undergo a strange transformation to produce four-part canons whose character attests to the thought/feeling and feeling/thought complexes invested in their intricately designed, fully concrete, contrapuntal expressions; just as the two-part *scorrevole* (fleeting) quasi-canonic/quasi-fugato interruption of the four-part canons shows yet another side—the lighter, more playful side of what is possible.

Among those works for which I devised titles that are composites of formal or gestural types, the *Sonata-Fantasia* is probably one of the earliest. It is the emotionally freer, more volatile and erratically changeable "fantasia" sections that enclose, embrace, and enfold the more formally organized three "sonata" movements. The following schematic sketch shows this relationship in the order of the seven sections that constitute this approximately twenty-minute work:

⌈ Prologue (Fantasia)
⌈ ⌈ Sonata I
⌈ Interlude A (Fantasia)
⌈ | Sonata II
⌈ Interlude B (Fantasia)
⌈ ⌊ Sonata III
⌊ Epilogue (Fantasia)

Prologue is a grand fantasia that establishes basic ideas. Interlude A extends and varies the fantasia character of the Prologue. Interlude B is itself a "fantasia" on the Prologue, presenting the latter's primary opening gesture in mirror inversion. Thus what was originally precipitous downward motion becomes a leaping upward—so long as musical sense and meaning are preserved. The Epilogue is a compressed recapitulation of the fantasia of the Prologue, as well as a recall of elements of the first of the "sonatas," ending on a rumination of the *cantus firmus* of the three-voiced Sonata I.

Everything changes with the arrival at Sonata I: texture, tempo, emotional character, and temperature. The three-voice texture, with the long-note cantus firmus in the middle, is patterned into three tiers, the top voice acting as an expressive commentary of fragmented lyric phrases, the third-tier bass made up of groups of rhythmic, distant, threatening rumblings. Only the cantus firmus is an unbroken, unperturbed, long-drawn-out line, while the framing top and bottom parts are kept remote—in a kind of restless background. Close intervallic motions in the cantus firmus aroused in me such strongly echoing associations with the opening measures of Schoenberg's *Klavierstück,* op. 23, no. 1, that I decided to quote the Schoenberg passages literally, sewing them into the context of my music. As Sonata I continues, I expanded on the cantus firmus and developed in the top voice, now in a high upper register of the keyboard, birdlike flutings as another kind of fantasia commentary on the continuing lyricism of the middle-register cantus firmus. Another brief passage from Schoenberg's op. 23, no. 1, is followed by a fantasia play on its different figuration, which in turn is succeeded by an extended variant on a lyric passage from the Prologue.

On the breakout at the close of Interlude A, Sonata II follows an intense, fiery series of tremolos that drop suddenly into exhausted rumblings suggesting a distant echoing of the bass voice under the cantus firmus of Sonata I. Essentially light and thin in texture, it is the first time the notation is reduced to two staves. The music of Sonata II has an entirely different tempo and emotional character from everything that has preceded it. This is indicated by the descriptive "Allegro scherzoso" at the head of the movement. What further distinguishes this movement structurally is the consistent use of hexachords expressed canonically in mirror inversion. These essentially two-part canons in mirror are fleeting in character but held together aurally by a hexachordal harmonic device I had already made considerable but different use of in my Second Symphony—something that can be called interlocking mixed major/minor tonal four-note chords hinged on major thirds (or minor thirds, depending on interpretation). Two such four-note chords bind the canonic imitation passages. Reading top down, the first is D, B♭/ B♮, G (or D, B♮/B♭, G); the second, B♮, G/G♯, E (or B♮, G♯/G♮, E). The suggestion that these groupings have some potentially definable relation to tonal harmonic properties is inescapable. However, this is not the place to do more than point to what underlies what is an arresting phenomenon.

With the arrival at Sonata III, marked "Molto lento, contemplativo, quasi parlando," we are at the contrapuntal heart of the work. Inasmuch as two canons of two parts, each in mirror inversion and of differing build and emotional temperament, are combined after their initial statement into a double canon of four parts (which invoke the use of the same four-part mixed major/minor chords that first appear in the Sonata II, Allegro scherzoso), this is the time to pause and discuss briefly the general use of canon in twelve-tone music.

Constructing with canons is a practice of composers of every period, including the modern. It is a way of thinking of music divorced from style and language; therefore, it is readily adaptable to pre-tonal, tonal, and post-tonal—that is, atonal—ways of composing. Its panhistorical nature rests in the principle of imitation and its devices. In medieval and Renaissance times, constructing with canons necessarily adapted itself to the strictures of modality and its various modes. During the baroque, classical, and romantic periods, canonic procedures adapted themselves to tonal considerations of voice leading involving consonance and dissonance. In the world of nontonal, emancipated dissonance, where earlier dos and don'ts no longer applied, a totally liberated dissonant palette of intervals came into play in twelve-tone and serial music. The canons of Sonata III reflect this— even though occasionally one does hear fleeting hints of the old tonal consonant agreement between intervals.

In one sense, the idea behind canon is quite simple. At the very least, a canon has two parts: a melodic statement followed by an identical answering statement— unless the answer is subjected to alteration via inversion or metric augmentation or diminution, or sounded at pitches of the scale other than that of the original statement. The canonic answer is a *diagonal* reflection of the initial statement entering at a selected specific metric distance from the starting point, a conversation between a melody and its alter-ego that confirms and reflects—a form of musical dialogue that is distinct from the kind of dialogue between, for example, a melody and accompaniment, or a subject and countersubject in fugal treatment.

After the first large statement of the four-part double canon, another contrapuntal device is introduced, that of a two-part invention running rapidly through essentially *pp–ppp* passagework marked *poco scorrevole.* This leads to an enlarged quasi-recapitulation of the four-part canon—the two-part canons out of which it is built now differently ordered—projected *con tutta forza*—that is, with maximum force. A brief return, marked *tranquillo,* of two-part canonic structures leads to the Epilogue, the final section of the *Sonata-Fantasia,* and a return to the freestyle fantasia character that enfolds the work. The play between the two opposites, fantasia and constructing with canons, provides the essential, emotional soul and designed structure of the entire work. This polarity of seeming freedom of expression juxtaposed with rigorous contrapuntal forms further establishes the poles between which the heightened intensities of the work move. They go from degrees of near chaos in the fantasia sections approaching densities of dissonance that admittedly pose a challenge to aural clarity, to highly structured, contrapuntal order reaching levels of abstract design and a return to clear aural perception. None of this is accidental or happenstance; all is purposed and purposeful.

The last page of the Epilogue suggests a reprise of the opening of Sonata I with its cantus firmus in long, close-intervaled melodic phrases whose weight of remembrance increases to the last notes. It was the same period in which I wrote *Sonata-Fantasia* that my mother died of cancer at sixty-two . . . much too soon . . . And her end was too long and too slow . . . It was for her I wrote those last remembering phrases . . .

Just as earlier I had enjoyed playing my Twelve Bagatelles for informal groups of people and in public, when opportunity arose, I took great pleasure in playing the *Sonata-Fantasia* once I had mastered its pianistic difficulties. At a composers' 1956–57 conclave held in the Midwest, I gave a performance to a large number of my colleagues, who responded enthusiastically. I recall two different occasions when I played the work for friends and colleagues in New York. The first, and clearest in my memory, was when I played it for William Schuman in his commodious office at Juilliard. Bill's reaction was incredibly warm and generous-hearted.

The second occasion was a visit to William Masselos,[1] a concert pianist solidly grounded in the traditional repertoire but fully conversant with new piano music, with a particular emphasis on new American piano music. I sought out Masselos because I hoped to enlist his interest in adding the *Sonata-Fantasia* to his repertoire. When I had finished playing the *Sonata-Fantasia* I recall sensing a tepid, uncertain, puzzled response—directly opposite to Schuman's. For some reason Masselos found it necessary to go off on a tangent about the "presenters" who invariably insisted that he play only old "warhorses," avoiding twentieth-century music like the plague.

Howard Lebow,[2] a courageous young pianist of that time, gave the first performance of the *Sonata-Fantasia* at Juilliard on March 3, 1958, and, not long after, took it on tour to almost every major European city and musical center. I have a distinct memory of Howard sending me a large sheaf of reviews in their original languages (German, French, and Italian) with translations, which I recall reading with a mixture of bemusement, annoyance, and serious irritation. Except for London, everywhere else Howard played the *Sonata-Fantasia*, it met with incomprehension and a generally negative response. The critics seemed not to be ready for a work of such size written in a still largely suspect language by an American composer they didn't know. One word summed up their overall assessment—"formless." Only the London reviewer seemed to have discovered some redeeming features in the work. Tragically, not long after returning from his European tour, Howard Lebow died in a car crash.

When I began writing the two-piano *Circles of Fire* for Sally Pinkas and her husband Evan Hirsch, Sally was busy learning the *Sonata-Fantasia* along with five of my other works she was scheduled to record for Gasparo.[3] Considering the range of styles represented in the six solo piano works composed over a period of five decades—from 1941 to 1984—from a youthful view of the old tonal world (*Variations on an Original Theme* [1941]) to a full-blown twelve-tone exploration in twentieth-century atonality (*Sonata-Fantasia* [1956]) to growing combinations and mixtures of both the tonal and atonal palettes (*Nach Bach* [1966], *Carnival Music* [1971], and *Partita-Variations* [1976]) to a final arrival of the tonal and atonal worlds understood apart from history (*Four Short Sonatas* [1984]), it was astonishing how Sally mastered each of them, revealing sure insight into their differing emotional characteristics. The strength of Sally's 1999 recording reflects her understanding of each of the works—the *Sonata-Fantasia* in particular. In the CD program booklet she describes the *Sonata-Fantasia* as "a dark and deeply anguished work," adding that it "demands the performer's ultimate emotional, intellectual and technical powers."[4]

CHAPTER 15

Some Things Saved for the End

At the heart of the differences between tradition and the avant-garde lies the problem of language. Schoenberg's atonal adventures early in the twentieth century were a direct attack on traditional tonal practice—intended or not. The idea as it grew in other—and later—hands was to wipe the slate clean: start all over again from scratch. But how? With a new language: one that excluded any and all vestiges of premodern tonal music, one that represented twentieth-century experience, outlook, and psychology. In the major European musical centers in Germany, Italy, and France there arose a "newer" avant-garde more destructive in its attitudes, born in the minds of a few young composers who were also powerful polemicists. Thus did serialism come about as an offshoot from Schoenberg's earlier twelve-tone method already a generation old by 1945.

The strange fact is that, initially, Boulez, Berio, and Stockhausen sought a consistency of interior control paralleling with its new serial logic the traditional internal functional controls of tonal movement practiced by nineteenth-century and earlier composers whose language the serialists sought to displace. Set against this quite large blind spot in post–World War II avant-gardism, it was quite opposite to the paradoxically expanding avant-gardism of the American composer Charles Ives, who produced his most effective works (*The Unanswered Question, Central Park in the Dark,* and the Fourth Symphony, among others) well before Schoenberg's twelve-tone music but not much before his freely composed atonal music (*Book of the Hanging Garden;* Three Pieces for Piano, op. 11; and Five Orchestral Pieces—all written in 1909). Ives—unlike the iconoclastic antitraditionalists of the post–World War II period whose labor was to find a different language base, one with a consistency that would replace the old tonal functional consistency—sought, through collage and montage and sharply overlaid juxtapositions of different dialects, a way of expanding the old tonal world by including it in the same contexts along with heavily chromaticized passages, highly charged atonal dissonance, misted-over melodic passages that lose their identity in the resulting polyphonic weave, as well as references to some of Ives's favorite Protestant hymns, popular songs of his day, and patriotic tunes—all thrown together. If there is one composer to whom my own way of working in what I call "dialects" owes inspiration, it is surely Charles Ives. Ultimately, the forbiddingly puritanical nature of the European avant-garde of 1945–50 could not support its negativism, nor the destructive inhibitions it laid on attempts at serialist musical speech.

In a culture that moves rapidly from one radical vision to another, the problem of language intensifies. Each new departure must concentrate on its single image in order to produce even a modicum of works sufficient to state the idea behind the new radical aesthetic. In such instances a single lifetime will suffice to represent what is intended. In a curiously deft way this describes the short life (1950–70) of the New York abstract expressionists as a whole, for they were one-idea painters for whom developing a vocabulary of different images combined and recombined in endlessly imaginative ways was out of the question: they would have had to abandon their recognizable trademark—brand-name individuality—for something more communal or generalized. Their flat, two-dimensional canvases—encouraged and praised by such critics as Clement Greenberg—were more than a rejection of continuing the traditional three-dimensional illusionism of painting. Rothko, Pollock, Kline, de Kooning, Hans Hofmann—each stubbornly went his own way, painting his own personal "inner landscape," a term that emphasized the absolute uniqueness of their separate psyches, their innermost subjective selves, an "I" form of visual autobiography. The New York abstract expressionist movement in painting couldn't help but express, among other things, the "vita brevis" part of the old Latin phrase "Ars longa, vita brevis." It inevitably stood outside the "ars longa" verbal figure by virtue of its historical brevity—biologically and artistically. "Ars longa" can be invoked only where tradition exists, and, for painting as an art, there was no long-standing American tradition, just as there was no such tradition worth speaking of where American music was concerned. A weak echo of a radical avant-garde movement in America, however, began around 1948 and ended with John Cage's death.

Cage's idea of random occurrence of sounds untouched by the human stain rested on thinly developed notions of chance, uncertainty, and indeterminism. By removing the human ego from his "music"—*sounds* would be more apt a description—he refused responsibility for results. In fact, he created a haven for anyone who had neither the ability nor the desire to acquire a real craft of composition. In a lesser way aleatory, as it came to be known, appealed widely but briefly. Here, too, there was no opportunity for invoking the "ars longa" clause. For an American in a hurry who identified with that side of American culture and its cult of the strange and the new—the short-lived immediacy that flickered brightly but briefly—there was sufficient justification for doing the radical thing. "Ars longa" was too locked into tradition to count for much in the klieg lights of American experience, its noise, its "Big Easy" self-satisfaction, its rejection of anything that couldn't be accomplished in a single lifetime.

For someone like myself who was engaged in the hard work of hammering himself into a real composer, all I've described thus far acted as an object lesson of what not to be or do. Striving for the near-perfection that would lead ultimately to becoming a true artist who would leave a legacy of valued, repeatable works had become a burning life ambition as early as 1942 and solidified into an expressible goal by the time I was in my early thirties. My ideas of tradition in Western music as it had evolved over almost a thousand years in Europe came only later when I developed something of an historical understanding of the function of tradition, particularly in relation to the negating energies of radical avant-gardism. All of my later efforts to think through my own relation to both tradition *and* avant-gardism entered deeply into my ideas about the problem of language—what was possible, what was not, what might work under certain conditions of use and design, what was meaningless under any condition. I searched for a rich, varied vocabulary that incorporated the traditions of the premodern with the "tradition" of the twentieth-century spirit of radical departures from the premodern.

Unconsciously, I realize now, I knew that hammering myself into an artist in music must have been no different in essence for any of my predecessors in music and other art media. I think, for example, of Brahms, who, despite his anxieties—perhaps even because of them—over the long reach of Beethoven's shadow, came to produce through relentless self-criticism and hard work the body of works that honor his name. I think of William Butler Yeats, who forged his work and himself out of the great English romantic poetry tradition, whose sources are Wordsworth, Coleridge, Keats, and Shelley. I think, too, of Wordsworth himself, who, less brilliant intellectually than his friend Coleridge, was a driven man and worked with ferocious intensity. The butt of much savage, satiric wit and parody on the part of younger colleagues, as he grew toward eighty, Wordsworth, when he died, did not flinch from his continued insistence on the highest standards of which he was capable.

But these are all Europeans. Where and who are the American artists, poets, and composers? Are there any that answer to these self-imposed, almost cruelly demanding standards of achievement? Hard enough to hammer oneself into an artist in any medium in a culture firmly rooted in the traditions of the art one sets out to master. At least you are digging in soil long cultivated. You can immerse yourself in a lifelong study of the works that move you, that inspire you with their imaginative power to attempt to reach their heights of craft and art—even if a good deal of the time you are dogged by intense feelings of doubt and despair that you can ever achieve the right to be counted among the company of those whose work means everything to you. But what if you have to dig in stone? What if the culture into which your birth hurls you—whether by accident or fate—lacks what you need most to build upon: a great tradition stretching back hundreds of years in an unbroken line of high achievement? What if you are born in the culturally barren, rock-bound utilitarian materialism of America of 1918? What is there in your own culture to sustain you, to challenge your best efforts, to nourish your most powerful hungers for creating a world more beautiful and ideal than the dull, gray grind you were tossed into at birth?

Surely it is the acme of paradox to introduce into this discussion of tradition— now with particular attention paid to the question of a national American musical culture—the name of Antonín Dvořák. In 1892, Dvořák came to New York to become the first director of the new National Conservatory of Music and stayed on until 1896. During that period he wrote his "New World" Symphony, which gives clear evidence of his genuine interest in American folk music. No American composer of the time came as close to capturing the spirit, the freshness and jauntiness, the melodic possibilities inherent in American folk music on the scale Dvořák did in his 1893 symphony. And that is the point of his concern for his American colleagues' relation to their own folk tradition and my conjectures concerning his involvement.

I recall reading a statement Dvořák generously addressed to his composer colleagues in which he said, in effect: lacking an American musical tradition comparable to the centuries-long European art music tradition, Americans ought seriously to consider using the varieties of their own national folk musics as sources of inspiration rather than continue emulating European art music. To whom did he address this friendly advice? My guess is he had in mind composers like Edward MacDowell, Horatio Parker, Ethelbert Nevin, Charles Tomlinson Griffes, Charles Loeffler, Dudley Buck, and John Knowles Paine. Certainly his advice was far from idle in terms of his own experience. Dvořák himself had made major use of his own folk traditions as sources for major works, and in writing his 1893 "New World" Symphony he revealed a keen ear for the chief characteristics and gestures of American folk music and adapting them to his purposes as Brahms did Hungarian music; Beethoven, Russian; Chopin, Polish; and Bartók, Hungarian and Romanian.

Unfortunately, we have no record of how his American colleagues reacted, or if they took any notice at all. Possibly they weren't even aware there was a problem. For, indeed, they faced a severe problem—in the philosophical, aesthetic sense rather than the surface "cultural" sense—endemic to America. From its earliest beginnings America never had its own self-developed traditions in music. Whatever Americans brought with them from the Old World was simply grafted onto the New World situation, where physical survival demanded all their energies to conquer what initially was wilderness. Understandably, composers of the late nineteenth century automatically looked to European standards in music and adopted European traditions, grafting them onto still primarily barren, untilled cultural soil. But in his enthusiasm to help his colleagues find a way out of their dilemma, Dvořák forgot the single most crucial necessity: to "own" a folk tradition (or any "tradition" for that matter), one must be born into it. Only in that way can it become a natural, unself-conscious language for a composer—as it did for Dvořák himself in Bohemia, Mussorgsky and Rimsky-Korsakov in Russia, Kodály and Bartók in Hungary, Georges Enescu in Romania. But whatever the musical virtues of America's early folk music—Indian ritual music, Negro spirituals, Appalachian mountain songs with roots reaching back to Elizabethan England—its wide varieties had not been "born into" by most of the American composers who were now teaching in universities such as Harvard and Yale. Simultaneously, however, the groundwork was being laid for the creation of a popular music tradition, fed by the vast American appetite for entertainment in music halls, theaters, bars, restaurants, and bordellos.

One day in the mid-1950s, a large collection of recordings issued by the Musical Heritage Society arrived on my desk at the publishing house. Whatever the reason, I was fascinated by the numerous works—mainly orchestral—this collection contained, and even more by some of the very composers Dvořák presumably had addressed in his published statement urging them to turn to American folk sources and away from the old European traditions for inspiration. I listened for many hours to these recordings. By the time I had gone through the lot I was left with a single impression of bloodless, tepid, uninspired stuff. It all sounded unmotivated, a musical counterpart of overpolite social behavior. Among these composers there were no Walt Whitmans or Herman Melvilles or Edgar Allen

Poes as in literature, no Albert Ryders, George Bellows, or Thomas Eakins as in painting.

Three composers who stood out from the rest had all studied in Germany: John Knowles Paine in Berlin, Horatio Parker in Munich, and Charles Tomlinson Griffes in Berlin. Griffes was the only one of the three whose gifts rose above his influences, which, in his case, seemed to flow from the French impressionistic sensibility of Debussy. Paine and Parker were clearly in the Brahmsian orbit, but without any musical personality. Their sole distinction lies in having had students who went on to leave a strong mark on early twentieth-century American music. Paine taught composition at Harvard, where Carl Ruggles studied with him; Parker taught at Yale, where Charles Ives was one of his students. Ives and Ruggles, each in his own idiosyncratic way, became important figures of an American, homegrown avant-garde that discovered atonality on its own without owing any specific debt to Schoenberg.

Yet no American tradition for art music took root—even in the next generation after Ives and Ruggles. Following the vastations of World War I in Europe, young Americans, hungry for music and the study of visual art in an atmosphere where tradition still existed intact, however shaken by the pre- and postwar shenanigans to displace the old traditions that hung on tenaciously, flocked to the major centers to pursue their work. Paris was the magnet that drew Aaron Copland, Virgil Thomson, and Walter Piston in the 1920s to study with Nadia Boulanger. Roger Sessions lived in Italy and Germany during the 1920s into the early 1930s.

By the end of World War II it was clear that the problem of a language fit for musical expression after the cataclysm of that rending war had reached crisis proportions. It was into this atmosphere of doubt, questioning, and uncertainty that I began my own quest in the late 1940s. And only in later years (the 1980s and 1990s) did I finally reach an understanding that there can be no art unanchored to a solid tradition.

Tradition grows silently and unself-consciously. A tradition is a collective way of working that catches fire without public pronouncements but with commitment, love, and enthusiasm for the work at hand. Those who leave behind a legacy of their best work, produced under devotion to the highest standards of craftsmanship, are the people who create in the generation that follows the love, respect, and admiration—even awe—for the legacy of which they are the fortunate heirs. This induces in them (and succeeding generations) the necessity of striving for the highest standards of achievement. Johannes Brahms loved and admired Johann Strauss's stellar waltzes; Puccini, the opera composer, had high regard for Franz

Lehár, the operetta composer; George Gershwin evidently experienced a kind of ecstatic revelation when he first heard Jerome Kern's music. At seventeen, I instinctively knew Gershwin to be a great composer—whether in his songs or in his *Rhapsody in Blue* or Piano Concerto in F—a "great composer" for me, then as now, whose music imprints itself on one's ear and soul permanently.

The point of departure for this crazy-quilt of people, stories, and events begins with a 2002 letter from Christopher Lyndon-Gee. With it came CDs of the first edits of three works recorded that spring with the Saarbrücken Radio Symphony Orchestra in their studios high up on the Halberg hill. When seen from our hotel room, the Halberg was the only truly picturesque vista in the city of Saarbrücken— that and the river Saar, which wound its way through the town. Gene and I enjoyed watching it, especially when the rains came and the river rose higher and higher, almost spilling over the closed adjacent roads and walkways. Christopher wrote:

> Dear George,
> . . . here finally are the results of Markus's work [Markus Braendle, chief recording engineer for the Saarbrücken Rundfunk Orchestra]—all of our work in Saarbrücken this last March and April [2002]. The orchestra sounds fine, Peter [Sheppard Skaerved] magnificent; yet I have to say that I will be sending voluminous notes to Germany. As a basic through-edit, each of the works is satisfactory. But I hear many spots where the ensemble is less than perfect. The tempi don't quite match up, the double-bass intonation is poor, or where I *know* that Peter played with more ease and poise in other takes. Fear not—we will worry at these until they are *right!* Meantime . . . steps along the way, this thorny and stony path (to heaven?) that we have all chosen.

He was alluding to edits of my Fifth Symphony for large orchestra, *Transcendental Variations* for string orchestra, and the restored version of the Violin Concerto.[1] I had been present at the recording of the symphony and the string-orchestra work and on March 17, 2002, at a Sunday matinee where Peter had given the world premiere of the concerto to a large audience in the Kongresshalle.

The year before there had been innumerable phone calls and letters between Christopher and myself. Two major preoccupations demanded close attention: first, who would be the soloist to record the Violin Concerto, and second, how to proceed with the concerto's restoration, which—of his own accord and with my encouragement—Christopher had undertaken to accomplish. Compared to finding a soloist, the restoration project proved to be far less problematic. The entire situation was fraught with the tensions and urgency of meeting preset deadlines. Naxos, with whom Christopher had a long association, had agreed to record the concerto.

At the same time, he had worked out the dates of the live premiere performance and recording sessions with Sabine Tomek, the *Musikchefin* of the Saarbrücken Rundfunk Orchestra.

Early in the search for the right soloist I had suggested Peter Sheppard Skaerved as a strong possibility. All I knew of Peter's playing was based on his work as first violin and leader of the London-based Kreutzer String Quartet, which had given a brilliant performance of my Third Quartet in London. There also had been some working sessions in Newtown Square where I helped Peter prepare the solo *Caprice Variations* for performance and, later, recording. Something told me he could do it and, in fact, needed only the chance to prove it. Christopher—who knew of Peter only as a chamber player—was initially quite cool to the idea, so I decided not to press the matter and let Christopher continue trying his way. After a few blind alleys, Christopher became quite excited when it appeared likely that he might be able to book Daniel Hope, another young English violinist being widely heard and recorded in Europe and hailed on all sides with much ado. All Christopher's negotiations till that point had been with an agent, without ever actually having a chance to meet Hope face-to-face to talk things over. Somehow, Hope continually eluded him.

Christopher was becoming mightily frustrated by Hope's elusiveness, and with each disappointment I began calling him Daniel "Hope-less." Then, in the midst of this frustrating stalemate and its attendant irritations, including increasing anxiety over the growing shortness of time, there came the sudden announce-ment from the agent that Hope had accepted an offer to become the violinist of the Beaux Arts Trio. Christopher immediately called Peter, who set to work to learn the concerto, which he formerly had told me he had loved since, as a boy of ten, he'd first heard the Stern recording. In one month's time, he mastered the work—musically, intellectually, expressively. When at last we all met in the Kongresshalle to rehearse that Saturday morning, March 16, 2002, there was electricity in the air. Peter proved his mettle beyond any doubts as the restored version came to life. In the days that followed I would quip that we constituted the second Anglo-American "invasion" of the European continent!

The recordings with Naxos, the connection with Sabine Tomek and the Saar-brücken Rundfunk Orchestra—how did they come about? Like all stories, these come from different directions and were brought together by converging circum-stances and intersecting interests—or simply by the determined will of a single individual, in this instance Christopher Lyndon-Gee.

Beginning in the late 1990s, Christopher began talking about a plan to record all my orchestral music—symphonies, concerti, and individual works. Klaus Heymann, the founder and owner of Naxos, responded positively. How this new project was to be achieved was entirely up to Christopher. His would bear the sole responsibility for securing the necessary interest backed up by firm commitments from whatever orchestra (or orchestras) met with Heymann's approval. Christopher kept me informed of all his initial efforts, none of which, unfortunately, panned out. Unperturbed, he stubbornly persisted in what I had begun to think of as an unreal, quixotic dream. No matter that he kept assuring me it was going to happen, most of the time I found myself unable to take him at his word: his intentions seemed too fraught with unpredictable contingencies and countless practical problems that would have to be met at every turn and resolved. Then, too, I wondered about the long years needed to come even close to realizing a plan of such scale. Besides, I was already in my eighties and keenly aware of the physical and mental diminishments that come in one's ninth decade. Were it not for the concrete reality of Heymann's support, I could almost have believed the whole idea was pure fantasy, that Christopher was "whistling Dixie," that he was, in fact, dreaming aloud. I asked myself over and over, from whence did this powerful conviction of the worth of my music spring? What had generated it, and when did it begin?

Then I remembered the first time we met in Chicago at the first performance of my Fifth Symphony. There I locate the origins of the initiating impulse that grew over the years into Christopher's desire to record my large works. It was on January 30, 1986, that Georg Solti led the Chicago Symphony premiere. Fate—what else to call such coincidences?—had brought this young Englishman to Chicago that weekend to audition for a post as assistant (or associate) conductor to Solti. Fate also decreed that he not be chosen. Had he been, I'm convinced, it would have changed his whole life in music, and perhaps mine. Would I be writing my final chapter this way? Impossible to know.

During the noisy hustle and bustle of the reception following the premiere, this young Englishman, bursting with the occasion's excitement, introduced himself. It was Christopher Lyndon-Gee—probably then in his middle twenties, full of youthful energy, an open, alive intelligence on his face. He had been deeply moved by my new symphony and had no hesitation in saying so in his offbeat, unself-conscious way. My family was with me, so I introduced him to Gene, our daughter Francesca, and her husband, and invited Christopher to join us. That moment, I'm convinced, was the starting point of the grand plan that hatched itself in Christopher's mind. Everything I've sketched thus far stemmed from that time: the experience of hearing the Fifth premiere and meeting my family and me in that relaxed, informal way apparently meant more to Christopher than initially showed on the surface. Only some years later, when he and his wife named their first child "Francesca" after our daughter, did I begin to realize how deep his emotional bond to all of us went.

I break off here to take a large step sideways by telling the story of *To the Dark Wood* (1985) for wind quintet. The commission came from what sounded like an impressive group that called itself the "Earle Page College Foundation of the University of New England, Armidale, Australia for the Promotion of Contemporary Classical Music." The foundation wanted to know if I would write a work for the "Canberra Wind Soloists." I was intrigued by the idea of writing a piece for musicians from "down under," perhaps even to attend the rehearsals and first performance and see something of another continent as remote as Australia. All that suddenly had great appeal. This despite the fact that until then I tended to shy away from writing wind-quintet music. More often than not I found its overall sound too dry for my taste. The dryness led to temperatures that went from cool to cold. I had heard too many lightweight, musically uninteresting pieces of nineteenth-century French wind music. Occasionally I warmed to a twentieth-century work, such as Paul Hindemith's brief, witty quintet or György Ligeti's later atonal venture, and had been repulsed by Schoenberg's 1924 twelve-tone, unbearably long and strenuous quintet for winds.

Cast against strings—especially orchestral strings—each of the instruments in a woodwind quintet—flute, oboe, clarinet, French horn, and bassoon—has great color, warmth, and appeal, but individual qualities I associate with each of them tend to become lost in constant wind-ensemble tuttis. Once I decided to accept the commission it was with the desire to find out if I could write a piece that would reveal, not conceal, the individual characters of the instruments by finding ways to open up the ensemble to as much dialogue and color as possible. I decided to write for five *solo* winds in order to find the best ways to show off their special qualities of sound and expression.

I still retain residual feelings and memories of the time I wrote *To the Dark Wood.* It was the summer of 1985. Afternoons were warm and hazy, shielded from the hot sun by the trees in the back of our house on Aronimink Drive in Newtown Square, Pennsylvania. I would sit on the deck that extended into the grassy back yard—sometimes I moved under the shade of our mimosa tree at a distance from the house—and fall into a reverie, melting into the stillness of the green scene around me. Beyond the back yard lay a dark wood of an old stand of silver beech, wild cherry, tulip trees, and a single great oak. These remnants of a once-great forest stood large and tall, irregular in their shapes and groupings. A sense of some intangible, not quite palpable mystery lay in that wood. I gave myself to it . . . allowed it to take over . . . until I felt I was there . . . *in* the wood . . . images began to form . . . I saw the ancient earth god Pan, ugly old Pan with his goat's horns and goat's hoofs and the body of a man—Pan, son of the god Hermes, the winged messenger—leading a parade of dancing nymphs and satyrs as he played his panpipes of woodland reeds. (Edith Hamilton describes Pan as "a noisy, merry god" and calls him "a wonderful musician."[2] Night noises in the dark wood were said to cause fear and "panic" in the heart of the uneasy traveler.)

Out of these imaginings and summertime reveries, I gathered together a body of ideas that became the woodwind piece. Some of it, following my inner imaginings and hearings of Pan and his noisy troupe, tended toward mildly insouciant, gentle, mocking gargoyle music. Some of it was taken from the sounds of the mourning doves I heard all around me—low, soft, chalumeau-register clarinet calls. The emphasis I placed on the French horn is best described in the program note I wrote for the first performance, given by the Canberra Wind Soloists in Armidale, Australia, on October 3, 1986:

> . . . there is an expressive tone which pervades and characterizes the atmosphere, the world within which [this] music takes place: the world of nature and the old mythology which still haunts the mind of man . . . The "calling" which is characteristic of this music is warrant of man's longing for a life which transcends rationalism with its arid, barren effects as well as of nature's longing for man's poetic healing sympathies. Both need each other to reach fulfillment; but in the frustration of that fulfillment there is a quality of sadness and darkness . . . it is the horn which is the wind instrument which best conveys not only the longing, sadness, and darkness I wanted to express, but also the nobility possible to those qualities.

On the inside of our copy of *An Armidale Album*, a historical account replete with photographs of this provincial university town and its founders,[3] is an inscription to Gene and me that captures the flavor of modesty combined with a touch of self-deprecation, and at the same time, an irresistible yet brash charm, which I found basic to the Australian temperament. This volume was given to us at our first meeting with representatives of the Earle Page College Foundation for the Promotion of Contemporary Classical Music. The two faculty members—both scientists—who took us to lunch were almost too respectful, but the sun of goodwill and conversation quickly melted the ice of awkward formalities and led to a startling revelation, when one of them said with a broad smile, "We . . . uh, yes . . . *we* are the 'foundation.' There's nobody else but us two." What else could follow this simple and surprisingly frank confession (delivered with a profound sense of relief) but a healthy release of laughter? The whole tale tumbled out:

how they loved music and felt this was their way of reaching out periodically and asking composers to write works for Australian performers. Clearly, two starry-eyed music lovers with a mission and the practical sense to make it work. The inscription read, "To George and Gene, from the EPC Foundation, loonies from down under, October 3, 1986." It put us at our ease for the whole time we were "down under" with the "loonies."

I remember fondly the Canberra Wind Soloists: flutist Vernon Hill, oboist David Nutall, clarinetist Alan Vivian, hornist Hector McDonald, and bassoonist Richard McIntyre—all of them thorough professionals and well-grounded musicians, each a unique personality, together giving off an air of openness and readiness for what lay ahead. It was evident at our first meeting that they had already done a great deal of work on the new piece and were enjoying bringing it to life. The groundwork was done; now it was my job to help them shape its overall design and refine and polish its niceties and nuances. Two of the players especially impressed me: Alan Vivian for his looseness and freedom of style of playing, and Hector McDonald, whose solidity and handling of the subtleties of both texture and tone color anchored the work by giving his part a strong, confident presence. There was no doubt at their first performance that the Canberra Wind Soloists had developed a strong affection for the *Dark Wood*. All in all, that first day in Australia—October 3, 1986—had its pleasures and rewards.

I brush past our travels up and down the eastern seaboard of the Australian continent—to Sydney, Melbourne, Brisbane, and the Great Barrier Reef—to get to our last and longest stop, the Canberra School of Music, where I crossed paths with Christopher Lyndon-Gee once again. Things had changed for him. Or so it appeared. He was now on the faculty of the school, teaching and conducting, and had married a charming Chinese woman who taught piano at the school. Christopher was the same engaging young man I'd met ten months earlier in Chicago, very energetic and active in the performance end of things. He conducted and played the piano parts in some of my larger ensemble pieces, performances in which members of the Canberra Wind Soloists also took part.

Canberra sits on a high, windswept plateau, and I remember vividly the early morning walks I took through suburban-like, tree-lined streets to the school from the cottage where Gene and I were housed. The walk—barely a mile long—was refreshing and invigorating in those mild October days. The air was wonderfully fresh and smelled of eucalyptus. What I marveled at especially were the birds, an incredibly exotic-looking variety I'd never before seen. Not only their vividly brilliant colors but their calls and songs, which enhanced their radiant appearance.

Most memorable was the picnic in the Australian bush that Christopher, a colleague of his, and their wives had organized. We piled into one car with baskets of food and drink and drove off to an area well inside a park preserve. The different look of the trees—mainly eucalyptus—and bushes on both sides of the roadway was fascinating. Once we arrived, we sat down to lunch. Suddenly, as though from nowhere, there appeared a large creature, almost as tall as a man. My Australian companions assured me there was nothing unusual about its unannounced appearance: it had been drawn by the smell of our food. "Just act natural," someone said. "Pay no attention." At first I thought I was looking at an ostrich, but my friends said, "No, it's an emu." As we ate and talked quietly, the emu, with long, slow, measured steps, strolled about the area, completely at ease; despite its almost comic design when seen up close, it moved with great, unhurried dignity.

Suddenly it began to rain in torrents. Big, fat drops. Hastily, we gathered up what was left of our picnic and made for the car, never looking back to see how the emu reacted. We were a short distance behind the car in front of us when, without any warning, from out of the bush came bounding a kangaroo, easily the size of a large man. It moved so quickly into the path of the car in front of us that the driver barely had enough time to come to a dead stop—unfortunately not soon enough to prevent his car from catching the kangaroo on a side of his big, reddish-brown-furred body, sending him spinning around wildly on the same spot, his arms flailing. I caught flashes of the terrified fright and bewilderment in the kangaroo's eyes as he spun about. Not much unlike a human's. But as soon as he had righted himself and found his balance, he was across the road, into the bush in seconds—and gone.

It was after the Australian experience that Gene and I made plans to arrive in Saarbrücken in March 2002, several days before the premiere of the restored Violin Concerto, and to stay for the following week of daily sessions recording both the Fifth Symphony and the *Transcendental Variations*. That would give us enough time to rest and to be as fresh as possible for the dress rehearsal with Peter. We arranged it this way not only because I wanted to be on hand to help guide Peter and Christopher through the concerto's intricacies, but also to make clear my ideas and feelings concerning the rarely discussed interrelations between tempo, gesture, and character, how gesture and character act on each other to arrive at the best tempo and—crucially important—clear articulation to make possible convincing musical performance. In the most basic terms, I wanted to be present for the first public performance of the restoration of the concerto—now the combination of final revisions I'd made in the 1970s and the painstaking labor undertaken by Christopher to track down the old cuts and, just as carefully, sew them seamlessly back into place. I knew I need not worry about the actual recording. Grounded as it was in the premiere performance, it came off splendidly. The concerto had taken on a glow that warmed my soul.

The dress rehearsal took place in the Kongresshalle just across the road from the hotel. As the members of the Saarbrücken Radio Orchestra came in, I was delighted to see they were mostly young men and women who gave off an alert freshness and an air of anticipation and energy. When I was introduced, I could sense they had been looking forward to my working with them. Since they had already recorded my Second Symphony and *Imago Mundi* in 2000 and 2001, it was clear they responded with pleasure to performing my music. As the rehearsal of the concerto began, I could see an immediate rapport springing up between Peter and the orchestra. Christopher gave most of his comments and suggestions to the orchestra in well-articulated German, the rest in English. Before we had even begun, I had urged Peter and Christopher to aim for an expansive, spacious projection; to clamp down hard only when the music turned fierce or wild; otherwise, to leave plenty of room for the solo violin to dialogue with the orchestra, especially in those frequent passages where wind and horn solos are in canon or obbligato relation to the violin. Peter's immediate grasp of the elasticity I wanted in his handling of the solo part was uncanny. He understood intuitively, and Christopher knew exactly how to provide the right orchestral tempo and pace to free Peter to play in an unfettered fashion.

All this suffused the masterful performances, both live and recorded, that resulted. There was a distinct air of celebration at the Hotel Mercure reception that Sabine Tomek had arranged. Both Peter and Christopher were heaped with kudos that made their faces shine with quiet triumph.

The daily recording sessions that followed brought a complete change of geography, ambience, and mode of work. Every morning for a week—mostly under dreary, overcast skies mixed with occasional wintry downpours—we took taxis to the top of the Halberg, where the Saarbrücken Rundfunk sat overlooking the town.

Wisely, Christopher started the first day's work by rehearsing and recording the four-horn *fantasia* central to the second episode of the Fifth Symphony. This section stands as an independent unit—mournful, grave, disjunct, overlapping, echoing fragments of horn calls, haunted and haunting, still reverberating distantly among the craggy peaks and passes of the Pyrenees, where Roland and his doomed band of knights once tried—but failed—to hold back the advancing tide of Arabs in hot pursuit of his king Charlemagne's army. Working directly with the SRO's four horn players remains one of the most deeply satisfying experiences of that entire week. They were unusually sensitive and responsive to every nuance and suggestion from either Christopher or myself, producing colors and textures I had imagined when I first wrote the symphony in the 1980s but had not heard sounding live—even from the great horns of the Chicago Symphony.

When the entire orchestra had reassembled, Christopher began the days-long process of rehearsing and recording what would be substantially long "takes" of the symphony from its opening measures. The ultimate goal of recording is to achieve, as convincingly as possible through electronic means, the special atmosphere and experience of hearing live performance in continuous, long-breathed musical sentences and paragraphs. I was keenly aware of Christopher's feelings about my Fifth. Not only was it the work that had brought us together, it was his opportunity to give it the fullness of its amplitude and inner spaces, to highlight its constantly shifting levels of alterations of textures and colors. Under his guidance, the men and women of the SRO turned those days into pure musical magic.

Enough of the week remained to realize to the fullest what I'd always known was locked in the notes of my *Transcendental Variations*. The performances it had previously received were unfortunately too perfunctory to reveal what it contained. The slowness of this otherworldly music exists on a plane far removed from the unimaginative, ordinary, professional performance. That in itself makes it virtually impossible to impart to the overpressured busy conductor who moves too quickly from concert to concert, style to style, historical period to period. Here, on top of the Halberg, Christopher and I, conferring at each stage of the work—to ensure its unhurried pace, to shape the theme and each variation's own unique growth and inner life, to emphasize each shifting pattern in texture and the heightening and lessening of tension—together we found ways of bringing to full realization the string orchestra's remarkable sensitivities to convey fully for the first time what I had originally intended.

We completed the recording of both works with time left over on the last day for Christopher to produce on the spot a quite special musical miracle. With the enthusiastic support of the orchestra, he announced quietly—and in English so that Gene and I would know what he was planning—that he was dedicating a "private performance" of the Fifth Symphony to Gene and myself in the time remaining. Words cannot describe the next half-hour's glorious outpouring of music and the emotions of our leave-taking of this supremely gifted ensemble of musicians.

All along, the plan had been to drive to Basel once we finished recording. In a rented car, with Christopher at the wheel, we left Saarbrücken on Saturday morning, March 23, 2002. Once out on the open road and fortunately with virtually no traffic, Christopher spread his road maps out on his lap, even covering the lower part of the steering wheel. I sat in the passenger seat alongside him. Gene, comfortably settled in the back seat, took in the scenery, which retained essentially the same between-winter-and-spring-look whether the signs and posters read in French or German. I grew increasingly apprehensive as the car drifted now a little to the left, now a little to the right, while Christopher continued checking his maps and correcting the drifting motion of the car. I couldn't refrain—hard as I tried—from showing a certain degree of nervousness and irritability. What a relief when we rolled into Colmar—a small town in old Alsace-Lorraine—in time for lunch, grateful we had made it in one piece.

The first time we had visited Colmar was to see Grünewald's amazing Isenheim Altarpiece with its moving panels. Its power and glory in paint was everything we had anticipated, and we needed a chance afterward to sit and reflect. It was midsummer, a particularly beautiful day, and fortunately we found an outdoor café just around the town square. Suddenly a thoroughly enchanting scene unfolded before us as we watched from ringside seats. A wedding party in several horsedrawn open wagons carrying bride and groom, bridesmaids, family, and friends, all dressed in their country-best finery, kept trotting 'round and 'round the circular plaza, singing and laughing joyously as they went.

Now, years later, we sat eating some lunch and recalling the memory of that delightful show, trying to convey its colors and delights to Christopher. This time we were warming ourselves with a steaming vegetable soup and an unparalleled quiche Lorraine.

Not long after leaving Colmar, we entered Basel, a wonderful old medieval city that Gene and I had grown to love. Resourceful as ever, Christopher found his way to Der Teufelhof, "The Devil's Lair," the same hotel—now considerably enlarged and modernized—where we had stayed the first time. After checking in, Christopher left for Saarbrücken to attend to other matters and would return to Basel in time for a panel discussion three days later.

Being in Basel once again brought with it special pleasures, among them the opportunity to revisit the art museum with its prize Klees and, quite close by, the comically zany water-fountain sculptures of the artist Jean Tinguely, who had been a dear friend of Paul Sacher and his wife. The strange configurations made by the twisting black pipes through which the water spouted in unexpected, constantly moving aerial designs were arresting in a clownish way. What gave us still greater personal pleasure was the chance to renew earlier ties of friendship with Felix Meyer, director of the Sacher Institute in Basel, his wife, Rosemary, and members of the staff. Over the years, Felix and I had developed a warm professional and personal relationship. I responded to his seriousness, his wide and broad knowledge of twentieth-century music—especially American (he had written

his doctoral dissertation in musicology at the University of Zurich on Charles
Ives's music). Above all, he was a man with impeccable taste in aesthetic matters
and, significantly, we were in basic agreement on the politics of the world.

The ostensible and, as it turned out, especially gratifying reason for this second
visit to Basel was to coach the academy students for their concert of some of my
chamber music and take part in a public interview with Christopher just before
the students gave their program. The entire afternoon had been organized by the
Academy of Music in direct association with the Sacher Archives. Seven students
performed four assorted pieces from the different tonal and atonal periods of
my work. Working with talented students is quite different from working with
professionals. First of all, one expects more technical mastery of the instrument
from a professional than a student performer; second, one hopes the professional
already has some idea of the language of contemporary expression, whereas one
really has no right to expect such familiarity from the still-developing student.
To my utter delight and surprise I discovered that among the seven brave young
musicians from different parts of the world who had elected to be part of the
proceedings, four of them demonstrated rare and precocious understanding of
my music—and at least two of these were surely of near-professional status, both
in technical proficiency and a highly developed sense of expressiveness. As it
turned out, Yael Zamir, a wonderfully gifted oboist, and Katia Abdeeva, a finely
polished pianist, gave a moving performance of *La bocca della verità* (The Mouth
of Truth), a twelve-tone work that makes great demands on both players; flutist
Satako Takezawa, clarinetist Iura de Rezende, and, again, Katia Abdeeva at the
piano brought out the strange poetry of my first collage music, *Contra Mortem
et Tempus* (Against Death and Time).

After so exhilarating an afternoon—what with the wide-ranging panel discussion that dealt with postmodernism and its essential enlargement of the expressive range of music by removing all barriers between the past and the present,
perfectly exemplified by the concert of my chamber pieces, which represented
differing intensities of the tonal and atonal worlds—Gene and I returned to Der
Teufelhof to rest. Inevitably, the need to eat grew too strong to keep putting it off,
so we went downstairs, where there was a charmingly informal dining area.

As though by the power of some magnetic force, each of our friends in turn
arrived there, all smiles, and joined us. First Christopher; then Maartan Brandt,
a friend and close associate of Christopher's; soon after, Felix. By some volition
all its own, these serial arrivals turned into a serial supper, everyone at some
stage of his or her meal—drinking and talking in high gear—a conviviality of a
special nature, a gathering of high-energy spirits, eminently compatible despite
individual differences in age and experience. A gathering of such spiritually like-

minded individuals can't help but produce some potent ideas, cogent insights that are absorbed into deep memory channels that serve, in time, to spread as a tremendously powerful remembrance of a great collective moment, keeping alive the sense of a profound commonality of feeling and thinking. That last night together was the perfect capstone to a second memorable visit to Basel. Having spent liberally of what I'd "saved for the end," early next morning Gene and I were homeward bound.

> A journey on the edge of day
> A circuit at the birth of night
> In tunnels of an endless gray
> Unknowing in their outward flight
> —Paul Rochberg

1912	Parents Anne Hoffman and Morris Rochberg immigrate to United States from Ukraine
1918	Born July 5 in Paterson, N.J.
1929	Family purchases a piano; begins lessons with Kathleen Hall
1933–34	Performs duo piano with second teacher, Julius Koehl, on WOR (Mutual Broadcasting Co.), New York
1933–41	Plays regularly in dance bands and combos, supporting himself through college
1937–69	*Book of Songs* for voice and piano (unpublished)
1939	Receives BA from Montclair State Teachers College, N.J.
1939–42	Studies at Mannes Music School in Manhattan with Hans Weisse, Leopold Mannes, and George Szell
1940–79	*Book of Contrapuntal Pieces* for keyboard instruments (unpublished)
1941	Marries Gene Rosenfeld August 18 in Minneapolis, Minn.; lives in New York City from September 1941 until November 1942, when drafted into the army
1941	*Variations on an Original Theme* for piano (revised 1969)
1943	*261st Infantry Song* and *March of the Halberds*
1944	Severely wounded in Mons, France, September 23
1944	Son Paul born September 28
1944	*Music for Gene and Paul* (unpublished)
1945	Discharged from army in July as Second Lieutenant, having received a Purple Heart and Oak Leaf Cluster
1945	Moves to Philadelphia, Pa., with wife Gene and son Paul
1945–48	Studies at the Curtis Institute of Music in Philadelphia, Pa., with Rosario Scalero and Gian Carlo Menotti
1946	Duo for oboe and bassoon (revised 1969)
1946	*Fantasia and Fugue* for orchestra (unpublished)
1946	*Four Songs of Solomon* for voice and piano
1946	*Two Preludes and Fughettas* from the *Book of Contrapuntal Pieces*
1947	*Orchestral Suite in Four Movements* (unpublished)

1947	Sonata no. 1 for piano (unpublished)
1948	Receives BM from the Curtis Institute of Music and is appointed to the faculty
1948–49	Studies at the University of Pennsylvania, Philadelphia, Pa., and receives MA
1948	Capriccio for orchestra
1948	*Sonata Seria* for piano (revised 1998)
1948	Trio for clarinet, horn, and piano (revised 1980)
1949	*Night Music* for orchestra
1949	Sonata no. 2 for piano (unpublished)
1949	Symphony no. 1 (three-movement reduction; fully restored 1977)
1949	Capriccio for two pianos (unpublished)
1949	*Five Smooth Stones* for soloists, chorus, and large orchestra (unpublished)
1950–51	Receives Fulbright fellowship and American Academy in Rome fellowship; Rochbergs spend year in Rome at the academy
1951	Becomes editor of publications at Theodore Presser Co., Bryn Mawr, Pa.
1951	*Concert Piece* for two pianos and orchestra (unpublished)
1952	Daughter Francesca born May 8
1952	String Quartet no. 1
1952	Twelve Bagatelles for piano (first twelve-tone work)
1952	Receives George Gershwin Memorial Award for *Night Music*
1953	*Cantio Sacra* for small orchestra
1953	*Chamber Symphony* for nine instruments
1954	Becomes director of publications at Theodore Presser Co.; leaves Curtis Institute
1954	*David, the Psalmist* for tenor and orchestra
1954	*Three Psalms* for a cappella mixed chorus
1955	*The Hexachord and Its Relation to the 12-Tone Row* published by Presser
1955	*Duo Concertante* for violin and cello (revised 1959)
1955	Fantasia for violin and piano (unpublished)
1955	*Serenata d'Estate* for six instruments
1956	*Arioso* for piano
1956	*Sonata-Fantasia* for piano
1956	Symphony no. 2
1956	Receives Society for Publication of American Music Award for String Quartet no. 1

1956	Receives Guggenheim fellowship
1957	Spends six months in Mexico under Guggenheim fellowship
1957	*Bartókiana* for piano
1957	*Blake Songs* for soprano and chamber ensemble (revised 1962)
1957	*Waltz Serenade* for orchestra (unpublished)
1957	Waltzes for string orchestra (unpublished)
1958	*La bocca della verità* for oboe and piano
1958	*Cheltenham Concerto* for small orchestra
1958	*Dialogues* for clarinet and piano
1959	*Duo Concertante* for violin and cello (revision; original 1955)
1959	Receives first prize, Italian International Society for Contemporary Music (ISCM) Competition for *Cheltenham Concerto*
1960	Becomes acting chair of Music Department, University of Pennsylvania
1960	*Time-Span I* for orchestra (unpublished)
1961	Becomes chair of Music Department, University of Pennsylvania
1961	Paul Rochberg becomes ill
1961	String Quartet no. 2, with soprano
1961	Receives Naumburg Recording Award for Symphony no. 2
1962	*Blake Songs* for soprano and chamber ensemble (revision; original 1957)
1962	*Time-Span II* for orchestra
1962	Receives honorary doctorate in music, Montclair State College, N.J.
1962	Receives National Institute of Arts and Letters Grant for String Quartet no. 2
1963	Trio (no. 1) for violin, cello, and piano (last twelve-tone work)
1964	Teaches spring semester as Slee Professor at SUNY at Buffalo
1964	Paul Rochberg dies November 22
1964	*Apocalyptica* for wind ensemble
1964	*La bocca della verità* for violin and piano (transcription of 1958 version for oboe and piano)
1964	*Zodiac* for orchestra (transcription of Twelve Bagatelles)
1964	Receives American Academy of Arts and Letters recording award
1964	Receives honorary doctorate in music, Philadelphia Musical Academy
1965	*Black Sounds* for winds and percussion (*Apocalyptica II*)
1965	*Contra Mortem et Tempus* for flute, clarinet, violin, and piano
1965	*Music for the Magic Theater* for large chamber ensemble
1966	Spends summer as composer-in-residence with Roger Sessions at Tanglewood, Lenox, Mass.

1966   *Music for "The Alchemist"* (staged at Lincoln Center, New York)

1966   *Nach Bach,* fantasy for harpsichord or piano

1966   Receives second Guggenheim fellowship

1967   *Passions According to the Twentieth Century,* theater work for singers, jazz quintet, brass, percussion, piano, tape, actors, dancers, and speakers (unpublished)

1968   Steps down as chair of Music Department at University of Pennsylvania, remains on faculty teaching composition and advanced theory

1968   *Fanfares* for massed trumpets, horns, and trombones

1968   *Tableaux* for soprano, two actors' voices, small men's chorus, and twelve players (text from *The Silver Talons* by Paul Rochberg)

1969   Duo for oboe and bassoon (revision; original 1946)

1969   *Eleven Songs* for mezzo-soprano and piano to poems of Paul Rochberg

1969   *Music for the Magic Theater* (small-orchestra version)

1969   *Prelude on "Happy Birthday" for Almost Two Pianos*

1969   Symphony no. 3: *"A Passion According to the Twentieth Century"* for vocal soloists, chamber chorus, double chorus, large orchestra (unpublished)

1969   *3 Cantes Flamencos* for high baritone (unpublished)

1969   *Two Songs* from *Tableaux* (transcribed for soprano and piano)

1969   *Variations on an Original Theme* (revision; original 1941)

1970   *Caprice Variations* (50) for unaccompanied violin

1970   *Sacred Song of Reconciliation* (Mizmor l'Piyus) for bass-baritone and chamber orchestra

1970   *Songs in Praise of Krishna* for soprano and piano

1971   *Carnival Music,* suite for piano

1971   *Fantasies* for voice and piano to poems by Paul Rochberg

1972   Spends summer as composer-in-residence at Aspen Music Festival

1972   *Electrikaleidoscope* for amplified ensemble

1972   *Ricordanza* (Soliloquy) for cello and piano in memory of nephew Robert Rochberg

1972   String Quartet no. 3

1972   Receives Naumburg chamber composition award for String Quartet no. 3

1972   Receives National Endowment for the Arts grant

1973   *Behold, My Servant* for a cappella mixed chorus

1973   *Imago Mundi* for orchestra

1973   *Ukiyo-E* (*Pictures of the Floating World*) for harp

1973	Concord String Quartet recording of String Quartet no. 3 receives Grammy nomination for "Best Chamber Music Performance"
1973	Receives second National Endowment for the Arts grant
1974	Concerto for Violin and Orchestra (revised 2001)
1974	*Phaedra,* monodrama for mezzo-soprano and orchestra (text by Gene Rochberg after the poem by Robert Lowell)
1975	Quintet for piano and string quartet
1975	*Transcendental Variations* for string orchestra
1976	*Partita Variations* for piano
1976	Symphony no. 4
1977	*Songs of Inanna and Dumuzi* for contralto and piano
1977	String Quartet no. 4
1977	Symphony no. 1 (five-movement restoration of 1949 three-movement version)
1978	String Quartet no. 5
1978	String Quartet no. 6
1979	*Slow Fires of Autumn* (*Ukiyo-E II*) for flute and harp
1979	Sonata for viola and piano
1979	String Quartet no. 7, with baritone, on poems by Paul Rochberg
1979	Receives first prize, Kennedy Center Friedheim Award for String Quartet no. 4
1979	Named Walter H. Annenberg Professor of the Humanities, University of Pennsylvania, Philadelphia, Pa.
1979	Recording of String Quartet no. 7 with Leslie Guinn, bass-baritone, receives Grammy nomination for "Best Chamber Music Recording"
1980	*Octet: A Grand Fantasia*
1980	Trio for clarinet, horn, and piano (revision; original 1948)
1980	Receives honorary doctorate of music, University of Michigan, Ann Arbor
1981	Quintet for two violins, viola, and two cellos
1981	Receives honor as Distinguished Pennsylvanian
1982	Teaches fall semester at Rubin Academy in Jerusalem
1982	*Between Two Worlds* (*Ukiyo-E III*) for flute and piano
1982	*The Confidence Man,* opera in two parts, libretto by Gene Rochberg
1983	Retires from University of Pennsylvania as Emeritus Annenberg Professor of the Humanities
1983	Concerto for Oboe and Orchestra
1983	Quartet for piano, violin, viola, and cello

1984	*The Aesthetics of Survival* published by University of Michigan Press
1984	*Four Short Sonatas* for piano
1984	Symphony no. 5
1985	*To the Dark Wood* for woodwind quintet
1985	Trio (no. 2) for violin, cello, and piano
1985	Receives Brandeis University Creative Arts Award Gold Medal of Achievement
1985	Receives honorary doctorate in music, University of Pennsylvania, Philadelphia
1985	Inducted into membership of American Academy and Institute of Arts and Letters
1986	Elected fellow of the American Academy of Arts and Sciences
1986	Receives Lancaster Symphony Composers Award
1987	Symphony no. 6
1987	*Three Cadenzas* for Mozart Concerto for Oboe in C Major, K. 314
1987	Receives Alfred I. Du Pont Award for Outstanding Conductors and Composers, Delaware Symphony, Wilmington
1987	Receives Andre and Clara Mertens Contemporary Composer Award, University of Bridgeport, Conn.
1988	Gene Rochberg commissions fourteen young composers to write pieces for piano based on themes from Rochberg's music for his seventieth birthday
1988	Sonata for violin and piano
1988	Suite no. 1 from *The Confidence Man* for orchestra
1988	Suite no. 2 from *The Confidence Man* for solo voices, chorus, and orchestra
1988	Receives honorary doctorate in music, Curtis Institute of Music
1988	Receives second prize, Kennedy Center Friedheim Award for Symphony no. 6
1989	*Ora Pro Nobis* for flute and guitar (*Nach Bach II*)
1989	*Rhapsody and Prayer* for violin and piano
1990	Spends spring in residence at Bellagio Study and Conference Center under Rockefeller Foundation
1990	*Muse of Fire* for flute and guitar
1990	*Summer 1990* (Trio no. 3) for violin, cello, and piano
1991	*American Bouquet* for guitar
1991	*Seven Early Love Songs* for voice and piano
1992	*Sonata-Aria* for cello and piano
1994	Receives honorary doctorate in music, Miami University, Oxford, Ohio

1995	Concerto for Clarinet and Orchestra
1996	Rochbergs move to Dunwoody Village, Newtown Square, Pa.
1996	Contracts with Paul Sacher Archive, Basel, Switzerland, to house manuscripts, sketches, and papers
1997	*Circles of Fire* for two pianos
1997	*Eden: Out of Time and Out of Space,* chamber concerto for guitar and ensemble
1997	Receives Distinguished Achievement Award, Longy School of Music, Cambridge, Mass.
1998	*Sonata Seria* for piano (original version 1948)
1998	*Three Elegiac Pieces* for piano (1947–98, 1945–98, 1998)
1999	Receives honorary life membership, Musical Fund Society, Philadelphia, Pa.
1999	Receives ASCAP Foundation Lifetime Achievement Award
2001	Concerto for Violin and Orchestra (revision; original 1974)
2003	Featured composer of the Music Festival of the Venice Biennale
2004	*The Aesthetics of Survival,* 2nd ed., published by University of Michigan Press
2004	*Five Lines, Four Spaces* completed
2004	Naxos recording of Symphony no. 5 receives Grammy nomination for "Best Classical Contemporary Composition"
2005	Rochberg's health fails May 2
2005	George Rochberg dies May 29 and is buried next to his son, Paul, at the George Washington Memorial Cemetery in Valley Forge National Historical Park, Pa.; *Transcendental Variations* is played in the chapel
2005	Memorial concert at Carnegie Recital Hall, New York, December 28
2006	Headstone engraved according to George Rochberg's instructions

George Rochberg
Composer
1918–2005
Contra Mortem et Tempus
Gene Rosenfeld Rochberg
Beloved Wife and Mother
1919–

2006	Rochberg honored April 6 at American Academy of Arts and Letters in New York City
2006	*The Aesthetics of Survival* receives ASCAP Deems Taylor Award for "outstanding print, broadcast, and new media coverage of music"
2009	*Five Lines, Four Spaces* published

AS84   Rochberg, George. *The Aesthetics of Survival: A Composer's View of Twentieth-Century Music.* Edited by William Bolcolm. Ann Arbor: University of Michigan Press, 1984.

AS04   Rochberg, George. *The Aesthetics of Survival: A Composer's View of Twentieth-Century Music.* Revised and expanded ed. Ann Arbor: University of Michigan Press, 2004.

Chapter 1

1. Hans Weisse (1892–1940), following study with Heinrich Schenker in Vienna, immigrated to the United States in 1931 and taught at the Mannes Music School and later at Columbia University. He was a teacher of Felix Salzer, who assumed his position at Mannes following his death. See David Carson Berry, "Hans Weisse and the Dawn of American Schenkerism," *Journal of Musicology* 20 (2003): 104–56.

2. Leopold Mannes (1899–1964), after studying physics and music at Harvard, taught theory and composition at the Mannes Music School (founded by his parents) from 1927 to 1931 and 1946 to 1948 and served in administrative positions (director, and eventually president) at the school from 1940 until his death. He also made a name for himself as a scientist early in his career: beginning in 1922, he experimented on color film processes with Leopold Godowsky Jr. in Kodak's research laboratories in Rochester, New York, and the result was the development of the Kodachrome Color Process in 1935.

3. William Blake, *The Marriage of Heaven and Hell* (ca. 1790–90), Plate 7, "Proverbs of Hell."

4. Quoted in George Rochberg, "Reflections on Schoenberg," *Perspectives of New Music* 11, no. 2 (spring–summer 1973): 62; reprinted in *AS84,* 51; *AS04,* 41.

5. George Rochberg, *Symphony no 2,* New York Philharmonic, Werner Torkanowsky (conductor), Columbia ML 5779 (1962), LP; reissued on *George Rochberg, Volume One,* CRI 768 (1997), CD.

6. Arthur Rimbaud, *A Season in Hell,* trans. Louise Varèse (Norfolk, Conn.: New Directions, 1945); Arthur Rimbaud, *Prose Poems from the Illuminations,* trans. Louise Varèse (New York: New Directions, 1946); Arthur Rimbaud, *A Season in Hell & The Drunken Boat,* trans. Louise Varèse (Norfolk, Conn.: Laughlin, 1961). All titles have been subsequently published in revised editions.

Chapter 2

1. Nicolò Paganini, *24 capricci per violino solo* (Milan: Ricordi, 1820).
2. *Daniel Kobialka Plays New Violin Music,* Advance Recordings W10601 (1969), LP.
3. Johannes Brahms, *Variationen über ein Thema von Paganini,* op. 35, for piano (composed 1862–63).
4. Sergei Rachmaninoff, *Rhapsody on a Theme of Paganini,* op. 43, for piano and orchestra (1934).
5. Witold Lutosławski, *Wariacje na temat Paganiniego* [Variations on a Theme by Paganini], for two pianos (1941).
6. Ludwig van Beethoven, *Variations pour le piano-forte* [Eroica Variations], op 35, for piano (composed 1802).
7. Ludwig van Beethoven, *Die Geschöpfe des Prometheus,* op. 43, for orchestra (composed 1800–1).
8. Anton Webern, *Wege zur neuen Musik* (Vienna: Universal, 1960); English trans. as *The Path to the New Music,* trans. Leo Black (Bryn Mawr, Pa.: Presser, 1963).
9. George Rochberg, *Caprice Variations,* Peter Sheppard Skaerved (violin), Metier MSV CD92065 (2003), CD.
10. George Rochberg, *Caprice Variations,* Zvi Zeitlin (violin), Musical Heritage Society (1978), LP.
11. George Rochberg, *Caprice Variations,* Eliot Fisk (guitar), MusicMasters Classics 01612–67133–2 (1994), CD.
12. *A Paganini: Virtuose Musik für Violine / Virtuoso Violin Music,* Gidon Kremer (violin), Deutsche Grammophon, 415 484–2 (1986), CD.
13. It was likely a still from the movie *Spring Symphony* (1983), in which Kremer appeared as Paganini.
14. George Rochberg, *Caprice Variations,* freely transcribed for guitar by Eliot Fisk (Galaxy Music, 1997).
15. George Rochberg, *Caprice Variations,* Eliot Fisk (guitar), MusicMasters Classics 01612–67133–2 (1994), CD.
16. Nicolò Paganini, *24 Caprices,* Eliot Fisk (guitar), MusicMasters Classics 01612–67092–2 (1992). CD.
17. *Caoine,* Michelle Makarski (violin), ECM 1587 (1997), CD.
18. *Elogio per un'ombra,* Michelle Makarski (violin), ECM 1712 (2000), CD.

Interlude 1

1. Charles Olson, "Projective Verse," in *Human Universe and Other Essays,* ed. Donald Allen, p. 52 (New York: Grove Press, 1967).
2. The performers were Patti Monson (flute), June Han (harp), William Anderson (guitar), Andrea Schultz (violin), Daniel Panner (viola), and Gregory Hesselink (cello).
3. *Spectrum New American Music, Volume II,* Contemporary Chamber Ensemble, Arthur Weisburg (conductor), Nonesuch H 71220 (1969), LP; Elektra Nonesuch 792222 (1990), CD.

Chapter 3

1. The 1951 film, produced by Walter Lowendahl, has been issued on DVD as *The Medium,* VAI DVD 4218 (2002).

2. Robert Whitney (1904–1986) was founder and conductor of the Louisville Orchestra from 1937 until 1967. In 1948 he began a program to commission and record new music.

3. Arthur Darack, music critic for the *Cincinnati Enquirer,* whom I met at Fort McClellan in Anniston, Alabama, while in the army.

4. George Rochberg, *Symphony no. 1,* First Edition Records, Louisville Orchestra, LOU-634 (1963), LP.

5. Laszlo Varga, principal cellist of the New York Philharmonic, who performed the solo for the 1953 premiere.

Chapter 4

1. American composer Wallingford Riegger (1885–1961).

2. Composer and teacher Ursula Mamlok (b. 1928), who immigrated to the United States from Germany in 1941.

3. George Rochberg, *The Hexachord and Its Relation to the 12–Tone Row* (Bryn Mawr, Pa.: Presser, 1955).

4. Alexander Uriyah Boskovich (1907–1964), an Israeli composer of Hungarian origin who adopted serial composition techniques late in his career.

5. Ezra Pound, *Make It New: Essays* (New Haven, Conn.: Yale University Press, 1935).

6. Even at that, many years later when the Concord String Quartet was performing it and eventually recorded it, I was still dissatisfied with the ending of the last movement. What resulted was an on-the-spot, improvised, different ending while the recording session was still in progress.

7. Efrem Zimbalist (1890–1985), composer and violinist, began teaching at Curtis in 1928 and was director from 1941 to 1968.

8. Arnold Schoenberg, *String Quartet no. 4, Opus 37,* Kolisch Quartet, Alco ALP 1005 (1950), LP reissue of a 78-rpm recording made in 1937.

9. René Leibowitz, *Schoenberg and His School: The Contemporary State of the Language of Music* (New York: Philosophical Library, 1949); Josef Rufer, *Composition with Twelve Notes Related Only to One Another,* trans. Humphrey Searle (New York: Macmillan, 1954); Ernst Krenek, *Studies in Counterpoint: Based on the Twelve-Tone Technique* (New York: G. Schirmer, 1940).

Chapter 5

1. George Rochberg, "Aural Fact or Fiction: Or, Composing at the Seashore," in *AS84,* 177–88; *AS04,* 187–98.

Interlude 2

1. William H. Gass, *Reading Rilke: Reflections on the Problems of Translation* (New York: Knopf, 1999), 59.

2. Rainer Maria Rilke, *The Duino Elegies,* trans. Harry Behn (Mt. Vernon, N.Y.: Peter Pauper, 1957).

3. Gass, *Reading Rilke,* 32.

4. See George Rochberg, *String Quartet no. 2 with Soprano* (Bryn Mawr, Pa.: Presser, 1971), 36.

5. Quartets by Earle Brown, John Cage, Christian Wolff, Lejaren Arthur Hiller, Jacob Druckman, Morton Feldman, Stefan Wolpe, Leon Kirchner, and George Crumb were released on *The Avant Garde String Quartet in the U.S.A.,* Concord String Quartet, Vox SVBX 5306 (1973), LP; reissued as *American String Quartets 1950–70,* Vox Box CDX 5143 (1995), CD.

6. George Rochberg, *String Quartet no. 2 (1959–61),* Concord String Quartet, Phyllis Bryn-Julson (soprano), Turnabout TV-S 34524 (1974), LP; reissued on *20th Century Voices in America,* Vox Box CDX 5145 (1995), CD.

7. George Rochberg, *String Quartet no. 3,* Nonesuch H-71283 (1973), LP; reissued on George Rochberg, *String Quartets 3–6,* New World Records 80551–2 (1999), CD.

8. George Rochberg, *Trio for Violin, Cello and Piano,* Kees Kooper (violin), Fred Sherry (cello), Mary Louise Boehm (piano), Turnabout TV-S 34520 (1973), LP; reissued on Albany TROY 153 (1995), CD.

Chapter 6

1. George Rochberg, "The Avant-Garde and the Aesthetics of Survival," in *New Literary History* 3, no. 1 (Autumn 1971): 71–92; reprinted in *AS84,* 215–31; *AS04,* 225–41.

2. Robinson Jeffers, *Roan Stallion, Tamar, and Other Poems* (New York: Modern Library, 1935), viii–x.

3. George Rochberg, *String Quartet no. 3,* Concord String Quartet, Nonesuch H-71283 (1973), LP.

4. John Rockwell, "What's New?" *High Fidelity and Musical America,* January 1974, MA-10–MA-32.

5. Robert P. Morgan, Review of George Rochberg, *Quartet for Strings, no. 3* (Concord Quartet, Nonesuch H-71283), *High Fidelity and Musical America,* November 1973, 115–16.

6. Linda Hutcheon, *A Theory of Parody: The Teachings of Twentieth-Century Art Forms* (New York: Methuen, 1985), 8.

7. Michael Walsh, "Kronos Quartet Passes the Test," *San Francisco Examiner,* March 28, 1980, p. 31.

8. Rockwell, MA-11.

9. Joseph N. Straus, "The Myth of Serial 'Tyranny' in the 1950s and 1960s," *Musical Quarterly* 83, no. 3 (Fall 1999): 301–43.

10. Ibid., 302.

11. Leon Botstein, "Notes from the Editor: Preserving Memory, Felix Galimir in Memoriam (1910–1999)," *Musical Quarterly* 83, no. 3 (Fall 1999): 295–96.

12. Straus, "The Myth of Serial 'Tyranny,'" 335.

13. George Rochberg, *Symphony no. 2,* New York Philharmonic, Werner Torkanowsky (conductor), Columbia ML 5779 (1962), LP; reissued on *George Rochberg, Volume One,* CRI 768 (1997), CD.

14. George Rochberg, *Quartets Nos. 4, 5, and 6 "The Concord Quartets,"* Concord String Quartet, RCA Red Seal ARL2–4198 (1982), LP; reissued on George Rochberg,

String Quartets Nos. 3–6, Concord String Quartet, New World Records 80551-2 (1999), CD.

15. George Rochberg, *String Quartet no. 7 (with Baritone, 1979),* Concord String Quartet, Leslie Guinn (baritone), Nonesuch 78017 (1983), LP.

16. George Rochberg, *Quintet for Piano and String Quartet (1975),* Concord String Quartet, Alan Marks (piano), Nonesuch N-78011 (1981), LP.

17. George Rochberg, *Quintet for Two Violins, Viola, and Two Violoncellos* (Bryn Mawr, Pa.: Presser, 1983).

Chapter 7

1. Igor Stravinsky, Concerto for Violin and Orchestra in D.

2. Arnold Schoenberg, Concerto for Violin and Orchestra, op. 36.

3. George Rochberg, *Concerto for Violin and Orchestra (1974),* reduced for piano by Stephen Paul Hartke (Bryn Mawr, Pa.: Presser, 1977).

4. Ralph Waldo Emerson, "Self-Reliance."

5. Alec Wilder, *American Popular Song: The Great Innovators, 1900–1950* (New York: Oxford University Press, 1972).

6. Leo Tolstoy, *What Is Art?,* trans. Almyer Maude (New York: Bobbs-Merrill, 1960).

7. Karl Haas (1913–2005), host of "Adventures in Good Music," a classical music radio program syndicated nationwide beginning in 1970.

8. Quoted in Thomas Flanagan, "Master of the Misbegotten," *New York Review of Books* 47, no. 15 (October 5, 2000), 18.

9. Elizabeth Hardwick, *Herman Melville* (New York: Viking, 2000), 102–3.

10. Hector Berlioz, *Evenings with the Orchestra,* ed. and trans. Jacques Barzun (New York: Knopf, 1956), 309.

11. George Rochberg, *Violin Concerto,* Isaac Stern (violin), Pittsburgh Symphony Orchestra, André Previn (conductor), Columbia M1012 (1979), LP; reissued on Sony Classical SMK 64505 (1995), CD.

Interlude 3

1. Lewis Thomas, "On Thinking about Thinking," in *The Medusa and the Snail: More Notes of a Biology Watcher* (New York: Viking Press, 1974), 154.

2. George Rochberg, *Piano Music,* Sally Pinkas, piano, Gasparo GSCD-340 (1999), CD.

3. Henry Corbin. *Mundus Imaginalis: or, The Imaginary and the Imaginal.* Translated by Ruth Horne (Ipswich: Golgonooza Press, 1976).

4. George Rochberg, *Circles of Fire: For Two Pianos, 1996–97,* Hirsch–Pinkas Piano Duo, Gasparo GSCD-343 (2000), CD.

5. Edward T. Cone (1917–2004), musicologist, theorist, and composer, who studied and taught at Princeton University.

6. For a fuller account, including Stravinsky's statement and my comments, see George Rochberg, "The Composer in Academia: Reflections on a Theme of Stravinsky," in *AS84,* 161–63.

7. Marcantonio Barone (b. 1962), a Philadelphia-based concert pianist.

Chapter 8

1. Dante Alighieri, *Vita nuova,* trans. Mark Musa (Oxford: Oxford University Press, 1992), 14.
2. Herman Hesse, *Steppenwolf,* trans. Basil Creighton (New York: Henry Holt, 1929), 40–41.
3. Ibid., 51.
4. Ibid., 52.
5. Ibid., 289–90.
6. Ibid., 307.
7. Ibid., 309.
8. *Music for the Magic Theater, for a Chamber Ensemble of 15 Players* (Bryn Mawr, Pa.: T. Presser Co., 1972).

Chapter 9

1. Primo Levi, *Si questo è un uomo* (Torino: F. DeSilva, 1947); English translation as *Survival in Auschwitz: The Nazi Assault on Humanity* (New York: Simon & Schuster, 1996). "If this is a man," the literal translation of the Italian, was used for the first English translation of the book (New York: Orion Press, 1959) and is a far better title. I know of only one other writer, the poet Czesław Milosz, who has understood the moral depths of the dilemmas that overcame the human species in the nadir of the twentieth century. In an essay on the situation of the intellectual in Eastern Europe he writes, "The work of human thought *should* withstand the test of brutal, naked reality. If it cannot, it is worthless. Probably only those things are worthwhile which can preserve their validity in the eyes of a man threatened with instant death" (quoted in Charles Simic, "A World Gone Up in Smoke," *New York Review of Books,* December 20, 2001, p. 14).
2. The text of Schütz's cantata is taken from Paul's account to King Agrippa of his apocalyptic vision of Jesus on the road to Damascus. "The story of Paul's conversion from adamant anti-Christian, Saul, to a follower of the Christian belief is mentioned three times in the Book of Acts. The literature on Schütz's composition cites Acts 9, verses 4 and 5, as the source of the text. In fact, the text is taken from Acts 26, verse 14. Only there do we find the second-sentence warning 'Es wird dir schwer werden, wider den Stachel zu Löcken' ('lecken' in Schütz)." Evan Linfield, "Rhetoric, Rhythm, and Harmony as Keys to Schütz's *Saul, Saul, was verfolgst du mich?*" in *Critica Musica: Essays in Honor of Paul Brainard,* ed. John Knowles (Amsterdam: Gordon and Breach, 1996), 239.
3. BWV 637 (from the *Orgelbüchlein*) and BWV 705 (from the Kirnberger Collection).
4. Czesław Milosz, *The Witness of Poetry* (Cambridge, Mass.: Harvard University Press, 1983), 79.
5. Ibid., 80.

Interlude 4

1. *Mountain Songs: A Cycle of American Folk Songs,* Paula Robison (flute), Eliot Fisk (guitar), Musical Heritage Society MHS 11239 (1987), CD.

2. The opening lines of William Wordsworth's poem "The World Is Too Much with Us."

3. Included on George Rochberg, *Eden: Out of Time & Out of Space,* Paula Robison (flute), Eliot Fisk (guitar), Chamber Music Society of Lincoln Center, Arabesque Z6745 (2000), CD.

4. William Shakespeare, *Henry V,* adapted and directed by Kenneth Branagh, Orion Pictures (MGM), 1989.

5. Included on Rochberg, *Eden: Out of Time & Out of Space.*

6. W. B. Yeats, *The Shadowy Waters* (New York: Dodd, Mead, 1905), 8–9.

7. Rochberg, *Eden: Out of Time & Out of Space.*

8. Lewis Thomas, "The World's Biggest Membrane," in *The Lives of a Cell* (New York: Viking Press, 1974), 145–48.

9. Ibid., 145.

10. Ibid., 147, 148.

11. Ibid., 148.

Chapter 10

1. G. Rochberg, "The Structure of Time in Music: Traditional and Contemporary Ramifications and Consequences," in *The Study of Time II: Proceedings of the Second Conference of the International Society for the Study of Time, Lake Yamanaka—Japan,* ed. J. T. Fraser and N. Lawrence (New York: Springer, 1975), 136–49.

2. George Rochberg, *Symphony no. 2; Imago Mundi,* Saarbrücken Radio Symphony Orchestra, Christopher Lyndon-Gee (conductor), Naxos 8.559182 (2005), CD.

3. D.H. Lawrence, *Apocalypse,* with an introduction by Richard Aldington (New York: Viking Press, 1932), 87.

4. *An Interrupted Serenade,* San Francisco Contemporary Music Players, Jean-Louis LeRoux (conductor), Grenadilla GS-1063 (1982), LP.

5. *Pictures of the Floating World,* Yolanda Kondonassis (harp), Telarc CD-80488 (1998), CD.

6. *Enchanted Dreams—Exotic Dances,* Geoffrey Collins (flute), Alice Giles (harp), Tall Poppies TP031 (1994), CD.

7. *Sue Ann Kahn Plays Schickele, Rochberg, Luening, Riegger,* Sue Ann Kahn (flute), Andrew Willis (piano), CRI SD 531 (1986), LP.

8. *Alexa Still, Flute,* Alexa Still (flute), Susan DeWitt (piano), Koch 3-7144-2H1 (1993), CD.

Chapter 11

1. George Rochberg, *Oboe Concerto,* Joseph Robinson (oboe), Zubin Mehta (conductor), New York Philharmonic, New World Records NW 335 (1986), CD.

Interlude 5

1. Robert Lowell and Jacques Barzun, *Phaedra and Figaro: Racine's* Phèdre, *Beaumarchais's* Figaro's Marriage (New York: Farrar, Straus, and Cudahy, 1961).

2. Ibid., 5.

3. Ibid., 8.

4. Edith Hamilton, *Mythology* (Boston: Little, Brown, 1942), 220.

5. George Rochberg, *Black Sounds, Cantio Sacra, Phaedra,* Boston Modern Orchestra Project, Gil Rose (conductor), Mary Nessinger (mezzo-soprano), Naxos 8.559120 (2002), CD.

6. D. H. Lawrence, *Apocalypse,* with an introduction by Richard Aldington (New York: Viking Press, 1932), 73.

7. George Rochberg, "Humanism versus Science," in *AS84,* 164–73; *ASo4,* 135–44.

8. Lawrence, *Apocalypse,* 76–77.

Chapter 12

1. Ludwig van Beethoven, *Sonata no. 9 in A Major for Violin and Piano, op. 47* ("*Kreutzer*"); George Rochberg, *Sonata for Violin and Piano (1988),* Maria Bachmann (violin), Jon Klibonoff (piano), Connoisseur Society CD 4178 (1990), CD.

2. *American Music in the 1990's,* Fischer Duo, Gasparo GSCD-349 (2000), CD.

Chapter 13

1. Quoted in H. C. Robbins Landon, ed., *The Mozart Compendium: A Guide to Mozart's Life and Music* (Borders Press, 1990), 151–52. My italics.

2. Alfred Einstein, *Mozart: His Character, His Work* (New York: Oxford University Press, 1945), 154.

3. Ibid.

4. Ibid.

5. George Rochberg, *Duo for Oboe and Bassoon* (Bryn Mawr, Pa.: Presser, 1980).

6. Dominick Argento, *Capriccio for Clarinet and Orchestra "Rossini in Paris";* George Rochberg, *Concerto for Clarinet and Orchestra,* Anthony Gigliotti (clarinet), Taipei Symphony Orchestra, Felix Chiu-Sen Chen (conductor), Bravo 20125 (2001), CD.

Chapter 14

1. Samuel Butler, *The Way of All Flesh* (London: Grant Richards, 1903).

2. Ibid., 451–52. My italics.

3. Michael Frayn, *Copenhagen* (London: Methuen Drama, 1999).

4. Werner Heisenberg, *Physics and Philosophy: The Revolution in Modern Science* (New York: Harper & Row, 1958; reprint ed. Amherst, N.Y.: Prometheus Books, 1999).

5. George Rochberg, "Indeterminacy in the New Music," *Score,* no. 26 (January 1960): 9–19; reprinted in *AS84* and *ASo8,* 3–15.

6. Rochberg, "Indeterminacy," 6.

7. Paul Celan, "Sprich auch du," English translation from *Poems of Paul Celan,* rev. and exp., trans. Michael Hamburger (New York: Persea, 2002), 69.

8. George Rochberg, *Trio for Violin, Cello and Piano,* Kees Kooper (violin), Fred Sherry (cello), Mary Louise Boehm (piano), Turnabout TV-S 34520 (1973), LP; reissued on Albany TROY 153 (1995), CD.

9. *Spring Music: Works by Baker, Rochberg, Rorem,* Beaux Arts Trio, Philips 438 866–2 (1994), CD.

10. George Rochberg, *The 3 Piano Trios,* Kapell Trio, Gasparo GSCD-289 (1998), CD.

Interlude 6

1. William Masselos (1920–1992), an American pianist who specialized in the performance of contemporary music.

2. Howard Lebow (1935–1968), American pianist, was a student of Edward Steurmann's (himself a student of Schoenberg's) at the Juilliard School and was teaching at the University of Massachusetts, Amherst, at the time of his death.

3. George Rochberg, *Piano Music,* Sally Pinkas (piano), Gasparo GSCD-340/2 (1996), CD.

4. Ibid.

Chapter 15

1. George Rochberg, *Violin Concerto (Revised Original Version),* Peter Sheppard Skaerved (violin), Saarbrücken Radio Symphony Orchestra, Christopher Lyndon-Gee (conductor), Naxos 8.559129 (2004), CD; George Rochberg, *Symphony no. 5; Black Sounds; Transcendental Variations,* Saarbrücken Radio Symphony Orchestra, Christopher Lyndon-Gee (conductor), Naxos 8.559115 (2003), CD.

2. Edith Hamilton, *Mythology* (Boston: Little, Brown, 1942), 44.

3. Lionel Gilbert, comp. *An Armidale Album: Glimpses of Armidale's History and Development in Word, Sketch, and Photograph* (Armidale, Aust.: New England Regional Art Museum Association, 1982).

304 *Index*

Rose, Gilbert, 219–20. *See also* Boston Modern Orchestra Project (BMOP)
Rosen, Nathaniel ("Nick"), 112
Rosen, Seymour (Sy), 122–23
Rosenfeld, Gene. *See* Rochberg, Gene
Rota, Nino, 125
Rothko, Mark, 261
Rudolph, Max, 78. *See also* Cincinnati Symphony Orchestra
Rufer, Josef, 72
Ruggles, Carl, 265
Russell, John, 169
Ryder, Albert, 265

Saarbrücken Radio Symphony Orchestra, 191, 266–67, 273
Sacher, Paul, 275
Sadoff, Simon, 66
Salzer, Felix, 4, 287n1 (chap. 1)
Salzman, Eric, 33
Sands, Diana, 216, 221
San Francisco Contemporary Music Players, 195
San Francisco Orchestra, 238
Sawallisch, Wolfgang, 237, 239–40. *See also* Philadelphia Orchestra
Scalero, Rosario, 5–6, 71
Scarlatti, Domenico, 72
Scheidt, Samuel: "Warum betrübst du dich, mein Herz," 221
Schenker, Heinrich, 4, 26, 125, 287n1 (chap. 1)
Schippers, Thomas, 47
Schnittke, Alfred, 238; Viola Concerto, 119; Cello Concerto no. 1, 119
Schoenbach, Solomon (Sol), 234
Schoenberg, Arnold, 12, 14, 26, 32, 53, 55, 66, 71–74, 80, 105, 131, 146, 229, 233–34, 260, 265; *Book of the Hanging Garden, The,* op. 15, 260; *Erwartung,* op. 17, 32, 243; Five Orchestral Pieces, op. 16, 243, 260; Five Piano Pieces, op. 23, 72, 256; Piano Pieces, op. 33, 73; *Pierrot lunaire,* 32, 105; Six Little Piano Pieces, op. 19, 72; String Quartet no. 2, op. 10, 92; String Quartet no. 4, op. 37, 72; Suite for Piano, op. 25, 73; Three Piano Pieces, op. 11, 72, 260; Violin Concerto, op. 36, 116–18; Wind Quintet, op. 26, 269
Schonberg, Harold, 96, 115
Schorr, Aaron, 34
Schubert, Franz, 101, 120, 124, 146, 203, 248
Schuller, Gunther, 22
Schultz, Andrea, 288n2 (inter. 1)
Schuman, William, 20, 80, 258–59
Schumann, Robert, 73, 82, 101, 108, 146

Schütz, Heinrich, 169, 174; "Saul, Saul, was verfolgst du mich," 170–72, 292n2 (chap. 9)
Scriabin, Alexander, 42, 254
Seattle Youth Symphony Orchestra, 200
Segovia, Andrés, 36
Sequitur (new music group), 44
Sessions, Roger, 6, 80, 139, 265
Shakespeare, William, 46; *Hamlet,* 149; *Henry V,* 179–80; *King John,* 22; *Romeo and Juliet,* 22; *Tempest, The,* 155, 206
Shapero, Harold, 54
Shapey, Ralph, 159. *See also* University of Chicago Contemporary Chamber Players
Shelley, Percy Bysshe, 70, 98, 126, 262; "Dirge, A," 231
Shelton, Lucy, 219
Shepard, Thomas, 21, 109
Sheppard Skaerved, Peter, 34, 144, 266–67, 272–73. *See also* Kreutzer String Quartet
Sherman, Robert, 111
Sherry, Frederick, 94, 250
Sherwin, Maggie, 201
Shiesley, Robert, 169
Shostakovich, Dmitri, 67, 215
Sibelius, Jean: Violin Concerto, op. 47, 118
Smith, Norman, 148
Smith, Susan DeWitt, 197
Sokol, Agatha, 200
Sokol, Mark, 93, 96, 100, 107–8, 115, 200. *See also* Concord String Quartet
Sokol, Vilem, 200. *See also* Seattle Youth Symphony Orchestra
Sokoloff, Vladimir ("Billy"), 197, 228
Solti, Sir Georg, 119, 121, 123, 191, 204–6, 268. *See also* Chicago Symphony Orchestra
Solzhenitsyn, Alexander, 215
Somers, Harry, 22
Sousa, John Philip, 209
Stalin, Joseph, 79, 105, 212, 214
Steinberg, William, 116–19. *See also* Pittsburgh Symphony Orchestra
Stern, Isaac, 129–30; and Violin Concerto, 75, 111, 116–17, 119, 121–24, 127–29, 205, 239, 267
Stern, Vera, 116, 129–30
Sterne, Teresa, 93, 101
Still, Alexa, 197
Stockhausen, Karlheinz, 260
Straus, Joseph N.: "Myth of Serial 'Tyranny,' The," 104–6
Strauss, Johann, Jr., 265
Strauss, Melvin, 83, 159. *See also* Buffalo Philharmonic

GEORGE ROCHBERG (1918–2005) composed six symphonies, three concertos, seven string quartets, and dozens of chamber and solo works over the course of a career spanning six decades. After establishing a name for himself as a modernist composer in the years following World War II, he grew dissatisfied with the expressive limitations of serial composition and began searching for a musical aesthetic that would allow him to build on the music of the past. Through explorations in his music and his writings, he arrived at a more inclusive compositional style that embraced both the old and the new, yielding groundbreaking works such as *Music for the Magic Theater* (1965), the String Quartet no. 3 (1972), and the *Concord Quartets* (1977–78). The revised edition of his collected writings on music, *The Aesthetics of Survival* (2004), was the recipient of an ASCAP Deems Taylor Award in 2006. In 2007, selected correspondence between Rochberg and Canadian composer Istvan Anhalt was published as *Eagle Minds,* edited by Alan Gillmor.

GENE ROCHBERG met George in 1938 while both were students at what is now Montclair State University. They married in 1941. After George's three years of military service, they moved to Philadelphia, where Gene studied at the Hedgerow Theatre School and the Barnes Foundation and was actively involved in theater and the other arts. She collaborated with her husband on a number of works, including the monodrama *Phaedre* (1974) and the opera *The Confidence Man* (1982).

RICHARD GRISCOM is head of the Otto E. Albrecht Music Library at the University of Pennsylvania. He served as executive secretary of the Music Library Association from 1992 to 1996 and edited the association's journal, *Notes,* from 1997 to 2000. He is coauthor of *The Recorder: A Research and Information Guide* (2003) and editor of *Music Librarianship at the Turn of the Century* (2000).

The University of Illinois Press
is a founding member of the
Association of American University Presses.

Composed in 10.5/14 Adobe Minion
by Celia Shapland
at the University of Illinois Press
Designed by Kelly Gray
Manufactured by Sheridan Books, Inc.

University of Illinois Press
1325 South Oak Street
Champaign, IL 61820-6903
www.press.uillinois.edu